S 1

THE SOCIALIST ECONOMIES
of the Soviet Union and Europe

THE SOCIALIST ECONOMIES
of the Soviet Union and Europe

MARIE LAVIGNE

translated by T. G. WAYWELL

MARTIN ROBERTSON

The original French edition was published in 1970 by Librairie Armand Colin, 103 boulevard Saint-Michel, Paris.

The revised English edition was first published in 1974 by Martin Robertson & Co. Ltd., 17 Quick Street, London.

ISBN 0 85520 043 X

Printed in the United Kingdom at The Pitman Press, Bath

CONTENTS

TRANSLATOR'S PREFACE

MARIE LAVIGNE'S *Economies Socialistes* was first published in 1970 by Armand Colin. For the purpose of this translation the author has since revised the book and brought both statistical material and commentary up to date. I have not attempted a literal translation, but an accurate though sometimes abbreviated rendering of the original into English which is acceptable to both informed layman and specialist. To keep down production costs, the exhaustive chapter bibliographies of the French edition have been left out, though the general bibligraphy, notes and references have been retained. The 'documentation' supplied by the author at the end of each chapter has been omitted for the same reason. It had the effect of giving a certain immediacy to the theme of the chapter in question in the form of selections from recent Soviet and East European publications, official documents, etc. Their omission, however, in no way detracts from the closely argued matter of the text and the interested reader can always refer back to the French edition, if necessary.

A notable feature of this book is the fine balance which Mme. Lavigne has achieved in her synthesis of social theory and practise in the U.S.S.R. and Eastern Europe. The organic relationship between theory and practice during the last half century is set in the historical perspective of societies in transition from capital to socialism. If the proper subject of political economy is the analysis of the mode of production and distribution of the social surplus on the basis of specific property relations, Mme. Lavigne achieves just that in a well-balanced study of the structure, operational mechanisms and international relations of the economies of socialist Europe.

The general picture which emerges is one of a number of societies in a post-capitalist situation working out their own individual solutions to the problem of establishing socialism on the basis of common ownership of the means of production. The diversity of their experience in the application of this principal appears to be at least as great as that of capitalist countries applying the principal of private ownership in the means of production. The myth of the socialist monolith is effectively, if indirectly, discredited.

The great diversity of economic activity both within and between each socialist country may surprise the uninitiated or those accustomed to the demonology often passing for political economy in Soviet affairs. Recent developments in economic reform apparently came as something of a surprise to the *illuminati* as well. Though that should not have been the case, in so far as the basic contradiction in most of these countries today, with all the economic ramifications it implies, had been clearly foreseen as a necessary though transient feature which would be carried through from the capitalist to the socialist epoch (Engels in *Anti-Dührung* and Marx in his *Critique of the Gotha Programme*). This contradiction, between collective ownership of the means of production on the one hand and a quasi-capitalist mode of distribution on the other, means the persistence of certain economic categories typical of bourgeois society, such as wages, bonuses and bank interest (though not private profit).

It is perhaps against this background that Mme. Lavigne's analysis is best seen: the attempt by one State, and then by several, to establish socialism on the basis of institutions which reflect both the fundamental principle of collective ownership of the means of production and the contradictory tensions of the new society, many of which were inherited from the past and will continue as long as the problem of relative scarcity persists. In this situation it is hardly surprising that many of the recent economic reforms are strongly reminiscent of the whip and carrot mentality of Bentham's 'felicific calculus', conceived originally in the philosophical context of Utilitarianism and nascent industrial capitalism. However, this process of adjustment to changing circumstances is merely one application of the Leninist principle of democratic centralism to the management of a socialist economy under new conditions, in which an attempt is being made to balance centralised economic control with optimum stimulation of enterprise initiative.

How these problems are solved, and particularly the paradox of collective production side by side with individual appropriation (so far in the field of consumer but not of capital goods) will depend largely on the rate of economic growth, on the elimination of scarcity and on the gradual substitution of social consumption funds for wage payments, about which Mme. Lavigne has some interesting things to say . . . .

I would like to acknowledge my wife Lucia's patient criticism of the translated text as it has emerged over the past months, together with the first-class work of my typist Kate Anderson and Elizabeth Paton's invaluable assistance in proof-reading.

Leeds, 1974

INTRODUCTION

'Socialist economy' is a common enough expression nowadays, and in so far as it covers everything outside the capitalist system is at first sight unambiguous.

However it is still little used by non-Marxist economists. The term 'collectivism' which has been in use in France for a long time first appeared at the end of the nineteenth century to describe an economic system founded on Marxist socialism, in which ownership of the means of production ceases to be private and becomes collective. Soviet Russia supplied the first concrete example after 1917. With the consolidation of socialism as a political and economic system in the U.S.S.R., followed by the creation after 1945 of a number of popular democratic states modelled for domestic and international political reasons on the Soviet Union, a 'collectivist system' came into existence. It is this regime which is sometimes referred to as the 'socialist system' or the 'socialist economies'.

However, since the adjective 'socialist' describes primarily a doctrine and a political regime, many writers are reluctant to apply it to an economic system. This reticence is very clearly expressed by André Garrigon-Lagrange:

> What we understand by a collectivist system, such as that existing in the U.S.S.R., is a regime characterised above all by the abolition in principle of private ownership of the means of production, the emphasis placed on the rôle of labour and the concentration of economic power in the hands of an authoritarian State committed to planning. Many, in describing such a system, speak of 'socialism', as a way forward towards communism. However, given the ambiguity of the term socialism . . . we prefer to revert to the unequivocal terminology of the nineteenth century and use the somewhat forgotten expression of collectivism.[1]

To avoid the ambiguous term 'socialism', economists have had recourse to unsatisfactory concepts, such as 'Soviet-type economies' or 'planned economies'. The first refers only to the particular country which began building socialism; it was followed later by others with common basic principles which they applied in different ways. The second concept emphasises a particular method of economic management—planning—which applies not only in all socialist countries but also in non-socialist ones. These two related concepts have led to circumlocutions such as 'economies in which planning is centralised according to the Soviet model'.[2] The expression 'Eastern country' is geographically ambiguous and quite inappropriate.[3] Where does the East begin and where does it end? Whereabouts is Cuba in the East? In conclusion let us quote the American economist Stanislaw Wellisz who prefers to use 'the prudent expression *economic system of the Soviet type* in order to avoid phrases like "communist economic system", "socialist economic system", or "planned economic system", all of which might lead to confusion' (p. 16; however the French translation of his book is entitled *Initiation aux économies socialistes*,[4] in apparent contravention of the author's intentions since he called the original *The Economics of the Soviet Bloc!*[5])

It is no use running away from the problem. We shall speak of socialist economies, but we shall define the expression first.

Contemporary definitions may be grouped around seven criteria, three of them political and four economic. Their common feature is that each one emphasises a single fundamental aspect of the socialist system.

Political Criteria

1. States which apply the principles of historical materialism belong to the socialist system.

The most simplistic version of this definition is the one which classifies under the socialist system states where the communist party is in power. In fact, of the fourteen states which at present make up this system, seven have no communist party as such: the ruling party is called the Socialist Workers' Party in Hungary, the Polish United Workers' Party in Poland, the Socialist Unity Party in the G.D.R., the Workers' Party in Albania and Korea, the People's Revolutionary Party in Mongolia, and the Workers' Party in Vietnam.

Even if one were to reject this interpretation and to take into account only the ideological basis of the regimes in question, the fact remains that there are several ideological variants of communism. Which one should constitute the basis of the 'true' socialist economic system?

2. In a socialist economy, the fundamental elements of economic policy are determined by the government, itself under Party control (whether or not the Party is called communist, is the only party or constitutes the dominant element in an 'alliance' or 'front' of socialist parties).

This definition purports to be more technical than the preceding one, but its inadequacy appears as soon as an attempt is made to analyse the rôle of the Party in economic life. The Party certainly plays an important rôle in all socialist economies. Above all, it establishes the general direction of economic policy, participates in the formulation of economic plans, determines economic reform and follows more or less closely the activity of particular sectors (in most socialist states, the Party is especially concerned with the problems of agriculture). The Party apparatus often includes sections concerned with general economic policy and control. But nowhere does the Party exercise *direct control* of economic activity; there is in all cases a specialised economic administration for this purpose.

If, in defining 'the socialist economy', exclusive emphasis is placed on the managerial role of the Party, one must logically conclude that there is a 'dilution of socialist principles' each time that, in some country or other, wider powers seem to have been conferred upon the professional economic administration. It will then be asserted that the 'technocratisation' of power has reduced the rôle of the Party and consequently initiated a 'retreat' from socialism.

3. Socialist economies are characterised by the participation of workers in the administration of economic life and in the management of production units.

This definition would make Yugoslavia the socialist economy *par excellence,* since this country has gone further than mere participation by organising all economic activity on the basis of direct self-management. In most socialist countries formal arrangements for worker participation in management operate through various institutions, trade union or otherwise, particularly within the framework of individual enterprises. In practice participation is fairly limited.

Nevertheless a socialist regime necessarily implies that every worker should feel concerned about the efficient operation of his own enterprise. At the same time he should experience a more general regard for the working of the economy in the social interest, an interest which is theoretically identical with his personal welfare. The idea of participation is an imperfect expression of this need. It is relevant to indicate the primary rôle attributed in all socialist economies to the means of control exercised by workers over the economic administration and units of production: information, publicity given to all scandals large and small and to the sanctions taken to eliminate them; the active intervention of the citizen in indicating possible improvements, from the operation of urban transport and the running of the local store, to the functioning of this or that ministry.

Economic Criteria

1. The aim of the socialist system is to ensure the fullest possible satisfaction of the constantly growing cultural and material needs of all members of society. The ultimate objective is the building of communist society in which 'all the sources of social wealth will flow abundantly and the great principle of "from each according to his ability, to each according to his work" will be realised' (Programme of the C.P.S.U., 1961, Part 2).[6]

This definition of socialist systems relates to their final objective: a classless communist system with complete equality between all members of society, where an abundance of goods will permit equal distribution according to need instead of unequal distribution according to work performed. But this form of affluent society still belongs to the distant future.

On the other hand, every 'capitalist' government has an economic policy designed to ensure the welfare of everybody; the objective is apparently identical. In these circumstances, the thesis of the ultimate convergence of the two systems becomes too easily seductive.

2. Socialist economies are planned economies.

This is the commonest and simplest definition. It implies the reciprocal definition of capitalist economies as market economies. But it is acceptable only if plan and market are mutually exclusive. This was the intention of those theses which demonstrated a diametrical opposition between planned socialism and liberal capitalism, or between the centralised economy, in which the plan established by a superior authority is imposed on all economic agencies, and the decentralised economy, based on exchange. This idea was developed mainly by contemporary liberal economists during the early period of socialism in Soviet Russia.[7] For these authors the socialist system is characterised by the absence of a market for capital goods, and the substitution of 'vertical' relationships between enterprises and the central planning authority for the 'horizontal' relationships between enterprises which exist in the market economy. They draw an antithesis between the two systems; on the one hand, there is the perfect rationality of the free market economy, leading to equilibrium of production and consumption and to the maximum satisfaction of needs; on the other, the absolute irrationality of the socialist economy, deprived of a market and therefore incapable of a rational allocation of productive resources, since planning cannot fulfil the functions of the market in this respect.

However since World War II the plan/market antithesis has become less clear. Many capitalist states now use planning methods to anticipate and orientate economic development. The growing public sector is the cornerstone of State intervention in the capitalist economy. Similarly socialist economies increasingly complement methods of direct imperative planning with tools of economic intervention based on the manipulation of market forces hitherto considered the exclusive province of capitalism (price policies, monetary and financial policies, etc.). In this way one arrives at the idea of market socialism, incorporated in the latest socialist constitution, that of the Czechoslovak Socialist Republic.[8]

Perhaps one should go much further and envisage the common evolution of the two systems, with the gradual erosion of the differences between socialism and capitalism ('industrial society' in the words of Raymond Aron, 'generalised economy' according to François Perroux, and 'convergence of the systems' according to Jan Tinbergen). We shall return to this much debated question in the conclusion of this work, but in the meantime it should be pointed out that to define socialist systems solely according to the criterion of planning would be to give too much importance to a method of economic action. Of course socialism implies planning, but the economic system which corresponds to it is socialist before being planned, and it is the essence of socialism which we must define.

3. Socialist economies are 'command economies'.[9]

This definition no longer refers to *method* (the plan) but to *means* (the tools of intervention whereby the objectives defined in the plan are achieved). Socialist systems are presented as economies in which State authority has recourse to a centralised administrative apparatus giving directives to base units which are simple executive agents.

The American economist Gregory Grossman, professor at the University of Berkeley, first systematised this notion and constructed a model of the 'command economy':

> The individual economic units (though probably only the firms and not the households) are ordered what, when, where, how, and how much to produce and consume. If done rationally at all, these commands (directives, orders, targets, 'plans') derive from some sort of conscious attempt ('planning') to coordinate the activities of the individual units and to direct the economy as a whole toward certain definite goals. The command principle implies several important things: relatively little independence or autonomy on the part of the individual economic unit; the presence of a superior authority that issues the commands and is capable of eliciting a minimal degree of compliance; very probably a hierarchical organisational structure; and a minimal amount of coordinative planning on which the commands are based.[10]

From this definition Grossman builds up an abstract system covering the different contemporary variants of economies of this type. He attempts particularly to integrate the tendencies towards administrative decentralisation which appear in all these systems:

> A *less-than-absolute* command economy, which we henceforth call simply a command economy, with relatively free household choice is of course the normal situation in the U.S.S.R. and other Soviet-type countries. Organisationally, it is a hierarchy; not despite some decentralisation but because of it, for . . . a hierarchical organisation in itself signifies some delegation of authority and hence some decentralisation.[11]

Another Berkeley economics professor, Benjamin Ward, carries the analysis further by describing the sociological implications of the concept and by defining a 'command society' as a 'form of economic organisation in which the allocation of resources is carried out by the extensive use of orders to produce and deliver goods.'[12]

Once more the criterion is too inflexible. Is it still a command economy when production units acquire extensive rights in questions of supply and marketing, when they can conclude contracts with suppliers and customers alike, as is anticipated in the economic reforms introduced in the socialist countries of Europe? At what point in the process of decentralisation does the 'command economy' disappear, and with it the socialist economy, if the two

concepts are identical? The proposed definition gives no reply to this question.
4. Socialist systems are characterised by a particular structure of production; they are economies in which priority is given to the growth of the capital goods sector.

Soviet economic policy was in fact based for a long period on the principle of priority growth in the capital goods sector. In general the economic policy of socialist countries has always been dominated in its first phase by a concern for rapid and vigorous industrialisation. In the case of countries already industrialised at the time of the socialist revolution, such as Czechoslovakia and the G.D.R., investment in heavy industry was increased. More concisely, this was the message spelled out by Lenin to the Eighth Congress of Soviets in 1920: 'Communism is soviet power plus electrification of the whole country.'

This is rarely put forward as an actual definition of socialism, but it is implicit in certain commentaries on present developments in the socialist systems. According to this line of argument, there is a retreat from socialism as soon as socialist countries begin to develop the consumer goods sector or try to balance supply and demand, etc. Planning and 'consumer sovereignty' are considered to be mutually exclusive.

All the preceding definitions contain elements of the 'socialist economic system', but do not give its essence in synthesis. That is why they fail to account for the diversity of these systems in time and space.

We propose the following definition: *the socialist system is an economic system founded on the socialist ownership of the basic means of production.*

This definition is supported by historical experience. Socialist revolutions have always included a programme of nationalisation, involving the expropriation of industrial capitalists and big landowners. This has made possible State direction of economic activity and planning.

The definition appears in every socialist constitution. It is true that the latest, that of the Czechoslovak Federation (1968), merely refers to the 'socialist economic system' (article 4), but the fact that it then gives an exhaustive list of State powers in economic matters implies socialist ownership of the principal means of production.

Moreover this 'official' definition of the socialist system is accepted by a wide range of experts. To quote Jean Bénard, professor at the University of Paris: 'At the risk of appearing very traditionalist, I would say that a society is socialist if, and only if, the principal means of production of that society are collectivised, that is to say if they are appropriated by the collectivity representing the society in question, and not by individuals or groups of individuals.'[13]

According to the Polish economist Wlodzimierz Brus:

The criterion for differentiating between capitalist and socialist economies is to be found in the basic relationships of production; in other words, and in conformity with Stalin's definition which in my opinion is broadly

xiv

correct, in: 1. the modes of ownership of the means of production; 2. the position in the production process deriving from this of different social groups; 3. the principles underlying the distribution of goods which are determined by these modes of ownership.[14]

Professor Gregory Grossman finds it necessary to complete his definition of the command economy with the following observation: 'We shall think of it as an economic system in which most productive assets are publicly owned, usually by the state or some division thereof.'[15]

In the words of Peter Wiles: 'Our definitions of socialism and of capitalism are exceedingly simple: public and private ownership, respectively, of the means of production. No apology is made for this; it is quite certainly the only logical and useful distinction.'[16]

There are two further propositions implied in this definition:

1. *A socialist economy exists only if there is socialist ownership of the principal means of production.*

'Socialist' ownership means ownership by the community as a whole. But until communism, the ultimate objective of socialism, is achieved, common ownership by the whole people will inevitably assume mediate institutional forms. In practice, this means State property and co-operative property. *State ownership* is generally applied to mining, the whole of industrial production (factories, plant, etc.), the means of transport, commercial organisations (in their entirety or in part according to the country), banking and financial establishments, and part of the agricultural sector. The soil itself is nationalised in only two socialist states, the U.S.S.R. and Mongolia. *Co-operative ownership* mainly covers the agricultural sector, and thereby craft enterprise as well.

Two observations must be made here.

Firstly, a conglomeration of group properties can never constitute socialist ownership. Nothing is more alien to socialism than the anarchist idea symbolised in the slogan 'the mine to the miners'. This concept was repudiated by Lenin at the very beginning of the Soviet regime: 'To legalise the ownership by the workers of a factory or a profession over their particular means of production, directly or indirectly, or to legalise their right to weaken or impede the power of the State to dispose of property, would be to deform the fundamental principles of Soviet power and to reject socialism entirely.' It is well to remember that, contrary to common belief, Yugoslav social ownership does not take the form of group property. The 1965 law on enterprises stipulates that workers must preserve intact the property of any enterprise put under their management. Neither is the property of agricultural co-operatives, to be found in all socialist countries, in any way the property of a particular group of peasants. It is not the co-property of the members, and the right of disposing of co-operative property belongs to the institution as such.

Secondly, the two concepts of socialist and State ownership are not identical. In other words, nationalisation does not automatically mean socialisation. This

is an essential point when one is considering whether or not certain economies
are socialist where the public sector is in fact dominant (Algeria, Guinea).
Even extensive nationalisation does not transform the country concerned into
a socialist regime if there is not at the same time a radical restructuring of
society. And history shows that such radical reform only occurs after revolution.

To what area does socialist ownership apply? To the basic means of
production.

Socialism does not therefore exclude personal property in consumer goods,
including durables. Socialist constitutions often list objects of personal property
to which citizens have a right: house, articles in common use, savings. One
may own both a principal and a secondary residence (although administrative
regulations often limit the area per person or family), a car and inherited
property. But all this property can serve only the personal needs of the owner.
It is illegal to lease part of one's house at speculative rents or to use one's car
for undisclosed operations in commercial transport.

On the other hand, socialism allows the personal ownership of means of
production which can be exploited by an individual employing no labour.
The plot of land allocated to the individual peasant is an illustration of this in
all socialist countries.

2. *Every economy based on this definition of socialist property must be
considered socialist.*

We can now bring in again all the criteria analysed above. Our criterion
synthesising them admits the following possibilities: different socialist
ideologies; different variants of economic power; different forms of mass
participation in economic management; different planning techniques; varying
degrees of flexibility in the management of the economy; evolving structures
in production; the realisation of the objective of socialism at different points
in history.

Fourteen states, which recognise each other as socialist in spite of their
political divergencies, conformed to this definition in 1970:
the Union of Soviet Republics
eight European states:
    the People's Republic of Bulgaria
    the People's Republic of Hungary
    the People's Republic of Poland
    the People's Republic of Romania
    the People's Republic of Czechoslovakia
    the German Democratic Republic
    the Federal People's Republic of Yugoslavia
    the Republic of Albania
four Asian states:
    the Mongolian People's Republic
    the People's Republic of Korea
    the People's Republic of Vietnam

the People's Republic of China
one American state:

the Republic of Cuba.

We shall limit our study to the socialist economies of Europe, since they comprise a homogeneous geographical area and have passed through similar stages of growth. In particular we shall deal with those seven European countries (U.S.S.R., Bulgaria, Hungary, Poland, G.D.R., Romania, Czechoslovakia) whose participation in Comecon since 1949–50 has strengthened their common development, and with Yugoslavia which has followed a parallel but original path during the same period. A study of the Asian socialist countries and of the Cuban Republic would be more appropriate in a work on the developing economies. Such a work is at present much inhibited by the difficulty of acquiring general and statistical information, and this is also true of one of the European socialist countries, Albania.

In Part I, we shall describe the *structural* framework of these economies as it is determined by socialist ownership of the means of production: economic institutions (chapter 1), management of the units of production and distribution, industrial enterprises (chapter 2), agricultural enterprises and commercial organisations (chapter 3).

Part II will be concerned with operational *mechanisms*: the strategy of growth and the means employed to achieve it (chapter 4); planning methods (chapter 5); tools of economic intervention (chapter 6). It will show how the growth objectives of planned development are achieved through a combination of planning techniques and tools of intervention borrowed from the market economy and put at the service of the plan.

Finally Part III will briefly describe the *international relations* which exist between socialist countries, and between them and the rest of the world. The problems of competition between systems which these relationships pose will be examined in the conclusion.

Part I

THE STRUCTURE OF
THE SOCIALIST ECONOMIES

1. Creation of Socialist Property
2. Administration of the Economy

ECONOMIC INSTITUTIONS

In 1944–5, a number of popular democracies came into being in Eastern and Central Europe: Albania, Bulgaria, Hungary, Poland, Romania, Czechoslovakia, Yugoslavia. The German Democratic Republic was added to the list in 1949. These countries established economic institutions along the lines of the Soviet Union which had preceded them on the path to socialism. In order to lay the foundations of socialist ownership, they first of all abolished private property in the means of production. Later, they created an economic administration to direct the various units of production.

1. CREATION OF SOCIALIST PROPERTY

The Origins of Socialist Property in the U.S.S.R.

Socialist nationalisation dates from the very beginning of Soviet power, i.e. from the time of the triumph of the Bolshevik revolution in November 1917. The principal stages of development were as follows:

26 October (8 November) 1917: *the abolition of private landed property* in the possession of large landowners and clergy: the land and means of production came under the control of peasant soviets. The 'decree on land' came immediately after the 'decree on peace'. Its adoption by the Second Congress of Soviets only a few hours after the fall of the Petrograd Winter Palace and the overthrow of the Provisional Government is a clear indication that a settlement of the agrarian question was the main worry of the new Soviet government. For several months the countryside had been aflame with

1

insurrection and the peasants had begun to share out the land spontaneously. Large-scale landed property was therefore abolished immediately and without compensation; the land was declared a 'national heritage . . . restored to all those who work it'; expropriated means of production were provisionally put 'under the revolutionary care' of the soviets. However, the decree did not expressly nationalise the land and upheld the rights of peasant smallholders who employed no wage-labour. The words 'nationalisation' or 'state-control' still did not appear in the law on 'land socialisation' which was passed on 27 January (9 February) 1918. It was this law that sanctioned the redistribution of the land and the rights of individual peasants. At the same time, it provided for the creation of state farms (in the shape of large pilot farms, stud-farms, etc.), and insisted on priority of state aid for collective forms of enterprise (communes, associations for joint cultivation of the soil, co-operatives). Nationalisation of the sub-soil was finally introduced on 29 May 1918.

14 (27) December 1917: *nationalisation of private banks*. The 1919 programme of the Russian Communist Party justified this measure *a posteriori* with a reference to French revolutionary experience:

> Avoiding the mistakes of the Paris Commune, soviet power in Russia immediately seized the State Bank, passing thereafter to the nationalisation of the private commercial banks. In this way, it transformed the bank, the centre of economic domination by finance capital and an instrument of political domination in the hands of the exploiting classes, into an instrument of working-class power and a lever of the economic revolution.[1]

1918: *the progressive nationalisation of industry*. Socialist appropriation of the industrial means of production would allow the state to 'take control of the economy', to employ a stock phrase. The somewhat ambiguous measures taken to socialise land-ownership were primarily of political significance, the nationalisation of the banks primarily symbolical, while the nationalisation of industry established the real economic foundations of socialism. There were several possible procedures: confiscation pure and simple, partial compensation of the former owners, or the gradual transformation of capitalist into socialist property through the implementation of various forms of 'State capitalism'. The first method was chosen, at least until the adoption of the New Economic Policy in 1921. However, in the weeks following the revolution various forms of takeover appeared possible; a decree of 13 December 1917 even anticipated the payment of compensation as a percentage of the capital invested by the expropriated owners, or as a percentage of shares held, in the case of companies. This decree was not applied, and at the beginning of 1918, in a decree of 21 January (3 February), the Soviet State explicitly announced the cancellation of its foreign debts. Nationalisation began from the end of 1917, being applied to those firms whose owners or managers refused to implement the provisions (adopted in 1917) on workers' control which arranged for the participation of representatives of the work-force in the management of factories and mills. The civil war, which marked the beginning of War

Communism, accelerated the movement: on 2 May 1918 the sugar industry was nationalised, on 20 July the oil industry, and on 28 June 1918 the whole of large-scale industry (important firms, with a capital value in excess of one million roubles, in the following branches: mining, metallurgy, metal processing, electro-technics, rubber, cellulose, wood, glass, tobacco, textiles, leather and hides, cement, flour-milling) as well as railways. A decree of 29 November 1920 pronounced the nationalisation of all industrial undertakings, whether they belonged to companies or individuals, employing more than five persons in the case of those equipped with mechanical power or more than ten persons where no mechanical power was in use.

22 April 1918: *foreign trade was declared a state monopoly.*

It was thus during the period of War Communism (1918–20) that nationalised (State) ownership of the means of production was formally established and that State direction of production and exchange was instituted.

But these legal and administrative provisions were adopted at a time when the country, already weakened by the war and shaken by revolution, was subjected to foreign intervention and civil war. Industrial activity declined and fell in 1920 to an index of 13.8 in relation to a base of 100 in 1913. The lack of raw materials and fuel, the paralysis of transport, the defection of trained personnel, the physical depreciation of capital which it was impossible to maintain let alone replace, were the obvious causes. The essential problem, however, was to survive: from this point of view, it was the state of agriculture which was the most critical. The peasantry (82% of the population in 1917, that is to say 130 million) was divided into three social strata: rich peasants or *kulaks*[2] who were immediately best placed to profit from the situation created by expropriation, 'middle' peasants, and poor peasants on whom Soviet power depended to consolidate its influence in the countryside. In fact, a decree of 11 June 1918 had created committees of poor peasants (the *kombedy*), with the function of organising the rural proletariat politically and of proceeding to further allocations of land, distributing to the poorest peasants not only land taken from the kulaks but also the cattle and equipment which would allow them to work the land. At the end of 1918, these committees, which had often used their power for the arbitrary settling of accounts, were dissolved and merged into the rural soviets, where the kulaks could play no rôle, since the Constitution of 10 July 1918 had deprived them of their electoral rights (article 23). In the course of the same year, steps were taken to ensure the provisioning of the towns: the establishment of a state monopoly in the corn trade, a decree of 13 May on the requisition of agricultural produce, the dispatch of workers' detachments into the countryside to collect corn, a new decree on 11 January 1919 on the requisition of foodstuffs. Agricultural production, like industrial production, collapsed, and in 1920 fell to one-third of its 1913 level; peasant disturbances and uprisings broke out all over the country.

Under these conditions, nationalisation was emptied of all content. It is difficult to visualise its significance for industry: the number of enterprises actually controlled by the economic administration (that is to say, by the central boards or *glavki* of the Supreme Economic Council created on 2 (15) December 1917), varied from month to month and has been estimated at one third of nationalised undertakings in 1920. The enterprises were in fact managed according to circumstances by local authorities (soviets), by committees of workers' control, and even by former 'capitalist' managements. The really socialist solution for agriculture would have been the nationalisation of the means of production and not merely of the land. The distribution of the land to the peasants after the expropriation of the big landlords and the maintenance of private property in capital equipment cannot be considered to be in conformity with socialist principles, especially in a context in which the 'socialisation' of the land decreed in law was a mere declaration of intent. Moreover, the agrarian measures passed on the night following the October Revolution had been pushed through during the Second Congress of Soviets by the Left Socialist-Revolutionaries, whose programme was much more popular with the peasant masses than that of the Bolsheviks. Land redistribution had satisfied a fundamental aspiration of the peasants; what would later exacerbate their discontent and foment revolt was not socialisation of the land, an abstract measure, but the nationalisation of domestic trade and the requisitions which deprived them of the fruits of their labour.

The first act of the New Economic Policy[3], adopted by the Tenth Congress of the Russian Communist Party in March 1921, was precisely to abolish the requisitioning of foodstuffs and raw materials and to replace it by a tax in kind, and authorisation for the peasants to sell their surplus freely on the market. Thus the N.E.P. broke immediately and at two points with 'War Communism': the nationalisation of domestic trade was implicitly abolished since free trade in agricultural produce was re-established, whilst the restoration of the market followed the previous abolition of all monetary transactions. For practical reasons, the Bolshevik party thus refused to radicalise War Communism, the theory of which had been outlined in 1919 by the economist Bukharin in his work on '*The Economy of the Transition Period*'. It was politically impossible to continue pressurising the peasants because of the risk of counter-revolution. At the same time there was insufficient Bolshevik personnel to assume the management of the nationalised undertakings.

The N.E.P. provided a pause in the building of socialism, allowing the regime to draw breath and prepare for total control of the economy. For industry the final objective was clear: complete socialisation of the means of production. The ultimate objective for agriculture was to be defined by Lenin in the famous article 'On co-operation' published in January 1923: without denying the importance of socialist state farms in agriculture, Lenin considered that co-operation could ensure the transition to socialism in the simplest way and in the way most accessible to the peasant. Of course, co-operation as such is not specifically socialist. The co-operative in a bourgeois regime can in no way be distinguished from a capitalist enterprise. But in the conditions of the dictatorship of the proletariat it is transformed and becomes a socialist mode of management: 'When social ownership of the means of production already exists and when the proletarian class has crushed the bourgeoisie, a regime of enlightened co-operators is a socialist regime.'

Thus socialisation of the means of production, the result of the first phase of the building of communism, was to lead to two forms of socialist property: State ownership in industry and in a deliberately restricted section of agriculture, and co-operative ownership in the rest of agriculture. This institutional distinction is fundamental to an understanding of economic thought in the U.S.S.R. It permeates Soviet economic theory, leading on occasion to analyses which have been uselessly complicated.

At the very beginning of the N.E.P. two different objectives were established. How would they be achieved, and above all in what period of time? The N.E.P. had begun with a major concession to the peasantry. But a settlement of the agrarian question, which according to Lenin could only be accomplished in one or two decades, was to be effectively postponed until the implementation of mass collectivisation in 1929-30, once the socialisation of industry had been completed.

THE SOCIALISATION OF INDUSTRY

The N.E.P. is usually defined as the temporary restoration of capitalism in the industrial sector. In fact this period (1921-7) was characterised by a series of complex measures which can be outlined in the following way: there was a partial and temporary restoration of capitalism in small- and medium-sized industry, controlled nevertheless by a socialist State using the methods of 'State capitalism'; large-scale manufacturing industry, on the other hand, the cornerstone of socialist power, was directed with ever-increasing efficiency by the economic administration, employing managerial techniques which would allow it to compete with private enterprise. In a way there was, therefore, mutual contamination of capitalism by socialism in small-scale industry, and the other way round in large-scale industry. This situation justifies and explains the question which Lenin put to the Eleventh Congress of the Communist Party in March 1922. 'Who will vanquish whom? (*Kto kogo?* in the short version allowed by Russian grammar), capitalism or socialism?

Denationalisation and State Capitalism

From 1921, the N.E.P. recreated the conditions necessary for the operation of a free market: the abolition of restrictions on monetary circulation and commodity exchange, the re-establishment of the freedom of enterprise by a decree of 7 July 1921 which allowed private persons to engage in craft activities and even to open small enterprises employing not more than twenty people; and finally, by a decree of 10 December, the denationalisation of firms employing less than ten workers which had previously come under State control. The same decree also authorised the Supreme Economic Council to denationalise establishments with ten to twenty workers if they could not be managed by government agencies under prevailing circumstances.

There was a parallel development of State capitalism. This concept is usually defined in socialist vocabulary as 'a specific form of the subordination of the activity of capitalist enterprises to the development of socialist appropriation'.[4] State capitalism implies a form of co-operation between the industrial bourgeoisie and the socialist State. The bourgeoisie has the choice of either accepting the conditions imposed by socialist power or expropriation pure and simple. It involves a compromise which is difficult to maintain. It implies, in effect, that the new regime needs the experience of national capitalist personnel or foreign capital, and that the social and political climate must inspire sufficient confidence in the capitalist class to dissuade them from emigrating or withdrawing their capital. In short, it rests on a contractual truce in the class struggle, each of the two factions not forgetting that if its immediate interest is more or less faithful adherence to the contract, its long-term objective is the elimination of the other. This assumes either a reconquest of power by the bourgeoisie or the consolidation of proletarian power. That explains why the notion is a highly ambiguous one. To Preobrajensky, who maintained that 'State capitalism is quite simply capitalism, and that it must not and cannot be understood in any other way', Lenin replied that with the installation of the Soviet regime State capitalism became 'three-quarters socialism', something which 'neither Marx nor Marxists could anticipate'.

According to the *Manual of Political Economy*, 'State capitalism, under conditions of proletarian dictatorship, is characterised by capitalist enterprises in industry and commerce, whose activity is defined by a contract with the socialist state and develops under its control.'[4] Various devices are possible: the leasing of State enterprises to private capitalists, concessions, especially in mining, contracts whereby the owner of a firm deposits part of his production with the State, mixed-economy enterprises, and contracts obliging private establishments to work to the order of the government with raw materials supplied by the latter.

In fact, during the period of the N.E.P. only the first two methods were extensively used. Leasing was applied to 3,874 enterprises (two-thirds of which were flour-mills). Rent was paid in kind until the end of 1922, later in money, and the contract always included an obligation to maintain capital equipment in a state of good repair. This system sometimes allowed former owners to return and manage an enterprise which had been taken from them: 26% of establishments leased in 1922 operated under such conditions. The length of the contract varied: in 1923, 22% of firms were leased for 1 year, 49% for 1 to 3 years, and 29% for 3 to 6 years. The position of these enterprises became less and less tenable. They were subjected to heavy taxation. From 1926 they were unable to obtain credit from the State Bank. Public service charges, especially in transport, were raised against them. Premature termination of contracts became more and more frequent towards the end of the N.E.P., above all for the flour-mills, since the Soviet government did not wish to leave this branch of industry, so important for feeding the population, in the hands of private capital.

Concessions were granted exclusively to foreign companies. During the period of the N.E.P., 144 contracts in total were concluded, 24 of which were in mining, 41 in the manufacturing industries and 36 in commerce. On 1 October 1928, 68 contracts were in operation, distributed by country as follows: 14 for Germany, 9 for the United States, 7 for Great Britain and Japan; other countries included Sweden and France. The most important of these concessions had been granted to a British firm, Lena-Goldfields, which was engaged in gold-mining, non-ferrous metals and forestry. Of the concessions granted in manufacturing industry, the largest was an enterprise producing ball-bearings and belonged to a Swedish company. Aggregate production within the concessionary sector in 1928 amounted to 0.6% of total industrial production. From 1928 the concessions gradually disappeared, either through the voluntary liquidation of the concessionary companies or through termination of the contract on the Soviet side when the foreign firm indulged in 'speculative' activities. However, on 1 January 1936, eleven concessions still remained.

The practice of leasing nationalised undertakings to private capitalists was abandoned much earlier; in 1928-9 the number of such private industrial concerns fell from 11,547 to 7,157, a reduction of 38.2%, while that of commercial undertakings fell by 45.4%. In 1930 all leased concerns came under the control of the economic administration.

The significance of private concerns in economic activity during the period of the N.E.P. can be appreciated from the following figures: in 1923-4, the private sector accounted for 33% of industrial production, in 1928 for 17%. It was essentially composed of small undertakings: at the beginning of 1926, 4,689 private concerns, or 84% of the total, employed less than 5 workers (only 2 had more than 250 workers).

From 1928, a specific form of socialisation was encouraged for small units of production and craft industries: regrouping into co-operatives. Frequently in the past small craftsmen had associated in so-called 'unofficial' co-operatives. The government now wished to give them an institutional framework. These small units of production were mainly situated in the countryside, and the objective of co-operation in this sphere was to support the collectivisation of farms from 1929. In 1928, 31.5% of workers in small-scale industry and the crafts were grouped in co-operatives, three-quarters in 1932. More than 70% of co-operators were in the countryside, so that side by side with the classical forms of co-operation (credit, supplies, sales, joint use of equipment) there appeared a specific form, the *promkolkhoz* or industrial collective farms of worker-peasants, an interesting institution which might have been developed later on had it not been for the decline of the co-operative craft workers.[5]

The return to private capitalism during the period of the N.E.P. was thus limited in time and in its objectives. Nationalisation was retained in large-scale manufacturing industry, but State enterprises were encouraged to model their management on capitalist methods.

Renationalisation and Market Socialism

The specific problem of the N.E.P. was to establish peaceful coexistence between State management and private initiative. How was this coexistence to be realised in industry? The State had to ensure a solid position for itself in the industrial sector, by means of nationalisation, in order to be able to retrieve the rest later, while giving nationalised industry the possibility of competing with the private sector.

Thus, whilst the decree of 9 August 1921 gave official sanction to the N.E.P., whose 'control lever is commodity exchange', nationalisation was consolidated a few months later. A decree of 27 October stated that 'all concerns which passed before 17 May of the present year into the jurisdiction of the organs of state power (central and local) are nationalised'. How would these establishments operate in competition with private industry?

The decree creating the N.E.P. replied to this question in advance in article 4: 'The enterprises will be managed on the basis of financial autonomy; the Supreme Economic Council must only take over control of enterprises if, in conformity with the general plan, they are supplied with material and financial resources by State organs or other means (free market, previous stocks, etc.)'. It was thus understood that the State would control the operation of concerns whose financial position appeared healthy to begin with. A resolution of the Eleventh Congress of the Party 'on financial policy' stated on 2 April 1922: 'In a situation in which commerce is tolerated and develops freely, the management of nationalised enterprises becomes substantially commercial.' State enterprises were placed in a situation analogous to that of private concerns: independence of management, direct relationships between economic units, the pursuit of profitability. During the period of War Communism, a decree of 4 March 1919 had placed all public enterprises under direct State supervision, their debts to the national bank being cancelled and transformed into grants. This text was abrogated and State industry removed from the budget. The only source of finance admissible for the whole of industry—private and public—became credit, long- or short-term according to whether it related to expenditure or working capital.

The operation of the public sector, like that of the private sector, was thus based on a compromise: control of industry through the economic administration (the Supreme Economic Council, its central sectorial boards or *glavki* and the regional economic councils or *sovnarkhoze*), but day-to-day management along the lines of private enterprise. This compromise came to an end with the final victory of socialist principles, prepared from the outside by industrial concentration and from the inside by the gradual erosion of enterprise autonomy.

In December 1921 a resolution of the Central Committee of the Party outlined the necessity of encouraging the regrouping of economic units: 'The Committee believes that the process of industrial decontrol and its adaptation to the N.E.P. has resulted in excessive industrial fragmentation, brought about by the speed of the operation itself. It is indispensable to terminate as quickly as possible the work of the Supreme Economic Council in the organisation and regrouping of industry, so as to ensure the completion by industry of the objectives fixed by the State.'

Integration began, in certain sectors of particular importance, with the creation of associations which had been decided upon in a decree of 12 August 1921: 'In a given branch of industry, the most important enterprises, technically well-equipped, rationally organised and situated, may be merged . . . into an independent association based on financial autonomy.' Trusts made their appearance in 1922, were legalised by decree on 10 April 1923, and displayed sufficient flexibility to be adapted to the N.E.P.—something the associations had been less successful in. They were also efficient enough in the hands of the public authorities to fulfil planning requirements. The resolution 'on industry' of the Twelfth Party Congress (23 April 1923) clearly shows the function of these organisations, which

> manage that fraction of the nationalised economy conferred upon them, within certain bounds of autonomy made necessary by existing market conditions and as previously defined by the higher organs of State administration . . . These economic groupings, like the enterprises of which they are composed, have as their fundamental aim the creation and realisation of a surplus value in the interests of State accumulation.

The same text continues:

> If each trust, in order to ensure the success of its work, must feel free in its general orientation and fully responsible for its activities, the State, on its side, must see in the trusts and the other associations agencies which are at its service. By these means, the State will remain in touch with the market as a whole and will be in a position to determine market orientation by a series of practical measures transcending the market influence of individual enterprises.

The trust had as its object the regrouping of large undertakings in the same branch of industrial activity, or the integration at regional level of concerns contributing to a specific line of production. In the middle of 1924, there were 133 central trusts and 345 local trusts. In both cases, the individual enterprise became a production section of the trust, lost its independent legal status and its right of immediate access to the market. The prototype of the trust of this period was 'Jugostal' (Southern Steel-Works), which regrouped the metallurgical enterprises of the south of the country with the coal-mines and coking plants which serviced them. Jugostal employed more than 35,000 workers and in 1929 accounted for two-thirds of cast-iron production in the U.S.S.R. In the textile industry, Noupravlenie was the most important trust, combining seventeen large linen factories to the north-east of Moscow and disposing of 33% of spinning capacity in linen. Trusts were formed, according to the same combination of sectorial and territorial criteria in the wood, cement, rubber and sugar industries. Final legal status was conferred upon them at the end of the N.E.P., by a law of 29 June 1927 on State industrial trusts, which defined them in article 2 in the following way: 'A State industrial enterprise, organised on the basis of a specific statute as an autonomous economic unit with independent legal status and share capital, forming an integral part of the State administration referred to in the statute; it will operate according to the principles of commercial accountancy in relation to the objectives defined by the appropriate administrative apparatus.' This law remained the basic text governing the activity of State enterprises until 1965.

At the same time as the trusts there appeared the syndicates, which were only brought under official regulation much later, in 1928: they were associations of trusts created to allow the trusts to implement a coherent commercial policy (supplies and sales). Thus there were syndicates in leather, textiles, salt, tobacco, the clothing industry, etc. Profiting from their monopoly position the syndicates sometimes had a tendency to raise prices, but this was checked by the government. They played a very active part in the process of renationalising economic life. In fact they were the means of gradually isolating the market trusts. From 1926 they stopped depositing with the trusts the product of the sales which had been effected on their behalf and began quite simply opening an account for them which recorded these sales. Conversely, the procedure was gradually introduced of appropriating raw materials in kind, by means of purchase vouchers, such as still exists in the Soviet system of supplying enterprises. That is why, quite naturally, the syndicates were absorbed after 1929 into the economic administration, of which they had been the advance apparatus.

During the course of the N.E.P. the autonomy of enterprises had been restricted from above, first of all by transferring to the trusts that freedom of management which had been previously granted to the individual concern, and later through the abolition of the commercial freedom of the trusts themselves. This largely involved the large units of production. In the case of small enterprises the instrument of reacquisition by the State was the Bank.

In the beginning, the New Economic Policy conferred considerable advantages on small-scale industry, especially by allowing it to establish prices which were high enough to cover operating costs and to accumulate capital for investment. At the same time, the fiscal burden was relatively light and became more onerous only from 1926. This price freedom led to a serious crisis in 1923, known as the 'scissors crisis'. As industrial prices rose, the controlled price of agricultural produce remained stable: the 'price scissors' opened more and more and created growing discontent in the countryside where the peasants could no longer obtain supplies of manufactured consumer goods and equipment. Industrial enterprises were faced with shrinking markets. To overcome the crisis the government took various measures (industrial price freeze, monetary stabilisation). From 1925, the situation improved: in that year, industrial production reached 73% of its pre-war level.

It was then that the State Bank began to circumscribe industrial activity more narrowly. It had been created on 12 October 1921. The national bank, solemnly instituted on the very day of the Revolution through the nationalisation of the former Imperial Bank, had been abolished in effect during the period of War Communism in March 1919, transformed into the 'general treasury of Communist society' and absorbed into the Ministry of Finance. Gradually the State Bank extended its control to all credit institutions (co-operative banks, local communal banks, mutual credit societies, banks specialising in long-term industrial credit). A decree of June 1927 required all specialised banks to communicate their financial position to the State Bank and to deposit all their liquid assets with it. The extension or restriction of credit became an efficient means of orientating industrial activity. As the Soviet economist Preobrajensky puts it so clearly: 'The State Bank during the period of proletarian dictatorship acted as an *agent provocateur* and betrayed capitalism to socialism by employing capitalist methods . . .'[6] As we have seen, the Bank entirely stopped extending credit to private enterprise in 1926. With regard to the nationalised sector, it practised a selective credit policy which accelerated the movement towards industrial concentration.

At the end of the N.E.P., through these various methods, one of the objectives of the policy had been realised: the socialist transformation of industry. But had the consolidation of working-class and peasant unity been achieved? This alone would permit the socialisation of agriculture. The answer to this question would be found in collectivisation, a problem to which the government could now turn its attention.

THE COLLECTIVISATION OF AGRICULTURE

In December 1927, the Fifteenth Congress of the Communist Party, which terminated the N.E.P. and defined the general lines of the first five-year plan (1928-32), also decided to go ahead with the systematic collectivisation of agriculture. The policy of the Party was clearly expressed. Agriculture would be socialised. In spite of the measures taken at the beginning of the Revolution, it was still based on private ownership. The redistribution of land had merely resulted in the fragmentation of holdings. Socialisation in this case was to assume a different institutional form from the form dominant in industry: co-operative ownership of the means of production. State ownership would be retained in the case of large experimental Soviet farms. This decision was the outcome of complex political struggles. It could be equally explained in terms of the condition of the Soviet peasantry at that time.

Land nationalisation and extensive common ownership of equipment in the Soviet Union are sometimes explained in terms of the Russian 'mentality', especially as land has remained in private ownership in the socialist countries of Europe. Such explanations are not convincing. Collectivisation 'succeeded' in the U.S.S.R. by means of extreme violence, methods which arrested the development of agricultural production for a long time.

The communal farm certainly existed in pre-revolutionary Russia. Readers of the nineteenth-century Russian novel will be familiar with the *mir* in rural life. This was a village community in forest areas where the land was first cleared collectively and then shared amongst the peasants. The land remained village property and was periodically redistributed. However this mode of farming, confined to a specific geographical area, was already in decline in the second half of the nineteenth century. Before the Revolution it comprised less than half the peasants of European Russia. Although irrational from an economic viewpoint, the *mir* was resuscitated by the Soviet regime as a means of socialist propaganda. In fact, although the resolution on 'socialist agriculture' of 14 February 1919, during the period of War Communism, insisted on the rôle of Soviet state farms (*sovkhoze*) as models for the socialist reconstruction of agriculture, the Party programme of March 1919 was more flexible. It began with an assertion of the supremacy of socialist agriculture:

> Soviet power, having completely abolished private property in land, has already begun to implement a series of measures with a view to organising socialist agriculture. The most important of these measures are:
> (a) the creation of Soviet estates, i.e. large socialist farms;
> (b) encouragement given to joint cultivation of the land;
> (c) State sowing of all unsown land, whoever the owner;
> (d) State mobilisation of all agricultural resources with a view to raising the level of knowledge in the countryside;

(e) encouragement given to agricultural communes as free associations of farmers for the joint large-scale cultivation of the soil.

The Russian Communist Party sees in these measures the only means of increasing the productivity of agricultural labour, and will therefore strive to ensure their thorough implementation and extension to the most underdeveloped regions of the country.

The Russian Communist Party anticipates the following measures in particular:

(a) State encouragement of co-operation in agriculture . . .
(b) widespread application of methods of soil improvement;
(c) systematic distribution of equipment to poor and middle peasants through hiring-agencies.

However, taking account of peasant attachment to private property, the programme then stressed the need to give direct aid to small farms. At the same time, it supported voluntary consolidation of peasant holdings:

In view of the fact that the small peasant farm will continue to exist for a long time, the Russian Communist Party will make every effort to introduce measures to raise peasant production. Notably:

(a) a more judicious distribution of land among peasants (abolition of gores and strips, etc.);
(b) peasants will be supplied with improved seed and artificial fertiliser;
(c) improved cattle breeding;
(d) the dissemination of scientific knowledge in agriculture;
(e) the dispatch of agronomists into the countryside;
(f) the setting up of national workshops for repairing agricultural equipment;
(g) the establishment of hiring-agencies, experimental centres, demonstration farms, etc.;
(h) the improvement of peasant holdings.

The Russian Communist Party bases all its work in the countryside on the proletarian and semi-proletarian sections of the peasantry. Above all, it organises them into an independent force, by creating in the villages communist groups, organisations for poor peasants, special professional associations of rural proletarians and semi-proletarians. In a word, it brings them closer to the urban proletariat and removes them from the influence of the rural bourgeoisie and the particular interests of the smallholder.[7]

The agrarian code of 1922 stated that the land was to be worked by the peasant household, but gave legal status to the *mir*, now called 'land association' (*zemelnoe obchtchestvo*). The rural community managed the land, the greater part of which was shared out among households. It could also purchase machinery, organise craft activities, and decide on the particular forms of organisation appropriate to the needs of the majority of its members. The peasants in the community had the right not to adopt the collective form of enterprise. In such cases, each family cultivated its own land, and only pasture, forest etc., remained common. If they wished to have a collective form of organisation, there were three possibilities: *toz*, *artels* and communes. The *toz* (society for joint cultivation) were temporary associations during periods of agricultural work: labour was collective, but cattle and implements remained private. These societies were the most elementary form of association and involved mainly the poorest peasants, who often possessed neither machinery nor draught-animals. The *artel*[8] was a true co-operative. Land, draught-animals, seed and agricultural implements were held in common, whilst the house and an adjoining plot of land remained individual property. It was this particular form of ownership which later became dominant. In the commune, on the other hand, everything was collectively owned: land, equipment, sometimes even housing and consumer goods. Of all collective forms of ownership in 1927, the communes represented 7.3%, the *artels* 46%, and the *toz* 46.7%. Taken together, they constituted only 0.8% of peasant holdings.

It was often difficult to draw the line between *toz, artel* and commune, especially as the peasant community could change from the one to the other. The authorities encouraged collectivisation under whatever name, and any rural community involved in some sort of collective farming soon came to be called *kolkhoz* or collective farm. The figures relating to the number of *kolkhozy* quoted in the statistics of collectivisation simply add together three heterogeneous types of farm. These figures only assume significance after 1932, when the *artels* already represented 95% of the total number of *kolkhozy*. The *artel* finally displaced the commune and the *toz* in 1935.

The confusion of rural structures during the N.E.P. period was also a result of the authorities' own uncertainty about which particular form was appropriate for the peasantry. At the beginning of this period, it was possible to distinguish three groups among the supporters of collectivisation: those who maintained that the objective of socialist agriculture was the creation of large Soviet farms, that is to say, corn, meat, or milk factories along the lines of nationalised concerns in industry. Then there were those who defended the communes and criticised the *sovkhoze* for perpetuating a system of wage-labour which ought to have disappeared in any authentic communist society. Finally, there were those who supported the Leninist contention that the most elementary forms of co-operation ought to be encouraged and more complex forms introduced gradually. All three were naturally opposed to the maintenance of an agricultural system based on private property, except temporarily during the strategic withdrawal of the N.E.P. period.

The supporters of the Leninist concept of co-operation could point to the vital traditions of co-operation in Russia. At the beginning of 1917, the co-operative movement comprised 13.5 million members (60 to 72 millions if we take their families into account). There were 51,000 co-operatives: 23,000 consumer co-operatives, 16,000 in credit, while 6,000 growers' co-operatives and 3,000 co-operative dairies were involved in the marketing of agricultural produce and marginally in supplying equipment, and finally, co-operatives in craft production. It was in this tradition that the origins of agricultural co-operation lay, and not in the backward and regressive *mir*. A decree of 16 August 1921 established the basis for co-operation in agriculture. The same year saw the creation of the pan-Russian Union of agricultural co-operatives (*Sel'skosojuz*). This was followed in later years by the establishment of associations of co-operatives in marketing, the purchase of equipment, credit, and, of course, consumer co-operatives as well. Onto this movement it was decided to graft the organisational framework of the *kolkhozy*: a federal council of the *kolkhozy* was set up alongside *Sel'skosojuz*, followed in 1927 by republican centres as the subsidiary apparatus of this council. The most important was the *Kolkhozcentr* of the largest of the Soviet federal republics, Russia. Later, after the completion of mass collectivisation, this hierarchical superstructure was abolished and its functions transferred to the People's Commissariat of Agriculture. It reappeared only in 1969.

It still has to be explained why collectivisation had to be forcibly imposed on the peasantry, instead of developing spontaneously from existing communal and co-operative traditions. The explanation is to be found in the political and economic circumstances of the time.

At the time of the Fifteenth Party Congress in December 1927, Stalin was opposed by two factions: the left represented by Trotsky and Preobrajensky, and the right led by Bukharin. According to Bukharin, who had completely changed his position since the period of War Communism, the proletariat in power had to maintain its alliance with the peasantry at all costs. At the same time, craft production in the countryside should be put at the service of socialism by developing the market, and the peasantry led gradually towards an acceptance of socialisation. For Preobrajensky, on the other hand, the building of socialism must pass through the stage of proletarian dictatorship based on a process of 'super-industrialisation'. There is a fundamental antagonism between the nationalised industrial sector and the peasant market economy, since the latter is based on the law of value of capitalist society and the former on the law of 'primitive socialist accumulation'. Socialist accumulation, of course, implies the transfer of resources from the peasantry into large-scale industry by various means: taxes in kind, unequal exchange based on low agricultural and high industrial prices. It also implies the socialist colonisation of agriculture by large state farms wherever possible and especially in underdeveloped areas.

Stalin, who until then had maintained a central position between these two extremes, took advantage of the 1927 December Congress to destroy the left opposition. However, from 1928-9, by embarking on a policy of mass collectivisation, he took up the programme of the left himself, radicalised it, and got rid of the right opposition at the same time. Apart from this political struggle, the basic reason for collectivisation was undoubtedly the need to solve the problem of agricultural supplies for the urban population. The N.E.P. had in fact succeeded in raising the level of agricultural production to 87% of its pre-war level by 1925 and to 21% beyond that level by 1927. Nevertheless in 1927 the proportion of agricultural production actually marketed was 50% below the 1913 level. There were two main reasons for this. In the first place, low free-market prices in agricultural produce tended to discourage sales. In the second place, the social composition of the Soviet peasantry had changed. Before the Revolution, the great mass was composed of poor peasants. Then the sub-division of the large estates had created a stratum of middle peasants. 67-8% of peasant families came into this category in 1925, according to Soviet statistics, and their first concern had been to raise the level of their own consumption. The *kulaks* comprised a third group. They constituted 4% to 5% of peasant families in 1925, and were in essence rich peasants employing wage-labour, leasing land and later even equipment. They alone were in a position to market a significant proportion of their harvest, but often preferred to do so by illicit and speculative methods rather than on the basis of contracts with the Soviet authorities. Under these conditions, the N.E.P. slogan of reliance on the poor peasant was totally inadequate: 'Reliance on the *bedniak*, the poor peasant; alliance with the *seredniak*, the middle peasant; struggle against the *kulak*.' A systematic policy of collectivisation and 'de-*kulak*isation' was therefore decided upon, involving the physical elimination, expropriation or deportation of the *kulaks*.

The various stages of collectivisation, and the terrible conditions under which it took place, have often been described: the violent assimilation of *kulak* and middle peasant leading to the deportation of whole villages; the collectivisation not merely of the means of production, but also of houses, cattle and poultry, provoking bitter resistance by peasants and the systematic slaughter of their own livestock as a means of keeping them from the *kolkhozy*. That is why there were less cattle in 1934 than in 1928. It took years for Soviet livestock production to recover. There was a temporary halt in the process. Stalin's spectacular article 'The Dizziness of Success', published in *Pravda* on 2 March 1930, criticised the excesses of those responsible for collectivisation at the local level and brought about a fall in the percentage of all farms collectivised from 59.3% to 23% within the space of a few weeks. But collectivisation was resumed from the end of 1930. It relied increasingly on the Machine Tractor Stations which had been introduced in 1929 as a means of modernising agriculture and organising the peasants politically. This second function of the M.T.S. was much in evidence in 1933, when 25,000 Party agents operated in political sections alongside the M.T.S. and inculcated into the peasants a 'respect for socialist property' and work discipline. A definitive form for the *kolkhoz* co-operative was finally adopted in 1935.

The figures speak for themselves: in 1927, 14,800 *kolkhozy* and 1,600 *sovkhoze* covered 2.7% of the cultivated area; in 1932, 211,100 *kolkhozy* and 4,337 *sovkhoze* accounted for nearly 88% of the cultivated area (cf. tables 1.1 and 1.2). The socialisation of agriculture was complete, the private sector insignificant. But in future two forms of socialist property were to coexist in Soviet agriculture. Complete nationalisation had failed. More precisely, it had not been attempted: the creation of a co-operative sector had raised enough difficulties by itself.

TABLE 1.1 [9]

THE STAGES OF SOVIET COLLECTIVISATION

	Number of *kolkhozy*	Collectivised farms as % of total	Percentage of total cultivated area occupied by *kolkhozy*
1927 (July)	14,800	0.8	—
1928 (July)	33,300	1.7	2.3
1929 (July)	57,000	3.9	4.9
1930 (May)	85,950	23.6	33.6
1931 (July)	—	52.7	67.8
1932 (July)	211,100	61.5	77.7
1937	240,000	93.0	—

TABLE 1.2 [10]

THE SOCIALISED SECTOR AS A PROPORTION OF THE SOVIET ECONOMY (%)

	1924	1928	1937
Of the national income	35.0	44.0	99.1
Of the gross industrial product	76.3	82.4	99.8
Of the gross agricultural product	1.6	3.3	98.5
Of retail trade turnover	47.3	76.4	100.0

Socialisation of the Economy in the People's Democracies of Europe

Two facts emerge from a comparison of the history of socialisation in the Soviet Union and in other socialist countries. In general nationalisation outside the U.S.S.R. was introduced gradually and not by measures passed immediately after the seizure of power. Moreover nationalisation was not applied to the land, and even in the industrial sector has remained more limited than in the U.S.S.R. In many of these countries, the process of socialisation in agriculture has not excluded a fairly important private sector by the side of the State or co-operative sector. These developments are summarised in table 1.3.

TABLE 1.3 [11]

THE SOCIALISED SECTOR AS A PROPORTION OF THE ECONOMY IN SOCIALIST COUNTRIES (%)

	Of the national income			Of the gross industrial product			Of the gross agricultural product			Of retail trade turnover		
	1950	1960	1966	1950	1960	1966	1950	1960	1966	1950	1960	1966
Bulgaria	—	99.5	99.7	97.5	99.1	99.5	65.0	99.1	99.6	94.3	99.9	99.9
Hungary	65.7	90.6	98.6	91.4	97.3	98.9	11.0[3]	77.0[3]	97.0[3]	61.0	98.8	99.1
Poland	54.0	72.4	78.8[1]	96.8	99.4	99.6[1]	8.0	10.8	13.3[1]	83.0	97.4	98.7[1]
G.D.R.	54.2	81.1	85.9	70.0	84.5	85.3	12.1	80.0	91.3	47.3	77.2	78.5
Romania	61.4	83.3	96.1	92.4	98.7	99.8	8.2	64.6	90.6	88.5	99.9	100
Czechoslovakia	81.0	98.0	99.1	96.1	99.9	100	17.0	90.1	90.5	91.7	99.9	100
Yugoslavia	—	77[2]	—	—	—	—	—	12.4[2-3]	14[3]	—	—	—

[1] 1967   [2] 1963   [3] cultivated area

NATIONALISATION IN INDUSTRY

The process of nationalisation was slower and more gradual than in the U.S.S.R. At the same time, although in the Soviet Union the key industries were nationalised in the months following the Bolshevik revolution, the N.E.P. initiated a temporary reversal of policy. There was no such interruption in the other socialist countries. This more prudent approach may be explained in two ways. In the first place, just after 1945 it was necessary to take into account the patriotic rôle played by the national bourgeoisie during the war and resistance against the occupying power. That is why the property of collaborators was nationalised immediately and that of patriotic capitalists only later. Secondly, for two or three years after the war, the communist parties shared power with others (socialists, agrarians). A dominant position within these coalitions was attained only gradually. Since the non-communist parties were generally in favour of limiting nationalisation to large-scale industry and to property recovered from the enemy or confiscated from collaborators, complete nationalisation could only be realised after they were eliminated from power.

The first stage of nationalisation took the form of workers' control. Even before the end of the war workers' councils had sprung up more or less spontaneously to take over the management of enterprises abandoned by their owners as Soviet troops advanced (Poland, Bulgaria, Czechoslovakia, Hungary). The workers' councils were given legal status during 1945 in establishments employing a minimum number of workers (five in Yugoslavia, twenty in Hungary, etc.). In East Germany workers' councils were recognised in 1946 by the Allied Control Council. In Bulgaria and Romania, the procedure was somewhat different: workers' control was guaranteed by State supervision of agreements concluded between trade unions and employers' associations.

The method of nationalisation differed from country to country. There were, of course, common characteristics too. The most significant of these was compensation for former owners, a feature which had been absent during nationalisation in the U.S.S.R., although the property of collaborators and occupying forces was confiscated without compensation. A Romanian law of 1948 also excluded émigrés from compensation rights.

The first stage of nationalisation everywhere involved mines, electric power stations, heavy industry, transport and communications, banking and insurance. Lists enumerating the enterprises concerned were often appended to the laws on nationalisation, and usually included all firms employing more than a minimum number of workers: 100 in Romania and Hungary (1948; reduced to 10 in Hungary the following year), 50 in Poland (1946). Smaller but economically strategic concerns were eventually added to the list. Conversely, certain sectors or types of enterprise were excluded: in Czechoslovakia, building, printing, the food industry, flour-mills and producers' co-operatives; in Poland, producers' co-operatives. In Yugoslavia whole sections of the economy were socialised in 1948 according to the productive capacity of the establishments concerned. The laws on nationalisation sometimes included special clauses. In Hungary in 1949, for example, it was stipulated that former owners of nationalised concerns had to be provided with employment in accordance with their profession and qualifications.

Nationalisation was considered to be complete between 1948 and 1952. In Bulgaria, by the end of 1948 the socialist sector was supplying 97% of industrial production, compared with 6% before the law on general nationalisation in 1947. In Czechoslovakia, 95% of industrial workers were occupied in this sector after February 1948. In Poland, from 1946, it accounted for 79.5% of workers and 86.5% of production. In Yugoslavia, the end of the process of nationalisation was marked in June 1950 by a speech by Tito, 'The factories to the workers', in which the head of state declared: 'There is not a single enterprise, factory or public institution in the hands of a foreign or national capitalist.'

A private sector continued to exist within almost all the socialist economies, but strict limits were placed on the dimensions of private enterprise, which was in any case always controlled by the State.

Examples:

In Yugoslavia, an individual cannot own an enterprise employing more than five workers; beyond that figure, the law on workers' management applies.

In Romania, Hungary, Czechoslovakia, Poland, there were different forms of state capitalism combining private and public capital until 1948-9: concessions (Romania), companies combining private and public capital (Bulgaria, Romania), state management of private enterprise with payment of dividends to shareholders and owners (Hungary, Czechoslovakia). These state-capitalist forms of enterprise have now disappeared.

In the G.D.R. in 1967, nationalised concerns still only represented about one-third of all enterprises. On the other hand, they supplied more than 85% of the gross industrial product and employed 83% of the labour force. In the G.D.R. after 1956 there was a particular form of enterprise to be found nowhere else in the socialist world. This was the partnership, with State participation organised by the Investment Bank of the G.D.R. These firms were managed by a private entrepreneur with personal liability for the efficient implementation of the production programme, within the framework of the State plan, as well as for maintaining the value of the firm's assets. The entrepreneur was paid a salary equal to that of the manager of a similar State enterprise and received a share of the profits in proportion to his invested capital. In 1967 these enterprises employed 12.5% of the total industrial labour force, accounted for nearly 10% of production, and on average employed 62 workers. At the same time, the G.D.R. was not without private enterprise as such, in the form of small family firms and craft workshops.

A Party offensive in February 1972 very quickly led to the almost complete liquidation of these enterprises. With the guarantee of retaining their managerial positions after nationalisation, the owners sold their enterprises to the State more or less willingly. According to a report published in *Neues Deutschland* on 28 April 1972, 94% of semi-State enterprises and 73% of private enterprises had been 'renationalised' by that date.

THE PARTIAL COLLECTIVISATION OF AGRICULTURE

In all the countries which turned to socialism after the war, the socialisation of agriculture took place without nationalising the land. Account was taken of the peasant's traditional attachment to the soil and attention paid to the immediate demand of 60 million peasants in Central and Eastern Europe, who just after the war expected only one thing from socialism: the expropriation of the great landowners and the redistribution of the land among the peasants. Thus the basic institutional principle of socialism, social ownership of the means of production, may exclude land from its field of application, provided the actual exploitation of the land is undertaken according to socialist principles. According to a Czechoslovak lawyer: 'Ownership of the land is not the essential and decisive factor in the socialisation of agriculture. The victory of the socialist economic system in this area does not depend unconditionally on the formal abolition of private property in land.'[12] The socialisation of agriculture does not therefore exclude private ownership of the land and can be achieved by grouping peasants into co-operatives, by encouraging the mechanisation of private farms through State encouragement and assistance, and by obliging peasant smallholders to work the land themselves.

Just after the war, and sometimes even before, the confiscation of the estates of the great landowners was followed by their division and redistribution to the peasants. In the inter-war period, agrarian reforms had been introduced in every country of Central Europe. With a few exceptions, however, these reforms did not result in a real restructuring of landed property. The exceptions were Czechoslovakia, Bulgaria and Yugoslavia. The small family farm was dominant in Czechoslovakia after 1937, where 1.5 million farms covered 98.3% of the cultivated area, and where 71% of them covered less than 12.5 acres, 25% from 12.5 to 50 acres, and 4% more than 50 acres. In Bulgaria in 1944, 90% of the peasantry occupied farms of less than 25 acres and produced 80% of the wheat crop. In fact the reforms were often implemented gradually and compensation paid to the landowner. The small peasant either could not pay or else paid by falling into long-term debt with the village moneylender. Moreover, the political influence of the landed aristocracy often prevented any implementation of the agrarian reforms.

The measures taken in 1945-6 were much more radical:
1. The land was generally confiscated without compensation and was

followed by its free redistribution to the peasantry. However, in Poland, Czechoslovakia and the G.D.R., the expropriated landlords were indemnified for a certain proportion of the confiscated land, and whereas poor peasants obtained land free of charge, middle peasants were obliged to pay.

2. The first land to be expropriated was that of foreign landowners (especially German; Hungarian in Slovakia), collaborators, émigrés, the land of religious orders, banks and companies, etc. In Yugoslavia, existing religious orders were allowed to keep up to 45 acres of arable land and as much forest. Later, landed property in excess of a legal maximum acreage was confiscated: 250 acres of any type of land or 125 acres of cultivable land in Poland, 113 and 63 acres respectively in Yugoslavia, 125 in Czechoslovakia and Romania, 50 to 75 in Bulgaria according to the region, 290 or 143 in Hungary according to social class of the owner (peasant or noble).

3. The expropriated land varied in importance from country to country: 50% of cultivable land in Poland, one-third in Czechoslovakia, 29% in Hungary, 15% in Romania, 8% in Yugoslavia, 4% in Bulgaria. The land was redistributed to the peasants, the State retaining a part of the confiscated area for the construction of state farms. Redistribution led to extreme fragmentation of holdings. In 1950 the proportion of farms of less than $12\frac{1}{2}$ acres was more than 75% in Romania, 60% in Bulgaria, Poland and Yugoslavia. If these countries were to avoid perpetuating a backward and unprofitable agriculture, it was vital to group the small farms into larger units which would be both economically more rational and politically closer to the socialist model.

The next stage was therefore collectivisation, which was generally both slower and less complete than in the U.S.S.R. Pre-socialist co-operative experience often made the introduction of collectivisation easier than it otherwise would have been. In 1945 there were more than 10,000 co-operatives of different sorts in Czechoslovakia, involving 80% of the peasantry. In Bulgaria at the same period, 11% of the rural population belonged to co-operatives. In Germany credit co-operatives were already in existence.

Generally speaking, more complex forms of co-operative evolved from the more elementary and incomplete types existing in the early period:
Retail and credit co-operatives or friendly societies (G.D.R.);
Co-operatives for the pooling of agricultural labour (mutual aid societies in Hungary and Romania);
Co-operatives for the pooling of equipment and labour, but not of the land, which remained the private property of the co-operators. In these co-operatives, income is divided partly according to labour supplied (60–90% of distributed revenue) and partly according to the amount of cultivated land belonging to each farmer (40–10%). Romania, Czechoslovakia, Hungary and the G.D.R. all passed through this stage of development. Indeed, this form of co-operative has in part been retained by the two latter countries;
Co-operatives for pooling all means of production, including the land. In

this case, income is distributed according to the labour performed, the peasant owning his house, a neighbouring plot of land, a few poultry and draught-animals. This form of co-operative is now dominant in all socialist countries, with the exception of Poland. It is worth noting, however, that in the G.D.R. and Romania the co-operatives actually own the land, whereas in Bulgaria and Czechoslovakia the peasant-owners put the land at the disposal of the co-operative, land, however, which they cannot alienate. In this case, the co-operative has a 'right of common use' over the land. In Hungary co-operative ownership of the land was only introduced in 1967.

Collectivisation was generally prepared for by the prior establishment of Machine Tractor Stations. These had a dual purpose. On the one hand, they accustomed peasants to socialist collective work. On the other, it became possible to cultivate large areas of land and to raise the yield of exiguous and fragmentary farms.

The systematic development of co-operation took place in two stages: from 1949-50 to 1953, and from 1956 to 1960. The pause between 1953 and 1956 was an almost complete halt in Poland and Yugoslavia. By the end of the second of these two stages, there was a high and stable level of collectivisation everywhere: 75% of the cultivable area in Hungary in 1961, 98% in Bulgaria in 1959, 60.8% in Romania in 1965, 63.9% of agricultural production in the G.D.R. in 1960.

The methods used to bring about collectivisation were less brutal than in the Soviet Union. Administrative coercion was nevertheless often employed, and it was the negative effect of these procedures on agricultural production which caused the authorities to relax their pressure in the middle of the decade 1950–60. The rich peasant, the equivalent of the Russian *kulak*, was particularly hard hit. He was subjected to a progressive income tax, obliged to sell a considerable percentage of his produce to the State at low prices, and was often refused the right of recourse to credit. In some countries, he was forbidden to belong to a co-operative. Share-cropping and mortgage loans, both practised before the war by rich peasants, were made illegal. Since the definitional criteria of the *kulak* are relatively arbitrary (an employer of wage-labour and owner of a large farm and equipment), and since the distinction drawn between rich and middle peasant was often subjective, the harassment and persecution of the rich was in reality often directed at peasants of modest means as well. It was then that the rural community as a whole opposed both administration and collectivisation.

Two socialist countries deliberately rejected a policy of co-operation in agriculture: Yugoslavia and Poland. In view of the fact that since 1948 Yugoslavia has in so many fields been committed to a non-conformist brand of socialism, it comes as no surprise to discover that much of its agriculture is still in private hands. And yet co-operative traditions in the Yugoslav republic of Slovenia can be traced back as far as 1856. The law on co-operatives was passed in 1946, but after several years of encouragement a further law in

1953 initiated their decline. It was this law which established the principle of voluntary co-operation and at the same time authorised private farms with an upper limit of 25 acres. In 1956 co-operatives still accounted for 46.7% of all farms, but by 1966 the whole of the socialised sector, co-operatives and state farms alike, hardly covered 14% of the cultivated area.

The Polish peasant seems to be even more adamant in his opposition to co-operation in agriculture. Even in 1955, the high point of co-operative expansion, it covered less than 10% of the cultivated area. The dissolution of the co-operatives was authorised in 1956. The number fell rapidly, from 9,076 in 1955 to 1,668 in 1960, and to 1,214 by 1966. In 1968, they were cultivating less than 1% of the land and supplying little more than 1% of gross production. Those co-operatives still in existence are little more than private associations of individual producers formed for the joint cultivation of the soil. However, to provide a socialist framework for peasant farming, an old Polish institution called the agrarian circle was resuscitated in 1956. This social and non-profitmaking organisation is of indeterminate duration and exists to inform peasants of government economic policy, to collate their suggestions and to advise farmers in matters of agronomy. It has no administrative power, and since 1959 its main function has been to manage and distribute investment credits from the agricultural development fund. In 1966 85% of the land was cultivated privately. The average farm was about 12½ acres, but 32.8% of farmers owned from only 1½ to 5 acres, and therefore belonged to that sociologically significant Polish class of worker-peasants.

Paradoxically, state farms in Poland occupy a more important place than in any other socialist country. In 1966, they accounted for 13.5% of the cultivated land and 13.3% of gross agricultural production. This situation is explained by the Polish recovery after the war of the western territories from which the Germans had been expelled. It was here that large state farms were established, the labour being supplied from other regions of the country.

Generally speaking, most socialist countries do not consider state farms to be the final stage in the process of socialising agriculture. Rather they are particular forms of agricultural enterprise, limited in extent, and with various objectives: the development of new regions (the clearing of virgin land), the promotion of new methods (pilot or experimental farms), the development of scientifically produced plant species. The proportion of the total area cultivated by state farms varies from 5% to 10%.

2. ADMINISTRATION OF THE ECONOMY

The socialist economic system is based on social ownership of the means of production. It is on this foundation and by means of specific institutions that the State is able to direct the economy in both the short and long term.

Broadly speaking, the management of the economy comprises several distinct concepts. In the first place, *planning,* which means 'determining for a fixed period of time the proportions and rates of growth of economic activity at the national, regional, sectorial and enterprise levels'.[13] Secondly, *administration,* which is the organisational apparatus determining the relations between on the one hand those agencies responsible for current management of the economy, and on the other units of production and distribution. Thirdly, the *judicial regulation* of economic activity. And finally, *control,* which 'consists in ensuring that the decisions of the economic authorities are correctly applied'.

Since these notions are often confused, it will be useful if we can distinguish between them clearly. *Planning* is in integral part of any socialist economy and is essentially a method of orientating economic activity. In all socialist countries, government planning departments are separate from the economic administration, do not receive directives from it (except occasionally for limited periods), and have no power over individual enterprises. Imperative planning does not mean direct interference in the management of an enterprise, but it does mean that the enterprise can be obliged to implement the plan established for it. In all socialist countries nowadays these direct means of administrative action are supplemented by indirect economic methods, the aim of which is to encourage enterprises to execute the plan not because they are obliged to but because it is in their interest to do so. This recent development does not necessarily imply a change in planning methods, but it radically transforms methods of administrative action. Another ambiguous expression in common use is 'centralised planning'. This really means not that the plan defines centrally every element of economic life, but that directives for implementing the plan are transmitted and controlled from the centre by means of a well-articulated administrative hierarchy. It is not difficult to visualise administrative decentralisation, or rather devolution, combined with the elaboration of the plan centrally. Conversely, it would be perfectly feasible for enterprises themselves to determine certain elements in their plan, but associated with a strengthening of administrative centralisation (this has been the case in the Soviet Union since 1965).

The *judicial regulation* of economic life is an important aspect of state management and must also be distinguished from the administration. It is important to know which law regulates the activity and freedom of enterprises and economic agencies: statutory law binding on the administration, which must respect 'socialist legality', or regulations reflecting a degree of arbitrary power on the part of the administrative authorities. On the one hand, there is public law which, as Soviet lawyers would say, regulates the vertical relationships between the administration and the various units of economic activity at a lower level. On the other hand, there is civil law regulating equal horizontal relationships between the units of economic activity. It is no coincidence that in all those socialist countries developing greater freedom of economic activity, the relevant law is increasingly civil law.

Finally, a *control* hierarchy completes the administrative apparatus and reinforces its efficiency. In those socialist systems where there is no real mass participation in the management of economic life (that is to say, everywhere except Yugoslavia), the system of control does allow workers to intervene at the moment when decisions are applied.

The principles of economic administration were first formulated in the U.S.S.R., which built upon them an institutional structure later exported to the other socialist countries of Europe. Since Soviet institutions were in no way suited to the dimensions and political and economic structures of these countries, there were naturally many difficulties and disappointments. However, with the introduction of economic reform into all the socialist states, the institutional framework has also tended towards diversification.

The Principles of Economic Administration

It is possible to distinguish two categories: political principles and technical principles. The first relate to the nature of the socialist system, and the second to the function of economic administration.

POLITICAL PRINCIPLES

These are 'democratic centralism' and 'party spirit'.

Democratic centralism, the 'pillar of the socialist political community',[14] is always referred to in Soviet texts as the primary organisational principle of the administration. According to Soviet lawyers this principle links the subordination of the lower administrative organs to the higher in economic planning and administration on the one hand, with the broad and simultaneous development of local initiative on the other. In other words, important decisions are taken centrally but do not preclude maximum autonomy in day-to-day management at the level of the enterprise. This principle had already been outlined by Lenin: 'Our task is to introduce democratic centralism into the economic sphere. We must bring about absolute co-ordination and unity in the functioning of economic enterprises . . . Moreover, centralism, democratically conceived, implies for the first time the free and full development of local initiative and action, as well as the diversity of ways and means for achieving the common aim.' The application of this principle implies a degree of equilibrium which is difficult to maintain. Too much centralism will crush local initiative and lead to the cumbersome bureaucratic procedures so often repudiated at the beginning of the economic reforms of the 1960s. On the other hand, too great an emphasis on the 'democratic' aspect of centralism means ignoring the general interest, anarchy and the non-implementation of decisions taken centrally. Stalinist bureaucracy and Yugoslav self-management at enterprise level are opposite examples of disequilibrium.

Democratic centralism is a political principle and cannot be understood in terms of centralisation and decentralisation, which are merely organisational techniques. In Marxist analysis, democratic centralism is organically linked to social ownership of the means of production, which in turn encompasses a fundamental contradiction. It assumes, in effect, a unity of interest of all members of society, whose products are entirely appropriated by the State – at least until communism has been fully realised. In fact individual and group interests are in no way consonant with each other, nor with the general interest as expressed by the State. Nor are the aims which they pursue identical. The function of the administration is to reconcile this multiplicity of individual interests and to direct the propensity of individuals and groups to optimise their own satisfaction into socially useful channels. Democratic centralism permits a dialectical solution of this problem. The democratic principle within centralism is made possible by the basic unity of interest brought about by the socialist revolution itself and its abolition of private property in the means of production. At the same time, centralism arises because it is impossible to satisfy the interest of all simply by means of the free play of individual and group interest. Hence the apparent internal contradiction between the constituent parts of the principle itself: imperative state planning and local initiative, economic directives and management autonomy.

Party spirit is the second principle common to socialist countries. This does not mean that the economic administration is subordinate to the Party, but that it must act in conformity with general Party policy. It is a mistake to assume that the Party controls everything. Of course, the Communist Party is the dominant force in society, whether it is the only party as in the U.S.S.R. or the main party in a political front. But the Party apparatus is in no way a substitute for specialised economic administration. The Party exerts influence at various levels. In the first place, the upper echelons of the Party machine (the Central Committee in the U.S.S.R.) take the important decisions in economic policy: such things as approving five-year plans, introducing economic reforms, etc. Similar political intervention is frequent at the most vulnerable points in the economy. In the U.S.S.R., for example, there is an annual or biannual plenary session of the Party to study current problems affecting agriculture. The Party has also an almost official right to scrutinise appointments to important posts in economic administration: heads of administrative departments, directors and managers in industrial concerns, in banks and state farms. These posts in the U.S.S.R. are enumerated on lists held at each level of the Party hierarchy by the corresponding committee (region, republic, etc.). The person appointed does not have to belong to the Party (another myth), but he must be acceptable to it. Finally, the Party intervenes in various ways at the level of the enterprise or farm: to solve problems of day-to-day management or maintain communist work discipline, for example.

This collection of economic functions normally exercised by the Party is by no means unimportant, but it does not justify identifying the Party apparatus with the economic administration. Insistence on Party spirit is intended mainly to stress that the administration must never become an autonomous body defining its own objectives. In other words, if democratic centralism properly interpreted guards against bureaucracy, Party spirit guards against technocracy.

TECHNICAL PRINCIPLES

Theoretically there are three systems of economic management: functional, sectoral and territorial.

Before beginning our analysis, it should be made quite clear that any choice between these different systems tells us nothing about the degree of centralisation in managing the economy. The territorial system is usually associated in people's minds with decentralisation and administrative flexibility, whereas the sectoral system is supposed to relate to a high degree of centralisation. Reality is often quite different. The territorial system involves actual decentralisation (or more precisely, devolution) when the local organs of the economic administration have extensive powers. On the other hand, it can equally well conceal considerable centralisation. This is the case where certain sectors lie outside the scope of the local organs or where local organs are subordinate to a further territorial hierarchy (regions, republics) to which they must refer most of their decisions. Conversely, a sectoral system can be combined with a high degree of devolution if the lower echelons of each sectoral administration (industrial ministry) have important powers and if the ministry confines itself to the general orientation of its branch of activity.

That this is no mere academic debate is shown by the perplexity of Western observers when the Soviet economic reforms were initiated in 1965. On the one hand, they were thought to be leading to greater flexibility in economic management. On the other, it was observed that reform of the enterprise was accompanied by an administrative reform which replaced the territorial principle (in existence between 1957 and 1965) by the sectoral principle (administration by specialised industrial ministries). This was not to reinforce the powers of the economic administration. On the contrary, it was to overcome the authoritarian and fastidious resistance to enterprise reform displayed by local administrative agencies.

One cannot help wondering whether it is in fact appropriate to evaluate the institutional development of the economic administration of socialist countries in terms of decentralisation. A loose[15] and normative definition (in which 'good' decentralisation is opposed to 'bad' centralisation) may lead to an interpretation of the reforms introduced since 1964–5 into the socialist countries of Europe as a not altogether successful attempt at decentralisation. If, however, we adopt the following more precise definition, one which is necessarily 'Western' since the word rarely occurs in 'socialist' texts, it must be concluded that the notion can be applied only to Yugoslavia: 'Decentralisation consists in conferring powers of decision on agents other than the instruments of central government, agents which are not directly incorporated into the vertical hierarchy of government and which are often elected by the citizens concerned.'[16] However in Yugoslavia this situation is not called decentralisation but self-management.[17] It is therefore preferable to adopt another notion, known to French law and particularly appropriate in the case of socialist institutions: devolution, which is the 'organisational technique of conferring important powers of decision-making onto agents of the central government at the head of various administrative divisions or departments.'[18] This is a technique which can be combined with three other technical principles, territorial, functional and sectoral.

To illustrate these three principles let us consider the management of a hypothetical clothing factory in the city of Minsk, which is the capital of Byelorussia (one of the fifteen Soviet republics).[19]

Pure-State Hypothesis of the Functional System

For each aspect of its management the enterprise will depend on a specialised government department, with which it will be in direct contact. It will depend on the services of the planning department for the drafting and execution of its short- and long-term plans; on the investment department for its capital projects (modernisation, extension, etc.); on the department of labour for problems relating to the work-force; on the department responsible for research and technical development for implementing innovations; on the department of finance, etc.

The economic administration cannot in practice be modelled on this pure-state hypothesis. Such a model implies a constant relationship between the production unit and a large number of administrative departments which would inevitably lead to the paralysis of management. There would certainly be an element of discord between the specialised departments – for example, between the departments responsible for labour and investment. Above all, a coherent policy of sectoral and regional development would be impossible.

We may conclude in the first place that any system of economic administration must include functional elements. There will always be a finance ministry and a central labour department, for example. In a socialist system, the functional department *par excellence* is the planning department, which has a special place in the whole process of economic administration. Secondly, the functional is always combined with the sectoral or territorial principle.

Pure-State Hypothesis of the Sectoral System
This time the enterprise will depend on a single specialised ministry (light industry) for all aspects of management. The ministry will lay down a plan, which will have been drafted with or without the participation of the enterprise and which will be co-ordinated with the macro-economic plan encompassing the plan of the ministry itself. The ministry will monitor implementation of the plan, determine supplies and customers, allocate funds from the budgetary credits it will have received, and specify labour requirements. The main drawback of this system is that it prevents any co-ordinated regional development, since each ministry is geared to the current management and future expansion of its own particular sector. In extreme cases, this can lead to absurd situations. For example, the hypothetical clothing factory referred to would not be able to establish direct relationships in a regional framework with its 'natural' partners, i.e. textile concerns as suppliers and commercial organisations as sales outlets. In the absence of co-ordinating regional departments a situation might occur in which the clothing factory was receiving cloth from a mill several thousand kilometres away, while a local mill was sending similar cloth to an equally distant clothing concern.

Nevertheless, a sectoral system of administration does have many advantages. Although a specialised ministry may tend to identify the general interest with the department of its own sector, it has a global view of the sector which can ultimately benefit the economy as a whole. The ministry will be very much concerned with the fullest possible utilisation of both human and material resources, implying in particular a rational distribution of specialists. It will be in a position to implement a coherent technical policy and the rapid diffusion of innovations. It will have within its jurisdiction enterprises with similar functional problems which it will be able to solve without duplication of effort. The compiling and utilisation of all sorts of information, an essential ingredient of economic administration in any planned system, will be made easier because the accounting and statistical data supplied will be homogeneous and easily assimilated. Finally, when establishing new enterprises or extending old ones, the ministry will be in a position to rationalise the size of productive units, and above all to profit from economies of scale. These are of course only potential advantages which can only be realised under an enlightened and innovating administration.

Pure-State Hypothesis of the Territorial System
The clothing concern in Minsk, like every other unit of production and distribution in the region, will depend for all aspects of its management on a regional economic administration. Whether or not this administration will be subordinate to a higher economic authority depends on the degree of centralisation of the system. It will co-ordinate the functional aspects of production, and will therefore both relate to central functional departments and have its own functional divisions. On the other hand, it will be considerably less well placed to co-ordinate the sectoral aspects of production. Experience shows that

the regional administration concerns itself mainly with local interests and takes little account of the general objectives which have been established for the different branches of activity.

Theoretically, a regional administration makes it possible to solve problems of development more easily and effectively than in the preceding system. A sectoral administration will be primarily interested in raw material resources and will neglect the rest, tending especially to rely on workers from outside the region to make up its work-force. A regional administration, on the other hand, will take account of the availability of manpower in quantity and quality, of markets, and of the specific advantages of the area. It will seek the optimal use of local resources. For example, it will consider the possibility of building a dam not only from the viewpoint of electricity supply, but also from the point of view of irrigation, etc. Since it is nearer the units of production, it will take decisions which concern them more quickly.

However, the regional system of administration can present difficulties: the region may wish to do everything and refuse to be confined to its own natural jurisdiction. In socialist countries, this system, when it has been partially applied, has been unable to realise a rational policy of regional development. The reason for this is that the various divisions of the economic administration were not established with regional development in mind, but on the basis of existing networks of local administration and Party. The application of the regional principle has therefore led to closer political control of economic life. It is evidently easier to exercise such control over local authorities than over a sectoral administration which can defend its autonomy in the name of technical requirements. The weight of this control was bitterly resented by individual enterprises. In the U.S.S.R., after the 1957 reform which created about a hundred *sovnarkhoze* or regional economic councils, production units were subordinated to a degree of tutelage which was reinforced by geographical proximity. This control was reluctantly accepted by enterprise managers, who saw a ministry which had been well aware of their practical problems replaced by an omnipotent local body soon to be accused of ineptitude. To all this was added the difficulty of combining regional economic management with planning at the national level.

Planning in all socialist countries implies sectoral divisions and makes use of relatively stable inter-sectoral coefficients. (The regional development plan merely completes the macro-economic plan established according to branches of economic activity.) Consequently, if information can only be collected through regional departments, the planners will be faced in each region by a very wide range of data which it will be difficult to aggregate. Once the plan has been finalised, it will have to be subdivided into regional units so that it can be transmitted to the local authorities responsible for its execution. All of this will involve a great waste of time. The planning bureaux will then be tempted to use unauthorised means to avoid these difficulties, which will inevitably bring them into conflict with the regional administration. It is for these reasons that the regional principle of administration has never operated for long in any socialist country.[20]

We can now examine the development and present state of the Soviet system of economic administration. We shall turn later to the systems in force in the European socialist countries.

The Soviet System of Economic Administration

The general line of evolution of the system was as follows:
  dominance of the sectoral principle from 1928 to 1957;
  dominance of the territorial principle from 1957 to 1965, with some 'contamination' from the sectoral principle after 1962;
  a return to the sectoral principle from 1965.

Only specialised economic institutions will be studied here. These institutions are responsible to the central organs of State administration (Council of Ministers of the U.S.S.R.) and of the government of the State (Supreme Soviet of the U.S.S.R.). Both of these have general economic functions. The Supreme Soviet approves the annual plan of economic development, the State budget, and the laws regulating economic activity. The Council of Ministers co-ordinates the activity of the ministers of the U.S.S.R. (above all, ministries with an economic jurisdiction). It takes the necessary measures to implement plan and budget and to strengthen the banking and monetary systems. The same institutional structure is to be found in each of the fifteen Union republics and the twenty autonomous republics, which have their own Supreme Soviets and Councils of Ministers. At a lower level, there are the local organs of State power (territorial, district and town Soviets), together with their executive bodies whose economic jurisdiction is very limited.

THE DOMINANCE OF THE SECTORAL PRINCIPLE: 1928-57

We shall not return to the question of economic administration before 1928. Its structure was briefly described earlier in connection with the history of the socialisation of the Soviet economy. During the period of War Communism (1918-20) the whole economic life of the country was subordinated to military needs. The powers of the Supreme Economic Council, which had been set up in 1917, were transferred the following year to a political body called the Workers' and Peasants' Defence Council. In 1920 this became the Council of Labour and Defence and stood at the apex of the whole apparatus of economic administration. With the introduction of the N.E.P., the Supreme Economic Council was called upon to direct and manage the nationalised sector. In addition to its functional sub-departments (plan, technical research, personnel), it comprised sectoral sub-departments or *glavki* which were to play an increasing part in the resocialisation of the economy.

The council was abolished in 1932. The problem of its reorganisation had been put as early as the beginning of the first five-year plan in 1928 and had been discussed in terms of reinforcing the sectoral principle. In the end the council was transformed into the People's Commissariat for Heavy Industry. Two other commissariats were created at the same time: Light Industry and Timber. By 1939 there were twenty commissariats. In 1946 they assumed the name of ministries. There were thirty-two of them in the period 1946-8 and thirty-one in 1956. The system then functioned almost entirely according to the sectoral principle:

Each ministry had its own functional sub-departments, and organised investment, supplies and labour within its own branch of activity. Indeed, the negotiating power of these ministries tended to circumscribe the rôle of functional agencies such as Gosplan and the finance ministry. Most influential were those ministries whose branches of activity were best placed in the network of growth priorities (coal, steel, engineering);

The system was highly centralised. Most of the ministries were all-Union, in the sense that they directed their enterprises from the centre. For secondary branches, the ministries were Union-republican, that is to say enterprises were controlled by ministries bearing the same name as the Union republics. Each ministry operated through a system of centralised agencies or *glavki* which corresponded to sectoral or territorial sub-departments. For example, the iron and steel ministry in 1946 had thirteen central agencies: special steels, iron and steel products, ferrous alloys, engineering, refractory products, ores, coke, timber, mining, and 'production'. The last of these agencies controlled nine important production units. In addition, there were two geographical agencies, one for the centre and south, and one for the Urals.

APPLICATION OF THE TERRITORIAL PRINCIPLE: 1957-65

In February 1957, at the instigation of Krushchev, a plenary session of the Party Central Committee decided to reorganise the management of the economy according to the territorial principle: 'The centre of gravity of industrial management must be shifted to the local level.'

The 1957 reform can be explained in several ways:

Political: a reversal of policy after Stalin's death in 1953; Krushchev's wish, as first secretary of the Party, to link his name to a liberal reform.

Economic: the qualitative performance of the Soviet economy was poor, in spite of high growth rates in production; many enterprises, especially in heavy industry, operated at a loss; greater flexibility might improve their management.

Administrative: the ministries had become more or less ungovernable fiefs.

There were three main strands in the reform of 1957: the abolition of the economic ministries; the creation of a regional economic administration; a strengthening of Party control over the economy.

Abolition of the Economic Ministries

The 1957 law abolished the sectoral form of economic administration. A few ministries survived, however. In 1962 there were nine, of which five were all-Union bodies (merchant navy, transport network, transport equipment, power, rocket construction) and four Union-republican bodies (geology, agriculture, finance, broadcasting). The ministerial form of direction was therefore preserved in rail and sea transport, and broadcasting; in strategic branches of the economy (geological prospecting, power, rocket construction); in agriculture, where the ministry controlled only the State sector; and finally, in finance, which came under a functional and not a sectoral ministry.

However on 23 November 1962 a plenary session of the Party Central Committee passed a resolution on economic reorganisation. This was followed by a law in December 1962 and by a number of decrees in the following year which indirectly re-established a sectoral-type administration. In fact, a sort of economic super-ministry was established at the all-Union level, the Supreme Economic Council, reminiscent of a similar institution liquidated in 1932. This directs and co-ordinates the activity of all economic agencies, including Gosplan. The following administrative bodies depend on the Council:

Functional administrations:

Gosplan, which is responsible for drafting long- and short-term plans;

The National Economic Council *(Sovnarkhoz)* of the U.S.S.R., which ensures the current implementation of the plan and effective direction of the economic administration. It is especially important in controlling the network of authorities concerned with the planned distribution of capital goods;

The State Committee *(Gosstroj)* responsible for investment;

The State Committee for the co-ordination of scientific research.

Sectoral administrations, which are in fact the reincarnation of the former ministries:

State production committees; to these must be added State committees by industrial sector dependent on Gosplan and concerned solely with planning, not with the management of enterprises (in fuel, metallurgy, chemicals, food industry, light industry, timber and paper industry).

The Creation of a Territorial Economic Administration

The law of 1957 anticipated the division of the Soviet Union into regions of economic administration (104 to begin with). These were to become base units for administrative purposes. Their agencies, national economic councils or *sovnarkhoze*, would have immediate control over enterprises in their jurisdiction. They would examine and transmit planning indicators to the enterprises under their control, scrutinise their progress, check the results of their management, intervene frequently during the course of the budgetary year to modify the plan, and they would also requisition resources. Their management was shortly to be disparaged as 'petty tutelage' and parochial.

The territorial principle was soon on the retreat. In 1960 a 'Republican *sovnarkhoz*' was established in each of the three largest republics (R.S.F.S.R., Ukraine, Kazakstan). Their purpose was to oversee the management of the regional *sovnarkhoze* which had formerly depended on the Council of Ministers of the Republic. At a meeting of the Party Central Committee in 1962, Kruschev declared that the *sovnarkhoze* were ill-adapted to their task. A Party resolution of 23 November reduced their number in an effort to arrest the development of a parochial mentality and the fragmentation of economic management. Only forty-seven remained. The territorial principle was further weakened by the fact that many sectors were completely free of *sovnarkhoz* direction: agriculture; the building sector managed by the Gosstroj; local industry dependent on local soviets. Moreover, by a decision taken centrally any given enterprise could be directly attached to a State committee. The liquidation of the *sovnarkhoze* in 1965 was thus the logical outcome of a development dating from their creation.

The Reinforcement of Party Control
The resolution of 23 November 1962 'on Party direction of the economy' laid down that at each level of the Party hierarchy there should be agencies for industrial and agricultural management, that is to say, territorial or regional committees and republican departments of the Central Committee. At the all-Union level four departments were set up: for agriculture, building and industry, chemicals, light industry. Such a system of control had existed in the past, but without this particular division of jurisdiction. In 1964 it reverted to its previous form, but without in any way weakening Party control.

PARTIAL RETURN TO THE SECTORAL PRINCIPLE: THE REFORM OF 1965

The administrative reform of 1965 passed with hardly a comment, since it coincided with the beginning of the reform of the enterprise (September-October 1965). It was nevertheless a significant element in the series of reforms of 1965, and comprised two aspects. The first of these was negative: rejection of the territorial principle. The second was positive: the system of ministries was re-established.

The Damocles' sword hanging over the *sovnarkhoz* finally fell at the end of 1965. After a report by Kosygin, chairman of the Council of Ministers, a plenum of the Party decided to liquidate the whole *sovnarkhoz* system: *sovnarkhoze* of the U.S.S.R., republican *sovnarkhoze*, the fifty regional *sovnarkhoze*, as well as the Supreme Economic Council standing at the head of the economic administration. These decisions received legal sanction in October 1965.

Sovnarkhoz management had led to economic fragmentation. The specificity of the different branches of economic activity had been ignored and their interests dissolved into those of the locality. At the same time, local administration was highly conservative. For example, a number of *sovnarkhoze* had displayed considerable hostility to the experimental scheme of direct contractual relationships between manufacturing industry and commerce, which had been introduced in 1964 with a view to future reform of the enterprise.

Henceforth the system of economic administration was much more straight-forward. It was based on the sectoral principle: within the framework of their particular sector, units of production would come under the direction of ministries. The latter would be responsible for the direction of enterprises and for the orientation of technical policy and applied industrial research within their sector.

The present structure can be described as follows: the sectoral principle is dominant; it is associated with certain territorial elements and comprises a strong functional base; the control factor has assumed greater importance.

DOMINANCE OF THE SECTORAL PRINCIPLE

The sectoral principle is applied through a complex system of ministries and is not merely a return to the system operating before 1957. There are two important differences.

Firstly, the proportion of economic activity controlled by all-Union ministries is substantially less than that dependent on the Union-republican ministries: between one-third and one-quarter of the national product. All-Union ministries control the following branches: mechanical engineering (coming within the competence of sixteen ministries); defence industry; gas and oil industries; three ministries for transport and one for transport construction; foreign trade.

The remaining sectors come under the jurisdiction of the Union-republican ministries: agriculture and the collection or purchase by the State of agricultural produce (two ministries); domestic trade; industry, comprising metallurgy, power apart from gas, oil and atomic energy, chemicals, light industry, food industry.

There has been a parallel sectoralisation of investment control, formerly in the hands of Gosstroj, the State Committee for Construction. Since March 1967 Gosstroj has been confined to functions of general planning and technical research. Investment policy has been transferred to four Union-republican ministries: for the construction of heavy-industry enterprises and the direction of major work in metallurgy and coal; for construction in chemicals and petro-chemicals; for construction in other industrial branches; for construction in rural areas. To these there was added in 1972 an all-Union ministry for the construction of oil and gas installations. The function of these ministries is to control the implementation of investment plans and the management of specialised construction enterprises. In 1965 three other specialised ministries with similar functions were created for particular sectors: transport construction; special construction and assembly work in the field of astronautics and military investment; rural engineering, mainly in land improvement and water conservation.

The fifteen Union republics establish Union-republican ministries which operate from Moscow. However, the republics are not all obliged to display the full range of ministries. Uzbekistan hardly requires a ministry of fishing. On the other hand, they may wish to create republican ministries corresponding to specific needs. Byelorussia is the only republic with a ministry for the peat industry.[21]

The second important difference is that ministerial powers were defined in a general regulation of 10 July 1967 and are confined to enterprises within their jurisdiction. They cover such things as planning, economic and financial management, and employment. In its relationship with the enterprise, the ministry does not merely have rights, but obligations too.

At the same time the regulation governing the activity of ministries holds them responsible to the 'Party, the state and the people' for the development of their sector, the quality of production and the satisfaction of consumer demand. It stresses also the dangers of ministerial isolation and the need to keep in touch with other ministries and departments. Finally, it is also stipulated that the U.S.S.R. ministry in Moscow, although it enjoys all-Union status, must respect the particular interests of the republics and take account of proposals advanced by republican councils of ministers. Similarly, the U.S.S.R. ministry has the right neither to create nor to liquidate an enterprise without first consulting the organs of republican power.

Thus the new-style economic ministry does not resemble its Stalinist predecessor. It has more duties and less power. It is anticipated that at some future date further protection will be given to the individual enterprise against possible ministerial encroachments by placing a screen between the base unit of production and the ministry itself. According to this scheme, a body representing enterprises within the same sector would receive and transmit administrative directives to the constituent enterprises. Such an innovation would constitute fundamental progress towards devolution of economic power. However, the U.S.S.R. is a long way behind other socialist countries in this respect. In other countries, as we shall see, economic reform has really transferred actual enterprise management to the level of the representative associations. In such cases, the organs of central government restrict themselves to matters of general economic orientation. In the U.S.S.R., on the other hand, the grouping of enterprises is merely intended to achieve greater concentration of production, since base units continue to be the mere recipients of ministerial directives. In fact not only has no ministry set up groups endowed with financial autonomy and a share of power, but in certain cases groups established before 1965 within the framework of the *sovnarkhoz* system have been abolished by ministries jealous of their own prerogatives, since the return to the sectoral principle.

However, although in 1972 there were only 880 associations grouping less than 4000 of the 50,000 enterprises in the U.S.S.R. and covering about 10% of total industrial production, a decree of the Party Central Committee and of the Council of Ministers of the U.S.S.R. in March 1973 stipulates that the restructuring of industrial administration must be completed between 1973 and 1975. The new administrative pattern will be either two-tier (all-Union or Union-republican ministry; association or combine) or three-tier (ministry; intermediate agency which may be a central department, a republican ministry or an all-Union industrial association; the base unit in the form of an association, a combine or an individual enterprise). The present structure may continue to exist in certain exceptional cases in light industry. On 2 March 1973 the jurisdiction, rights and obligations of the all-Union and republican associations were defined. After this decisive intervention, the movement towards concentration will doubtless gain momentum in spite of the resistance which has held it back for so long.

THE SECTORAL PRINCIPLE AND ITS RELATIONSHIP WITH CERTAIN ASPECTS OF THE TERRITORIAL AND FUNCTIONAL PRINCIPLES

Quite apart from the degree of devolution implicit in the establishment of Union-republican ministries, two further aspects of the territorial principle need to be mentioned. In the first place, the reform anticipates a local policy in the development of consumer industries. It has been suggested that the latter could be municipalised by being brought under the control of the local authorities (local soviets), which are in the best position for adapting this type of production to demand. Secondly, although territorial economic administration was abolished in 1965, the territorial principle has been strengthened in the area of planning. In fact, the plan is established on the basis of a division into eighteen regions corresponding to economic complexes, which are moreover much more rational than the previous administrative divisions of the *sovnarkhoze*. The aim of this regional planning is to counterbalance the sectoral orientation in economic management.

However, equilibrium has not yet been achieved, and since reform numerous demands have been made, particularly in the upper echelons of the republican hierarchies, for a better co-ordination of sectoral plans within the territorial framework.

The functional element is maintained through various State committees. A chart of the economic administration would assimilate State committees and central administrative organs fulfilling the functional principle. There are five committees with especially important functions:

State Planning Committee or Gosplan: Gosplan is responsible at the all-Union level for the formulation of long- and short-term plans. It must at the same time co-ordinate the development of all economic sectors and regions of the country. It has the further task of improving planning methods. Gosplan controls general implementation of the plan and must facilitate any necessary adjustments during the period of its execution. It has the additional function of liaising with the planning organs of other socialist countries and with the various departments of Comecon.

It possesses a complex internal structure based on both sectoral and functional principles. Thus it has sections according to industrial branch corresponding to the planning departments of the sectoral ministries with which they are in close contact.

Apart from the all-Union Gosplan, the Gosplan apparatus comprises a hierarchy of local and republican agencies. Each republican Gosplan formulates its plan on the basis of the general scheme laid down by the all-Union Gosplan. The jurisdiction of the republican Gosplans was extended as a result of the economic reforms, so that now only planning for the defence industry lies outside their scope.

State Committee on Construction or Gosstroj: This committee is concerned with the technical and methodological control of investment. Construction enterprises now depend on specialised ministries.

State Committee for Material and Technical Supplies: This committee was established in 1965 and is the main instrument of intersectoral co-ordination. Employing 600,000 people, it controls the exchange of 25,000 types of intermediate product which it supplies to enterprises and work-shops. In this field, the ministries merely serve to concentrate and synthesise the requirements of their respective enterprises, which they then transmit to the committee which will subsequently distribute the products via its twenty-one central boards.

State Committee for Labour and Wages: This old institution was created in 1933 from the People's Commissariat of Labour. It is in fact a ministry of labour.

State Committee for Science and Technology.

In aggregate there are fourteen committees. To the functional administrations we should certainly also add the Banks (State and Investment), and the Central Statistical Board of the U.S.S.R.

CONTROL

Control by the masses over economic life is an essential element in the functioning of Soviet economic institutions. Lenin put it like this in 1917: 'Verification and control are essential to the organisation and functioning of the first stage of communist society.'

It should be noted that this is not a reference to mass participation in the direction of the economy or in the management of production units. Self-management is non-existent in the U.S.S.R. The role of workers' organisations, basically the trade unions, is to participate in fixing wages and to manage the social security system. More particularly, the trade unions will share in fixing wage rates at occupational level, determining the selection of wage categories at enterprise level, establishing productivity norms and so on.

The real meaning of popular control is the following: workers should be supplied with information on any malfunctioning of the economy; the revelation of minor and major scandals; an obligation on the authorities to eliminate the causes and effects of mistakes, illegal acts, fraud, etc., which may have been perpetuated in the course of economic activity.

It is extremely difficult to ensure the efficient operation of such control. One would have to overcome natural apathy, protect individuals revealing inadequacies, or, where there was no question of repressive measures being taken by a particular administration, create forms of control which were really popular and not merely integrated into the administrative hierarchy.

It is not surprising, therefore, that the organisation of control has been modified more than a dozen times. For a long time control oscillated between two extremes: mass spontaneity on the one hand, and control through Party agents working within the party apparatus on the other. Workers' control was in fact established in certain enterprises in the capital from the time of the Revolution. From 1920 it was institutionalised and known as the Peasant and Workers' Inspection. Party surveillance in this area began with its own Ministry of State Control, which operated until 1934 in concert with the Peasant and Workers' Inspection. From 1962 to 1965, surveillance passed into the hands of the Party-State Control Committee.

A median solution has usually been found, that is to say, the organisation of control under the aegis of a State department. This was the Committee of Soviet Control between 1934 and 1957, which was revised, suppressed and reconstituted several times. Since 1965 the responsible authority has been the State Committee of Popular Control. The latter consists of a specialised apparatus supported by groups of voluntary workers who, in the guise of control groups or committees, are to be found in enterprises, shops, public establishments, the administration and so on. In Moscow alone in 1969 there were 35,500 control groups comprising 205,000 voluntary popular inspectors.

The objective of control is to check systematically that Party and government directives have been implemented by economic units and departments. Similarly, it implies an all-out struggle against anything which might impede the realisation of planning objectives: 'violations of state discipline, parochialism, administrative routine, wastage, embezzlement, all attempts to deceive the State and impair socialist property.' The law on control specifies that the widest publicity should be given to its work, above all through the media of press, radio and television. Offenders once informed of the complaints against them may be sued if they do not immediately make good the damage, and in any case are always liable to disciplinary measures within their own organisation.

The efficiency of the control apparatus assumes constant and regular use. Sometimes the control hierarchy resorts to campaigns in areas where public opinion is particularly sensitive. In July and August 1968, for example, there was a general check on shops and restaurants in Moscow. Subsequently, 1200 establishments were invited to improve their organisation.

The problem of 'economic delinquency' is closely related to that of popular control. The masses' right of scrutiny over the way in which the various authorities manage socialist property is exercised through the control apparatus. The efficacy of this control will therefore depend largely on the attitude of individuals and social groups towards the property which the Revolution seized from private capital and which Lenin urged them to respect in these words: 'Protect and preserve, as you would your own eyes, the land, bread, factories, equipment, products and means of transport which henceforth belong to you all!' In all socialist countries collective morality includes a new ethical value—a conscious commitment to the preservation of socialist property. This has a corollary in the new set of crimes relating to this property. The extent of these crimes and the community's disapproval or tolerance of them are an important element in economic life.

In the U.S.S.R. economic delinquency has always been an object of concern for the authorities and has always been subject to heavy penalties. After the Revolution and during the civil war, crimes against socialist property were perpetrated either by individuals bent on sabotaging the regime or by speculators of all kinds. Otherwise they were simply the result of deprivation and poverty. These conditions persisted until after World War II.

What is difficult to explain is the damage done to socialist property in an expanding economy where primary needs have been more or less completely satisfied and where state ownership of the means of production is unquestioned by the vast mass of the population. How can one explain the growth of delinquency to the point where the Soviet authorities had to reimpose the death penalty for the most serious economic crimes in 1961-2?

Certain crimes may in themselves appear relatively trivial: the book-keeper helping himself from the till, the worker taking away materials to do odd jobs in his own or his neighbour's home, or the collective farmer rearing his private cow on collective hay. This sort of delinquency can be explained partly in terms of the self-interest motive analysed by criminologists and partly by the inadequacy of certain services in the Soviet Union. What is serious, however, is the community's general toleration and even tacit approval of this sort of crime, an attitude which could well lead to a lowering of public morality. Such a situation is far more dangerous in a socialist than in a capitalist state. In the latter attacks on private property, which constitute most economic breaches of the law, are at least implicitly condemned by the owners.

In 1968 several surveys were carried out in this area. In one of these, involving a state farm, a tractor factory and a dairy-product factory, the following question was put to the employees: 'Is there in your enterprise a careful and conscientious attitude towards socialist property?' Only 68.5% of the workers replied in the affirmative, the percentage falling to 23.5% in the case of management. A further significant fact was that the percentage of positive replies was much higher among older personnel than among newer workers. The criminologists on the inquiry interpreted this to mean that the older the employee the more accustomed he is to a negligent attitude towards socialist property! Among factors leading to delinquency, workers gave priority to 'the unconscientious behaviour of management with regard to raw materials, semi-finished and finished products, etc.' This is no surprise in view of the fact that many economic infringements of the law have no judicial sequel, because the management does not wish to denounce its workers or else deliberately covers up for them, either out of direct complicity or because the director has no wish to appear as the head of an enterprise of dubious morality.

Another survey produced similar results. It covered a group of textile concerns in the Moscow region, where the theft of fabrics by employees had reached worrying proportions. The investigation was this time confined to workers found guilty of theft. Apart from direct motives of self-interest, 97% explained their act in terms of the absence of control by management. 30% declared that their colleagues had seen them commit the offence without showing any sign of disapproval.

In a system based on social ownership of the means of production, such phenomena cannot be considered as merely secondary. The question is can the absence of a collective consciousness vis-à-vis this property be explained in terms of a hangover from the capitalist past? Or can it be more adequately explained in terms of an institutional system which does not involve workers directly in the management of production, something which would give them a greater interest in the protection of social wealth?

Systems of Economic Administration in the Socialist Countries of Europe

Very generally speaking, it would be fair to say that until 1957 the European socialist countries modelled the administrative framework of economic units on that of the U.S.S.R. Yugoslavia[22] was the exception, rejecting the Soviet model as early as 1950. The Soviet reform of 1957 precipitated certain divergencies within the system. Most of the socialist countries followed the Soviet Union, replacing the sectoral by the territorial principle only to abandon it a few years later. Others, such as Poland, maintained their own system of economic administration.

Moreover, nowhere did the administrative reforms introduced in all these countries as in the U.S.S.R. after 1965 result in such significant reversals of policy as in the Soviet Union itself. The reform had three main characteristics. Firstly, it increased the power of the central authorities in their control over the general orientation of economic activity (sectoral ministries). Secondly, day-to-day management of enterprises was based on a system of industrial associations. It was this feature of reform in the socialist countries which most clearly distinguished it from the Soviet reform, which has still not established intermediaries between the ministry (or its departments) and the enterprise.

Thirdly, it placed greater emphasis than in the U.S.S.R. on worker participation in management and control.

THE STRENGTHENING OF THE CENTRAL ORGANS OF ECONOMIC ADMINISTRATION

In most of the countries there was a return to the system of sectoral ministries. In 1965 the G.D.R. abolished its National Economic Council and established eight industrial ministries based on its former divisions, a Ministry of Material Supplies and an Agricultural Council. The abolition of the Economic Council reinforced the rôle of the State Planning Commission, and also of the State Committee for Research and Technology on account of the significance attached to applied industrial research in the G.D.R. Bulgaria reinstated its ministries in 1966. Poland and Hungary also have an economic administration of this type. Romania modified the structure of its ministries in the same direction and placed at the head of the whole administration a Higher Council for Economic and Social Development, which is dependent on both the Council of State and the Party Central Committee and thus reinforces the managerial rôle of the political authorities. In Czechoslovakia administrative reform was only introduced on 1 January 1971, combining five sectoral ministries and functional departments at federal level. The power of the economic departments of the two Czech and Slovak republics is very limited. It is worth noting that as a general rule the administrative system is far less complicated in the socialist countries of Europe than it is in the U.S.S.R. Not only are these countries much smaller geographically but their economies are far less diversified and so the number of ministries required is much reduced, to less than a dozen on average.

It is certainly true that in all of these socialist countries of Europe, the central administration (ministries or boards) no longer have direct control over enterprises. They must now concentrate their attention on the general problems of economic development. The centre of gravity in the management of enterprises has been transferred to the level of the industrial 'association'.

THE INDUSTRIAL ASSOCIATIONS: AGENCIES OF DIRECT CONTROL OVER ENTERPRISE

These associations are based on the concentration of enterprises within the same branch of activity. Although they may have different names in the different countries, their functions are identical: to bring the management of enterprises within a specific group under the same control.

In the G.D.R. there were 80 associations in 1958 (84 in 1968), comprising nearly 2,000 large units. In 1964 they accounted for 13% of all concerns and supplied 72% of gross production. There were 8 associations in the mining and power sector, 5 in metallurgy, 6 in the textile industry, 8 in chemicals, and 34 in engineering. They are known as the V.V.B. or *Vereinigungen Volks-eigener Betriebe*. These associations, financially autonomous since 1964, have responsibility for planning production, fixing prices and organising the supply and sales of enterprises within their jurisdiction, as well as for centralising financial management. They receive directives from their particular ministry, which they then classify and pass on to the enterprises in their branches. They alone are responsible to the ministry for the results achieved in their group. German experience has shown the utility of these groupings in at least two fields: investment and foreign trade. It is possible for the associations to devise a coherent long-term investment policy. They have an internal financing fund derived from a proportion of the profits and the depreciation allowances of the constituent enterprises. Enterprises also have a technical research fund levied on their turnover. The principle of non-budgetary self-financing of investment was agreed in 1967. The share of the budget in financing the whole of industrial investment fell from 59% in 1963 to 6% in the plan of 1970. As for foreign trade, it is the association which contracts for deliveries with the suppliers and customers of the group. Equally, the associations may deal directly on foreign markets or through the joint establishment of subsidiaries or import-export offices. From 1968 there was a further development along-side the associations: the establishment of combines or vertical integration, especially in furniture, metallurgy and electrical engineering. One of the most important is the clock- and watch-making combine, Ruhla. In 1972 the thirty-seven combines already in existence accounted for a third of global industrial production and half of industrial exports.

The same sort of association is to be found in most of the other countries. Czechoslovakia had developed a more elaborate system based on two types of association. The first, the *trusts,* were organised along the lines of horizontal branch integration. There were seventy-three of these at the beginning of 1968. The second, the *Konzern,* of which seventeen were set up, were established on the principle of vertical integration. Because of some resistance on their part, individual enterprises subsequently gained the right to leave the association, provided they then came under the control of the competent ministry. From the summer of 1968, dozens of enterprises expressed their wish to withdraw from the association to which they had been attached. This was in conformity with the terms of the action programme of the Czechoslovak Communist Party of 5 April 1968. According to the programme: 'Enterprises must have the right to determine the activity of these groups, the right to leave them and to create others, and the right to enter other groups which will fulfil more efficiently the functions of concentration and specialisation of production.' Since 1969 the freedom of enterprise in this respect has probably been restricted. It seems too that the functioning of the trusts has not been entirely satisfactory. From the beginning, the trusts tended to act rather like pressure groups, attempting to obtain concessions from the ministry for their particular branch of activity (permission to raise prices, credit facilities, fiscal advantages, etc.). This is doubtless a general risk involved in socialist cartelisation. The associations display a tendency to behave like monopolies and to abuse their position of strength. A similar situation arose in Hungary, where the reform introduced in 1968 authorised enterprises to form their own associations in addition to the 300 which had been in existence since 1962. The reforms replaced the previous centralised distribution of capital goods with a free market, and certain production associations profited from their monopoly position by imposing their own prices and conditions on customers. The Hungarian authorities reacted by dissolving a dozen trusts. There are still a score of them, besides twenty-five associations and nearly twenty joint-stock companies mainly engaged in foreign trade. Associations created on the initiative of firms can only have limited objectives (joint research programmes, the production of spare parts, advertising, etc.). They have no independent legal status. These precautions against excessive concentration have no real effect in a country where there are less than a thousand industrial enterprises altogether and where industry is relatively the most concentrated in the world.

This negative aspect should not be forgotten in any analysis of the effects of administrative devolution coupled with the economic concentration of industrial units.

WORKER PARTICIPATION

One of the most interesting aspects of the association is worker participation in their administration. The association is of course directed by a chairman appointed and dismissed by the minister, and the chairman likewise appoints and dismisses the managers of enterprises in his group. However he is almost always assisted by a consultative body containing a number of worker representatives. In Poland they are called colleges, in Bulgaria economic councils, in the G.D.R. councils comprising workers, managers and specialists, and in Czechoslovakia boards of management. This consultative body is kept informed of the economic and financial results of the association, and must be consulted on matters concerning the use of its resources, particularly in the area of 'internal financing'. In Romania further progress has been made. The managing board of the association is no longer an advisory but a deliberative body, one-third of which represents the ministry, one-third the management of the group, while one-third are trade-union representatives of the workers.

In every case worker participation is organised through the trade unions and takes place at the relatively high administrative level of the industrial association. The reforms have hardly improved direct participation in the day-to-day management of enterprise. This has been put into effect only in Yugoslavia, where the whole system is based on self-management. In the other countries workers' councils involved in enterprise management have had an only episodic existence, and that usually during periods of crisis. A pale reflection of them is to be found in the various types of committees and discussions which have an advisory capacity in some areas of activity. On the other hand, the trade unions everywhere constitute a powerful and organised force, but their function is to defend the professional interests of the workers and not to participate in management.

In the Soviet Union the workers' councils were still-born in 1918. A nationalisation bill, never actually implemented, included management by elected factory councils which would be competent to establish plan and budget, draft internal administrative procedures for the unit of production, and take part in all important decisions. In the socialist countries of Central Europe, workers' councils also appeared during periods of crisis. In Hungary the draft constitution for the councils drawn up in October 1956 conferred important powers on them. They would be able to take decisions on all production problems and determine the distribution of income within the enterprise. The councils would also elect management committees to work alongside managers, and they would be responsible for the general progress of the enterprise. The law on councils passed at the end of 1956 was already more limited in scope and was subsequently abrogated in 1957. Existing councils were dissolved. In Poland, the first councils appeared in September-October 1956 and received legal sanction in November of the same year. By the end of 1957 they covered one-quarter of Polish enterprises, employing half the labour force. Numerical success, however, concealed the general ineffectualness of the councils, which were welcomed by neither trade unions, Party, nor enterprise management. In fact they began to disappear from 1959 as a result not of liquidation but of absorption by a new institution created in December 1958. This was known as the 'assembly of workers' autonomy' and was composed of delegates from the union branch in the enterprise, from the Party cell and from the workers' council. Thus institutionalised, the workers' council assumed a purely formal rôle. In the G.D.R., the workers' committees formed spontaneously in 1956-7 were all dissolved in 1958.

Ten years later and in similar circumstances, there appeared in Czechoslovakia a movement in favour of establishing councils, outlined in the action programme of the Czechoslovak Communist Party of 5 April 1968. This document even recommended that councils should be empowered to appoint and dismiss both directors and higher management. It indicated quite clearly that they would not be mere extensions of the trade unions, but that they would be elected bodies composed of delegates representing the work-force and outside representatives of economic and social interests (such as banking). This scheme was never implemented.

The emphasis given in the action programme of the Czechoslovak Communist Party to the difference between the workers' councils and the trade unions is explained by the fact that in socialist countries trade unions play a very restricted part in management. Representing the vast mass of workers, their main function lies in the social sphere where they possess considerable power: the management of social security, the formulation and supervision of labour laws, collective wage bargaining, etc. It is significant, for example, that in the U.S.S.R. worker participation in the formulation of the plan and in the control of its execution is effected through a weak body of little prestige known as the 'standing committee on production'. It was established by decree in 1958 and comprises representatives of the trade union, management, the Party and workers elected at their own general meeting. The committee meets once or twice a quarter to hear reports by the management on the progress of the enterprise, and to voice opinions on the organisation of production and the fixing of technical norms. Similar institutions with the same functions exist in the other countries: production committees in the G.D.R., assemblies of workers' autonomy in Poland, production committees in Hungary.

Prospects for the further development of worker participation in the socialist countries outside Yugoslavia appear very limited. There are two possible solutions. The first is that there will be a move towards the Yugoslav system. Some countries have tried this at certain periods in their history, coinciding with a clear rejection of the Soviet model of socialism. However, the effective and powerful operation of workers' councils inevitably implies rejecting the principle of unitary management of enterprises by a body of functionaries belonging to the economic administration. This in turn challenges the political base on which the whole of this administration system rests. That is the reason for their disappearance in Hungary and the G.D.R., their still-birth in Czechoslovakia, and their absorption in Poland. The other alternative is to enlarge the rôle of the trade unions. Hitherto such attempts have failed. An analysis of the activities of trade unions in all the socialist countries leads to one main conclusion: they show very little interest in questions directly related to production, probably because they know the limits of their powers. The workers count on their union to guarantee their job. Works' committees generally and systematically oppose redundancy, even where it is technically justified. They expect the union to obtain advantages in such areas as housing on workers' estates, holiday vouchers for rest homes, etc., and to defend their interests in labour disputes. Only on one point did the economic reform change this generally passive approach. Trade unions have everywhere been brought into the process of determining bonuses or other forms of profit sharing in the different enterprises. Here they have sometimes been very effective.

In the European socialist countries, worker participation in the management of enterprise is therefore only very indirect. And this is in spite of collective ownership of the means of production, and in spite of the substitutes for participation by means of different forms of control within the enterprise and mass mobilisation outside it, in an effort to ensure effective execution of the plan.

The weakness of participation is generally reflected in lack of interest. It is this weakness which probably explains, in part at least, those phenomena described in the socialist press as 'shortcomings in work discipline' or a 'weakening of the spirit of socialist emulation', tendencies which can lead to a general slackening of effort by workers. We shall consider in the next chapter whether the Yugoslav example of self-management offers a possible solution.'

Chapter 2

1. Enterprise Reform in the U.S.S.R.
2. Enterprise Reform in the Socialist Countries of Europe

ECONOMIC UNITS
THE INDUSTRIAL ENTERPRISE

In every socialist country the primary function of the economic administration is to direct the basic units of the economy according to planning strategy and the principle of socialist ownership. These economic units will cover industrial and agricultural enterprises, commercial organisation and transport services. The ultimate objective of the administration is to ensure implementation of the plan. The main difficulty here is to harmonise the interests of different economic agencies (individuals or groups).

In capitalist society it is the market mechanism, competition, which tends to resolve antagonistic interests. In the socialist system, the abolition of private property in the means of production does not automatically eliminate such conflict, and if the economic agencies do not spontaneously act in the general interest, the State will have to ensure that they do.

The situation obviously poses two problems. The first, concerning the philosophy of the system, is to discover how representative of the national interest the general interest defended by the State and its apparatus really is. An investigation of this problem lies outside the scope of the present text, and we shall not pursue the matter here. The second problem concerns the means employed by the administrative apparatus to attain its objective of harmonising different interests. This means achieving a balance between the centre and the 'periphery', between the interests of different groups and economic units, between the individual interests of workers and those of their enterprise and so on.

There has been a tendency in socialist countries to develop in the same direction. From the authoritarian regulation of all economic life, they have passed to methods of control which link the direct and centralised administration of economic units with autonomy of management at enterprise level. A corollary of this development is increasing reliance on material incentives to reinforce or replace administrative directives. Underlying the whole process is the following observation, gradually accepted everywhere: the basic economic unit will more readily respond in the direction required by the authorities as a result of its own immediate material interest than as a result of administrative compulsion.

At the beginning and end of this historical process there are consequently two different notions about the management of economic units.

1. *The authoritarian approach*: here any 'collective' form of material incentive in enterprise management is excluded. Only the individual self-interest of workers is taken into account and utilised by means of wage and bonus adjustments. The economic unit is an administrative tool and must obey orders transmitted downwards through an administrative and hierarchical chain in which it is the last link. Whether the hierarchy is founded on the sectoral or territorial principle makes no difference. Mistakes by enterprise directors are punished with disciplinary measures against the individuals responsible. The failure of management results not in bankruptcy of the concern but in its reorganisation under a new director.

The application of this authoritarian approach led to disappointments and miscalculations in the execution of the plan in every sector of economic life: agriculture, commerce, and industry. In agriculture, failure was explained away with references to the climate, meteorology, the peasant mentality, and the 'inferior' nature of co-operative as compared with state ownership.

Gradually the idea developed that only by transforming the administrative framework of the individual enterprise could management and results be improved.

2. *The approach combining centralised control with management autonomy*: in the interests of efficient plan execution economic units must be given more freedom of management and a material stake in this management. Managerial autonomy and a collective material interest in the enterprise go together: if the enterprise has greater freedom, there must at the same time be a tangible objective for the work-force of the establishment, the realisation of which will coincide with the best possible implementation of the plan. This objective will be profit maximisation within the enterprise. Profit is thereby called upon to play a primary rôle in socialist economic management. We shall see why this new rôle of profit cannot be interpreted to mean a 'return to capitalism'.

We have deliberately not opposed 'plan' with 'market', just as in the last chapter we avoided opposing 'centralisation' with 'decentralisation'. As we shall see, whatever name may be given to the economic reforms in the socialist countries themselves, such as 'new mechanism' or 'new system', they are based on a combination of planning and market forces, the second being subordinate to the first. We must also be clear about what is understood by 'market'. It should not be thought that the socialist economies are passing from total planning to perfect competition. On account of their industrial structures, which are comparable to those in developed capitalist countries, the 'socialist market' could only be one of monopolistic competition. The problem is that of utilising the specific mechanisms of the latter for and through planning.

This particular approach was first conceived and discussed in relation to industrial enterprise, to which this chapter will be devoted. However the movement for reform has spread to other units of production and distribution in the state or collectivised sector. This extension of reform will be studied in the next chapter.

1. ENTERPRISE REFORM IN THE U.S.S.R.

The reform of the enterprise, decided at a plenary meeting of the Communist Party Central Committee at the end of September 1965, was introduced gradually from January 1966. By 1970 it applied to more than 36,000 enterprises accounting for 83% of industrial production and more than 91% of total profits.

The process of reform passed through three stages: a criticism of the previous situation; a series of decisions taking account of the proposals put forward during the preceding years; the progressive application of the reform.

Criticism of the Traditional Situation of the Enterprise

This criticism revealed a divergence of interest between enterprise and administration which the central authorities had been unable to reconcile within the traditional authoritarian framework defined above.

SUBORDINATION OF THE ENTERPRISE TO THE ADMINISTRATION

Within this framework the enterprise is a unit of production managed by a single director who is appointed by and is responsible for his management to the organs of the economic administration. These organs determine almost every item of his management by imposing a series of tasks, the fulfilment of which is carefully checked.

At the same time, the enterprise enjoys what is called *khozraschyot*, formally at any rate. We shall translate this as 'financial autonomy', but it is an extremely hard concept to define; Soviet writers at least escape the problem of translation. We propose the following definition of *khozraschyot*: The enterprise, a productive unit endowed with legal status for accounting purposes, is responsible for its management to the agencies of the economic administration, and within a given framework of economic activity laid down by the plan must cover its working costs by its revenue and if possible make a profit.

Commentary on this definition:

'The enterprise is a productive unit endowed with legal status for accounting purposes': even during the most authoritarian and centralised periods of enterprise management, the Soviet firm was always an individual unit from the accounting point of view, with its own balance sheet, trading account and reserves.

'It is responsible for its management to agencies of the economic administration': administrative interference varies directly with the degree of authoritarian centralisation. This type of 'petty tutelage' means that the administration can use or abuse its rights with impunity, without being accountable to the enterprise in question. It can, for example, impair the efficient management of the firm by modifying the current plan or by transferring part of its reserves to another concern.

'Within a given framework of economic activity laid down by the plan': the plan is the base of the firm's activity. It takes the form of a production programme, a technical plan and an estimate of expenditure and revenue. This is the *tekhpromfinplan* (technical-industrial-financial plan) which may reach dozens of pages in length, or even several hundred in the case of large firms.

The tasks imposed on the enterprise are formulated in terms of indices (sometimes called indicators in contemporary Sovietology). An index is a figure showing the enterprise what it must accomplish (planned index), and the administration what the enterprise has in fact accomplished (the accounting index, which at the end of the period is related to the planned index).

Before enterprise reform the indices were both detailed and numerous, tying the enterprise to a variety of objectives. The growing complexity of the management of industrial enterprise made it increasingly difficult to co-ordinate the indices, especially as they were calculated and imposed from the centre. The indices covered four areas.

Production: the index was often fixed in terms of the total value of production, which the firm would then attempt to maximise by every possible means; by using the costliest raw materials so as to raise the total value of production, or by manufacturing those articles which were easiest to produce, often at the expense of quality and finish. It was essential to be able to display a total product of high aggregate value, even if quality or variety did not satisfy the consumer.

Enterprise folklore is prolific and one could easily produce a thick volume of stories published by the newspapers on the ways firms implemented the plan according to the established indices. Increasing the value of the product by using expensive raw materials or by adding useless extras was a sore point with consumers for a long time. For example, it was difficult to buy plain wooden kitchen stools because the production of this simple article was not to the advantage of firms, who preferred to make painted chairs so as to raise their gross index. Generally speaking, everyday consumer goods were often pointlessly ornate, since the motif on a plate or decoration on a dress made possible a higher product value without really increasing the cost to the enterprise. A consumer once complained in his daily newspaper that he could not find electric wire extensions in the shops which were not embellished with porcelain beads at both ends—which buyers soon threw away. Sometimes raw material norms were imposed, but it was always possible to get round them: a clothing factory was obliged to use a particular cloth to make coats; to raise the value of the coats, it hit on the idea of using for the lining a material costing twice as much as the cloth on the outside.

A second way of raising the total value index in the case of a firm producing a wide range of products was to concentrate on those which were easiest to make. Thus a clothing factory might prefer to concentrate on adults' rather than children's clothes, since the latter require proportionately more work. One particular category of product which was always disadvantageous from the point of view of the total production index was the manufacture of spare parts, which are not very rewarding in terms of indices but which require much labour. That is why, even when there was no shortage of a particular article, it was impossible to buy spare parts for it. Consequently, a black market in spare parts developed between individuals and between firms.

The index can also be fixed in kind: so many metres of cloth, so many tons of steel or machinery, so many units, etc. The reaction by firms to planning in kind had highly deleterious effects on the economy as a whole. For example, the fixing of an index in linear metres for cloth encouraged textile enterprises to narrow the width of the product, while a tonnage index in engineering produced heavier and bulkier machinery.

Costs: the target here took the form of a cost reduction index in relation to the previous planning period. However, the pursuit of cost reduction tended to produce lower-quality products.

Enterprise personnel: the wages fund, the division of the work-force into categories, the total number employed, the productivity of labour and wage rates were all planned.

The management of productive capital: planned indices established norms for the use of equipment and raw materials. Moreover, the plan decided the firm's suppliers, as well as the type and quantity of purchases to be obtained from each supplier.

This type of enterprise plan was criticised on many counts. There were three main criticisms.

Firstly, it was drafted without the participation of the enterprise concerned. Formally the plan was drawn up only after a process of consultation. This involved a draft plan for the firm drawn up by the planning agencies on the basis of the results of the preceding year. Enterprise counter-propositions to the administrative hierarchy followed and subsequently final approval of the plan (*cf.* chapter 5). In practice the plan was imposed from above by the administration, which had a profound mistrust of the individual enterprise, considering *a priori* that the firm tended systematically to overstate its needs and to understate its real productive potential.

Secondly, the plan was more or less arbitrarily revised during the period of its implementation. The firm could never be sure of the stability of the indices which had been allotted to it.

Thirdly, traditionally, planning targets had to be exceeded. The bonuses linked to plan implementation were progressive and were designed to encourage overfulfilment of planning objectives. (This implies that the plan was not an accurate reflection of real industrial potential and that it had not been scientifically formulated.) The effort to exceed planning requirements was a permanent one but tended to intensify towards the end of the planning period, when the whole economy would be in a state of feverish activity. When firms were unable to reach the targets of their particular plan, rather than submit to the unpleasantness consequent on non-fulfilment, they would resort to various methods of cooking the accounts. The most common was to include in the present planning period the results of the first week or fortnight of the following one, in the hope that the deficit could be made up later.

'It must cover its working costs with revenue': even during periods of considerable centralisation of management the enterprise had a degree of autonomy in day-to-day management. On the other hand, it had none at all in the field of investment. It was allocated a statutory sum and almost all its investment was financed from budgetary sources. The firm was not concerned with investment policy (extension, modernisation, etc.) and had to make 'prudent and economical' use of the productive capital it possessed with a view to covering its costs. However, as we shall see, the no-deficit principle had many exceptions.

The costs of the firm were essentially composed of:

Wages: the wages fund was planned. Every fortnight the State Bank released a sum equal to the wages bill (on the basis of the plan, of which it had a copy) as well as sums for the many bonuses to be paid for exceeding the production plan, for productivity, for cost reductions, etc. The last-mentioned sum was released on production of relevant enterprise vouchers.

Expenditure on raw materials: the Bank had at its disposal all documents relating to enterprise supplies. It paid suppliers after checking that the purchases made did in fact correspond to the allocation of raw materials established in the plan. All payments between firms had to be made through the Bank. Moreover, it exercised close control over stock management and the accumulation of abnormal stocks. Since the enterprise was never certain of its supplies, stock accumulation was a common policy, as the firm attempted to build up reserves in case of need.

Capital charges: until reform they remained negligible, since the firm paid no interest on its productive capital. The only capital charge was depreciation, the rates of which were very low and the base (balance-sheet value of the assets) generally under-valued. It should be noted that the systematic undervaluation of capital has a theoretical basis. Value theory and its implications for the value of capital goods will be examined later.

Sales receipts were also fixed in advance since they proceeded from the quantities produced (established in the plan) and from the selling prices determined by the state. The firm had no marketing problems since its customers were already earmarked in the plan. They had to take its product even if it did not correspond to their needs (especially in quality; the only recourse of the customer was then to protest to the economic administration). The firm's receipts were thus guaranteed, and they had to be paid in their entirety into the State Bank.

'And if possible make a profit': the notion of enterprise profit was not suddenly discovered by Soviet economists during the discussions which preceded reform. Profit has always existed as an element in the management of enterprise. But before reform it was a secondary element for several reasons.

In the first place, profit was not traditionally an important index in the plan. What mattered to the firm was to fulfil and if possible improve on the production and cost reduction plans, for it was basically to these two indices that the bonuses paid to workers and management were linked.

Secondly, even with exemplary management the firm was not always in a position to make a profit. Owing to a policy which systematically depressed prices for capital goods, enterprises in this sector often ended up with a deficit which was then made good by the State. This was the category known as 'planned deficit' enterprises. They were especially common in the extractive industries.

Thirdly, the enterprise which made a profit often kept very little of it. On average, it had to pay 70% of its profit into the budget in the form of a 'profits tax'. This was not a fixed coefficient but a distribution tax. Its yield was determined by the administration (ministry or *sovnarkhoz*) which distributed it arbitrarily among the enterprises within its jurisdiction. The result was that some enterprises were totally exempt, while others were obliged to hand over 90% or more of their profit. Moreover, the administration could make deductions, practically without limit, from the surplus of profitable concerns in order either to cover the deficits of other enterprises or to build up reserves. The meagre residue (1%–6%) was paid into an enterprise fund, the use of which was closely controlled. This same fund received 20%–50% of any 'excess profit' eventually made beyond planning expectations. As a general rule, the 'enterprise fund' was so small that the enterprise had no interest in making a profit.

CRITICISM BY ECONOMISTS

Criticism developed after 1958–60 within the framework of a general renaissance of economic science, which was characterised by new and fertile discussions on value theory and price formation (1957–8), and on the measurement of investment efficiency (1958).

It is natural to ask why the criticism appeared at that particular point in time. The observation that 'something was wrong' with the Soviet system was older still. It was implicit in the general criticism of the Stalinist personality cult which came to the fore in 1956. At a time when the finger of accusation pointed straight at Stalin and his system, it was possible to believe that merely to abolish administrative control over the economy by ministries and to replace it by *sovnarkhoz* control would solve the problem of enterprise management. That was an illusion soon belied by the facts, since *sovnarkhoz* control over enterprises was just as oppressive and meddlesome. In fact the whole economy was suffering from a permanent conflict of interest between enterprises and the planning administration. Mutual recrimination was the result.

Firms accused the economic administration of 'petty tutelage'. Between 1957 and 1965 control agencies such as the planning departments, the State Bank, and the *sovnarkhoze* were reproached for the multiplicity of their directives and controls and for their continual interference in the management of firms without being legally accountable for mistakes.

On the other hand, the administration accused enterprise of routine, lack of dynamism and innovation, and systematic camouflage of their potential and resources. The administration further maintained that the plan was usually badly executed from a qualitative point of view.

The result was a general climate of mistrust and hostility. On the principle that the enterprise was faking its results and always trying to cheat, the administration reacted by overloading enterprise with targets. If the plan seemed to have been executed too easily, production targets were raised. As soon as profitability increased, the administration mopped up the profits. On the other side, enterprises naturally tried to defend themselves. They exerted pressure on the administration. There were no 'pressure groups' as such in the U.S.S.R., but firms, especially the large ones, did have 'link-men' operating between themselves and the administration, whose job was to obtain modifications to the plan, additional credits, supply vouchers and so on. The firms gave each other mutual support. For example, reciprocal credit although illegal was not unknown; a supplier could always delay sending his invoice. Similarly, they would tide each other over by means of the clandestine sale of supplies directly to each other. The stocks surplus to requirements referred to above were especially used for this purpose.[1]

Of course not all enterprise directors spent their time devising means for slipping through chinks in the planning system. The vast number of administrative procedures and prohibitions made rational and smooth enterprise management impossible even for those directors with the greatest sense of the general interest. One might say that they were obliged to cheat in the interests of plan fulfilment.

Thus, in the system just described, the authoritarian direction of enterprise compromised the general interests of economic development, on two counts in particular. Firstly, in spite of detailed planning, production was not geared to the needs of consumers of either capital or consumer goods, simply because the system could not guarantee efficient preparation or execution of the plan. In the second place, in spite of the alleged rational and systematic allocation of productive resources to avoid the wastage of capital goods, many were either squandered or made useless.

Gradually a new concept emerged in an attempt to solve these contradictions. If the constraints weighing down upon enterprise were lightened and if firms could be induced with appropriate material incentives to select the most efficient combinations of production factors within the framework of the plan, then the interest of the firm would coincide naturally with that of society as a whole.

The starting point was a forceful article by Professor E. Liberman, 'Plan, Profit, Premiums', which was published in *Pravda* on 9 September 1962. Liberman was later kept in the limelight by the Western press, but his rôle as the 'father' of economic reform should not be exaggerated. He was chosen as the spokesman of a new current of thought which had many other representatives. As a teacher of political economy at the University of Kharkov in the Ukraine, it could be shown that in the U.S.S.R. not everything necessarily comes from the capital and that his theses had a scientific and objective basis.

His propositions were as follows. Enterprises must be encouraged to execute the plan as precisely as possible without superfluous controls. (Contrary to some mistaken interpretations there is no question of 'freeing' the enterprise from the plan.) The enterprise would be free to choose the means best suited to this objective, and only two indicators would be imposed from above. The first indicator would be the value of production sold in each main category of manufacture. The firm would then try to fulfil the plan not arbitrarily but by producing saleable commodities, especially as overfulfilment of planning requirements would no longer be advantageous to the firm, which would now be 'rewarded' for strict implementation of the plan. On the other hand, to avoid lethargy at the planning stage, the firm would be rewarded for exceeding planning targets in relation to the previous year. The aim is to encourage the firm to submit a draft plan involving the full utilisation of resources without camouflaging its reserves.

The second indicator would be the ratio of profit to capital investment (profitability index). To maximise this indicator the enterprise would on the one hand attempt to increase its profits in absolute terms, and on the other economise on its capital investment. A natural consequence would be better management of capital assets. All other plan indicators would be freely determined by the enterprise itself (productivity, cost, raw material utilisation norms, etc.).

These proposals are interesting but somewhat general. If they are to be effectively applied a number of other conditions must be present.

To judge the enterprise on the value of the product actually sold has no sense if at the same time the administration continues to determine the outlets for this product. It is only meaningful if the enterprise itself is obliged to look for customers and to fill the orders they place. It was for this reason that Liberman and others proposed replacing administrative links between manufacturing enterprise and commercial organisations by direct links, at least for consumer goods. These relations would be based on contracts approved by the administration *a posteriori* and not *a priori* as had formerly been the case.

It is equally senseless to declare that the enterprise is free to organise production with complete autonomy if it continues to depend for supplies on the administrative allocation of capital goods.

To introduce the profit motive as an essential incentive implies a price reform which would allow firms to make profits in reality. It also implies fiscal reform. No firm will be induced to maximise profits if it knows in advance that almost all will go to the government. A further implication is that the enterprise will be able to make effective use of its residual profit in the interest of the whole personnel.

The Liberman scheme thus appeared seductive but inadequate. Consequently, it was attacked not only by conservatives, but also by progressive economists who underlined the limited nature of the reform suggested by Liberman. The most interesting theses were those developed by the academician Nemtchinov who emphasised two points: the need for price reform and the complete transformation of relations between enterprise and administration. This transformation would involve replacing the directive plan imposed from above with a command plan negotiated contractually between enterprises and the agencies of the economic administration.

Discussion of these proposals lasted three years and was interspersed with a number of spectacular press articles. Two such were the article by the academician Trapeznikov in *Pravda* on 17 August 1964 entitled 'For Flexible Enterprise Management', and Liberman's reply on 20 September 1964 'More on Plan, Profit and Premiums'. Reform was decided upon at the end of 1965, the way having been prepared by a number of economic experiments carried out on individual enterprises in different parts of the country. The most famous of these involved two clothing firms in Moscow and Gorki called Mayak and Bolshevichka. From July 1964 they acquired the right to establish their production programme on the basis of contracts concluded directly with shops and only later approved by the planning departments. Their performance was assessed according to their fulfilment of the sales and profitability plans.

Reform of the Enterprise: the Decisions of 1965

The reform was adopted following a decision by the plenum of the Central Committee on 29 September 1965. Two resolutions were adopted on 4 October 1965. The first was the resolution on socialist State enterprises. This text applies to all industrial enterprises, to building concerns, to transport, and to state farms or *sovkhoze*. It codifies the rights and obligations of enterprise. Hitherto enterprises had operated under the decree on State industrial trusts of 29 June 1927, numerous articles of which had either been amended or had fallen into disuse. The second resolution was the decree on the improvement of planning and the strengthening of economic incentives in industrial production.

Whereas the resolution codifies the rights and obligations of enterprise in a general sense, the decree organises the concrete application of the reform which must be progressively extended to the whole of industry. The resolution has immediate effect for all enterprises. The decree applies only to those brought within the ambit of reform.

The various measures of the reform can be grouped under two heads:

Measures Satisfying the Demands of Enterprise: Enterprises had complained about administrative tutelage. The reform diminishes this tutelage by reducing the number of planned indicators imposed on the enterprise by planning agencies. However, this move was less radical than that proposed by progressive economists. The compulsory indicators are:

1. A sales output indicator which replaces the gross output indicator. Generally there is a single indicator. However when there is a diversification of production within the enterprise the sales output indicator is supplemented by indicators, expressed in physical units, for the main products.
2. Profitability (the ratio of profit to total capital investment).
3. The total wages fund; however, the precise categorisation of personnel will no longer be imposed from above.
4. Total payments into the State budget.
5. Total centralised investments. To this were added two further indicators: one for the extension of productive capacity, to ensure the efficient use by the enterprise of investment funds allocated to it; one expressing the basic objectives of enterprise modernisation.
6. Material and technical supply: the volume of deliveries of raw materials and equipment to the enterprise.

The detailed application of these indicators as well as the formulation of indicators established previously by the authorities (costs, productivity, etc.) are the work of the enterprise itself.

Moreover, the administration is forbidden to modify plans during the period of their execution. More important still, in addition to the annual plan, enterprises will have a medium-term quinquennial plan.

Measures Satisfying the Administration: These are measures to improve the drafting and execution of plans by means of enterprise incentives designed to maximise profits in the interests of both the enterprise and the economy as a whole. To understand the complex operation of this mechanism one must analyse firstly, the behaviour enterprise is supposed to adopt in response to the economic stimulus, secondly, the means employed to induce this behaviour, and, thirdly, the tangible objectives of the enterprise itself.

The enterprise is induced to function efficiently on the basis of a rigorous plan. The incentive mechanism comes into play at two points: when the plan is at the drafting stage and when, at the end of the planning period, the enterprise is assessed on its results. In the first place, the enterprise must be induced to submit a plan ambitious enough to ensure the full employment of its resources. In the second place, it must implement the plan correctly.

To achieve the first of these objectives, the payment norms which the enterprise may make out of its profit into the stimulation funds are determined in two ways: for every 1% planned increase in sales or profits in relation to the preceding year; as a function of the planned level of profitability. Thus the enterprise knows in advance that the greater its sales, profit and profitability, the greater will be the payments it can make into its different funds.

However to ensure implementation of the plan payments from profit into the stimulation funds can only be authorised once the plan has been executed. Plan implementation is assessed at the end of each quarter. If the plan is overfulfilled the enterprise can make additional payments into its funds, but only at lower rates. In other words, contrary to pre-reform practice, over-fulfilment of the plan is not encouraged. Conversely, if the plan is not executed fund payments will diminish *pro rata*.

The enterprise is guided towards economically desirable behaviour (from the viewpoint of the administration) through the pursuit of profit, which thus becomes the motor of enterprise activity.

However it is not a question of just any profit or of profit at any price. The authors of reform had every reason to fear that enterprises, if they were encouraged purely and simply to maximise their total profit, would be tempted to do so at the expense of judicious management of their productive capital. In fact Soviet enterprises, by dint of long tradition, had acquired the habit of considering that their fixed and circulating capital cost them nothing or almost nothing.

Since they acquired equipment and raw materials through the material and technical supply agencies, firms were only made directly aware of the scarcity of such goods by the difficulty of obtaining from the relevant departments the documents necessary for the purchase of machinery, basic products, etc. This scarcity was not reflected in costs. The undervaluation of all the elements of productive capital had its corollary in low capital-goods prices, negligible rates of depreciation, short- and medium-term interest rates rarely higher than 2%, and above all in the absence of any return on invested capital.

To give enterprise an economic rather than an administrative incentive to reduce its capital expenditure to a strict minimum, a new element was introduced into the reform mechanism: a charge on fixed and circulating assets, or a tax on capital, at a rate of 6%. At the same time, the enterprise is encouraged to maximise not total gross profits (receipts minus production costs) but the profitability index or profit-capital investment ratio.

These two instruments of economic action (charge on assets and profitability index) operate simultaneously and in the same direction. This can be seen from the following hypothetical outline of a firm's profit distribution:

1. Gross profit (sales receipts − production costs) ...... 820,000 roubles
2. Priority payments:
   (a) charge on fixed and circulating assets .... 420,000 roubles
   (b) interest .... 50,000 roubles

   470,000 roubles

3. Net profit (1)−(2) .... 350,000 roubles
4. Payments into stimulation funds .... 100,000 roubles
5. Profit balance .... 250,000 roubles
   of which a proportion to be paid into State budget 200,000 roubles

The enterprise must first make certain priority payments out of its gross profit, notably the charge on assets and the payment of short- and medium-term interest to the State Bank. Net profit (3) is of interest to the enterprise for two reasons: it is from this source that it will derive its stimulation funds; the profitability index will be calculated on the basis of this particular expression of profit.

The magnitude of the index Pn/K or the ratio of net profit to invested capital, will depend on two things. Firstly, on the size of the numerator: thus the firm is induced to maximise sales (i.e. the indicator of output sold) and to minimise its charges, including interest and asset charges. Secondly, on the size of the denominator: it is in the firm's interest to reduce expenditure on capital investment.

In this way the maximisation of profitability mechanism introduces the main indicators and elements of enterprise management in just the proportions necessary to obviate a senseless race to accumulate profits.

This leaves the question why the enterprise will necessarily seek to maximise its rate of profit. Why should it not look for the easy way out by drafting an unambitious plan involving no annual progression and by settling for mediocre results? This involves the whole question of the enterprise's self-interest.

The answer is to be found in the reform itself. All the workers of an enterprise have a collective and individual interest in improving its performance, since the results obtained will have a direct repercussion on their personal income through the bonus system, which represents a significant proportion of their pay. According to estimates made before the initiation of reform bonuses constituted on average 10% of pay. In fact the enterprise finances three stimulation funds from its net profit: material incentive fund for paying individual bonuses to enterprise personnel; fund for social and cultural measures and for housing construction which serves as a source for financing social aid programmes and collective investments for the benefit of all workers (the building of workers' houses, children's playgrounds, holiday homes, the organisation of cultural pastimes, etc.); production development fund for the limited internal financing of minor modernisation schemes, technical innovations, etc., and thus for the extension of productive capacity.

If these incentives are to serve their purpose the workers must feel the effects of them. In other words, the advantages obtained must be great enough to justify the additional effort involved. From this standpoint two conditions must be fulfilled. There must be a revision of wholesale prices so as to guarantee a normal profit to firms, and there must be fiscal reform with a view to reducing the tax on profits. In principle these changes were anticipated in the reform. The Central Committee resolution of September 1965 indicates that a revision of prices is in progress and that in the meantime the economic reform will only be applied to profitable concerns. New wholesale prices for all industry were to be introduced on 1 July 1967 (see chapter 6 for details). Tax reform would proceed from the introduction of the charge on productive capital which according to the decree of 4 October 1965 would become 'the main form of payments into the budget and the principal source of centralised state finance' (article 21). In the profit distribution table reproduced earlier there appears on the last line 'a proportion to be paid into the State budget'. The very name of this payment, however, implies that it was to be relatively insignificant and residual. In fact, in the spirit of the initiators of the reform, it was to be stabilised as a percentage of profit much lower than the former appropriations had been.

The application of the reform was to belie this optimism, just as it was to disappoint many other hopes born from the decisions of 1965.

Reform of the Enterprise: Its Application (1966-70)

The reform was introduced by stages so that its gradual extension to the whole of industry would not dislocate economic activity. Let us look at the methods of its application and its first results.

THE METHODS OF APPLICATION

There were three reasons for the slow and staggered implementation of reform:

A political reason: reform was decided upon just one year after the fall of Krushchev, who had been severely criticised for the style of his innovations. One need only remember (*cf.* chapter 1) the administrative reform of 1957 which precipitated a sudden transition from the sectoral to the territorial principle in the administration of industry, and the subsequent numerous revisions of this reform between 1957 and 1964. The new administrators wished to proceed in a radically different way, step by step, introducing the reform first of all to a number of selected enterprises so that any eventual mistakes would not have repercussions on the whole of the economy and so that the experience gained in the first attempts would serve as an example in the later stages.

An administrative reason: the 1965 decisions were not merely concerned with reforming enterprise management. They also introduced administrative reforms such as the abolition of the *sovnarkhoze* and the institution of sectoral ministries. At the same time they anticipated the reform of wholesale prices which was to be completed in two years. Moreover, the U.S.S.R. was about to implement its five-year plan for 1966-70. The magnitude of this programme made all the more dangerous any precipitate implementation of enterprise reform.

An economic reason: the reform was not to be applied immediately to any enterprise. Any firm to be brought within the scope of the reform had to fulfil the following conditions:

1. It had to be profitable at existing prices and under normal conditions of management. This excluded most heavy-industry firms.
2. It had to have a stable outlet for its production and a satisfactory supply situation. The first of these would make it possible to plan the output sold indicator without too much difficulty. The fact that this market situation is still far from being achieved underlines how difficult it is to apply the reform in a context in which the administrative distribution of capital goods is retained.
3. The enterprise had to be in a healthy financial situation and to have satisfactory relations with the State Bank.
4. The firm had to possess a management enterprising enough to accept the risks implicit in any new experiment.

The stages of reform were as outlined in table 2.1 below:

TABLE 2.1[2]

APPLICATION OF ENTERPRISE REFORM IN THE U.S.S.R.

Year	Number of enterprises transferred to the new system	Percentage share of these enterprises in industry			
		of the total number of enterprises	of total production	of the labour force	of total profit
1966	704	1.5	8	8	16
1967	7,248	15	37	32	50
1968	28,850	54	72	71	81
1969*	36,000	75 approx.	83	—	91

*provisional figures

It was the revision of wholesale prices, completed on 1 July 1967, which made is possible to speed up enterprise reform, especially by applying it to heavy industry. For example, in 1968 a large segment of the engineering industry was brought within the aegis of reform. 1969 saw reform in certain branches of the extractive industry (particularly oil), in non-ferrous metallurgy, and in petro-chemicals. The reform has not yet been applied evenly in all regions. The growth areas in this field have been the western republics (the Baltic republics, Byelorussia, Ukraine, Moldavia), but the introduction of the new system has been slower in Transcaucasia and Central Asia.

THE RESULTS

Table 2.2 outlines the annual progress of enterprises incorporated into the new system in relation to industry as a whole, as reflected in certain basic indicaors. Published statistics only cover the years 1966–8.

TABLE 2.2[3]
THE RESULTS OF ENTERPRISES INCORPORATED IN THE NEW SYSTEM

	1966 in relation to 1965		1967 in relation to 1966		1968 in relation to 1967	
	All industry (1)	Enterprises in the new system (2)	(1)	(2)	(1)	(2)
Gross Production	+ 8.6	+ 10.5	+ 10.0	+ 10.7	+ 8.1	+ 8.3
Sales	—	+ 10.5	—	+ 11.5	—	—
Profits	+ 10.6	+ 23.3	+ 22	+ 24.5	+ 14	+ 15
Labour Productivity	+ 5.2	+ 8.0	+ 7.0	+ 8.2	+ 5.0	+ 5.6

In the first year the difference between enterprises transferred to the new system and the whole of industry is considerable for all comparable indicators. This is because the best enterprises in each sector were chosen to inaugurate the reform. The difference in the growth of profit between 1965 and 1966 is particularly significant. The difference in the following two years is less marked. The reduction of the gap was especially noteworthy in 1967, a year of rapid expansion for the whole of industry.

In 1969 no official statistics were given for enterprises operating within the new system, but the year was characterised by a general slowing down of growth. Aggregate industrial production rose by 7%, profit by 10% and productivity by 4.8%. A number of Soviet economists attribute this slackening to the unsatisfactory application of economic reform. Official statements have tended to confirm this interpretation, especially at the plenary session of the Party Central Committee held in December 1969. Moreover, implementation of the reform was deliberately slowed down during the second quarter of 1969 following instructions from the inter-ministerial commission responsible for its organisation.

It is hardly an exaggeration to say that at the beginning of 1970, four years after it had been launched, economic reform in the U.S.S.R. was in an *impasse*. The main reason for this was undoubtedly that reform had been grafted onto a system of economic planning and control which had not been modified in any radical sense. This explains the contradictions which appeared in the system, at first only marginal as reform affected relatively few enterprises, and then so violent that the whole mechanism seized up.

An analysis of the numerous reports, conferences, books, declarations and commentaries on the economic reform by Soviet writers and personalities makes it possible to classify these contradictions under four heads: contradictions between legality and reality; contradictions between conservatism and the spirit of reform; contradictions between the freedom of management granted to enterprise and the maintenance in many areas of a control system pre-dating reform; the paralysis of methods of industrial stimulation.

The first two types of contradiction are those most frequently referred to, since they tend to produce the most glaring scandals. However, they are perhaps less serious than the others since they can be overcome in due course, whereas the last two challenge the very basis of reform.

The Contradiction between Legality and Reality

The relations between economic administration and enterprise developed over several decades according to a simple formula: the enterprise had no rights, the administration had all rights. Economic reform changed everything on paper: the enterprise now possesses important rights vis-à-vis the administration.

Unfortunately administrative organs are still in no way accountable for their actions, whereas enterprises may incur heavy material loss in the case of inefficiency. There is no way in which the enterprise can resort to litigation in the case of conflict with an administrative agency; State arbitration and economic tribunals only cover litigation between enterprises. The only way for enterprise directors to make their voice heard is through the press. If a newspaper gets its teeth into a particular story and requires an explanation, the administration will sometimes make amends, especially if the newspaper happens to be *Pravda*, *Izvestia* or the *Economic Gazette,* the economic weekly of the Party. It should be added that each enterprise depends on several different administrative agencies and the directives of one often contradict the arrangements of another. For example, an enterprise might begin the year with production and supply plans closely co-ordinated. During the course of the year the ministry might modify its production programme. It would then be necessary for the firm to revise its purchases of raw materials, semi-finished products, etc. However the State Committee for Material and Technical Supplies might refuse to change the order forms issued at the beginning of the year.

In fact ministries have an annoying habit of modifying enterprise plans during the course of the year, even though this is formally prohibited by the resolution of October 1965. Every ministry counts above all on complete plan fulfilment at the end of the year, and if an enterprise within its jurisdiction appears to be overstretched it will transfer some of its work to a more reliable concern. Thus productive units which may have already received the final draft of their plan very late (at best in November for the following year) have no guarantee that the indicators established for them are permanent and can expect abrupt changes in their objectives. Modifications are especially common in firms working for export. Another violation of the rights of enterprise occurs where ministries continue to impose indicators abolished by the reform, such as norms for working capital, numbers employed, or an indicator for gross production, concurrently with one for output sold. Since reform many enterprises have consequently seen a rise and not a fall in the number of their compulsory indicators. Finally, the ministries are very jealous of their absolute power and maintain their enterprises in a state of feudal dependence, forbidding any individual approach to the world outside. Thus in *Pravda* on 6 September 1966 the director of a firm making valves complained that he was unable to satisfy general demand for his products although he had large stocks of the finished product. The reason was that his ministry (with jurisdiction over engineering products for the chemical and oil industries) prohibited him from supplying firms outside its sector before fulfilling all the orders planned for firms within the ministry's ambit. For the same reason ministries regarded unfavourably the establishment of direct contractual links between enterprises. It is true that the resolution on enterprise had maintained an administrative procedure in the distribution of capital goods. But at the same time it had stipulated that direct contracts would apply in the case of consumer goods. This should mean that the plan for enterprises producing consumer goods should be established on the basis of demand as determined by the commercial organisations which are their customers. In fact, contracts have been relatively few. Moreover, the two pilot clothing firms which as early as July 1964 had begun to organise production on the basis of contracts concluded with shops had to abandon the procedure after reform as a result of opposition by the ministry on which they depended.

The resolution of 9 April 1969 on the delivery of consumer products confirms again the right of enterprises and shops to enter into a direct contractual relationship. It does not seem to have been applied any more effectively. Similarly ministries have been opposed to the concentration of enterprises into associations, even though the principle of concentration had been vigorously defended by Kosygin in September 1965. Not only were there no new associations after 1966, but those in existence were either dissolved or reduced to a state of impotence, the ministry dealing with constituent enterprises over the head of the management of the association. More specifically, on 1 June 1969 there were 510 associations in the U.S.S.R. covering 2,211 enterprises, or about the same number as in 1964. This dismantling has been particularly systematic in the Leningrad region where the powerful industrial base was reorganised and concentrated during its *sovnarkhoz* period in 1957-65. The industrial ministries, whose omnipotence seemed threatened by the size of the Leningrad firms, fragmented the associations by placing their subsidiaries under the control of different central managements, in accordance with the principle 'divide and rule'.

The ministries were not alone in their opposition. Other administrative agencies displayed similar contempt for the law. A good example is the State Bank, which hindered the free use by firms of their stimulation funds, particularly funds for socio-cultural and housing programmes. It refused to release funds for the purchase by an enterprise of a second-hand bus to be used by its staff on Sunday outings. It prohibited other firms from employing this fund to pay for workers' sport and theatre entertainment, to buy presents for the New Year tree of employees' children, etc. In spite of all this, the regulations are quite clear: the enterprise has the right to use the fund to finance any collective social or cultural activity. The Investment Bank also behaved illegally, and arbitrarily allocated enterprise production development funds, in principle controlled by firms, for unauthorised uses such as refuse dump improvements.

Thwarted in these ways by the administrative apparatus, firms often failed to respect their obligations to each other. Contractual discipline was particularly slack. Enterprises are always linked by contract to suppliers and customers. For the most part these are contracts renewing a sales (purchase) order made by the material and technical supplies agencies, since direct contracts remain the exception. Before reform these contracts were very often incorrectly fulfilled. However, this did not have serious consequences for the injured party. For the defaulting party punishment for non-implementation was generally a fine and, according to well-established practice, enterprises tended to let each other off. After reform non-fulfilment of contracts had more serious consequences for the injured party. For example, delay in the delivery of raw materials might imperil plan execution and cause an enterprise to lose important bonuses. A delay in payment by the customer has the same effect because output is not considered to be sold until it has been paid for. Before reform the dispatch of an order to the customer constituted plan fulfilment. Fines paid by defaulting suppliers or customers are often much lower than the cost of the damage caused. A decree of 27 October 1967 increased an enterprise's accountability for the non-fulfilment of contractual obligations. However, dynamic and well-managed concerns still complain that as far as the execution of planned indicators is concerned they are still at the mercy of the insolvent customer, the supplier who does not worry about delay, and the transport firm which is not prepared to load, unload or convey goods on time.

This leads us to the second type of contradiction: between the spirit of reform which should animate all economic agencies and the conservatism so deep-rooted in bureaucratic tradition.

The Contradiction between Conservatism and the Spirit of Reform

The reform demanded from enterprise directors a certain degree of courage and the will to abandon traditional practices of dissimulation towards the administrative hierarchy. In its turn, the hierarchy would recognise the enterprise's new independence. This had certain implications.

In the pre-reform sense of the term, the 'good' director would return from negotiating the plan with the ministry and would convene a meeting of his managerial staff. There he would announce that he had obtained a plan of 1 million roubles whereas the enterprise was really capable of producing goods worth 1½ million, that he had extorted supply vouchers for 20 new machines whereas 10 such already lay unused in a warehouse—but you never know, better to have too many than too few! He would add perhaps that he had managed to raise norms for stocks. Then everyone would down *champanskoe* and congratulate such a prudent director.

Reform required completely different behaviour by directors if they were to succeed. Henceforth they would have to proceed openly, propose realistic plans and stop covering themselves by accumulating hidden reserves. They were also urged to display imagination and initiative, and to improve the quality and range of product offered to customers.

Some did so, especially in the enthusiasm of the first year. But too often things were made difficult for them. The clothing firm wishing to produce dresses in washable, non-iron, synthetic material had to struggle to deal directly with suppliers of material and to use the colouring chosen by its research department. At the same time, it had to have its patterns approved by fifteen authorities and wait three months to sell the dresses to the shops because the price of the new articles had not yet been fixed. When the dresses finally began to appear in the ready-to-wear departments, it was winter and the customers didn't want them any more. The road haulage firm which broke with tradition and began to look for return freight for its lorries, which had formerly returned empty, met with administrative obstacles placed in the way of its marketing initiative. Finally, progressive enterprises were bitterly disillusioned when they came to prepare the plan for the second year of the new system. It was obviously not possible for them to draft a sales and profits plan considerably higher than the previous year, for they had already mobilised their reserves and formulated a capacity plan for the first year of the reform. Since in the new system payment norms into stimulation funds depend on the annual growth of the planned indicators, the prospects for such payments in the second year were far less rosy. Enterprises then understood where their interest lay. As on previous occasions they should propose moderate increases in indicators, even if they could do better. In this way they would leave a sufficiently wide margin to stop the plan 'treading on their heels' so to speak.

The administration has not really abandoned its traditional mistrust. It still suspects that the enterprise which has done well in a particular year could have done even better. Apart from its overtly illegal acts, the administration interferes daily in the life of the enterprise, by means of controls, inquiries, questionnaires, requests for information and so on. An example is the exasperation of a saw-mill director in Arkhangel: not only did he have to send a daily report on production and stocks to the ministry (by telegram) as is the general rule, but he had to reply to inquiries such as these: 'Urgent: draft a complete report on the number of public lights in your town'; or 'How are you implementing your current community service plan: the river ferry service; the needlework and dressmaking classes?' (*Izvestia,* 13 February 1970). The unfortunate man just could not understand why a saw-mill director was expected to know the number of street lights in his town, or why he should participate in advancing the domestic accomplishments of the female population. Another example is the chief engineer of a metallurgical combine in the Urals who appealed for help in the *Economic Gazette* of November 1969, no. 48. The administration had organised a series of checks on the 'culture' of production, the speed of installing new productive capacity, progress in the field of invention and rationalisation, the actual state of labour and material resources, the fall in 'fluidity' of management, the collection of scrap-iron, and the initiative of young workers in technical progress. For each operation it was necessary to establish a committee, convene several meetings, draft reports and minutes, and give a monthly account of the results. The engineer wondered if it might not be a good idea to replace the steel production plan by a control fulfilment plan!

This enormous bureaucracy obviously absorbs considerable resources. It explains the swollen numbers employed in the central administrations and in the higher management of firms. Staff are after all necessary for sitting in committee, drafting and duplicating reports, and replying to inquiries. It also helps explain high and useless telephone and telegraph costs, the abuse of talks and symposia, the large number of 'missions' to Moscow by enterprise managers who visit central administration departments several times a year, either officially or on their own initiative. All these points are brought out in a decree of 13 October 1969 issued by the Party Central Committee and the Council of Ministers 'on measures for improvement and economies in the functioning of the administrative apparatus'. This decree requires an immediate reduction in all useless administrative expense and in the numbers of administrative personnel at all levels, from ministry to enterprise. It stipulates that in all these areas there should be a total saving of 1.7 milliard roubles in 1970. This sum represents 1.1% of the country's total budget and is exactly equal to aggregate administrative expenditure itemised in the budget for the same year. The attempt to solve the problem of bureaucracy by resolutions is dubious as resolutions do not change attitudes. Bureaucracy and routine, however, like administrative illegality, are external obstacles to the successful application of the reform. The undermining of reform by its own internal contradictions could prove to be more critical in the long run.

The Contradiction between the Freedom of Management in Enterprise and the Maintenance of the Previous Control Apparatus

We shall begin with a story. There was once a director of a firm manufacturing photocopiers, who was open to new ideas and who managed his factory with great efficiency. The firm prospered by producing machines of excellent quality. One day he came across an article in an economic review vaunting the merits of publicity in a socialist regime. 'Good', said the director. 'Since publicity is no longer a shameful capitalist category and since here it is a vehicle of progress, I shall advertise too.' His research department brought out a fine advertisement, reproducing the most modern photocopying machine in the factory and including a short description of its speed, its durability and the economies it would bring to the user. The only thing missing was the shapely secretary who appears in similar capitalist advertisements. The advertisement was sent to several technical magazines which gave it suitable prominence. Orders began to flow in almost immediately. These were accompanied by a furious letter from the department for precision machines, which is one of the twenty-one central boards of the State Committee for Material and Technical Supplies. The director was informed that to advertise his products was a stupid idea since their market had already been fully determined in the plan and that to fulfil additional orders was impossible. It only remained for the unfortunate director to send a letter to his potential clients, photocopied no doubt, explaining why he could not satisfy the demand . . . and to meditate on the virtues of advertising as a vehicle of progress.

This edifying story illustrates clearly a major contradiction of the reform. The indicators imposed on the enterprise are now relatively few. Within these limits the Soviet enterprise is invited to act autonomously and to operate like a well-managed capitalist concern. The different elements of the reform have been mutually adjusted so as to harmonise the material interest of individual production units and the economy as a whole.

This is all very well, but everything depends on whether the enterprise can use this autonomy effectively, even assuming the presence of ideal conditions such as a respect for legality and an enlightened administration free of bureaucratic impedimenta.

This is very often not the case. A few examples will show why. As some economists pointed out when the reform was being prepared, if an indicator of output sold replaces that of gross production for the individual enterprise, the objective is to encourage it to produce according to demand. In other words, the firm must gear production to the quantity, quality and variety required by consumers. A further objective was to create a healthy spirit of competition between enterprises, since those making articles of inferior quality or of a specification not in accordance with demand might not be able to sell their output. In this case, of course, they would also fail to fulfil their plan.

For the output sold indicator to be effective it is obvious that enterprise markets must be neither imposed nor guaranteed. In fact this condition does not apply even within the terms of the reform itself for the capital goods sector. Enterprises in this sector do not find their own customers. These are allocated by the material and technical supplies departments. Of course the customer can refuse to take a faulty machine or low-quality raw materials. But he had that right before the reform. It was a right he tended not to use, for refusal of a particular consignment would lead to numerous formalities and in no way guaranteed replacements. The introduction of the output sold indicator has not made machines more productive, nor fertilisers supplied to agriculture more effective, nor the material delivered to the clothing industry more varied and attractive. Metallurgical factories continue as in the past to supply castings which do not conform to specification. The castings then have to be worked up on the spot, a task which employs more than half the labour force in engineering.

In the consumer-goods industry things should be different since the reform authorises production units to conclude contracts directly with shops. But even when contracts have been agreed (which is not often the case) it is difficult to adapt production closely to demand because raw material suppliers do not always deliver the products needed by the enterprise. Secondly, prices are still imposed: wholesale prices for units of production, retail prices for shops. These prices are fixed by different procedures (*cf.* chapter 6) and there is no price co-ordination at wholesale and retail level for the same article. Thus an article which is in great demand by consumers may be a profitable line for producing firms but may not be ordered by shops because the margin between wholesale and retail price is too narrow for them to make a reasonable profit. On the other hand, firms sometimes refuse orders for articles which would sell well, but whose cost price is hardly covered by the wholesale price. It is for this reason that enterprises insistently call for a degree of price flexibility, especially for new products. Ideally they would like to establish their own prices, perhaps within a certain price bracket. Hitherto the economic authorities have always opposed such a move. It is a field in which socialist countries outside the U.S.S.R. have adopted a different policy, deliberately it seems.

Consequently, in spite of reform, the main defects of the previous system have been perpetuated. Enterprises produce with impunity articles which consumers do not want. Others cannot function normally because raw material deliveries are either insufficient or do not conform to specification. The mistake of the economic authorities has been to consider all these cases in isolation and to try to solve problems administratively in each area by means of sanctions and the transfer of management. What they really need to do, however, is to recognise the contradictions inherent in the reform itself. An example of how not to solve the problem is the decree published in *Izvestia* on 12 December 1969 'on the development of production, the extension of choice and the improvement in the quality of domestic porcelain and earthenware for 1970–5'. One cannot by administrative decree miraculously remove those obstacles blocking the smooth functioning of reform.

Another area of fictitious autonomy is labour management. Wages are fixed by statute, according to occupation, qualifications, etc. This, linked to the centralised determination of the wages fund, practically removes the firm's freedom of manoeuvre. With a given wages fund the enterprise can in theory choose to have either a limited number of highly specialised and well-paid workers or a greater number of less-qualified and lower-paid ones. In fact this choice hardly exists since employment structure in the enterprise will be determined by the type of production itself. It could certainly try to reduce its labour costs in absolute terms by lay-offs linked to the rationalisation of production. It would then come up against trade-union resistance supported by efficient legislation protecting workers against all forms of dismissal. A further obstacle to reducing the labour-force is that the wages fund is planned according to the actual number of workers employed in any given unit of production. An enterprise dispensing with workers surplus to requirements cannot hope to maintain its wages fund intact so as to raise the pay of its personnel the following year. Since 1967 there has been an experimental departure from this rule in several enterprises. The firms in question have a wages fund which is planned at a given level for several years ahead. They can then follow the employment policy of their choice. If they reduce their labour-force, wages-fund economies go to those workers remaining with the firm.[4] But this experiment is limited for the time being, since the trade unions are hostile to a measure which would certainly bring considerable unemployment if it became general. Finally, enterprises have another reason for not restricting their outlay on labour. The material incentive fund and the fund for social and cultural measures and housing construction, paid out of profits, are calculated as a percentage of the wages fund. Other things being equal, the size of bonuses and other advantages for the personnel will depend on the size of the wages fund. This is one of the paradoxes of the reform. In principle the enterprise is encouraged to economise from every point of view to reduce its costs. On the other hand, the material incentive mechanism leads it to increase its outlay on wages. The inter-ministerial committee responsible for implementing the reform took more than three years to realise this. At the end of 1969 it decided that for 1970 the ministries would fix the stimulation fund totals independently of the wages fund. It was hoped that this would lift the incentive system out of the rut into which it had sunk.

The Paralysis of Stimulation Mechanisms

The reform is based on the material interest of the enterprise in improving its results. In spite of the revision of wholesale prices completed in 1967, which made many branches of the economy profitable for the first time, two circumstances paralysed the functioning of the material incentive system. The first was the absence of radical tax reform. The second was that enterprises found it impossible in practice to use a large part of their stimulation funds.

The Soviet tax system will be studied later (chapter 6). But it should be pointed out that the difference between the former appropriation from profits and the new payment of the disposable profit balance is purely nominal. Both are distribution taxes, and the ministries, like the *sovnarkhoze* before 1965, divide the burden arbitrarily between the enterprises in their jurisdiction. This particular contribution to the budget is equal in many sectors to 60% to 70% of profit after as before reform (*cf.* table 2.3). It is drafted in advance into the plan of the enterprise (the compulsory budget payments indicator). Consequently, and contrary to the impression given by the profit distribution scheme outlined earlier, it in no way resembles a residual balance left after the financing of the stimulation funds. The economic administration uses the budget payments indicator in the same way as the other enterprise indicators. If during the year the ministry notices that an enterprise is very likely to exceed expected profit margins, it will not hesitate to increase the 'disposable balance'.

TABLE 2.3[5]

PROFIT UTILISATION OF INDUSTRIAL ENTERPRISE (%)

	1965	1966 (a)	1966 (b)	1967 (b)	1968 (b)
Total Profit	100	100	100	100	100
Paid into budget	71	74	73	69	67
of which:					
appropriation from profits ... (+ disposable balance to be paid into budget for enterprises in new system)[1]	71	74	69	56	45
charge on assets			4	8	17
rent payments[2]			—	5	5
Remaining at the disposal of enterprises	29	26	27	31	33
of which:					
allocated to investment[3]	9	6	4	7	10
contribution to stimulation funds ...	6	7	9	11	14
allocated to the extension of circulating capital and to the planned losses of other enterprises	10	8	14	13	9
other (contributions to ministerial and departmental reserves) ...	4	5			

(a) Enterprises not transferred to the reformed system.
(b) Enterprises transferred to the new system.
1. In the transition period enterprises transferred to the new system had to pay two taxes.
2. See chapter 6 for this tax, which concerns only particular types of enterprise.
3. Not internal financing. *Cf.* chapter 6.

In these conditions it is hardly in an enterprise's interest to maximise its profits: the game is not worth the candle. The profit stimulation mechanism (the subtle interaction of the profitability indicator and the charge on assets) tends to slip into neutral gear. The charge is only a negligible proportion of the financing expenses of enterprise. For most firms the payment into the budget of the disposable balance is from three to ten times greater than the aggregate charge. Some writers have suggested that the rate of the charge should be considerably increased, to 10% or even 15%. Others expect a great deal from the re-evaluation of industrial balance sheets on 1 January 1972, which should raise the value of productive assets and consequently the basis of the charge. These measures will not radically alter the situation. Enterprises are indifferent to the charge. It costs them little. At the same time, the two-year exemption which is granted for equipment purchased by means of credit or out of internal capital resources does not encourage modernisation because the gain is too small.

Thus burdensome taxation blunts the edge of whatever appetite an enterprise might have for increasing its profits. But what about the workers? Are they aware of the advantages to them of the stimulation funds?

One must distinguish between the three different stimulation funds. The material incentive fund poses no insoluble problems. But the same cannot be said for the socio-cultural and production development funds.

The material incentive fund (50% of aggregate funds in 1967) is a source of bonuses for workers and trained personnel (engineers, technicians, clerical staff). For the workers it is an additional source of bonuses. They receive increases and supplements incorporated into their wage paid out of the wages fund and not from profits. The payment of these bonuses is usually automatic and is rather like the thirteenth month. In 1968 they constituted from 8% to 10% of industrial workers' wages. On the other hand, for trained personnel the material incentive fund is the main if not the only source of bonuses. The underlying philosophy is clear: trained personnel can directly influence the dynamism of the firm and are held to be more responsible for collective results than the workers for whom the collective material incentive mechanism introduced by the reform has little meaning. The right to bonuses paid out of profit is hardly an incentive for workers to improve their production, for two reasons. Firstly, they can be sure of receiving the ordinary bonuses from the wages fund. Secondly, the additional bonuses they might expect are not high. After the reform they reached an average of a little more than 3% of wages in firms covered by the new system. Trained personnel should be more sensitive to material incentive bonuses, since in 1967 they raised pay by an average of 20%. But the inducement had little effect even on them.

In the first place, enterprises felt that the method of establishing the material incentive fund was pointlessly complicated. It will be remembered that in the last analysis the fund is derived from profit and is calculated according to wage norms based on at least two indicators: profitability; and either sales or profit at the discretion of enterprises. 70% of firms chose sales, which is an interesting comment on their confidence in profit! Some writers have suggested that the method of calculation could be simplified by basing it entirely on the mass of profit. The authorities do not favour this solution, since it would precipitate an unhealthy race to accumulate profit and would not adequately relate the size of the fund to fulfilment of the plan.

In the second place, the firm is no more free of uncertainty in this area than in other aspects of its management. The norms for establishing the stimulation funds are defined by each ministry and in the first year were made to measure for each enterprise. From 1967-9 group norms were calculated, applicable to several enterprises in the same branch of activity where operational conditions were similar. The norms vary from one year to the next in a direction or in proportions which do not always correspond to the efforts and results of enterprise. The size of the stimulation funds naturally varies with them.

Finally, the system gives a very clear advantage to small firms. In 1967 enterprises employing from 200 to 500 persons were able to pay bonuses equivalent to 13% of their total wage fund. Enterprises with more than 10,000 workers only reached 8%. Smaller-scale enterprises can integrate profit or sales increases more easily into their plan than the large units, and they risk less in case of failure. Thus they can obtain more advantageous norms in the establishment of funds.

More generally, the introduction nowadays of a system of material incentives encounters a certain indifference among workers. It is doubtless very ethical for members of a socialist society not to run after money. But there is perhaps more to it than that. Workers' incomes have now reached a level which makes it possible to satisfy basic needs. At the same time the State provides a large number of free services. Why earn more? To change one's flat. It wouldn't make any difference, since norms for living space rigorously limit the area allowed per person. To buy a car, perhaps? In this case there are waiting lists years long. It isn't money which is short but supply. To have a good holiday? Holidays don't cost much in the Soviet Union. But what is difficult is getting a residence voucher guaranteeing a place in a hotel or rest-home. Perhaps to buy the thousand-and-one gadgets that brighten up daily life and make it a bit easier? The shops are especially short of such articles. Consequently the average Soviet citizen today seeks leisure rather than money. This can hardly be said to favour collective dynamism at work. That is why in the Soviet Union the value of material inducements is now seriously questioned for the first time. The problem is what can replace them.

A sort of sociological sclerosis is beginning to paralyse the limbs of the incentive system. As for the two other enterprise funds, the obstacles are purely material.

The socio-cultural fund (an average of 17% of the total stimulation fund in 1967) and the production development fund (33%) should in principle be used as a source of social or economic investment. However, the enterprise cannot in general acquire purchase vouchers for the goods corresponding to such investment (building materials, machinery, etc.), which is not catered for in the official plan. It seems that in most cases these funds are quite simply transferred to the central investment fund of the ministry. This is in flagrant violation of their original purpose.

The following case appeared in the *Economic Gazette*. A firm wanted to build a small block of workers' flats. Fortunately, its socio-cultural fund was large enough to cover all expenses. First of all it contacted a firm of architects to obtain a plan and an estimate. The firm replied that its order book was full, that it had to complete those projects which came within the scope of planned building operations, and that it could not accept an unofficial individual order. Unless . . . perhaps they could come to some arrangement. Perhaps out of the forty proposed flats the enterprise could leave one at the disposal of the firm of architects? It really would be most convenient, since a young office colleague had just arrived and hadn't yet found accommodation. The enterprise accepted the terms. It was take it or leave it. Once the plan had been established the enterprise contacted a building firm. Same initial refusal, for the same reasons: our annual building plan is complete, and we can only embark on projects itemised in the general investment plan. However, since it's you, we might make a special effort, in return for a few flats in your block, of course. That shouldn't put you out too much! The same thing was repeated at every stage: for installing gas, electricity and waste disposal units. The block was finally finished. Half of it was occupied by families from outside the enterprise.

It is easy to understand why in these circumstances the personnel of an enterprise are unresponsive to the advantages of such a fund. It has been proposed that the fund should be used mainly in the form of loans to co-operatives building flats for co-ownership, since they can obtain material allocations more easily. Unfortunately there is no legal authorisation for use of the fund in this way.

Similar obstacles stand in the way of the production development fund and reduce to almost zero the practical possibilities of internal financing.

The general impression left by these early results is negative. The situation of the firm is not radically different from before the reform. Bureaucracy, routine and indifference explain this half-failure. But it must also be admitted that even in ideal conditions the reform could not be effectively applied in its present form. The autonomy of management and the incentive rôle of profit are counteracted by the whole system of planning and economic control, which has been touched up but in no way fundamentally modified. The problem is how to get out of this *impasse*.

The only coherent general work on the subject is that of a young economist researching at the Economics Institute of the U.S.S.R. Academy of Sciences, B. Rakitskij.[6] Analysing the application of the reform, Rakitskij observes that enterprise autonomy is either impeded or destroyed by the maintenance of burdensome controls in numerous areas. In that case one might well ask why the control apparatus is not dismantled. The answer of course lies in the anarchy and disorder which would be an immediate consequence. In the present situation such fears are probably well founded. Since enterprises are used to being allocated raw materials and equipment, it is difficult to predict exactly how they would react if suddenly faced with a free choice of sources of supply. Out of habit some would doubtless contact the same supplier, merely increasing their demands, which the supplier, in a position of strength since there is still a shortage of capital goods, would probably ignore. Others would try placing small orders simultaneously with different suppliers. This would probably cause some temporary disruption of their production programme. In another area, if the obstacles to the effective utilisation of the production development fund were removed, it might in the end compromise general investment policy. A further problem is that complete freedom in managing the labour-force might result in numerous lay-offs and general unemployment, together with a rise in pay for skilled personnel.

These are weighty arguments. But Rakitskij does not believe that a socialist state wishing to implement a particular policy of economic growth and social development when productive resources are relatively scarce must necessarily practise an authoritarian policy of economic control. According to him, the reform has been a partial failure because it has not been accompanied by structural transformation. It is not suited to small-scale enterprise. In 1967 one-third of Soviet firms employed less than 100 workers, produced 4.6% of total production and disposed of 3.4% of productive assets. These enterprises are not in a position to resist administrative encroachments or to oppose continuous changes in their plans. They would be no better off if they were free to obtain supplies, negotiate sales contracts or introduce a long-term modern-isation policy. What is necessary is a reorganisation of the structure of industry. More specifically, an intermediate agency should be created, an association of enterprises, standing between the ministry and the individual enterprise. Different types of enterprise association have existed in the U.S.S.R. in the past (trusts, combines). But such groups were not integrated economic units. They were merely stages in the administrative hierarchy, transmitting directives from the centre. The new associations which Rakitskij would like to see developed would act both as shock-absorbers between administration and enterprises and as intermediaries between different enterprises. They would be responsible for the group's external relations. This would mean dealing with the material and technical supplies agencies, centralising orders for the products of the group and eventually establishing central supplies and sales departments such as existed in Soviet industry before 1929. They would also be well placed from the point of view of investment policy. Associations, since they can offer better security than the individual enterprise, are in a position to negotiate more favourable credit facilities with the Bank. Similarly, suppliers would adhere more rigorously to estimates and delivery dates for the powerful association than for the small firm. Inside the group, the association could institute a policy of research and innovation. A research department may be costly and useless for a small unit, but a worthwhile investment for a large one. Such an innovation could be introduced into a particular enterprise of the group without undue risk, since any temporary fall in profit proceeding from the introduction of new measures would not be borne by a single firm but by the whole group. The ministry would establish aggregate planning indicators and payments into stimulation funds, and budget for the association as a whole. One of the functions of the association would be to adapt and allocate these to particular enterprises within the group. Finally, it could realise economies of scale by improving the organisation of production, centralising the accounts system and so on.

All these advantages have been experienced by those associations already in existence. As we have seen, the various economic administration agencies fear such associations and are opposed to their creation. They take shelter behind the argument that monopoly kills the spirit of competition. Since this spirit is almost totally absent, the risk is obviously minimal. The development of associations is without any doubt the way to save reform in the U.S.S.R. So far, it has hardly begun. Other European socialist countries, however, have systematically introduced such a system. This is especially the case in the G.D.R.

Addendum

At the beginning of 1973, reform applied to 43,000 enterprises (87% of the total) and accounted for 94% of production.

The mechanism of economic reform has been modified twice within the framework of the 1971-5 five-year plan. Moreover, since the beginning of 1973, the restructuring of Soviet industry into associations seems to have entered the phase of actual implementation.

1.   A decree of 21 June 1971 attempts to improve planning and economic stimulation in industry. It aims to ensure better qualitative fulfilment of the plan both in methods and results, and to give a quinquennial framework to enterprise activity. The plan is to be fulfilled mainly by raising the productivity of labour. An additional compulsory indicator has therefore been introduced for enterprises: increased labour productivity, calculated annually for the period 1971-5 with 1970 as the base year. The intention is also to guarantee quality of production: since 1972 enterprises have had a second additional indicator requiring the 'production of new products which correspond technically and economically to the best results of foreign and national techniques'. These two indicators are in addition to those introduced by the reform. The shortcomings of the reform are therefore to be corrected not by an extension of enterprise autonomy but by increasing its obligations. On the other hand, to avoid penalising the most dynamic enterprises as happened in 1966-70, the time-scale for economic units is now more flexible. By drafting ambitious

annual plans they had tended to reduce their possibilities for the following year. To rectify this situation for 1971-5 minimum annual indicators have been established for each enterprise constituting 'slices' of the quinquennial plan. If the enterprise drafts an annual plan which is more exacting than the base indicators, it will have the right to increase payments into its stimulation funds. This would be the case, for example, if the 1974 slice of the five-year plan anticipated an increase in production of 7%, but the enterprise proposed 8% when drafting its 1974 annual plan. The stimulation funds are then normalised throughout industry by the ministries. Enterprise stimulation fund norms are established for each ministry for the five-year period. The ministry is authorised to create a reserve not greater than 10% of total funds. The reserve will make possible a more flexible regulation of incentive funds over the five-year period between enterprises within its jurisdiction.

2. The creation and use of the material incentive fund (43.3% of total stimulation funds in 1971) and of the fund for social and cultural measures and for housing construction (17.7%) were modified in a decree of 23 May 1972. This has meant an improvement of the way in which the second of these funds may be used, in an attempt to suppress the abuses mentioned earlier. At least 60% must be allocated to its original purpose: residential construction, crèches, day-nurseries, either by the individual enterprise concerned or in co-operation with other enterprises and municipalities. The enterprise construction fund may be supplemented by long-term credit not exceeding 50% of the total. If the enterprise co-operates with a municipality, the latter cannot claim more than 6% of the accommodation constructed for housing people from outside the enterprise. Similarly, not more than 2% of the accommodation can be allocated to the managerial and maintenance staff of the property. Further permissible fund allocations are enumerated: the purchase and maintenance of rest homes, tourist centres, holidays for the best workers, improved canteen meals, and the purchase of specialised vehicles such as ambulances, travelling libraries and cinemas. On the one hand, enterprises have obtained a guarantee that the funds will be used for their own needs. On the other, there are more constraints on fund utilisation.

3. The resolution of 2 March 1973 on industrial associations must give some satisfaction to the supporters of this particular form of organisation. As for the functions transmitted to the associations they are essentially those outlined by Rakitskij and mainly concern supplies, research and investment policies. It is still not clear, however, whether the undoubted increase in the autonomy of these associations will not be at the expense of the constituent enterprises, which, although retaining their independent legal status, must transfer some of their resources to the association. The association will have a centralised stimulation fund comprised of three separate funds as in the case of individual firms, together with a number of specialised funds: research, adoption of new techniques, plant extension, financial aid to constituent enterprises, depreciation reserves.

One experiment, followed with keen interest, which apparently served even more in promoting recent developments than the activity of the thousand or so associations existing in 1972, was that relating to the ministry of precision instruments, automation and command systems. Its eleven central departments were transformed into associations in 1968. In 1970 it acquired financial autonomy and a management structure identical in every way with that of an enterprise. At the same time, anticipating the 1971-2 decrees, its financial and economic indicators were based on five-year planning norms. The transformation of a whole ministry into an enterprise is somewhat surprising. In effect, the U.S.S.R. has set up a sort of I.B.M. with a complete monopoly.

The effects of this industrial concentration will not be felt until 1975, which is the deadline for establishing associations. The other aspects of economic reform continue to be discussed, and its implementation criticised, along the same lines as before: the irresponsibility of the administration in exceeding its rights and that of enterprises in not fulfilling contractual obligations; the lack of freedom in marketing and the acquisition of supplies; the limited rôle of profit as an incentive. On this last point, the proportions in the final distribution of profit have varied little since 1968 (*cf.* table 2.3): the budget still takes the lion's share (62% in 1971, i.e. 45% under 'disposable balance to be paid into the budget' and 17% under 'charge on assets'); of the 38% remaining at the disposal of enterprises, 14% goes to the stimulation funds as in 1968.

2. ENTERPRISE REFORM IN THE SOCIALIST COUNTRIES OF EUROPE

It is possible to draw a useful distinction here between the members of Comecon on the one hand, and Yugoslavia on the other. The Comecon countries (Bulgaria, Romania, Hungary, Poland, G.D.R., Czechoslovakia), although in many ways different from the U.S.S.R., have developed along similar lines. On the other hand, Yugoslavia radically modified its economic system after 1950 by basing enterprise activity on the principle of self-management.

The Comecon Countries

In all these countries the pre-reform situation was similar to that in the U.S.S.R. Authoritarian centralised planning and control fettered the enterprise. The productive unit had no collective interest in its results.

As in the U.S.S.R. the initial cause of reform was a growing awareness that the traditional system was incapable of ensuring sound economic development. With the exception of Romania the growth rates of national income and industrial production were everywhere in decline from 1961 (*cf.* table 4.1, chapter 4).

As far as reform procedure is concerned, there is one common element throughout. The initial impetus was given by a Party decision following a Central Committee meeting: in 1963 in the G.D.R. after the Sixth Congress of the Socialist Unity Party, in January 1965 by the Central Committee of the Czechoslovak Communist Party, in July 1965 by a plenum of the Central Committee of the Polish United Workers' Party, in April 1966 by the Central Committee of the Communist Party of Bulgaria, in May 1966 by the Hungarian Socialist Workers' Party, and in October 1967 by the Communist Party of Romania. Methods of implementation were decided later at the highest administrative level, generally after public discussion of the scheme in the press, at meetings and so on.

There were considerable differences in the way the reform was introduced. From this point of view it is possible to classify countries into two groups.

Firstly, the countries which chose to introduce the reform gradually and to implement its various elements at intervals (i.e. price revision, re-evaluation of enterprise balance sheets, etc.). In this category were Bulgaria, Poland and the G.D.R. In Bulgaria the general principles of the new system were published in December 1965 and approved in April 1966. In 1967 65% of gross industrial production was supplied by enterprises in the new system, which became general the following year. In Poland the decision was taken in July 1965 and the reform applied to most sectors and enterprises in 1966. However the various components of reform were introduced successively: the reorganisation of investment financing in April 1966, price adjustments on 1 January 1967 (not a general revision of prices, since this had been done in 1960), the adoption of the law on enterprise associations at the end of 1966, the regularisation of the bonus system in 1967. In the G.D.R. the reform began in 1963 with a search for new methods of plan formulation. In 1964 new wholesale prices were introduced and financial autonomy conferred on enterprise associations. The charge on productive capital was tried out and later made general. The reform was gradually extended to the rest of the economy in 1965–6 (industry, domestic and foreign trade, agriculture, transport). The economic administration was reorganised at the beginning of 1966, and the enterprise endowed with new legal status in 1967.

Secondly, those countries opting for detailed theoretical preparation of reform, experimentation at various levels, followed by its introduction wholesale: Hungary, Romania. In Hungary, after the decisions of May 1966, the parts of the new system were assembled over a period of eighteen months (the reform of prices, foreign trade and planning). The new system was introduced in its totality on 1 January 1968. In Romania preliminary experiments were carried out with seventy-one enterprises in 1967. The new system came into operation on 1 January 1968. However it seems that for the first year the reform was only really applied to foreign trade.

Czechoslovakia is a special case. At first sight it seems to belong to the group which introduced reform gradually. In fact the first stage merely consisted of a series of measures of economic recovery, since it was in Czechoslovakia that the downturn in the rate of growth of the national income had been most marked in the period 1963–4. In 1963 there had actually been a fall of 2%, and an increase of only 1% in 1964 as against an increase of 5.5% and 6.2% respectively for the whole of Comecon. The new system was introduced on 1 January 1967, after an experimental period in 1965 and 1966. However, political developments, especially from the beginning of 1968, influenced the direction of reform. The action programme of the Czechoslovak Communist Party of 5 April 1968[7] pointed out 'the mistakes and gaps in the implementation of the economic reform programme', and explained: 'Enterprises faced with market requirements must be free to take decisions on all questions directly concerning the operation and management of the enterprise. They must be free to respond creatively to market demand. Market demand and economic policy will operate in the direction of greater economy in production and of beneficial structural changes.' These changes were not accomplished. They were not even formulated in detail. The events of August 1968 and their consequences completely halted reform and economic activity in general for several months. In May 1969, at a plenary meeting of the Party Central Committee, Husak recognised that they would have to begin all over again: 'It is necessary to examine critically the course taken by economic reform, its stages and measures, with a view to finding a clear starting point.'

At present there are three main elements in the general orientation of reform. Firstly, greater flexibility in the management of firms is in principle subordinated to efficient plan fulfilment. However new conceptions of planning do tend to give much more freedom to firms than is the case in the Soviet Union. Secondly, increasing reliance is placed on economic and financial mechanisms in the orientation of enterprise activity. The rôle of the market becomes very much greater. Thirdly, the reform has made direct participation in foreign trade easier. It is this which distinguishes these countries from the U.S.S.R., and which can be explained by their much greater dependence on foreign trade as such.

At the same time, administrative reform has left a far less bureaucratic framework for firms to operate in than in the U.S.S.R. (*cf.* chapter 1), since the associations have assumed considerable importance as intermediaries between the central administration and productive units.

NEW PLANNING IDEAS

The plan remains the basis of economic activity. At the central planning level the emphasis is on the long-term plan, which is necessarily less detailed than the annual plan. For this reason the drafting of the annual plan is undertaken at enterprise level, where there is a real degree of autonomy. All socialist countries draw up very long-term plans in an effort to anticipate demographic and economic growth rates, to calculate changes in industrial structure, and to forecast future technical developments and so on. These plans are established for ten- to fifteen-year periods. In general they have a five-year realisation term and overlap with the following five-year period. In all these countries there is also a five-year plan integrated into the framework of Comecon. Its continuity is guaranteed by an extension into the next two or three years. Finally, there is everywhere an annual macro-economic plan. In the U.S.S.R. this annual plan is virtually the blueprint for the whole economy, on which enterprise planning is based. This is not the case in the other socialist countries, where the rôle of the enterprise in drafting the plan is much more important on two counts.

In the first place the firm has a real say in the formulation of its plan. This is true even where the plan once drafted as a result of different consultation procedures is imposed on it by administrative decision. In Poland the draft plan is submitted to firms, who then produce counter-plans. The first experiment with counter-plans was in 1966, when 90% of enterprises took part. This particular experiment was not a complete success, largely because the initial plan was detailed and so thorough that it was difficult for enterprises to establish alternatives. Since then the counter-plan has been modified and organised at association level. From its own sectoral administration the association receives an outline plan reduced to a few indicators (value of gross production, export objectives, labour productivity, investment). At that point it collects the proposals of its constituent enterprises and on this basis formulates draft plans. From the plan finally accepted by the administration it then establishes a certain number of directional indicators for its enterprises. The Polish example is an illustration of the rôle played by the associations in a real extension of enterprise autonomy. When firms submit individual counter-plans to the administration the whole procedure is a sham. But the association, acting as a sort of screen between the individual enterprise and the administration, is in a position to negotiate real plan variants.

In the G.D.R., enterprises can also present counter-plans to their associations, and the latter likewise to the ministries. The economic reform anticipates a gradual reduction in compulsory indicators and should take final shape in 1971. A new principle was introduced in 1969. Henceforth the enterprise will be responsible not only for current operations and results, but for expansion, including such things as market research and technical progress. This will also be a responsibility of the association. Quantitative indicators will become of secondary importance in relation to financial norms based on the profit indicator, and in relation to the new technical plan which will synthesise plans for modernisation, expansion and the progress of the firm and its group.

In the second place, the enterprise directly drafts the plan for a range of indicators which is often much wider than in the U.S.S.R. However, it is possible to classify countries into three groups. In the first group, the G.D.R., Poland and Romania are subject to a relatively imperative planning system, in which a fairly high number of indicators are imposed on enterprises through the medium of the associations, with the possibility of submitting counter-proposals. In the second category, Czechoslovakia and Bulgaria have strengthened the planning element within reform, as a reaction against early developments conferring considerable autonomy on enterprises. Finally, it is in Hungary that the market mechanism has evolved furthest.

Before analysing these mechanisms, one further significant difference between the U.S.S.R. and all other European socialist countries needs to be underlined. The liberalisation of the exchange of capital goods, almost nil in the U.S.S.R., already exists in these countries at the level of the associations, which ensure supplies and sales for their group. It could be maintained that the individual enterprise is still not really free to look for suppliers or customers. However Soviet experience has shown that freedom of exchange between firms cannot be introduced all at once without seriously disrupting the distribution of raw materials. The choice then was between repudiating such liberalisation, as in the U.S.S.R., or creating an organised market between important groups, as in the other socialist countries, with the concomitant risk of monopoly.

ECONOMIC AND FINANCIAL MECHANISMS

The reforms attach considerable importance to economic and financial means of directing enterprise activity: prices, taxation, credit. Their purpose is to prevent enterprises from using their resources, and especially their profits, in a manner detrimental to the interest of the state. This is particularly important now that firms are more or less free to establish their own plan and organise their own productive activity.

Orientation Through Prices

In the U.S.S.R. enterprise reform was accompanied by price reform. The aim was to ensure a normal profit-earning capacity for all enterprises, so that profit could become a real incentive. This concern is also found in the other socialist countries, but combined with the desire to introduce a degree of price flexibility wherever possible as a function of market fluctuations or of the relationship of supply to demand.

> *Examples:* Four types of price have been established in the G.D.R.: fixed (for goods and services essential to production and to living standards, such as basic raw materials, equipment, food products); 'ceiling' (goods where rapid technical progress is likely to lead to a fall in production costs); 'calculated' (by firms, mainly for spare parts and small-scale auxiliary production); 'negotiated' (for goods made to order or research work required by an enterprise from some specialised agency).
>   In Czechoslovakia a three-tiered price system was introduced in 1966-7: fixed (for the most important industrial products); a price bracket (maximum

and minimum) for a number of other products; free. At the beginning of 1967 the percentage of products sold in these different price categories was 64%, 29% and 7% respectively. However, on 1 January 1970, a moratorium froze prices at their level of 30 August 1969, the intention being to reform the price structure during the five-year period 1971-5. In Hungary, wholesale prices are either fixed or confined to a maximum upper limit (for most basic products), or free within certain limits (negotiated between enterprises). Since 1 January 1968 retail prices have fallen into four categories: fixed (20% of output sold), with a ceiling (30%), bracketed (27%), free (23%).

The liberalism of such price determination is more apparent than real. The freedom of the enterprise relates only to negotiated prices (in the G.D.R. and Hungary) which cover only small-scale production. Experience has shown that whenever a ceiling or bracket was established, prices soon stabilised at the maximum level, which is equivalent to fixing prices administratively.

Orientation through Financial Policy
As far as the fiscal system is concerned, the other socialist countries differ from the U.S.S.R. in one respect, and have a clear lead in another.

The taxing of profits is less arbitrary than in the U.S.S.R. In three countries (Bulgaria, Hungary, Czechoslovakia) budgetary payments out of profit take the form of a proportional or progressive tax, the actual rates varying from country to country. They are not levied at the discretion of the administration as is the case in the U.S.S.R. In the G.D.R. and Poland, as in the Soviet Union, enterprises make budgetary payments which vary according to results and which are defined by individual norms. However, they have more guarantees against abusive appropriation by the authorities.

The tax on capital was first introduced in Hungary (from 1964). It was introduced into the G.D.R. in stages between 1964 and 1968, and is now to be found everywhere except in Romania. Apart from its purely fiscal aspect, it has the function of encouraging the efficient management of productive capital. This is especially important in those countries (Bulgaria, Hungary, Czechoslovakia) where there is no centrally determined indicator for the use of fixed and circulating assets.

It should be added that in Hungary and Czechoslovakia there is a tax on wages. This is to prevent a too rapid rise in wages which might result from the freedom of enterprises to determine the total wages fund and from the full-employment situation existing in these two countries.

Budgetary policy is an important aspect of economic reform in so far as investment by enterprises must derive either from internal financing or from borrowing, and not as in the past from budgetary subsidies.

In the U.S.S.R. too the financing of investment will in the future proceed increasingly from non-budgetary sources. However the actual planning of investment will remain highly centralised, whereas in the other socialist countries there is a clear evolution in the direction of enterprise (association) autonomy in capital formation. In fact the associations have to establish development funds, plan the investment of their enterprises, and negotiate medium- or long-term credits with the banks.

As a general rule, the investments of associations and enterprises are programmed and enumerated in greater or lesser detail in the macro-economic plan. In Hungary, only large investments of national interest are included in the plan and financed out of the budget (the construction of new enterprises, large infrastructure projects, etc.); the investments of firms appear in the plan as large accumulations of capital by branch of activity.

Finance from non-budgetary sources is becoming increasingly common. Those sources are depreciation, enterprise funds and credit. The reform anticipates the creation of development funds everywhere, either in the individual enterprise or within the association. Credit is also an indirect means of orienting investment otherwise freely planned by enterprises.

Examples:

In the G.D.R. a 'bank for commerce and industry' has been set up within the framework of reform. Its purpose is to grant medium- and long-term credit to enterprises where this is justified by the expected return on investment.

In Czechoslovakia enterprise investment is largely financed by borrowing at an annual rate of 6%. The state bank set up a selection department organised in conjunction with the enterprise associations to examine requests for credit from the point of view of economic viability. Assuming equal viability, preference was given to the investor able to reimburse the credit earliest. However, this competitive system was abolished in 1971 and replaced by the administrative authorisation of credit according to the macro-economic advisability of the project in question. If the proposed investment is finally incorporated in the plan, it can be financed by long-term credit up to 60% of the total estimate.

Profit

In the U.S.S.R. profit is seen as a means of ensuring efficient plan fulfilment. It is in the enterprise's interest to maximise profit (or the rate of profit, profit/ productive capital). If it does so and if at the same time it fulfils the essential planned indicators (especially output sold) it acquires the right to dispose freely of a percentage of its profit, which will vary to the degree that the plan has been fulfilled. The work-force itself is directly affected, since bonuses depend on satisfactory results in relation to planning requirements and on the level of profit, which is the source of bonus funds.

The same concept is to be found in the G.D.R., Poland and Romania. The bonus is linked to plan fulfilment. On the other hand, there are different mechanisms for encouraging the full utilisation of plant capacity when the plan is drafted. In the G.D.R., for example, if the enterprise fulfils or exceeds the plan established by its association, the total bonuses to which it is entitled are less than if it fulfils or exceeds a counter-plan of its own which is more demanding than the initial one.

The same is not true of Czechoslovakia, Hungary and Bulgaria, where at the beginning of reform enterprises were placed in a market situation and where profit maximisation is seen as an objective independent of plan fulfilment. In other words, the revenue of the firm which it can use freely is not linked to plan fulfilment. This is only logical, since in these countries the plan imposed on the enterprise is made up of a very small number of compulsory indicators. The consequence is that the enterprise will gain or lose according to the efficiency of its own management. In the case of bad management, not only might there be no bonuses, but wages themselves might be cut. This particular approach has been completely abandoned in Czechoslovakia, considerably modified in Bulgaria and retained with a few changes in Hungary.

Examples:

In Czechoslovakia from 1967 to 1969 the basic concept was gross revenue (receipts less the cost of raw materials and depreciation). From this revenue the enterprise first had to pay state taxes, interest on bank loans and contributions to its technical development fund. Only then, from the balance, could it pay its workers out of a single remuneration fund. This was divided into a basic wages fund out of which employees received a monthly advance corresponding to a normal wage, and a gross revenue participation fund which was the source of annual bonuses. The ratio between the two funds was generally 9 to 1. The enterprise could practise an autonomous policy in employment and wages. It could, for example, choose to have a large number of poorly paid workers or fewer employees with a higher average wage.

This system was abandoned in 1970. The official reason was that it tended to create wide inequalities between enterprises and encouraged unjustified wage differentials. A net revenue concept (gross revenue minus basic wages) was substituted for that of gross revenue. However the direct planning of all wages has not been reintroduced, and the enterprise is simply required to respect current wage rates as determined by collective agreements. Take-home pay is still indirectly regulated by income tax.

In Hungary in 1968-9 a 100% basic wage was guaranteed in all circumstances only to industrial workers, even in the case of poor enterprise management. Middle management and directors had their incomes guaranteed at levels of 85% and 75% respectively. At the same time, there was a further improvement in the complex mechanism designed to stimulate the interest of personnel in the results of production and simultaneously to limit excessive general increases in income (wages and bonuses). The gross profit of the enterprise was divided into two parts: a profit-sharing fund, taxed progressively (from 40% to 70%); a development fund, bearing a proportional rate of taxation (60%). The division of the two funds is based on the ratio of the firm's total wages to its capital. To ensure that the profit-sharing fund is not too low in capital-intensive sectors, the total wages bill is multiplied by a coefficient of from 1 to 8, according to the sector, in establishing the ratio. After tax has been paid, a deduction is made from each of the two funds (10% and 12.5% respectively) to finance the reserve fund of the enterprise. Only then can the funds be used for paying bonuses or for internal financing. Since 1970 a ceiling has been imposed on bonuses of 25% of the basic wage for all categories of personnel. In addition to the proportional tax on wages, the enterprise pays a progressive tax on the annual increase in wages, which may rise to 400% of any increase. This tax is calculated in such a way as to prevent both an increase in the average wage and an excessive recruitment of badly paid workers, which would make it impossible for the firm to raise its average wage while employing too much labour.

In Bulgaria in 1966-7, the enterprise financed a residual wages fund which was equal to its gross revenue after deducting taxes, bank interest and payments into its stimulation funds. This system worked so badly that in 1968 it was found necessary to return to a more classic form of wage determination: the enterprise would pay rates by occupation and category as approved by the Council of Ministers; the total wages fund would be planned once again.

ENTERPRISES AND DIRECT ACCESS TO FOREIGN TRADE

Direct access to foreign markets is the logical consequence of the greater freedom of enterprises in all aspects of their activity. It corresponds also to the much greater dependence of the non-Soviet socialist economies on foreign trade. The ratio of imports to national income is 3.7% for the U.S.S.R., but 35% for Hungary, 30% for Czechoslovakia, 28% for Bulgaria, 25% for the G.D.R., and 12.5% for Romania (1964).

The reforms have tried to encourage firms to export. In most countries, foreign exchange receipts are partly left at the disposal of the exporting firms —mainly to allow them to import machinery and raw materials. Poland is the only country where the workers receive part of the export receipts in the form of bonuses.

Hungary has gone furthest in this field. Not only do enterprises have an interest in exports, but the international market has a stimulating effect on the domestic market. With this in mind, the state has established foreign trade multipliers, or conversion rates of the results of transactions in currency on foreign markets. In 1968 the rates were fixed at 40 forints to the rouble and 60 forints to the dollar. The prices of exported goods are thus based on actual receipts in foreign currency converted into forints, and those of imported goods on actual expenditure in foreign currency. Previously foreign trade organisations settled their accounts with exporting or importing firms on the basis of domestic prices, and then either cashed the difference or bore the loss in relation to foreign prices. The new method makes it possible to allow international prices to exert some influence on domestic prices and consequently widens the scope of market mechanisms, which in the other countries are limited to internal economic activity.

In the second place, the reforms have partially or totally abolished the screen between enterprises and foreign markets. To avoid the fragmentation of foreign trade, access to the international market has generally been reserved for enterprise associations. They sometimes intervene directly. In Bulgaria, for example, two associations, Bulgarplod for preserves, fresh fruit and vegetables, and Rhodopa for meat produce, combine the production, processing and export of food products. Other associations export agricultural machinery (Agromachina), ships, tobacco, beet, etc. In Poland the Polfa association combines eleven pharmaceutical enterprises and has complete autonomy in matters of foreign trade. More often than not, the associations operate on foreign markets through specialised subsidiaries or export-import offices. Both these are especially well-developed in the G.D.R., which in 1966 had 170 export offices in 40 countries. Alternatively, the associations may set up joint-stock companies. An example of this is the Czechoslovak company Centrotex, which combines several associations in the textile industry—wool, cotton, linen, jersey, clothing. A further possibility is the conclusion of contracts between associations and foreign trade organisations. In Czechoslovakia the Jablonex organisation, which is responsible for exports in jewellery and crystalware, has contracts with production units.

Sometimes large firms have the right to buy and sell abroad on an individual basis. This has been the case in Hungary since 1957, and since 1968 the system has been extended to about a hundred enterprises (electrical and medical equipment, rolling-stock, engineering). There were fifty-one such units in Poland in 1966, and just over a dozen in Czechoslovakia at the beginning of 1969. These firms sometimes have a world-wide reputation: Skoda of Czechoslovakia, Carl Zeiss Jena of the G.D.R. The latter has contracts in 102 countries.

Even if the State everywhere retains its monopoly of foreign trade, the growing trend towards direct contact with international economic activity must have internal repercussions, even if the only results are to familiarise an increasing number of firms with competition, marketing, the problems of advertising, after-sales service, etc.

AN APPRECIATION OF THE REFORMS

Each country is a special case. The two countries where developments have been least clear are Romania and Czechoslovakia, both characterised by highly centralised planning and limited enterprise autonomy in day-to-day management and investment policy. They represent economies of the pre-reform Soviet type.

In all the socialist countries, the drafting of the 1971-5 five-year plans was an opportunity for evaluating and adjusting the reforms in hand: revision of the price and incentive system (Poland), greater industrial concentration (Bulgaria), re-establishment of wage and price control (Hungary), increase in the number of planned indicators imposed on firms (especially with the aim of accelerating technical progress), more enterprise and association responsibility for fulfilling contractual obligations.

In no socialist country has it been possible to maintain completely the initial direction of reform. This is true even of the G.D.R. and Hungary, where the

...d introduced an efficient and well-balanced system conferring a
...ôle and extensive autonomy on associations, and the latter an original
...ination of planning and market. The new mechanism in Hungary in
...ticular was unable to develop its full potential. Pressure built up in several
areas and obliged the authorities to reintroduce direct controls to prevent
serious disequilibrium. Investment demand was very high, and since there
had been no administrative regulation of the exchange of capital goods since
1 January 1968, the consequences were serious: the rupture of traditional
contractual relationships; the speculative accumulation of stocks by users
rushing to buy up scarce raw materials; the abuse of monopoly power by some
producers; supply difficulties in the case of small firms. Labour scarcity exerted
an upward pressure on wages. To oblige firms to resist this pressure there was
a tightening of taxation on pay and direct control of wages. Finally the freedom
conferred on enterprises in the field of foreign trade, in conditions of excessive
demand for capital and consumer goods, brought about a large increase in
imports. In spite of an intricate system of import duties and taxes, the balance
of trade developed a considerable deficit. Thus Hungarian economic policy
wavers uncomfortably between market and plan. It cannot give free play to
market mechanisms without compromising the general orientation of the plan.
At the same time, the reimposition of precise controls constitutes a threat to
the intricate mechanism of the reform itself.

Yugoslavia

Yugoslavia occupies a special position among socialist countries by virtue of the
fact that since 1948 it has been outside the Soviet socialist bloc and since 1950
has reformed its economic system on the basis of self-management. The
Yugoslav enterprise is no longer subject to control or administrative planning.
Decisions on current activity and enterprise expansion are taken autonomously
by its own workers. Orientation of enterprise activity by the state is indirect.

THE ENTERPRISE AND SELF-MANAGEMENT

In July 1950 a law on enterprise management modified the 1946 law on
enterprise so as to bring it into harmony with new principles of workers'
management. At present, the organisation of enterprise is determined by a law
of 1965, promulgated two years after the new constitution of 1963 which
defined the basis of self-management in article 10.

According to the 1965 law the Yugoslav enterprise belongs to no particular
category; it is simply self-managed. Thus it is neither State, nor nationalised,
nor public; it is neither federal, republic, nor local. It is a working organisation,
and the means of production are social property. The State cannot dispose of
the means of production, nor transfer them to other enterprises, nor does it

finance the enterprise. However the enterprise does not own the means of production either. It merely manages them and must maintain them unimpaired (article 17 of the law).

An enterprise is not created administratively. It may be established from the division of an existing enterprise, on the initiative of a local community or group of citizens, or by the decision of one or several enterprises to found a new unit of production. The initial capital is usually advanced by a bank, which decides whether or not the new project is viable.

With a few exceptions, the disappearance of an enterprise is not the result of an administrative decision either. An enterprise may disappear as a result of a merger, integration or absorption. An enterprise can also be declared insolvent, but only after some reorganisation has been attempted by the bank, local community or another autonomous enterprise. This is especially true if the enterprise in financial difficulty has particular social significance, when temporary assistance may be necessary to give it time to get back on its own feet.

The enterprise is self-governing. Direct self-management by the working community is compulsory only in units with less than thirty workers. It can also be made mandatory by a decision of the work-force in units of between thirty and seventy employees. Beyond that a self-management apparatus has to be established, comprising workers' council, management committee and director. The workers' council may have anything from fifteen to eighty members who are elected by a workers' meeting for two years. Members are re-eligible for election once only. It meets publicly from four to six times a month. The presence of the director is mandatory. The management committee is elected by the council, of which it is the executive body. The director is an *ex officio* member of the committee, which has a minimum of five members elected for one year with the possibility of re-election. Since 1968 the appointment, dismissal and tenure of office of the director have been determined by the workers' council and management committee.

The functions of these organs of self-management are defined in articles 48 and 49 of the law. According to observers of meetings of workers' councils in various enterprises, it would appear that the workers are far less interested in those functions linked to the drafting of plans and production programmes, the approval of balance sheets and trading accounts, than in functions linked to the distribution of enterprise revenue, particularly when it concerns the distribution of bonuses or the allocation of social investment (residential construction especially).

Self-management carries with it the risk of conflict. The most obvious is the conflict between the general interest and the group interest of the enterprise. A further risk, which has only become apparent in recent years, is that of conflict between national and foreign interest as soon as the enterprise obtains the right of free recourse to foreign capital for further expansion. Finally an even more fundamental conflict is now emerging—between the very principle of self-management and the development of the private sector.

Self-management and Conflict

The most common criticism of the self-management system is that it tends to oppose the narrow interests of a particular group of workers to the general interest of the country as a whole.

Within the self-management framework enterprises are free to determine their particular economic activity. In other words they are free to expand along the most profitable lines and to neglect those less profitable sectors which may nevertheless be essential to economic growth. They are also free to establish prices as a function of supply and demand. Similarly they may opt to combine into different sorts of association or merger, which brings the risk of monopoly power in certain sectors. It is especially in the field of income distribution that the powers of the organs of self-management are at their widest.

The law anticipates the possibility of conflict and attempts to moderate enterprise power in several ways. For example, according to article 19 of the law on enterprises, the enterprise is obliged to operate as efficiently as possible with a view to obtaining the best results for both enterprise and community. Article 28, which is a sort of mini anti-trust law, prohibits mergers or associations which might damage the general interest as defined by the law. It is in the spirit of the system to encourage healthy competition between enterprises. At the same time, they must not be allowed to 'damage socialist economic relationships' or 'to create unequal business relations'. In the case of enterprise mergers, it is in fact questionable whether real workers' control can be maintained in the face of the growth of the enterprise, and whether this does not undermine the very basis of self-management. It seems that concentration creates difficulties arising from conflicts between workers' councils in individual units on the one hand and central councils on the other.

The concentration of enterprises in Yugoslavia did in fact accelerate between 1956 and 1970. In 1970 3.3% of enterprises accounted for nearly 50% of gross industrial production and nearly 60% of all workers were employed in enterprises with more than 1,000 employees. In a large enterprise, self-management must relate to at least two levels: the establishment and the firm. As a result of the fifteenth amendment to the constitution adopted in 1968 workers acquired the right to determine the internal organisation of the self-management system. In large enterprises this right, originally designed to reinforce self-management by workers, was paradoxically appropriated by the firm's technocracy. In some enterprises the powers of the management committees were transferred to business committees composed of managerial personnel. In others the workers' committee at enterprise level became the exclusive province of engineers and management. By way of reaction against this tendency, several constitutional amendments were adopted in 1971. Amendment 21 protects the right to self-management of the smaller units constituting the larger enterprise. It even allows the base organisation, corresponding to a technical unit of from forty to eighty workers, to secede from the enterprise, provided it does not prejudice the rights of workers elsewhere in the firm. Amendment 22 confirms the right of the organs of self-management to determine mergers and associations between their own enterprise and others (including financial institutions).

Income distribution is the chosen ground of self-management, and it is here above all that the law imposes restraint on enterprise initiative. The first obligation is to maintain the capital managed by the enterprise. From gross revenue there must therefore be first a deduction for depreciation, for which the law establishes a minimum rate. Secondly, the enterprise must fulfil its social obligations, notably by paying taxes. Since 1965 the Yugoslav enterprise has not been required to pay a tax on profits. It pays tax on its productive assets, at a rate varying from 2% to 3.5%. A further obligation is the payment of interest on bank loans and the repayment of debts on maturity. At this point the enterprise distributes its revenue between individual workers' incomes, which are subject to tax only at this stage, and various funds. The exact proportions of this distribution are imposed administratively and are defined in the articles of the enterprise. The articles themselves are drafted by the workers' council, which is subject to administrative control on this point.

The purpose of obliging the enterprise to establish funds is to prevent all the revenue being distributed to workers. This particular obligation constitutes an insurance against risk: by means of a reserve fund into which must be paid a proportion of revenue equal to 2% of annual working capital, until the reserve fund reaches 10% of working capital; further payments are made into the reserve fund of the commune or republic. The obligation also guarantees the future expansion of the enterprise by internal financing (out of the business or functional fund designed to finance productive investment). Equally, it makes possible certain social investments out of the collective consumption fund.

The constitutional amendments of 1971 maintain these limits on the right of the organs of self-management to distribute enterprise revenue. If amendment 21 declares that enterprise revenue belongs entirely to the firm which is responsible for determining the criteria for distributing this revenue, it also affirms that these criteria must conform to agreements signed with socio-political collectivities such as the communes. Moreover, if necessary, the law can regulate such distribution directly, especially to provide for future expansion over and above the needs of internal financing. The amendment has introduced two important principles: the right of every worker to a minimum income sufficient for 'his security and social stability'; an obligation of mutual assistance between economic units. This obligation can lead to levies on enterprise revenue either for social purposes (funds for unemployment insurance and retraining) or for general economic objectives.

Table 2.4 shows the distribution of the revenue of Yugoslav enterprises since 1964. There is a clear trend towards an increase in the share of personal incomes.

TABLE 2.4[8]

REVENUE DISTRIBUTION IN YUGOSLAV ENTERPRISES (%)

	1964	1965	1966	1967
Personal incomes	53.9	54.9	55.5	57.8
Economic funds (for expansion, depreciation)	31.4	33.9	31.4	30.9
Social funds	5.2	4.9	7.2	5.9
Other	9.5	6.3	5.9	5.4

The regulations described above do tend to limit any tendency towards narrow self-interest on the part of enterprises. But they do not eliminate inequalities between workers' incomes, which are still considerable between branches and particularly between regions.

The logical development of self-management since 1967 has created a new type of conflict: between the national interest and foreign interests. This is because Yugoslav enterprises have the right to turn to foreign capital as a source of finance.

Previous legislation already allowed the Yugoslav enterprise to invest jointly with one or more other Yugoslav enterprises. For the first time in September 1968, operating through the banks, an enterprise invited private savers to subscribe to a loan. The enterprise was a car firm assembling Fiat cars in Yugoslavia. The debentures placed with the public earned interest at 6% and gave their owners a preferential right of participation in a lottery for the purchase of a car on favourable terms.

However in such cases the operation was still purely national. From 1967, on the other hand, Yugoslavia seemed to swing towards capitalism as such, when she opened up her territory to foreign investment. The risk is sufficiently real for the law to surround foreign investment with a series of conditions and limitations:

Foreign capital can only be invested in an existing enterprise. The firm retains its legal status as a self-managed unit. In other words, it cannot become a limited liability company, a partnership, etc. Foreign capital must not constitute more than 49% of the total capital of the enterprise, which remains in complete control of all managerial functions.

The contract linking the Yugoslav enterprise with its foreign partner must be entered in the official business register.

Certain sectors are closed to foreign investment: banking, insurance, commerce, transport, services (communal and social), with the exception of the hotel trade.

The contract is temporary and must indicate the date when the foreign investor will have been entirely reimbursed (by annual payments from revenue).

The foreign investor can only transfer the return on his capital after paying profits tax at 35% (this tax is levied only on foreign investors) and after reinvesting at least 20% of his profits.

Recent legislation has tended to strengthen the rights and widen the field of action of foreign investors. In 1971 the twenty-second amendment to the constitution expressly guaranteed the rights of investors over their capital. In future these rights cannot be curtailed by any law or act once the contract has been concluded. In the same year regulations were introduced making it possible in certain cases for foreign capital to exceed the previous 49% limit imposed on foreign investment in any given enterprise. Moreover special arrangements have sometimes been made to accommodate profits tax (i.e. lowered to less than 35%), or the obligation to reinvest.

A first evaluation in 1972 indicated that over a five-year period foreign investment had been slight. Fifty-two contracts had been concluded and the average share of foreign capital in a joint enterprise had been 26%. The main investors were German and Italian firms, covering 50% of capital invested in Yugoslavia. The main branches affected were cars (53% of capital), chemicals (16.7%), and rubber (7.5%). Two-thirds of this capital were invested in the two most developed republics, Slovenia and Croatia, which is a good indication that the legislation of 1967 is no remedy for the problems of regional under-development.

Finally, self-management can be vitiated by the development of the private sector. Until 1971 this sector was tolerated outside agriculture in certain craft activities and services (catering, hotel trade), with an upper limit of five on the number of workers employed in any enterprise. Amendment 14 to the constitution, without substantially modifying the economic weight of the private sector, marks a profound change in attitude towards this form of activity. In the first place, the freedom of the individual to work with private means of production is rather vaguely *guaranteed*, provided the particular activity in question accords with the methods and potentialities of individual labour. The self-employed worker no longer belongs to a suspect category outside the community of workers in self-managed enterprises. In principle they all have the same socio-economic status and the same rights and obligations. In the second place, just as he has been socially reintegrated into the community of workers employed in autonomous enterprises, economically he can now collaborate with the socialised sector through various forms of association, and is thus able to share in the management of affairs of joint concern. In the third place, the amendment authorises the employment of salaried personnel in excess of the legal maximum limit where necessary. It gives an institutional frame-work to the relationship between small employers and their workers: the contract of employment must conform to a collective agreement concluded between the relevant trade union organisation and the corresponding economic committee on which private employers will be represented. Private enterprise is thus recognised and institutionalised. It is no longer marginal and temporary.

Are we likely to see the reappearance in Yugoslavia of the small shareholder as well as the small employer? Amendment 22 states in article 5 that enterprises may draw on the financial resources of private capital. In addition to repayment of the principal, private capital would receive interest or 'other advantages'. However, proof of debt would not confer a right of participation in management. The other advantages, if they include a share in revenue, might be compared to a sort of dividend.

These regulations do not threaten the system of self-management so long as the permitted expansion of the private sector is strictly controlled. It is probable that private enterprise will develop in areas requiring little capital investment in premises and equipment and where demand is strong: tourism, and especially road transport and building. According to a survey conducted among potential temporary emigrants in 1971, 13% declared that their purpose in going to work abroad was to be able to set up a small business on their return with the savings they hoped to accumulate.

INDIRECT MEANS OF ECONOMIC ORIENTATION

In Yugoslavia there is no specialised economic administration directing enterprises, nor any imperative planning of their activity.

The plan is simply a document providing information on the country's economic potential and defining its general proportions: relationship between consumption and investment, relationship of economic growth between different branches and regions, relationship between the volume of foreign trade and national income, etc. On the basis of the federal plan each republic and commune drafts its own individual plan. Any conflict of interest is settled by arbitration at a higher level.

The economic reform introduced in 1965 is very different from the reforms in the other countries, since it did not constitute a fundamental break with past practice. This was already characterised by an absence of imperative planning and by the important rôle played by indirect methods of direction: prices, taxation, incomes policies and, especially, credit.

In principle price control is limited: before September 1965 20% of industrial wholesale prices were free, since then 48%; after the reform free prices accounted for 74% of retail turnover. From 1966 to 1968 there was a moderate annual increase in prices of 5%. Then inflation developed, and in 1970 the general price level rose by 10.5%, and in 1971 by 16.5%. The government reacted by strengthening controls, followed by a price freeze which was renewed several times until April 1972. In May of the same year, a law on the social control of prices established the principle of price freedom, the general level to be determined by world prices and supply and demand. At the same time, the law authorises the use of the price freeze or the establishment of ceiling prices. For industrial prices it introduces a contractual procedure between enterprises and socio-political organisations. The procedure, which was intended to cover income determination as well, does not seem to have been applied satisfactorily. On 1 January 1973 a general incomes freeze was introduced at the average level reached in the period January-October 1972. There was a parallel freeze of the prices of many industrial goods. On the other hand the prices of services and food were raised, administratively.

Financial policy operates through a complex system of subsidies and incentives for certain products, and above all of grants to the less developed regions. The aim is to reduce income disparities between workers in different branches and regions.

Finally, it is the development of the banking system which dominates the present evolution of the Yugoslav economy. Selective bank credit has become the main instrument for determining investment priorities. Until 1963 a federal investment fund financed investment centrally, according to procedures and criteria analagous to those in the other socialist countries. In 1963 it was relieved of this function by nine specialised banks (a federal bank, six republican banks, and two banks for autonomous regions). Controlled by the federal or regional political authorities, they continued to apply a coherent investment policy. Since 1965 the investment banks have only granted loans according to commercial criteria. In addition to these banks there are commercial banks established jointly by enterprises and public collectivities. In 1968 there were ninety-six banks, seventeen of which were authorised to deal in foreign currency. As a result of concentrations their number has since diminished; fifteen banks account for two-thirds of total deposits. The law on banks and credit operations of December 1971 has tended to reduce the financial power of the banks, by conferring on the founding enterprises a much more extensive right of participation in their management. Enterprises and local collectivities responsible for establishing a bank retain their original investment, intervene in the management of the bank and share in the distribution of its revenue. It had been necessary, in fact, to pre-empt excessive concentration of power in the hands of the banking system. Whereas in 1963 credit covered 9.1% of investment in enterprises, the figure had risen to 43.8% in 1967 and to 53% in 1970, when its share in the financing of circulating capital also reached nearly 35%.

Credit is regulated by means of the classical tools of monetary policy typical of the capitalist system: bank rate, compulsory deposit reserves (32% in 1970), rediscount ceilings, regulation of short- and long-term credit.

To the problems inherent in indirect regulation of economic activity in Yugoslavia is added the difficult task of achieving a balance between the powers of the federation and the republics. The constitutional amendments of 1971 were intended to strengthen the powers of the republics. But the definition of federal jurisdiction is so vague as to allow any interpretation. Amendments 25 to 28 enumerate the basic elements of a single socialist market: the issue of money, the nature (but not the total) of tax receipts, the price system, planning, foreign relations. However, this could justify either a high degree of centralisation or of devolution in economic policy according to circumstances.

In any assessment of the Yugoslav version of market socialism there are several black spots. Two are particularly worrying:

Firstly, the opening of the economy to foreign competition has certainly led to a healthier economic situation, but brought with it inflationary tendencies which could only be contained by resorting to a price freeze. Exports were stimulated by successive devaluations of the dinar (four times since 1962, two of them in the wake of the dollar devaluations of December 1971 and February 1973). But the foreign debt is still considerable, even though in 1972 the balance of payments was positive for the first time since the war. The convertibility of the dinar could not be implemented in 1970 as had been hoped. And although enterprises have now completely free access to foreign markets, State intervention in the form of import duties and export subsidies is by no means negligible.

Secondly, the present system seems unable to deal with unemployment. In recent years in the non-agricultural socialised sector unemployment has been running at about 10% of the active population. The Yugoslav government has had to encourage emigration. According to the March 1971 census there were 670,000 Yugoslavs working abroad, or 15% of the non-agricultural active population. They are a not insignificant source of foreign currency earnings (something less than 700 million dollars in 1971; in the same year commodity exports earned 1,800 million dollars). At the same time, of course, they help alleviate the unemployment problem. 60% of them work in the Federal Republic of Germany. Their departure is organised by the Federal Labour Office. Since 1965 agreements have been concluded with France, Austria, Germany, Sweden, Holland and Belgium in an attempt to regulate the conditions under which they emigrate.

Apart from the chronic difficulties specific to the Yugoslav economy, self-management has not yet reached the apex of the economic and social pyramid of which it is the official base. The 1971 congress on self-management held in Sarajevo underlined the necessity for self-management in all social movements. But it did not explain how self-management would operate beyond the enterprise and local organs of power, that is to say beyond the daily horizon of most workers and citizens.

ECONOMIC UNITS
COMMERCIAL ORGANISATION
THE UNIT OF PRODUCTION IN
AGRICULTURE

The economic reforms introduced into the socialist countries are not limited to changing the position of industrial enterprise in relation to the economic and planning authorities. They affect the whole of economic activity. In this chapter we shall examine their broader application mainly in the light of Soviet experience.

In the U.S.S.R. the resolution of 4 October 1965 on socialist State enterprises of production applies to State enterprises in industry, building, agriculture, transport and communications. On the other hand, commercial enterprise still came under the resolution on State commercial enterprises of 17 August 1927. But the economic reform decided on by the Party Central Committee in September 1965 has as its objective the whole of the State sector and the whole of production and distribution. Consequently, by the end of 1972 the following sectors had been brought within the aegis of reform: 7,800 *sovkhoze* (out of 15,500, producing 54% of total output in the state agricultural sector); 550 building enterprises representing nearly one-quarter of all activity in the industry; the whole of rail, river, sea, road and air freight transport; 45,000 shops (18% of the total covering 35% of retail turnover).

The procedure for introducing the reform was similar to that followed in industry: gradual extension to the whole sector.

The objective of the reform is also similar: to substitute for the authoritarian control of units of production and distribution a more flexible form of control which will make it possible, in the general interest of plan fulfilment, to combine management autonomy and a direct interest in the results of economic activity. These principles are of course adapted to the specific requirements of each sector. For example, in the building trade, the problem is to encourage

99

building firms to complete work quickly and without unnecessarily exceeding the agreed estimates. In transport, freight must be moved quickly and at the lowest cost.

The co-operative sector underwent a similar radical transformation, begun even before that of the state sector. In our analysis of the ways in which the reforms were implemented, we shall use as examples the organisation of distribution in the State sector and the collective farm or *kolkhoz* in the co-operative sector.

1.   THE STATE SECTOR: DISTRIBUTION

At this point the reform poses the fundamental problem of the function of the market in the socialist system. Before reform the traditional function of the commercial sector had been to supply consumers at the lowest possible cost with goods manufactured in the productive sector. Commercial enterprise was the passive intermediary between production and consumption which were planned centrally.

This notion reflected a period when the supply of capital and consumer goods was less than the demand for them. The limited range of products available to the consumer made it relatively easy to distribute them centrally. The limited supply meant that all goods marketed found a buyer.

Economic development changed the whole situation. The authorities became aware of this phenomenon at the end of the 1950s, just as the problem of reforming the entire economic system was coming to the fore. The growing diversification of production was increasing the number of goods whose distribution had to be planned centrally. There was growing congestion in the centralised system of distribution itself. The increase in supply led in some cases to a saturation of demand, to which supply could not react quickly since the market was not structured to link supply and demand. This was a function of the planning authorities.

Within the context of reform and in relation to the distributive sector, it would have been logical to recognise the importance of commerce and to re-establish a real market as an active intermediary between production and consumption. But there is too much resistance to such a development.

As far as capital goods are concerned, the establishment of a relatively free market would threaten the very basis of the plan. If firms could buy or sell capital goods and the means of production freely the whole of the present system of investment planning would be undermined.

In the case of consumer goods, we have already seen that reform included the creation of direct links between production and distribution, by introducing contracts between enterprises and commercial establishments approved *a posteriori* by the planning departments. But bureaucratic opposition meant that this particular legal innovation was never anything more than a dead letter.

Apart from such opposition there is in the U.S.S.R. a basic mistrust of the commercial system, which is looked upon if not as entirely superfluous to economic life at least as a sort of foreign body which must be contained within strict limits if it is not to become a parasitical burden as under capitalism. Until recently advertising was still considered to be a shameful practice, and although it made its appearance in the U.S.S.R. a little while ago, commerce still bears a certain stigma.

The Distribution of Capital Goods: Material and Technical Supplies

The system for distributing capital goods was conceived during a period of acute shortage with a view to satisfying certain priority needs defined in the plan.

The point of departure is the plan, which establishes centrally the needs and resources available for these goods in the form of double entry tables or balances (*cf.* chapter 5). This collection of material balances, by product, is the result of production plans drafted by enterprises, rectified and synthesised by planning departments.

The evolution of this mode of distribution has led to the creation of a ponderous administrative machine increasingly incapable of guaranteeing supplies which meet the needs of enterprise. Partial reform tends merely to attenuate its deficiencies.

THE INSTITUTIONAL FRAMEWORK

Before 1957 each ministry had its own central sales and supplies departments with local branches. Altogether there were 6,000 supply and 3,000 sales agencies. The ministry organised this distribution on the basis of instructions from Gosplan which allocated customers and suppliers to it. This method of organisation brought ministries and planning departments into conflict and a high degree of administrative fragmentation in the distribution of the means of production.

Between 1957 and 1965 a complicated system was introduced to prevent regional administrations from helping themselves to the scarcest products. Fourteen central inter-republican administrations were established alongside Gosplan to distribute basic products. Less important goods were to be allocated by supply administrations attached to the republican Gosplans.

It was from this system that there emerged in 1965 the state committee for material and technical supplies or Gossnab, a sort of distribution ministry for intermediate goods which would be independent of both ministries and Gosplan. This plethoric administration, employing 600,000 people in 1967, comprises twenty-one central boards by product and thirty regional boards. How does it function?

THE SUPPLY SYSTEM

For enterprise directors the problem of supply is a source of constant anxiety, even within the framework of reform. Hence their constant tendency to inflate requirements so as to be sure of obtaining at least the necessary minimum.

The following is a typical example of the procedure involved. An enterprise needs five machine-tools of type X. It places an order with its ministry. If the ministry approves, the order is transmitted to Gosplan and Gossnab, and finally reaches the central board for the supply of machine-tools.

Let us assume that the demand is met. The enterprise will then obtain a purchase voucher, corresponding to a sales order delivered to his supplier. It is only at that moment that the enterprise can conclude a contract specifying details of delivery.

The procedure is far from perfect. In the first place it would be extremely difficult to obtain a purchase voucher for the five machines. This often involves the enterprise in a great deal of trouble, including the employment of more or less official representatives to wangle the purchase voucher out of the supply department. Everything depends on the pressure that can be brought to bear. Secondly the procedure is a long one in itself and may last several months. A third disadvantage is that the voucher is issued for one year. The same procedure must therefore be repeated annually, even where suppliers vary little from year to year as in the case of raw materials. A further drawback is that the delivery is often late or defective. The contractual obligations of the supplier were very weak until 1967. In that year they were reinforced, but apparently without much real effect. A resolution of 9 April 1969 on the delivery of technical goods, constituting in effect a new contractual code for deliveries, increases the responsibility of the supplier in the case of goods whose quality falls short of contractual specifications. At the same time, it lengthens guarantee periods and introduces an important innovation in the case of bulk deliveries. Previously a customer ordering in bulk often found in the delivery goods which were quite useless, but which still had to be paid for if he wished to keep the rest. Now he can refuse to take any delivery which has not been clearly specified in the contract. The way this new regulation is applied will depend a great deal on the relative bargaining power of the two parties.

The enterprises themselves are in no way satisfied with supply procedure. Apart from its clumsiness, its two main defects are incoherence and inaccuracy, the inevitable result of the growing mass of goods to be distributed.

Incoherence proceeds from lack of co-ordination between the various agencies of Gossnab, and especially between the central and territorial agencies. The situation is made worse by ministerial interference. In theory the ministries no longer have the right to organise the distribution of intermediate goods and should always proceed via Gossnab. In fact they have retained their own supply departments and illegally exercise the functions of purchase and supply on behalf of their own enterprises, in the name of the specific needs of their sector. For example, pitchforks are distributed by the central board for metal supplies, shovels by the ministry of mechanical engineering for building, roads and waste disposal, and axes by the ministry of mechanical engineering.

Paradoxically, inaccuracy has been increased by the reform itself. Before reform, Gosplan planned the resources and uses of nearly 18,000 basic products. Since then it has been responsible for the central planning of 1,500 to 2,000 products through the system of material balances. The central and territorial boards of Gossnab take care of the other 25,000 products (13,000 come under the central supply boards and 12,000 under the territorial boards). This unification of planning and distribution for most intermediate goods, linked to a degree of decentralisation, is excellent in itself. But the Gossnab agencies do not practise the material balances method and usually proceed by renewing the previous year's plans, since their main concern is to guarantee a full production programme for enterprises and the allocation of enough customers to absorb the goods produced. They do not define the structure of distribution. This they leave to the enterprises within the framework of contracts concluded through the purchase voucher system. But since the entire market for intermediate goods is a sellers' market, suppliers are in a position of strength and hardly make any effort to deliver goods according to the precise specification demanded by customers.

The reform of this system of distribution thus appeared to be a matter of some urgency, especially after the introduction of enterprise reform. Management autonomy, even after reform, certainly appeared to be obstructed by the administrative distribution of capital goods.

SUPPLY REFORM

There is an attempt to base this sector on commercial principles so as to supply enterprises quickly, from stable sources and without useless intermediate agencies. Actual achievements have been rather slight.

Two decrees, one on 27 January 1967 and the other on 28 April 1969, introduced a relative decentralisation of the distributive apparatus. In other words, they increased the distributive powers of the territorial boards.

In 1969 there were fifty-six territorial boards. Their purpose was to become commercial intermediaries between suppliers and users of capital goods and to analyse the supply and demand for them within their area of competence. A further (and as yet unfulfilled) function was to establish product balances indicating both necessary imports and possible exports from the region. By the end of 1972 half of them had acquired financial autonomy and had been transformed from administrative to commercial organisations. In 1968 they were already organising the distribution of 74% of production covered by Gossnab, through their 4,000 local branches. Their activity, however, is still narrowly circumscribed on the one hand by the central boards of Gossnab and on the other by ministerial supply departments which tend arbitrarily to redistribute purchase vouchers or sales orders already placed by the territorial boards.

Two other innovations are more important, though of limited application. Where continuous relations already exist between suppliers and customers, it will be possible to conclude direct contracts without recourse to purchase vouchers. However an extension of the wholesale trade is envisaged for goods produced in sufficiently large quantities.

Direct contracts are only an extension to the capital goods sector of the procedure already in use for consumer goods. 3,900 such contracts were concluded in 1967 and 5,500 in 1968, covering 800 products. In 1969, for example, 21.5% of total deliveries of metal products, 25% of cement, and 11% of chemical products were dealt with in this way. It is anticipated that such contracts will apply mainly to the distribution of fuel, building materials, crates and metals. These products have common characteristics. Their weight means that it is desirable to economise on transport costs. Since consumer demand varies little from year to year, it will be possible to draw up contracts for periods of three to five years, with annual adjustments where necessary. The direct contract system makes it possible to meet the precise specifications imposed by customers in these cases. Computer studies at the Gossnab research institute attempt to determine the most rational links between suppliers and customers and encourage the establishment of direct contracts on a scientific basis.

In 1969 the wholesale trade in capital goods was confined to 600 experimental 'shops'. It covered two product groups: fuel for industrial motors and enterprise lorries; enterprise surplus stock sold on commission.

In any case, enterprises tend to place their hopes in the improvement of planned supplies rather than in the new method. What they require above all is an adherence to guarantees of stable and regular supplies, which are often given on paper but rarely respected.

This bureaucratic and centralised system of supplies now exists only in the U.S.S.R. In most of the other socialist countries the function of distributing intermediate goods has been transferred to the enterprise associations introduced by the economic reform. The associations draft the supply plan of their enterprises in relation to the production programme and conclude the necessary contracts. A general plan of product distribution is established by the central planning departments, but it is not mandatory on the associations. The problem might arise of a discrepancy between the general supply plan and actual distribution resulting from the contracts concluded by the associations. In theory such distortions are avoided by means of special agencies called supply offices in the G.D.R., and purchase-sales groups in Czechoslovakia and Poland. They are not public administrations as in the U.S.S.R., but commercial organisations with financial autonomy. Their function is to co-ordinate the activities of firms or associations producing intermediate goods of the same type but which come under different associations. Furthermore, they must distribute orders and negotiate with customers. In Hungary, economic reform went further and freed exchange in capital goods, with certain special exceptions. In 1968 the exceptions covered fifty-eight products representing 20% of the total turnover of this sector. The system has been retained in spite of certain stresses during the first year of its operation, due to a very heavy demand for such products as special steels and synthetic textiles.

It might be asked why the U.S.S.R. does not follow these apparently positive experiments. In the first place, her industry is still not organised into enterprise associations and the dispersion of productive units makes it difficult to pass to more flexible forms of distribution. The progressive implementation of the programme of concentration begun in 1973 will doubtless make it possible to rationalise the supply system. Secondly, the size of the Soviet Union poses problems which are unknown in the other countries, such as the number and range of its products and the enormous distances they have to travel. The authorities fear there might be serious dislocation of the circulation of intermediate goods if the strict control of distribution were abandoned.

The Retail Trade in Consumer Goods

In the U.S.S.R. this sector comes largely under State control, whereas in the other socialist countries small-scale private commerce is relatively more important. Institutionally a distinction is drawn between so-called State commerce (shops depending on the Soviet Ministry of Domestic Trade) and co-operative commerce (shops depending on the Central Union of Consumers' Co-operatives). In 1967 they represented 68% and 29% respectively of the total turnover of domestic trade, as they had done for the previous ten years or so. In fact there is only a formal statutory difference between them. The co-operative sector comprises the rural retail network in industrial goods, and co-operative shops are managed in much the same way as State shops in the towns. On the fringe of this State system there is a free sector, which will be discussed later in relation to agriculture. This is the urban *kolkhoz* market where the peasants (or the *kolkhozy* themselves) sell the agricultural produce of their private plots of land (or, in the case of the *kolkhozy*, those products not purchased by the State).

The planning of commerce has remained detailed and centralised. 404 types of product are distributed at the federal level and cover 60% of the total turnover of retail trade. Notable among these products are flour, sugar, meat and meat products, textile and clothing products, shoes. The organisation of the distribution of most remaining goods is done at the level of the republics. Only for a very small number of articles is the supply to shops free, such as matches or watches.

In spite of the resolution on enterprise and the resolution of 9 April 1969 on the delivery of consumer goods, it is evident that the possibility for enterprises to sell their products directly to shops remains largely theoretical. Direct enterprise-shop contracts are still the exception.

Distribution at the retail level itself is also unsatisfactory. Once again the reform tried various palliatives.

DEFECTS IN THE PRESENT SYSTEM

These can be grouped under three heads:

Firstly, the retail trade does not act as an intermediary between production and consumption. It does not transmit consumer demand to firms, since that is a function of the planning departments. Nor is it adequately equipped to pass on information to the consumer.

Since the introduction of enterprise reform, attempts have been made to establish a link between production and consumption. In 1966 a federal institute was set up to research market demand. In an effort to determine and anticipate demand, sociological and economic surveys have multiplied from two sources. The first of these is the statistical information supplied by commercial organisations. The second is the analysis of the family budget. Since 1965 family budget analysis has covered a sample 25,000 families of industrial and other workers, together with 26,000 peasant families. Analysis is by family type classified according to size, income, parents' occupation, etc. The commercial statistics are not very meaningful, since they provide information on what consumers have bought and not on what they wanted to buy. The family budget surveys have the same disadvantage. They make it possible to identify important variations in the pattern of consumption, such as a relative fall in food purchases and a rise in expenditure on clothes, domestic and cultural items.

There is a parallel development of informative advertising, designed to give the customer information on new products and to familiarise him with different brands. But such efforts to inform producer and consumer are limited. Above all, they exist outside the commercial system as such. To give an example of the consequences of this lack of co-ordination: at the end of 1968 in Moscow one could often see on publicity hoardings an advertisement for take-away meals which housewives were invited to buy in restaurants: 'Instead of wasting your time in the kitchen, buy take-away meals: they taste good and are no more expensive.' Many Moscow housewives would willingly have followed this advice. Unfortunately all the restaurants had put up another sign: 'No take-away meals today'.

The second defect is that although the planning of production has been improved by enterprise reform, it still cannot guarantee that supply is adapted to consumer needs.

Planning often remains routine. Consequently production does not react quickly enough to the saturation of the demand for certain products. Conversely the marketing of new products is very slow. The planner too frequently assumes that what has been sold in the past will find a market in perpetuity. Demand of course changes. From 1953 to 1960, for example, the sale of watches doubled and that of sewing-machines tripled. But from 1961 to 1968 the former rose by only 18% and the latter fell by 62%. During this period firms continued to produce the same planned models of watches and sewing-machines, and shops continued to buy them under a system of orders imposed from above. It was only when stocks achieved prodigious heights that planning agencies took note. Demand can change even in the case of a product in common use for which there is normally a stable market. State shops once pointed out to the planning departments that they had accumulated abnormally large stocks of cooking salt. Consumer research explained. The fall in the consumption of salt in towns is linked to rising living standards and to the consequent reduction in salted foods produced at home, since housewives now prefer to buy fresh produce. Once again it took many months to change supply schedules. Conversely, it takes a long time for new products to reach the shops. The demand for modern detergents in 1967 was only 3% satisfied because enterprises did not have enough material interest in their production and because shops were not insistent enough in demanding them.

Moreover, planning procedure is slow. Enterprises receive plan confirmation after considerable delay, so that there is a permanent time-lag between the appearance of seasonal products on the market and the moment when the user needs them. In the clothing trade, for example, winter apparel comes into the shops in summer, and *vice-versa*. The Soviet consumer certainly cannot live like the proverbial and improvident cricket. In July one must buy skis and order a winter coat. In December it is time to think of buying beachwear.

The unpleasant effect on the consumer of planning according to a gross product indicator has already been described. Although this has now been officially replaced by the total sales indicator, it is still frequently used in practice.

Finally, production planning is no better co-ordinated for consumer goods than it is for capital goods. The results are often exasperating for the Soviet consumer. The following examples can be quoted from the Soviet press: twice as many skis as ski-boots; sausage meat but not enough skins; matches but not enough boxes; biros but too few refills; tape-recorders but no tapes; suspenders without belts; toboggans without runners.

As the third and final group of defects, the actual functioning of the retail trade leaves much to be desired. During years of scarcity the shops had no difficulty in selling all the goods they received. They are not suited to the present situation in which the consumer has become more difficult to please on account of the wider choice now available. Staff are ignorant of the elementary rules of stock management. Even in those rare cases where shops can obtain supplies directly from firms, they often prefer to go through the administrative channels of distribution for fear of ordering too much or too little.

The commercial network is too thinly spread. The lack of shops means purchasers lose a great deal of time, especially in the new urban residential areas and suburbs. The queues observed by Western commentators are not necessarily due to an absolute scarcity of goods. They are explained by the scarcity of shops, the traditionally slow service and the irregular supply system which tends to glut the market intermittently with exceptionally large quantities of a given article, so that customers rush to buy before it is too late. Add to this the limited range of industrial goods in rural shops and we can understand why peasants selling their produce on the *kolkhoz* market increase the strain on urban shops, as they try to buy what they cannot find in the village or market-town.

The idea of a commercial service as such hardly exists. House-to-house deliveries are unknown, as are orders by telephone, mail-order sales (except for a few isolated experiments) and after-sales service. When such services are introduced the administrative method of their application is sometimes not conducive to greater consumer satisfaction at all. A furniture shop was once persuaded to introduce a delivery service. To make this profitable it decided to make the service compulsory for everyone, including the customer living next door. Accompanied by two stalwart friends, the man came to buy and remove a chest of drawers, only to hear that he would have to wait two months for compulsory delivery!

Credit sales are hardly developed. In 1967 they represented 5.7% of commercial turnover in consumer durables, in spite of a low rate of interest varying from 1% to 2% according to the period of the loan, which may extend to twelve months. Purchasers of consumer durables are usually willing to pay cash once it is their turn to come off the waiting list.

The picture is even blacker for services than for the distribution of goods. The demand for all kinds of services is growing. At the same time, prices are low and vary little whatever the quality of the service. The number of establishments in this sector is inadequate. The result is queuing at restaurants, cafés, cinemas, theatres and hairdressers. It takes days for the plumber to come or for a dress to be returned from the cleaner's; weeks or even months for the coat ordered at the dressmaker's, or for the vacuum-cleaner or car to be repaired. To jump the queue a special recommendation or tip is required. Once again the authorities have tried to put things right by administrative means. A decree published in *Izvestia* (27 December 1968) enumerates measures for improving services. In particular it mentions the establishment of service centres in the new towns for repairing domestic appliances, flat maintenance, washing, baby-sitting. It goes on to recommend the development of services ordered by telephone, more expensive express services, repairs on the instalment plan, and the hiring of domestic appliances. All excellent ideas, no doubt. But in Moscow in 1969 there was only one baby-sitting organisation for 6 million inhabitants, and 13 service stations for tourist cars!

COMMERCIAL REFORM

Reform of the commercial enterprise began at the same time as that of the industrial enterprise. By the end of 1972 it covered 45,000 shops (out of nearly 700,000).

As in the case of industrial enterprise it first involved a simplification of planned indicators. Compulsory indicators will in future be turnover, profit, inventory of principal goods, investment and State budget payments. The commercial enterprise itself will freely plan distribution costs, wages fund and stocks, all of which had been imposed administratively before reform. It will establish stimulation funds out of net profits, as a function of turnover plan completion.

The first results of the reform were hardly satisfactory. The incentive rôle of profits in this sector is negligible, since retail prices are low. Unlike wholesale prices, they were not revised. The average rate of commercial profit (ratio of profit to turnover) was only 1.9% in 1971 (0.61% in catering). At the same time, the reform is often ignored by the authorities. Thus the departments of the State Bank still control the stocks of commercial enterprise.

Moreover, as in the industrial sector, commercial enterprise does not yet seem to have assimilated the new frame of mind required by the reform. They act neither as capitalist shops bent on sales promotion, nor as socialist organisations concerned with the optimal satisfaction of the needs and demands of the population. Traditional practices are applied to fulfil formal plan requirements in turnover and profit. Shops are to be found using the illegal method of joint sales, especially as New Year approaches or in the frenzy of buying which precedes 1 May. Two articles, one in demand and the other not, are sold together. Two examples quoted in the Soviet press were a good bottle of Armenian brandy sold with an unsolicited Soviet 'port', and a manicure set with a cumbersome box of tools. A further ploy is quite common at the end of the financial year. If shops realise that the turnover plan will not be met, they will sell for cash articles which are in great demand but not yet in stock. In December 1969, for example, a shop sold several dozen fictitious refrigerators with a promise of delivery in ten days. In fact the customers had to wait several weeks.

2.　THE CO-OPERATIVE SECTOR: AGRICULTURE

The co-operative sector is at present composed exclusively of agricultural co-operative enterprises or *kolkhozy*. As we have seen, the so-called co-operative commercial sector is in fact managed according to the same rules as State commerce. Craft co-operatives were abolished in 1960.

The planned management of co-operation in agriculture has always been one of the main concerns of the Soviet authorities, for two reasons.

Firstly, agricultural policy in both capitalist and socialist countries is one of the most difficult aspects of economic policy. Its objective is to regulate production. But whereas industrial production can be planned with some precision, meteorological uncertainties are still an insurmountable obstacle to agricultural planning. The problem is all the more intractable as over-production is just as much to be feared as scarcity. A further objective is to regulate farm incomes. Pressure in this area mounts as the incomes of other workers are increasingly guaranteed.

In capitalist countries the State influences production by encouraging particular types of crop, and income levels by guaranteeing prices and outlets.

In a socialist system, production is influenced through planning. Soviet experience has shown that whenever agricultural production has been planned without taking account of the hazards peculiar to agriculture, planning objectives have never been achieved. Moreover the attempt by the authorities to implement plans at whatever price brought such a negative response from the peasantry that it seriously jeopardised future growth in agriculture. For example, over-ambitious plans in livestock produce encouraged peasants to slaughter breeding cattle in an effort to supply the quantity of meat required. Prestigious plans for fodder production brought about the harvesting of cereals before they were ripe. In the U.S.S.R. since 1965 a much more realistic method of planning for basic agricultural products has been introduced. This means planning not the whole of production, but that part which must go to the State. In other words, the risks of production will in future only affect peasant consumption.

As far as income is concerned, until the end of the 1950s the authorities tended to consider that the Soviet peasant could live from the produce of his personal plot of land, both by direct consumption and by the sale of his surplus in the town market. Only in the last few years has it been found necessary to guarantee peasants a stable income and therefore a reasonable profit to the co-operative farms themselves.

The second reason is that agricultural policy in the U.S.S.R. has been complicated by the fact that it applies to two forms of property. Parallel with the co-operative farms there are the *sovkhoze* or state farms, in the form of

TABLES 3.1a to 3.1f[1]
AGRICULTURAL STATISTICS

3.1a   Number of farms at the beginning of mass collectivisation and at the present time

	1927	1940	1950	1971
Kolkhozy (in thousands)	14.8	236.9	123.7	32.8
Sovkhoze (in thousands)	1.4	4.2	5.0	15.5
Farms of poor and middle peasants (in millions)	23.7	3.6	0.7	0.04
Kulak farms (in millions)	1.1	—	—	—

3.1b   *Kolkhozy*: average dimensions

per *kolkhoz*

Year	Kolkhoz families	Area under cereals (thousands of hectares)	(a) cattle	cows in (a)	pigs	sheep and goats	Tractors converted into 15 hp. units, and including those of the M.T.S. and R.T.S. until 1960
				Head of Livestock			
1928	13	0.04	5	2	2	7	0.2
1940	81	0.5	85	24	35	177	2.4
1945	83	0.4	72	16	12	167	1.8
1950	165	1.0	224	56	98	546	6
1971	439	3.2	1,332	426	983	1,684	63

3.1c   *Sovkhoze*: average dimensions

per *sovkhoz*

Year	Total number of workers	Area under cereals (thousands of hectares)	(a) cattle	cows in (a)	pigs	sheep and goats	Tractors (15 hp. units)
				Head of Livestock			
1928	134	0.8	97	32	31	403	2
1940	330	2.8	592	229	459	1,420	24
1945	281	1.7	389	118	138	1,135	15
1950	334	2.6	562	170	500	1,530	26
1960	745	9.0	1,957	689	1,715	4,280	103
1971	587	6.1	1,971	697	1,200	3,562	125

3.1d   A comparison of total production and State deliveries in selected agricultural products (millions of tons)

	Product				Delivered to the State			
	1950	1960	1968	1972	1950	1960	1968	1971
Cereals ...	81.2	125.5	169.5	181.2	32.3	46.7	69.0	64.1
Cotton ...	3.5	4.3	5.9	7.1	3.5	4.3	5.9	7.1
Sugar beet .	20.8	57.7	94.3	72.2	19.7	52.2	84.2	64.3
Potatoes ...	88.6	84.4	105.2	92.6	6.9	7.1	11.5	11.6
Vegetables .	9.3	16.6	19.0	20.8	2.0	5.1	9.0	11.5

3.1e   Distribution of the cultivated area by category of farm (%)

	1928	1971
Total area under cereals in all categories of farm	100	100
of which:		
sovkhoze and other state farms	1.5	47.8
kolkhozy	1.2	49.2
personal plots of collective farmers and workers ...	1.0	3.0
private farms and farms of other social groups ...	96.3	0.0

3.1f   Share of the personal plot of peasant and worker in total production and in State purchases of agricultural products (%)

	1940		1960		1965		1967	
Products	Share of total production (a)	Share of State purchases (b)	(a)	(b)	(a)	(b)	(a)	(b)
Cereals ...	12	3	2	—	2	—	2	—
Sugar beet ...	6	6	—	—	—	—	—	—
Turnsoles ...	11	5	4	—	2	—	2	—
Potatoes ...	65	37	63	24	63	27	63	19
Vegetables ...	48	2	44	7	41	7	41	5
Meat	72	37	41	13	40	9	38	13
Milk	77	34	47	7	39	4	38	4
Eggs	94	93	80	37	67	26	63	19
Wool	39	24	22	14	20	14	20	13

model enterprises, pilot farms in developing areas, and experimental centres. Stalin's aim, and to a lesser extent Krushchev's, was for the State sector gradually to absorb the collective sector. Today's policy seems to be to maintain the present balance between the two forms of property, whilst standardising as far as possible the management of farms and the condition of the peasantry across the two sectors.

The present position is given in the following statistics (tables 3.1a–3.1f). In the U.S.S.R. in 1971 there were 15,500 *sovkhoze* covering 94.4 million hectares under cereals or 47.8% of the total area. 32,800 *kolkhozy* covered 96.9 million hectares or 49.2% of the total area. The remaining 3% are the auxiliary plots of the peasantry. In that same year there were 16 million *kolkhoz* workers and 9 million on the *sovkhoze*.

Sovkhoz management is subject to the same rules as industrial management, their labour force coming under the head 'workers and employees' in official statistics. The reform of the state farms was determined in a decree of 13 April 1967 on the total financial autonomy of the *sovkhoze*. It was introduced gradually, to 400 farms in 1967 and to nearly 3,000 by the end of 1968. By the end of 1969 it covered 4,000 farms, and in 1972 extended to 7,800 *sovkhoze*. Its objective is apparent from the title of the 1967 decree. The various elements of the reform are very similar to those for industrial enterprise. Compulsory plan indicators have been reduced in number. In future these will be limited to an indicator of production in kind, to the total wages fund, to the ratio of profit and productive capital, and to the volume of investment. Secondly, there has been an increase in selling prices to guarantee the profitability of any *sovkhoz* under average management. Thirdly, the *sovkhoz* will have easier access to credit. Finally, the profit incentive will play its part by means of an encouragement fund linked to the degree of plan fulfilment. In fact, after paying the budget charge on productive capital, the *sovkhoz* finances three funds similar to those in industry, together with an additional insurance fund against bad harvests.

The *kolkhoz* system was based until 1969 on a statute of 17 February 1935 defining the agricultural *artel* or co-operative. According to this statute, the *artel* had free use of the nationalised land in perpetuity. Buildings, equipment and livestock would be exploited collectively. Control of the co-operative was in the hands of the general assembly (an assembly of delegates in large *kolkhozy*), which elected the executive council and its chairman. Choice of the chairman was in fact closely controlled by the Party. The co-operative farmer had the right to own his house, a strip of adjacent land, livestock and equipment. The extent of the strip and the quantity of livestock authorised changed from period to period. In 1969 the area of the strip varied from 0.15 to 0.50 hectares according to the region. The collective farmer also had grazing rights on *kolkhoz* land. However, he was not alone in this. Of the surface area covered by the auxiliary strips, three-fifths were owned by collective farmers and two-fifths by workers and other employees. This last group comprised *sovkhoz* workers as well as elements of the rural intelligentsia such as teachers and doctors. The reason for this toleration of private property is political, economic and social. Politically it constitutes a safety valve for the traditional resistance of the peasants to absorption into the co-operatives. Economically the private holding is the most flexible source of supply for the urban market in potatoes, vegetables, poultry, eggs and dairy products. Socially the existence of the private holding and the income it was supposed to afford the peasant tended to serve as an excuse for the State not to provide a guaranteed minimum wage in the *kolkhoz* sector.

The *kolkhoz* constitution of 1935 which had been approved by the second congress of co-operative farmers remained in force for thirty-five years. A decree of 28 November 1969 established a new type of *kolkhoz* constitution based on the decisions of the third federal congress of co-operative farmers meeting from 25 to 27 November. This constitution incorporates most of the reforms relating to *kolkhoz* economic activity after 1965. They mainly concern the organisation of production, the distribution of *kolkhoz* revenue, the pay and state insurance of co-operative farmers. However, there is very little change in the legal status of the *kolkhoz*. The *kolkhoz'* free use of the land in perpetuity is reaffirmed, although the land itself remains State property. This is merely a reiteration of the terms of the land legislation which had codified agrarian law in December 1968, based until then on a law of 1928. In particular the new constitution forbids the unjustified withdrawal of cultivable land from the *kolkhoz* for non-agricultural purposes. At the same time, it establishes compensation procedures where *kolkhoz* land is reduced or temporarily allocated to other specific uses. Similarly it maintains the right of the co-operative farmer to a strip of land adjacent to his house, 0.50 hectares at the maximum or 0.20 hectares on irrigated land. The *kolkhoz* family may also own a cow and yearling calf, a bullock less than two years old, a sow and litter of three months or two porkers, up to ten goats and sheep taken together, bee-hives, poultry and rabbits. The new constitution retains the former principles of internal kolkhoz organisation. Its main contribution is that is adapts them to the present situation of the co-operative farm. First of all, it eliminates all the legal terms which characterised the institution in 1935. Next, it takes account of the fact that in 1969 the average *kolkhoz* no longer consisted of a small village of less than a hundred families as in 1935. By 1969 it usually covered a dozen or so villages composed of more than 400 peasant families. The new constitution therefore anticipated new forms of management as a function of the size of the co-operative.

The basic managerial structure remains the general assembly or legislative body, and the executive council and chairman elected by the assembly as in the 1935 statute. However, the new legislation attaches considerable importance to the smaller, secondary assemblies of co-operative farmers. In fact, the direct democracy of the *kolkhoz* general assembly, suited to small units of production, cannot function efficiently in large-scale co-operatives. Consequently, extensive control over day-to-day management has been conferred on these secondary assemblies (generally coinciding with a village), which elect a council and chairman to represent them at the higher level of *kolkhoz* management. Finally, to prevent any abuse of power by chairman or council, a control commission is elected for three years by the general assembly.

As a sort of adjunct to the new legislation, the third congress of co-operative farmers established kolkhoz councils, to be elected at every regional level from rural district to republic. At the same time, it elected a federal council which met for the first time in March 1970. This decision established a number of agencies which among other things will be responsible for the management of social security, a function which for workers and employees of the State is exercised by the trade unions. In fact trade unionism in Soviet agriculture exists only in the nationalised sector (one of the largest of the twenty-five union organisations in the Soviet Union). Until 1970 there was no organisation at national level responsible for the State insurance fund established for co-operative farmers in 1964. It is not surprising that the first meeting of the *kolkhoz* federal council was mainly concerned with examining the problems of managing this fund. One may also assume that the *kolkhoz* councils, and particularly the federal council, will contribute to rationalising the monetary payments made to co-operative farmers since 1966. This might be done by means of a wage determination procedure similar to the one in which the trade unions participate at federal level for workers and employees of the nationalised sector.

In spite of the rapprochement of the nationalised and co-operative sectors, the institutional organisation of the *kolkhoz* still bears the weight of tradition. The historical origins of the *kolkhoz* system and the political conditions of its implementation weighed heavily on its economic progress. This development can be divided into two periods, separated by the reforms of 1965.

Development of the Kolkhoz System until 1965

1958 was a turning-point in this development. Before 1958 State pressure on the *kolkhozy* was very strong (through its policies on incomes, prices, taxation, farm equipment). As a result of reforms introduced from 1958, the attitude of the authorities became more liberal, but without much practical effect.

BEFORE 1958: THE POLICY OF CONSTRAINT

The attitude of mind of the authorities towards the collectivised peasantry was one of complete mistrust. The *kolkhoz* as a unit of production and the co-operative farmer as a producer were to be coerced into serving the needs of industrialisation.

To this end the following means were used:
1. A system of compulsory deliveries to the State was accompanied by the imperative planning of production, sowing, harvest dates, etc.
2. Prices: until 1953 the prices paid to the farms for compulsory deliveries were always less than the cost of production. Higher prices were paid for deliveries over and above the quota (from 30% to 50% for vegetable products and 120% for livestock produce). In fact, planned compulsory deliveries were on such a scale that there was hardly any surplus for additional deliveries.

Prices were raised in 1953, but the distinction between the two types of delivery was maintained.

3.   Taxation: the *kolkhoz* itself was taxed first. The tax, levied on the gross income of the previous year, was proportional and levied at different rates according to the source of income (sale of cereals or agricultural products for industrial purposes). Since the tax was on gross income, it had to be paid even by those *kolkhozy* which were in deficit. It was particularly burdensome when bad harvest followed good.

As for the co-operative farmers, until 1953 they were subject to a highly progressive income tax. Since then they have had to pay an agricultural tax based on the cultivated area of the individual private holding at a fixed rate per 1/100 of a hectare.

4.   Pay in the *kolkhoz*: pay was effected through the complicated *troudoden* system. Its chief characteristic was that it was neither guaranteed nor exclusively (even partially) monetary. The system was based implicitly on the notion that the peasant could not possibly die of hunger since he had his own small-holding and could live from its produce. Basic monetary needs would be covered by selling the surplus product of the same holding on the urban *kolkhoz* market.

The *troudoden* was an abstract unit of pay based on a standard day's work. It was calculated at the end of the year after harvest receipts. Disposable income was calculated after deducting material costs of production, the payment of taxes, insurance payments, and additions to the joint fund. The balance, if it existed, was divided in both kind and money among the co-operative farmers according to the number of days worked by them during the year. The right of sharing in the distribution of *kolkhoz* revenue was not automatic, but depended on contributing a minimum number of work-days. This was to dissuade farmers from devoting almost all their time to their personal plots. Work-days were weighted according to the difficulty of the task involved. For example, the daily rate for hand-reaping might have been two *troudodni* and for preparing sheaf-bonds a half *troudoden*. The following is an example of the way in which individual income might have been calculated: assume that the net annual revenue of a particular *kolkhoz* was 240,000 roubles, that it comprised 800 persons each having contributed an average 150 *troudodni*, ie. 120,000 *troudodni* (in toto). The *troudoden* would then be worth 2 roubles. If the 240,000 roubles were composed of 120,000 roubles in cash and 120,000 in kind (wheat, potatoes, etc.) each co-operative farmer would receive on average 150 roubles in money and the same in the form of wheat, etc. These he would normally receive on one occasion at the end of the year, unless his *kolkhoz* were sufficiently prosperous to make advance payments during the previous twelve months. He could never be absolutely sure of just how much he would receive.

5.   The organisation of agricultural work: the authorities' distrust of co-operative farms, thought to be politically unreliable, led in 1931 to the creation of the Machine Tractor Stations (M.T.S.). Their purpose was to provide the

desired managerial framework for the *kolkhozy*. Originally every M.T.S. had a political assistant director. A parallel function was to perform agricultural work on behalf of the *kolkhozy*, thereby preventing them from acquiring their own equipment. The work of the M.T.S. was paid in kind with a proportion of the harvest. For the State this amounted to a supplementary source of agricultural supplies.

AFTER 1958: THE POLICY OF LIBERALISATION

Kruschev's post-1958 policy *vis-à-vis* the *kolkhoz*, although liberal in intention, maintained the system in a narrow straitjacket. On the one hand it was hoped that the *kolkhozy* would become profitable and motivated towards plan fulfilment. On the other it was feared that once they began to prosper they would put their own self-interest before that of the State. The distinguishing features of this policy were as follows:

1.   The planning of agricultural production remained very detailed. However, compulsory deliveries, akin to confiscation, were abolished. From 1961 the local agencies of the State committee for agricultural deliveries were empowered to conclude delivery contracts with farms on the basis of the plan.

2.   The double price system was abolished at the same time as compulsory deliveries. New prices were introduced in 1958. They were economic prices, calculated regionally, and were intended to cover costs and guarantee adequate farm profits under normal conditions of management. These prices were stable in normal harvests, but could be modified in the face of exceptionally good or bad harvests. Although excellent in principle the reform tended in practice to introduce a high degree of incoherence into the price structure. This was due to the difficulties of suddenly introducing a rational method of calculating cost prices (never before undertaken in the *kolkhozy*) and rates of profit, and of establishing a rational zoning system, etc.

3.   The *kolkhoz* tax burden was lightened. The tax was still based on gross revenue and in principle was fixed at the single rate of 12.5%. To encourage livestock breeding there was a tax relief of 80% on revenue from the sale of animal produce.

4.   In 1958 the principle of a guaranteed fixed money wage was established to replace the *troudoden* gradually. However the principle was never implemented for the simple reason that the *kolkhozy* did not have the resources to make wage payments possible. In 1964 the pay of the co-operative farmer was less than three-quarters that of the *sovkhoz* worker.

5.   The M.T.S. were liquidated (though they continued to exist as Repair Tractor Stations for two or three years). Their equipment was sold to the *kolkhozy* which from 1961 were able to purchase new equipment directly from agencies of the Agricultural Technical Centre (*Sojuzsel'khoztekhnika*), the equivalent of the State Committee for Material and Technical Supplies in the industrial sector. One of the reasons for the agricultural price rises in 1958

had been to allow the *kolkhozy* to purchase their own equipment.

The 1965 Reforms

In spite of the 1958 measures the agricultural situation deteriorated until 1965. The rate of growth of agricultural production fell. Between 1950 and 1954 the index of agricultural production rose by 22%; between 1955 and 1959 by 49%; but between 1960 and 1965 by only 14%. The policy of intensive agriculture could not be carried through in the absence of sufficient farm income to buy machinery and fertilisers.

The 1965 reforms constituted a considerable improvement in the position of both *kolkhoz* and farmer alike.

THE EFFECTS OF THE REFORM ON FARMS

A plenum of the Party Central Committee adopted a resolution on 26 March 1965 criticising the whole of previous agricultural policy and strongly recommending more freedom in *kolkhoz* management. The resolution was followed by a series of measures in April and May 1965 introducing the following changes:

1. A new concept of agricultural planning. The discussions preceding the reform had revealed two possibilities: to retain imperative planning directed from above; to organise agricultural supplies on the basis of contracts freely concluded between farms and state collection agencies. These were in fact the same options as in industrial planning. The solution finally adopted was a compromise: apart from perishable produce, centralised planning would be maintained; the plan would continue to establish the total volume of agricultural production expected, by product, but only the sales plan would be compulsory for the *kolkhozy*. The volume of total production would simply be an indicator within the macro-economic plan. The sales targets imposed on the *kolkhozy* were more realistic. They would be fixed for a five-year period in the form of an annual average indicator (for example, 55.7 million tons a year for cereals, 8.5 million tons of meat a year). They are in fact a minimum requirement which has usually been exceeded. In 1966 the *kolkhozy* sold 75 million tons of cereal to the State, and 10.3 million tons of meat; in 1967, 57.2 and 11.5 million respectively; in 1968, 69 and 11.9 million. But in 1969 only the delivery target for meat was exceeded, with 11.7 million tons sold to the State. For the first time the sales of cereal, 55.5 million tons, did not reach the target figure. At the same time, State collection agencies have greater responsibility for any deviation from contracts concluded with the *kolkhozy* (as from 1 January 1968). Nevertheless the contract system does not operate satisfactorily. Contractual relations between collection agencies and *kolkhozy* are not always equal. Sometimes the agency managers are able to oblige *kolkhoz* council

chairmen to sign blank contracts and later to impose targets beyond their real capacity.

There has thus been a development similar to that in industrial planning. As in industry, the main indicator for production planning is output sold. Other *kolkhoz* indicators cover investment, especially in irrigation and land improvement financed from the State budget, and deliveries to tractor and agricultural machinery units.

2. Price advantages are conferred on *kolkhozy* selling products to the state over and above delivery targets. Prices are from 50% to 100% higher for these additional sales, according to the type of product. As a consequence there has been a tendency for the *kolkhoz* rate of profit to rise: 20% in 1964, 27% in 1965, 35% in 1966. Such rates of profit may appear high in relation to industry. However, unlike industry, the *kolkhozy* must purchase equipment entirely from their own funds. The state will assume responsibility only for costly items of infrastructure.

3. A considerable alleviation of the tax burden. *Kolkhoz* income tax was completely revised in April 1965. Since then it has been a 12% tax on current annual net income, levied over and above a 15% profit level and payments made into the State insurance fund which was established in 1964. To ensure that no *kolkhoz* escapes from the tax by distributing all its net income in the form of pay, the tax also covers wages above 60 roubles per month per *kolkhoz* member. The rate is then 8%. In other words, only the prosperous *kolkhozy* pay the tax: those whose rate of profit is over 15% (the ratio of net revenue to costs) and pay their members above the minimum guaranteed industrial wage.

4. The *kolkhozy* now have certain financial facilities. Debts prior to 1965 have been cancelled and there are greater opportunities for short- and long-term credit. In 1966 the system of advances against future crops practised by the collection agencies was abolished and the *kolkhozy* authorised to use direct bank credit, especially to obtain finance for the payment of wages. This was related to the introduction of a guaranteed wage in the *kolkhozy* on 1 July 1966.

5. The *kolkhozy* are encouraged to develop their non-agricultural activities. The period 1966-7 marked a significant change in the attitude of the authorities towards the *kolkhozy*. Fear of a disguised resurrection of private enterprise had led to the repression of extra-agricultural activities within the *kolkhozy*. Now they can be undertaken by 'inter-*kolkhoz*ian organisations' grouping several units of production: for the construction of small electric power stations or irrigation networks; for building construction; for the establishment and operation of units processing agricultural products; for managing artificial insemination and incubation units, etc. At the same time a decree of 16 September 1967 gave the go-ahead to the development of auxiliary or craft enterprises in the *kolkhozy* to employ labour during the off-season.

It is quite clear that the *kolkhoz* sector is no longer considered one to be pressurised, but as an autonomous element of national economic activity whose development must be stimulated through a system of material incentives.

THE EFFECTS OF REFORM ON *KOLKHOZ* MEMBERS

1.   Various measures have tended to bind the *kolkhoz* farmer more closely to his co-operative. Even before the 1965 reforms, a law of 15 July 1964 introduced a system of retirement and disability pensions for *kolkhoz* members who until then had no allowance for sickness, accident or old age. Among other things, this law had the effect of limiting the drift of families from the countryside. Retirement age for men and women was fixed at sixty-five and sixty years respectively. In 1967 the age limits were in both cases lowered by five years, extending to *kolkhoz* members the system applicable to other workers and employees. In the second place, as we have already seen, the principle of a guaranteed monthly wage was recommended to the *kolkhozy*, to take effect from July 1966. However, on this second occasion, the recommendation was actually implemented, thanks to the credit facilities granted to the *kolkhozy* at the same time, and also to the fact that the general profit level of the *kolkhozy* had been raised. In 1967 the average daily wage of the *kolkhoz* worker was already 3.25 roubles, which was 50% more than in 1964 and 90% of the *sovkhoz* wage (which in turn was on average 75% of the wage of the industrial worker).

2.   A more favourable policy was adopted towards the individual private holding. It was encouraged in various ways from the end of 1964, particularly in the field of stock breeding: taxes on private livestock breeding were abolished and credit facilities granted to peasants for the purchase of cattle. This amounted to an implicit recognition of the economic value of the private holding in agriculture, whose contribution to overall agricultural production is by no means insignificant. The new *kolkhoz* constitution of 1969 outlines the precise rights of *kolkhoz* families in this area of activity.

However, in spite of these measures, it is doubtful whether Soviet agriculture has achieved a satisfactory level of equilibrium. Between 1968 and 1969 agricultural production fell by 3%, and by 4.6% between 1971 and 1972. These results were due to meteorological factors rather than to mistakes in general economic policy or to bad farm management. It is nevertheless disquieting that the U.S.S.R. is not self-sufficient in agricultural products, food or raw materials, in view of the fact that 30% of the active population is employed in agriculture and that the proportion of total investment allocated to it is steadily increasing (15% between 1950 and 1960, 18% between 1961 and 1970).

The purpose of the authorities is clear: to bring industry and agriculture closer together. The industrialisation of agriculture must be continued. This means more electrification, more mechanisation and a greater application of chemical knowledge to production. It also means developing the transport network and techniques of preserving and processing agricultural produce.

Because of an inadequate road network, the absence of preserving units on farms and an insufficient number of lorries, large quantities of fruit and vegetables go to waste each year without being marketed. The cities are short of milk, eggs and poultry not because production is inadequate but because there is no effective marketing mechanism. Hence the staggering profits of individual peasants who have no hesitation in flying hundreds of miles to sell a few boxes of tomatoes to housewives in the capital.

In the second place, there has been an official move towards greater concentration in farming. But this time concentration has not taken the form of regrouping the *kolkhozy* as between 1950 and 1964, when their number fell from 123,000 to 38,000. Nor does it mean the transformation of *kolkhozy* into *sovkhoze* (about 20,000 co-operative farms were absorbed into the state system between 1950 and 1964). It has taken the form of *kolkhoz* associations and the creation of agro-industrial complexes combining both agricultural and industrial activities. We have already seen that for some years the State has been encouraging farms to establish enterprises for processing agricultural produce, building material enterprises using local resources, and enterprises producing crates and packing-cases, as well as encouraging them to develop the skills of local craft-workers. The farms have sometimes abused this freedom. For example, according to the 1969 report on plan fulfilment, certain *kolkhozy* found their auxiliary activity so rewarding that they neglected their main function. However, isolated abuses such as have occurred will certainly not cause the Soviet authorities to change their general policy, especially as for them the development of agro-industrial complexes is a first step towards a profound transformation of rural life, towards the urbanisation of the countryside. The ultimate objective is to harmonise as far as possible the living conditions of both town and country, to provide in both an equivalent network of free or commercial services. In fact cultural, educational, medical and commercial services are much less in evidence in the countryside than in the towns. The introduction in 1965 of agricultural pensions has still not provided the co-operative farmer with a pension equal to that of the industrial worker. Recent measures to raise the standard of living of the peasants have reduced the drift from the land, but young people continue to leave (in 1967 the average age of the agricultural worker was fifty years). Teachers with qualifications in agriculture are likewise reluctant to remain in the countryside. The authorities seem to be expecting a great deal from an ambitious project which, in effect if not in form, is an extension of the 'agro-town' concept formulated in about 1950-1 at the end of the Stalinist period. The intention is to restructure rural localities by concentrating the habitat, building urban-type housing estates with facilities such as running water, electricity, gas, improved roads and commercial and cultural services. A village reconstruction plan was formulated for 1970-5. It seems to have been implemented so far mainly in the *sovkhoze*, which here as elsewhere are being used as both model and testing ground. It remains to be seen whether such radical changes will be accepted by the peasants, deeply attached to their traditional environment and especially to the individual home.

In the other European socialist countries agricultural policy has evolved in similar fashion. From authoritarian control of agriculture, designed to appropriate resources necessary for industrial development and at the same time to ensure political supervision of the peasantry, these countries have developed more flexible forms of administration based on the use of economic instruments of control. Like economic policy in general since 1952, agricultural policy in Yugoslavia has followed a unique path. Its objective has been the modernisation of a backward agriculture. However, it was decided not to impose a socialist transformation on existing structures, but simply to encourage flexible forms of association between individual producers, and between the latter and co-operative farms which represent almost 14% of the total cultivated area. Agriculture is proportionately more socialised in Yugoslavia than in Poland.

It should be noted that agriculture is not equally important in all these countries. The G.D.R. and Czechoslovakia are primarily industrial countries. Agriculture employs 15.5% and 21.4% respectively of the active population (1966), and contributes 11.9% and 12.6% to national income. Problems of agricultural policy are therefore easier to solve in these two countries. Their main concern is to ensure adequate imported food supplies to supplement domestic production. In the four other European member-countries of Comecon, agriculture employs between one-third and one-half of the active population, and provides between one-fifth and one-third of the national income. Bulgaria, Romania and Hungary are net importers of agricultural products. Poland almost achieves equilibrium in its agricultural trade balance, but imports large quantities of wheat (mainly from the U.S.A.). National agricultural policies are obviously influenced by these differences.

Apart from Poland, legal and administrative structures in the socialist countries tend to be similar. As in the U.S.S.R., the socialised sector is dominant everywhere except in Poland (*cf.* chapter 1) where private farms cover 86% of the cultivated area. But the balance between state and co-operative farms is not the same. The State sector is most important in Romania and Czechoslovakia, covering 30% of cultivated land. The proportion is 20% in Hungary, 13% in Bulgaria and Poland, and 7% in the G.D.R. Except for Poland the co-operative sector covers the largest area (from 60% to 85% according to the country).

Co-operatives and state farms have always depended on a single administration (ministry or a higher agricultural council), whereas in the U.S.S.R. *kolkhoz* and *sovkhoz* have for long been under the control of different administrations, because of the particular political problem of the *kolkhoz* sector. Some years ago the agricultural administration extended its jurisdiction beyond the field of production to the collection and processing of agricultural produce, and to the supply of industrial materials and equipment to the agricultural sector. This makes possible a more coherent solution to marketing and supply problems in agriculture. At the same time, as in industry, the concentration of farms in the form of co-operative associations has been encouraged in several countries (Bulgaria, Romania, Hungary). These associations are managed by elected councils which represent and defend co-operative interests *vis-à-vis* the administration. In addition they have responsibility for farm purchases and sales with outside bodies, and have the power to draft bills or regulations concerning agriculture.

The Planning of Production
All the European socialist countries, like the U.S.S.R., experienced a period
of authoritarian planning in agriculture. Such planning was linked to a
system of compulsory deliveries imposed on farms and paid at very low
prices. These methods were abandoned everywhere in the period 1960-5.

At present the accent is on long-term production planning. In the G.D.R.
a general outline of agricultural development has been drafted for the period
up to 1980. Similarly in Czechoslovakia there is an economic-technical
outline of developments in agriculture until 1980. Bulgaria and Poland have
twenty-year plans. These drafts are not of course concrete directives. They
indicate general trends in the structure of production, the development of
the labour market, technical innovations and so on. More precise indications
are contained in the five-year plans for the main products (cereals, potatoes,
sugar-beet, meat, dairy produce, etc.). Current farm activity is determined
by the contracts concluded with collection agencies. As a general rule, no
compulsory delivery is directly imposed on farms. The collection agencies
purchase a given quantity of produce for the State. They place their orders
after direct negotiations with farms, which (since 1965) lead to contracts
renewable several times a year. Farms thus have a guaranteed and stable
market. In Poland contracts are concluded between local authorities and
peasants (since most farms are privately owned), and contain details of
price, quantity, quality and time of delivery.

The substitution of contractual procedures for authoritarian directives
implies the development of indirect means of State intervention in farming,
especially via the price mechanism.

Agricultural Prices
During the period of authoritarian planning any prices policy was inevitably
subordinated to the process of industrial accumulation by means of state
appropriation of agricultural surpluses. The prices paid for compulsory
deliveries were often lower than production costs. Higher prices were fixed
for deliveries above the compulsory quota.

After the adoption of a contractual procedure for sales, single prices were
established (regionally differentiated) for each product, usually at a higher
level than costs. This reform of agricultural prices took place in 1960 in
Czechoslovakia, Bulgaria and Poland, in 1964 in the G.D.R., and in 1965
in Hungary. For certain products (especially livestock), prices had to be kept
low so as not to exert upward pressure on retail prices. In this case farm
deficits were made good out of subsidies. In most of these countries the
collection agencies are free to negotiate prices for certain categories of
product, such as fruit and vegetables in Bulgaria and Romania. In Czechoslovakia and Hungary they can do so for deliveries in excess of the quantities
agreed in the contracts.

Supplies of Agricultural Equipment
Towards 1960 the Machine Tractor Stations which had been set up everywhere after the war, following the Soviet pattern, were abolished, except in
Poland and Romania. Their retention in Poland is due to the small size of
the private holdings, which do not possess costly equipment and which can
be indirectly controlled by the administration in this way. In Romania their
continued existence is due to the more authoritarian concept of economic
control generally prevalent in that country.

In the G.D.R., Czechoslovakia, Hungary and Bulgaria M.T.S. equipment
was sold to the co-operative farms either at very low prices or with generous

conditions of payment. Since then the farms have been able to buy equipment and supplies at generally low prices and under a simplified procedure.
Almost all centralised allocations of industrial products to agriculture have
been replaced by a direct sales system organised through wholesale distribution agencies. Co-operatives finance purchases out of their own resources or
by having recourse to credit. For example, in Bulgaria and Czechoslovakia
they establish development and technical progress funds for this purpose. In
Bulgaria they can obtain twenty-year loans at 2% per annum, and in
Hungary thirty-five-year loans at 1%. In the G.D.R. it is medium-term
credit which is most used (from three to five years, with a rate of interest
of from 1.5 to 3%); similarly in Czechoslovakia.

Taxation
As in the U.S.S.R. the tax burden on farms has been considerably lightened.
A land or income tax is used as a means of equalising conditions of management and of bringing up to the average level farms operating in an
unfavourable geographical situation or soil conditions. These farms benefit
from tax reductions and exemptions, and often from subsidies or price
advantages supplementing the tax concessions. On the other hand, better
placed units of production are taxed more heavily.

The Pay of Agricultural Workers
The co-operatives of the socialist countries used to pay their members
according to the *troudoden* system borrowed from the U.S.S.R. However
they began to modify it much earlier.
    Pay was mainly in money after 1953 in Czechoslovakia, 1962 in Romania,
1963 in Bulgaria and 1964 in Hungary. Attempts to guarantee it were made
at a very early date: in 1958 in the G.D.R., where farms received a special
State grant to guarantee a fixed and regular wage, eventually to be
supplemented by bonuses; in 1963 in Bulgaria, where a central guarantee
fund was financed jointly by State and farms; from 1964 in Czechoslovakia,
on the basis of a detailed pay scale according to occupational category; from
1961 in Hungary. Farms were able to resort to short-term credit to pay
their workers regularly in spite of the sporadic and seasonal nature of their
receipts. Since the middle of the 1960s they have applied different methods
to interest their members in the results of production (gross receipts or
profits), and have established bonus funds similar to those in industrial
enterprises.
    Finally, State insurance for agricultural workers was often introduced
several years in advance of the Soviet Union: 1957 in Bulgaria, 1958 in
Hungary, 1959 in the G.D.R., 1964 in Czechoslovakia, 1966 in Romania.
It is usually less generous than social security for industrial workers, but its
field of application is just as wide. The state insurance system includes
retirement pensions, disability pensions, sickness benefit, family allowances
to compensate the loss of a bread-winner and so on. The retirement age in
most of these countries is a few years older for peasants than for workers.
Usually it is sixty years for women and sixty-five for men. This rapid survey
would seem to show that the European socialist countries have treated their
peasantry more generously than the Soviet Union. There is no doubt, in any
case, that they have considerably shortened the period of political constraint,
economic exploitation and social discrimination imposed on the co-operative
sector.

Part II

OPERATIONAL MECHANISMS IN THE SOCIALIST ECONOMIES

---

Chapter 4

1. The Strategy of Development

2. Growth Factors

3. Growth and Structure of the Economy

ECONOMIC GROWTH

The first objective of the socialist economies is economic growth. The ultimate aim is the welfare of all. This is expressed in the basic economic law of socialism: 'The ever-increasing satisfaction of the growing material and cultural needs of the people by means of the constant development and improvement of socialist production.'[1] In a socialist system, production can and must grow indefinitely in both quantity and quality ('development' and 'improvement'). The needs of the population, also expanding indefinitely, are themselves a causal factor in this progression.

A glance at the results achieved by the European socialist economies will show that at first sight this objective has been systematically pursued (table 4.1). For the whole of this chapter we shall use the official statistical sources of the socialist countries. One might certainly have reservations about the way

TABLE 4.1[2]

NATIONAL INCOME: ANNUAL RATES OF GROWTH (%)

	1951 -67	1951 -55	1956 -60	1961 -65	1966 -70	1971 - 75 (plan)
Members of Comecon (total)	8.2	10.7	8.3	6.1	7.3	6.0 - 6.5
Bulgaria	9.6	12.2	9.6	6.7	8.7	8.0 - 8.5
Hungary	5.7	5.7	6.0	4.5	6.8	5.4 - 5.7
Poland	7.1	8.6	6.6	6.2	6.0	6.6 - 6.8
G.D.R.	7.7	13.2	7.4	3.4	5.2	4.8 - 5.1
Romania	9.8	14.2	6.6	9.1	7.7	11.0 - 12.0
Czechoslovakia	6.0	8.1	7.0	1.9	6.8	5.1
U.S.S.R.	8.8	11.3	9.2	6.5	7.2	6.5 - 7.0
Yugoslavia	8.8	8.4	11.8	7.3	6.7	7.5

these data are calculated and about their significance. The note on Soviet statistics in the appendix deals with this problem. In face of the almost impossible task of recalculating all these figures, it would seem reasonable to take them as they are in the official collections. At the same time their 'directions for use' will be clearly displayed, especially in connection with the main aggregates of national income accounting, since these do not correspond to standard Western practice.

In spite of a slowing down in growth rates after 1960, it is evident that the European socialist economies are developing more quickly than the industrialised capitalist countries. The question as to why this is so is not of mere scientific interest. The reply to it necessarily has political implications, since it concerns the final outcome of the competition between the United States and the Soviet Union, as well as the attraction of the socialist system for the Third World. Consequently there are many different approaches to the analysis of socialist growth, often politically motivated.

The historical approach emphasises the backwardness of the countries in which socialist revolution took place. Starting from a low level and given a systematic policy of industrialisation they were able to realise a very rapid rate of growth in the early period. Once this first phase was complete, however, there was a tendency for growth rates to diminish, as can be seen from a comparison of rates in the initial take-off period with those of today. This explanation is borne out by a comparison of growth rates between countries. Those economies which were initially the most underdeveloped (Bulgaria, Romania) expanded more quickly than the others. But this particular explanation cannot account for detailed differences in rates of growth, both geographically and over time. Above all it ignores the great initial diversity of situation in the various countries. Just after World War II there was a marked contrast between Yugoslavia, Romania and Hungary on the one hand, and Czechoslovakia and the G.D.R. on the other. The first group were hardly industrialised and their agriculture was characterised by the domination of large landowners, overpopulation and low yields. The other two had a history of industrialisation, a skilled labour-force and a thriving heavy industry. Poland was at an intermediary stage of development, with abundant mineral resources insufficiently exploited and an important agricultural sector plagued with rural unemployment. As far as Russia is concerned, and it is to her that the rapid growth/low take-off point argument should best apply in principle, it should be remembered that at the end of the nineteenth and beginning of the twentieth centuries the State had pursued a vigorous policy of industrialisa-tion based on foreign loans. The Soviet Union inherited a productive capacity which in 1913 comprised the most up-to-date technical innovations. It was the advanced technical level of her industry which made it possible for the Soviet Union to live off existing industrial capital, almost without replacement, until the beginning of the first five-year plan.

Interesting among the historico-political analyses is the thesis of Alexander

Gerschenkron.[3] According to this line of argument the history of Russia since Ivan the Terrible has been dominated by territorial expansion and the political ambition of her leaders to achieve at any price the economic and cultural levels of the West. Since the material and human resources at their disposal were inadequate for the purpose, periods of spectacular growth (the epoch of Peter the Great, the industrial capitalism of 1890-1900, the first two Soviet five-year plans 1928-37) were followed by stagnation or at least by a slackening of expansion once political pressure was relaxed. For Gerschenkron this pattern of growth is always voluntarist and imitative. Through the centuries only the models and the figures in power have changed: the American mirage follows the fascination for the European West, and Stalin is the heir of Peter the Great.

This thesis implies a philosophy of history which goes beyond the limits of economic analysis. However it does have the advantage of underlining the importance of the political system as a factor in development. In the socialist states, the political authorities (and especially the Party leaders) hold economic power and can take decisions affecting the general orientation of growth and can implement these decisions through a network of economic agencies within the administration. Growth would then be the logical result of action inflexibly geared to this objective. Socialist institutions do eradicate a certain number of obstacles which in the capitalist system tend to limit the possibilities of State action in the economic sphere. The absence of a competitive market eliminates risk. Socialist managers are not faced with problems of uncertainty. Inventions spread quickly, since within the country there is nothing like a patent system conferring legal protection. There are no monopolies with interests running counter to those of the State[4]. The period of centralised authoritarian planning, which came to an end between 1960 and 1965 in most of the countries to which this outline applies, coincides with the period of most rapid growth. However we still have to explain how the socialist planners were able to achieve their objectives, since their determination, however strong, could not bring about such development alone.

A conscious policy of growth presupposes a *strategy*; it is based on material and human resources which constitute the *factors* of development; it tends towards a specific economic *structure* at the sectoral and regional levels.

1. THE STRATEGY OF DEVELOPMENT

The Soviet policy of growth, which initially served as a model for other socialist states, is based on Marx's theory of reproduction as developed by Lenin, who applied it to socialist conditions.

The Theory of Socialist Reproduction

The object of this theory is to define under what conditions 'simple' and 'extended' reproduction take place during the continuous process of production and exchange. By simple reproduction is meant the reconstitution of the material product created during a particular year by replacing the material and human capital incorporated in the product. Extended reproduction implies an increase in that same product.

Let us first define the product. In physical terms it is the total mass of material goods produced during a specific period (a year), which can be divided into two categories: capital goods (raw materials, semi-finished products, machinery, etc.); consumption goods (personal and collective). In value terms it is the sum of the values of gross production (without deducting intermediate consumption) in all branches belonging to the sector of material production. This aggregate of values can be divided into two parts:

1. The value transferred to the product by those goods used up in the production process. This transfer is complete in the case of goods used up immediately (materials) and gradual in the case of equipment whose wear and tear is reflected in depreciation charges.

2. New values created by labour.[5] According to Marx:

$$P = P_1 + P_2 = c + v + m$$
$$P_1 = c_1 + v_1 + m_1; \quad P_2 = c_2 + v_2 + m_2$$

where
P = total product
P_1 = production of capital goods
P_2 = production of consumption goods
c = capital spent on the wear and tear of equipment and on the use of raw materials (transferred value)
v = capital spent on wages
m = surplus value, created by labour alone
$v + m$ = new values created in the period, where v is the 'necessary product' (for the reproduction of labour power) and m the added product.

We shall meet this definition of the material product again, in connection with price determination (*cf.* chapter 6), and above all in connection with planning methods (chapter 5). It is the basis of every national accounting system in the socialist countries, expressly called the material product accounting system, in which the fundamental aggregate is the gross social product. This aggregate differs in two fundamental ways from equivalent aggregates in Western systems of national accounting, for example from the standard gross national product aggregate.

In the first place, it includes all intermediate consumption. In fact the theory of reproduction on which socialist national accounting has been constructed implies an analysis of the whole of exchange relations involved in the formation of the product, including those within the productive sector. The result is that socialist statistics concerning the total product are not comparable with Western gross national product statistics which represent the sum of added values minus intermediate consumption. Data on gross industrial production are calculated in the same way. This method tends to swell the product of branches of production nearer the final consumer, which must contain more 'transferred' value than the product of branches at an earlier stage of transformation. At the same time, industrial production will be greater in the more specialised units of production, since their product will already have passed through numerous stages of transformation.

In the second place, the gross social product is defined as the whole of the production of material goods. This material criterion in socialist accounting is highly restrictive. The following constitute the various branches of material production: industry, building, agriculture, forestry, wholesale and retail trade, those sections of transport and communications necessary to material production. Services are excluded, as is the 'productive activity' of State and local administration. It should not be forgotten that in a socialist system the public administration has extensive functions. Thus all the services of the hotel trade, which is administered by the municipalities, are excluded from the total product.

Marx defined the process of simple reproduction in Book II of *Capital*, but gave only a summary account of extended reproduction.

Simple reproduction presupposes a static economy, with no investment: the new values created in a given period $(v + m)$ must be consumed. To achieve a position of equilibrium, demand must be equal to supply in each of the two departments of production: capital goods and consumption goods. Since the total demand for capital goods is equal to the sum of capital goods used up in the preceding period (given that there is no new investwent), we have:

$$c_1 + v_1 + m_1 = c_1 + c_2 \qquad \boxed{v_1 + m_1 = c_2}$$

The same result is arrived at by analysing the demand for and supply of consumption goods:

$$c_2 + v_2 + m_2 = v_1 + m_1 + v_2 + m_2 \qquad \boxed{c_2 = v_1 + m_1}$$

This relationship is thus the equilibrium equation of simple reproduction: the new values created in department 1 must be equal to the consumption of capital goods in department II. Oscar Lange expresses the same thing graphically in the following way:

$$c_1 + \boxed{v_1 + m_1}$$
$$\boxed{c_2} + v_2 + m_2$$

Under conditions of extended reproduction, the new value is not entirely consumed. A proportion is allocated to investment. Consequently the sum of capital goods used up in time t' will be greater than the sum of capital goods used up in time t, so that we have:

$$c_1' = c_1 + \Delta c_1 \qquad c_2' = c_2 + \Delta c_2$$

As previously, equilibrium will exist when supply and demand are equal in each of the departments of production. It will be achieved only if the new value created in department $I(v_1 + m_1)$ is greater than the consumption of capital goods by department $II(c_2)$:

$$c_1 + v_1 + m_1 = c_1 + \Delta c_1 + c_2 + \Delta c_2$$

$$v_1 + m_1 = c_2 + \Delta c_1 + \Delta c_2 = c_2 + \Delta c$$

$$v_1 + m_1 - c_2 = \Delta c$$

$$v_1 + m_1 > c_2$$

By how much must the new values created in department I exceed c_2? Extended reproduction presupposes that surplus value m (or the net additional product) is partly allocated to an increase in expenditure on capital goods, hence $q = \dfrac{\Delta c}{m}$. A further part of m will be allocated to the increase in expenditure on wages required by the expansion of production: $z = \dfrac{\Delta v}{m}$. The balance p will be used to increase consumption; we shall thus have $q + z + p = 1$, and in each of the two departments $q_1 + z_1 + p_1 = 1$ and $q_2 + z_2 + p_2 = 1$.

The product formulae can then be written as follows:

$$P_1 = c_1 + v_1 + q_1 m_1 + z_1 m_1 + p_1 m_1$$

$$P_2 = c_2 + v_2 + q_2 m_2 + z_2 m_2 + p_2 m_2$$

And the equality between the supply and demand of capital goods:

$$c_1 + v_1 + q_1 m_1 + z_1 m_1 + p_1 m_1 = c_1 + c_2 + q_1 m_1 + q_2 m_2$$

$$v_1 + z_1 m_1 + p_1 m_1 = c_2 + q_2 m_2$$

or $c_2 + q_2 m_2 = c_2 + \Delta c_2 = c_2'$ (or the total demand for department II capital goods at time t') and

$$v_1 + z_1 m_1 = v_1 + \Delta v_1 = v_1'$$

Hence: $$c_2' = v_1' + p_1 m_1$$

Thus capital goods expenditure by department II is equal to a fraction of the new value created by department I: wages and that proportion of the net additional product going to consumption.

The same result is obtained on the basis of equality in the supply and demand of consumption goods.

In Lange's[6] notation we would write:

$$c_1 + q_1 m_1 + \boxed{v_1 + p_1 m_1 + z_1 m_1}$$

$$\boxed{c_2 + q_2 m_2} + v_2 + p_2 m_2 + z_2 m_2$$

It should be noted that this theory, devised for the capitalist economy, was intended primarily to explain crises of overproduction. For example, in the simple reproduction hypothesis, production in department I might be too great in relation to the demand for capital goods. Such a situation would be reflected in a surplus of new values created in $I(v_1 + m_1)$ over expenditure on capital in II (c_2). Equilibrium would not be achieved. It is worth stressing too that the Marxist scheme of reproduction is only valid for a closed economy, without foreign markets. This condition substantially circumscribes the validity of Marx's analysis for the capitalist system, as Rosa Luxembourg was to point out later.

Marx's formula was adopted and developed by Lenin, and later by Soviet economists with the aim of supplying some indication of the strategy of growth required in a planned economy. The socialist economy is not free from all disequilibrium, which can occur as a result of exchanges between department I and department II. To take the analysis further, it is necessary to complete Marx's initial scheme by first introducing the dimension of time. In other words, the 'productive consumption' of the net added product m, qm in the symbolic notation given above, does not take place at the same time as its unproductive consumption. In the course of productive consumption, the periods of use of capital goods are not identical. Secondly, one must abandon the hypothesis of the invariability of the rate of accumulation $(q = \Delta c/m$; $q_1 = 0.5, q_2 = 0.3$ in the examples given by Marx) and of the organic composition of capital $(c/v$; according to Marx $c_1/v_1 = 4$ and $c_2/v_2 = 2)$ or the coefficient of capital intensity according to one's terminology.

It was on this last point that Lenin's contribution was of capital importance for subsequent theories of growth in the Soviet Union. According to Lenin it is impossible to deduct anything from Marx's scheme about the rate of growth in each of the two sectors. Each develops along parallel lines. The theory takes no account of technical progress, which leads to a continuous growth in the ratio c/v.

Lenin developed the consequences of this new hypothesis in one of his first articles, written in 1893, 'On the Problem of Markets'.

Taking the model of extended reproduction given by Marx, he shows that with the same initial data for the base year one arrives very quickly, after only three or four years, at very different results if the organic composition of capital is raised at different rates.

But why reject a constant c/v? Because technical progress operates through an expansion of investment (new construction, modernisation). It is therefore necessary to increase the production of capital goods not only to ensure the development of existing productive capacity at present technical levels, but also to incorporate new, additional fixed capital into this productive potential. It might be objected that this does not necessarily lead to a rise in the ratio c/v. To this argument Lenin replies that technical progress, by definition, means an increase in the productivity of labour, i.e. an increase in production per worker by means of better technical equipment in the work process. Capitalists would never spend more on capital if they did not simultaneously economise in the use of labour power. Thus v increases in absolute value, but at a slower rate than c. This effect of technical progress will be evident both overall and within each individual sector: $\dfrac{c_1 t_0}{v_1 t_0} < \dfrac{c_1 t}{v_1 t}$ (in the algebraic example developed by Lenin, which is not reproduced here, $\dfrac{c_1 t_0}{v_1 t_0} = 4$, as in Marx; but from the fourth year in the process of reproduction we already have $\dfrac{c_1 t}{v_1 t} = 5$); $\dfrac{c_2 t_0}{v_2 t_0} < \dfrac{c_2 t}{v_2 t}$ (in the algebraic example, $\dfrac{c_2 t_0}{v_2 t_0} = 2$, $\dfrac{c_2 t}{v_2 t} = 2.12$; the growth in capital intensity is relatively less marked because the search for technical progress is directed above all at the development of department I). Lenin therefore concludes in his article that 'in a capitalist society the production of capital goods increases more quickly than that of consumption goods', since each year it is necessary to allocate a greater proportion of the total accumulation fund (Δc) to the production of capital goods: Δc, increases more quickly than Δc_2. Thus production in department I increases at a quicker rate not only because initially one must invest more there in order to incorporate advances in technical progress, but also because more is reinvested proportionally than in department II. Consequently, the hypothesis of the invariability of accumulation rates in the two sectors must also be abandoned: the ratio q_1/q_2 will rise.

Such was the main modification made by Lenin to Marx's scheme. It is worth noting that like his predecessor he bases his argument on constant prices, that is to say physical quantities. The value of the capital goods unit, like that of the consumption goods unit, is invariable.

It could be asked whether Lenin thought that this demonstration was only valid for capitalism. One would think so from another article written shortly afterwards, 'A Definition of Economic Romanticism'. When speaking of the more rapid development of department I, he says: 'that corresponds perfectly to the historic mission of capitalism and to its specific social structure: the first consists precisely in expanding the productive forces of society (production for production), the second excludes their use by the mass of the population.' However, Lenin's commentators have not interpreted his thought in this way. They have usually maintained that any economy experiencing an industrial revolution and substituting machines for manual labour necessarily follows a similar line of evolution.

Even if, contrary to what is suggested in the quotation in the previous paragraph, it is admitted that Lenin was basing his argument on the technical and not on the exclusively social characteristics of capitalism, it is clear that his demonstration implies an hypothesis of extensive development (the creation of new productive capacity) and dispenses with intensive methods of promoting growth (an increase in production by a better use of existing capacity, by more efficient combinations of labour and capital). This hypothesis was doubtless still valid for Russia in 1917. But could it still be retained for countries on the way to socialism after having reached an advanced state of industrialisation?

The question did not arise when Stalin adopted the law of priority growth in capital goods production and transformed it into a dogma to be imposed on planners. The law was applied as a basic rule of economic policy from the beginning of five-year planning in the U.S.S.R. The whole question was to be raised again, much later, in the criticism levelled against this law by the economists of the socialist countries of Europe.

The Law of Priority Growth in Department I

The law can be formulated in the following way: in modern conditions of large-scale production, a faster rate of growth of production in department I than in department II is a necessity. This objective law, independent of human volition, operates under both socialism and capitalism, since technical progress leads to the production of ever more machinery and raw materials for use in the two departments. For any developing economy the priority growth of department I is automatic. However it is only under capitalism that this law comes up against a contradiction. Productive potential exceeds the capacity of the market to absorb the product. Hence crises of overproduction[7]. Under socialism this could not be the case, since, according to Stalin, it is consumption which stimulates production; the law thus operates through the creation of productive capacity to satisfy increased consumption in the long run.

According to this classical interpretation of the law, one must work in the same direction by systematically investing more in department I. This was the main characteristic of Stalinist policy, which succeeded in promoting rapid industrial growth at the expense of consumption (at least in the short-term).

After Stalin priority growth for department I was not immediately challenged, though the voluntarist interpretation of the law was. It was admitted that without ceasing to invest more in department I, growth in department II could be accelerated at the same time. In other words, there could be a diminution in the rate of growth of department I in relation to department II. It was also admitted that within department I it was possible to develop not only those branches manufacturing capital goods for department I itself (such as iron and steel in the Stalinist period), but also those branches whose products are used in the consumption goods sector (chemical industry, engineering, etc.).

Such considerations may appear to be scholastic. But it should not be forgotten that in the Soviet Union all investment policy has derived from this concept. For the same reason opposition to the theory towards 1960–1 was something more than a mere scholastic debate between economists.

The controversy which developed then was not about the advisability of priority investment in department I, but about statistical verification of the law. The question was whether or not in an expanding economy there was in fact automatically more rapid growth in department I.

A reply to this question cannot be based on an analysis of a socialist economy, since there the law is sustained by an economic policy directed to that end. It must be based on an analysis of a capitalist economy, where the law operates as part of the natural scheme of things, in theory. That is why Soviet economists set about analysing the American economy, and in particular the structure of production in that economy.

These analyses have demonstrated that contrary to Lenin's thesis the co-efficient of capital intensity (or the organic composition of capital in Marxist terminology) does not necessarily rise. An examination of American statistics shows that over more than a century this ratio has remained stable. Over the last eighty years it has even decreased. One must conclude either that the law of priority growth is not necessarily true for an expanding economy, or that its corollary, the tendency for the organic composition of capital to rise, is inexact. The second deduction makes it possible to preserve the law. That is why certain Soviet economists have opted for this interpretation, by demonstrating that the index of the organic composition of capital does not in fact rise because the two elements of 'constant capital' (c in the gross product formula)—fixed capital and circulating capital—vary inversely with each other. Where fixed capital per product unit tends to rise, circulating capital (raw materials, power) falls.

A further consequence of the law of priority growth in department 1 is that the gross social product rises more quickly than the national income. If it is admitted that technical progress leads to a more rapid growth of expenditure on equipment (c) than on wages (v) in the product, ($c + v + m$) must inevitably grow relatively more quickly than ($v + m$). On this point it is particularly difficult to verify the facts statistically for capitalist economies, since their national accounting does not include an aggregate for the gross social product. It has been carried out for the U.S.S.R. and the socialist countries, but has not led to any penetrating discoveries. The results have in fact varied according to the weighting of product and income indices and according to the base year used. An example would be the calculations (table 4.2) relating to seven countries in the period 1951–66 (base 100 in 1950), in base-year prices.[8]

According to these figures, for at least four countries (Poland, G.D.R., Romania, Czechoslovakia) the excess coefficient is so weak as to be inconclusive, and in the U.S.S.R. operates in the opposite direction.

It is worth noting, finally, that statistical verification of the law of priority growth in department I does not involve a direct comparison between the rates of growth of the two sectors. It is effected indirectly by analysing the ratios c/v or $c + v + m/v + m$. A comparison of the two products is in fact very difficult, even within the confines of the socialist economy. The national accounting system only distinguishes between capital and consumption goods in industry, industrial production being divided into two corresponding groups, A and B. Production in other branches of activity, and especially in agriculture, is not divided into the two departments. Usually the relationship between A

TABLE 4.2

EVOLUTION OF GROSS PRODUCT AND NATIONAL INCOME
INDICES

	Gross social product (1)	National income (2)	Excess coefficient (1)/(2)
Bulgaria (final year 1965) ...	454	390	1.16
Hungary (final year 1964) ...	272	230	1.19
Poland (period 1958–64) ...	159	146	1.09
G.D.R.	347	330	1.05
Romania	457	454	1.01
Czechoslovakia	271	252	1.08
U.S.S.R.	381	393	0.97

and B in a given country is taken to be an indication of the relationship between departments I and II. This of course is a completely arbitrary hypothesis and may falsify structural comparisons for a given country (between two periods), as well as between different countries.

Consequently, for some years the debate has tended to shift away from the 'objective law of growth' and towards a discussion of those economic policies most likely to promote it.

Actual Growth Priorities

The origins of Soviet growth strategy are to be found in the great debate which between 1925 and 1928 opposed the so-called left and right factions of the Communist Party, of which Stalin was to be the final arbiter.[9] The right faction, represented by Bukharin, emphasised the rôle of agriculture in growth. Agricultural production, which by 1925 had reached pre-war levels, would rise at a faster rate if the confidence of the peasantry were restored as a result of re-establishing the market and abolishing the system of requisitions. In this way a surplus would be created for export and for industrial development (agriculture supplied industry with raw materials for processing and with food for a growing labour force). Industry would in turn be able to increase its sales to the agricultural sector, where it would find an expanding market (agricultural equipment, consumption goods). Once an exchange circuit had been established between the two sectors, it would tend to expand without interruption. The leftists opposed this argument with their own thesis. Their political spokesman was Trotsky and their theoretician the economist

Preobrajensky. For them the capital requirements of industry for future growth would be infinitely greater than the capital which had been required in the reconstruction period. Then they had been satisfied with merely replacing existing equipment. Now resources had to be mobilised for new, additional investment. The problem was where to find this socialist accumulation. This would certainly be in the surplus created by the agricultural sector. However, it was no use waiting for the peasants to transfer this surplus freely to the State to serve the cause of industrialisation. Experience under the N.E.P. showed that the rate of consumption of the agricultural product within agriculture had a tendency to rise with any increase in that product. Rapid and purposeful socialisation of the agricultural sector would therefore precede a policy of industrialisation financed by the agricultural surplus produced—if necessary by forcibly restricting consumption.

After politically destroying the left faction of the Party in 1927, it was nevertheless its policy that Stalin decided to adopt. The general collectivisation of agriculture in 1929–30 was followed by systematic industrialisation from the time of the first five-year plan in 1928. This was based on the massive priority growth of heavy industry, with the aim of overtaking as soon as possible the United States, by then the most advanced of all capitalist countries. The obsession with making up lost ground was almost certainly also connected with defence considerations, but these were not the dominant factor.[10] The same theme recurs in innumerable later documents, especially in the Communist Party programme adopted at its Twenty-second Congress in 1961: 'The Communist Party of the Soviet Union proposes to increase the volume of industrial production in the next ten years by about two-and-a-half times, and to overtake the level of industrial production in the United States.'

This industrial ideology was reflected in the highly ambitious targets of the first two five-year plans for basic production. They were what the American writer, Naum Jasny, called bacchanalian planning, when he pointed out that the production figures fixed in 1932 for 1937 for electric power were in fact only achieved in 1951; the 1937 targets for oil were reached in 1955 and for cast-iron in 1952.[11]

Whatever may be thought of the methods used, it must be recognised that the policy of forced industrialisation made rapid economic growth possible (although lower than targets, which were deliberately fixed at a very high level). According to Soviet sources the national income grew at an annual rate of 14.1% between 1928 and 1940 (compared with an annual average of 8.8% in the period 1951–65). During this period the production of capital goods rose tenfold and that of consumption goods more than fourfold.

The U.S.S.R. imposed this particular strategy of growth on its socialist partners after World War II, using different political means but similar economic methods. There was consequently a parallel development of economic structures: a tendency for the agricultural labour force to move into the industrial sector, the concentration of investment on industry and a considerable growth of the share of this sector in the national income, and a rise in the proportion of the national income allocated to investment (*cf*. tables 4.10, 4.15 —4.18). Economic growth rates apparently justified this strategy, at least until 1960 for the national income as a whole and for gross industrial production. The picture is much blacker for agricultural production.

But after 1960, in every European socialist country except Romania, growth rates declined. It was this situation which led to the introduction of economic reforms in the planning and management of enterprise activity. It amounted to an admission by the political authorities that the slowing down of growth had been mainly due to institutional factors: to centralised and authoritarian planning, to the stifling of enterprise initiative by the bureaucracy. We have already discussed the remedies which were applied: greater flexibility in control methods, recourse to economic incentives to encourage better management. The growth policy itself was not questioned. Industrial branches manufacturing capital goods still have priority, a policy which is now tempered however with some concern for increasing the growth of consumption industries. The intention is to bring the growth rates of the two sectors closer together and to reduce the relative advantage of department I.

For some economists in the socialist countries the Soviet mode of growth itself was the cause of the diminution in growth rates in the period 1960–5. The law of priority growth in department I implies, in a country in the first stages of development, an *extensive* type of growth: increased production is obtained from a growth in the labour force, by expanding productive capacity from the creation of new units, or from the development of hitherto neglected areas. This model was suited to Soviet conditions in 1928: an enormous country with an abundance of unexploited natural resources and a surplus labour force in agriculture. However in the European socialist countries of the post-World War II period what was necessary was *intensive* growth, with the replacement of existing capital by improved means of production or better utilisation of existing capital. This was particularly the case in those countries already possessing an industrial infrastructure (East Germany, Czechoslovakia, and even Poland). Such a policy would have obviated the problem of the shortage of manpower, from which Czechoslovakia suffered in particular, since it had no reserve of unemployed labour in the countryside.

It is interesting to consider the arguments advanced by Czech economists[12] against the policy of extensive growth, since they have been the most ardent critics of the transposition of the Soviet model to the popular democracies.

According to their view this type of growth is inefficient, in so far as it puts a brake on technical progress. It is based on the transfer to industry of an underemployed and unskilled work force from agriculture, and on the use of the net revenue of existing enterprises (and often of their depreciation funds as well) to finance the establishment of new units of production. The new units thus have to operate with unskilled labour and with equipment manufactured according to outmoded techniques in old factories which will have been unable to modernise. Labour productivity will remain at a low level, particularly as workers who at first might have been stimulated by the possibilities opened up to the national economy, tend to be quickly discouraged by the stagnation of their standard of living. They no longer willingly accept the sacrifices which they are asked to make for the benefit of future generations. Then it becomes necessary to strengthen the authoritarian character of planning, which leads to either political crises or a halt in growth.

In the second place, far from allowing a regular and proportioned rate of development, extensive growth promotes disequilibrium and fluctuations in activity[13] (*cf.* table 4.3 for all the countries concerned). This is the thesis of J. Goldman, who, in his studies of Czechoslovakia, Poland, Hungary and the G.D.R., has observed alternate periods of high growth (1951–2, 1959–60) and periods when growth has slowed down (slight in 1954–6, considerable in 1961–3). His observations and analyses are confirmed by those of some Polish economists[14] (notably J. Pajestka). According to Pajestka, the origin of these fluctuations is to be found in the authoritarian planning mechanism responsible for the strategy of extensive growth. The planner fixes on a high rate of growth, since his objective is to maximise production. He links to it a level of investment (ratio of investment to national income) which tends to be all the higher since he intends to give priority to the heavy industrial sector where the coefficient of capital (capital/product ratio) is itself high. In practice, there is not necessarily any direct relationship between the plan for financing the investment and the corresponding material resources (raw materials, equipment, etc.). In such conditions there will tend to be an excess demand for capital goods (resulting from the plan) in relation to their supply. Consequently, it will be difficult to complete those operations outlined in the plan which have actually begun. This will lead to the freezing of resources over increasingly long periods of time. Similarly, in order to establish new units of production within the framework of extensive growth, it may be necessary to neglect the replacement of equipment and modernisation in old enterprises. The result is a decrease in the total productivity of capital, until it reaches that critical point which represents the trough of the quasi-cycle.

This argument illuminates the difficulties inherent in planning investment which are common to all socialist countries and which economic development itself tends to aggravate. In a relatively non-industrialised economy, it is possible to avoid the problems of choice by concentrating investment on a small number of sectors to which all other sectors are subordinate. The most characteristic example is the construction of the Ural-Kouznetsk metal combine in the U.S.S.R., which in 1933-7 absorbed one-quarter of all productive investment.

But this does not explain why there should be a quasi-cycle. The movement cannot be self-perpetuating. The planner could, for example, correct the disequilibrium by reducing the number of new projects so as to complete current ones. Similarly, there can be no automatic recovery. Any new acceleration of economic growth presupposes that the planning departments have taken note of mistakes in the general orientation of activity and have rectified them. This might eventually take the shape of radical economic reforms such as took place in the socialist countries after 1965.

One might ask, finally, whether the premise is correct, and whether concentrating on department I necessarily requires extensive growth. This

TABLE 4.3[15]

A. GROWTH FLUCTUATIONS IN THE SOCIALIST COUNTRIES OF EUROPE (excluding the U.S.S.R.)

Year	Annual growth rates (all countries)			Annual growth rates of national income by country							
	of the national income	of industrial production	of agricultural production	Albania	Bulgaria	Hungary	Poland	G.D.R.	Romania	Czecho-slovakia	Yugo-slavia
1951	14.8	17.7	10.2	—	41	17	8	22	31	10	10
1952	4.8	15.8	-8.2	—	-1	-2	6	14	5	11	-15
1953	10.3	13.0	11.7	—	21	13	11	5	15	6	20
1954	5.3	8.4	0.4	—	-1	-4	10	9	-1	4	3
1955	10.5	10.3	8.8	—	6	9	9	9	22	10	13
1956	1.9	7.2	-4.0	1	1	-10	7	4	-7	5	-1
1957	11.9	10.3	11.7	14	13	23	11	7	16	7	23
1958	6.7	10.9	-1.7	7	7	6	6	11	3	8	2
1959	8.7	11.4	5.9	19	22	7	5	9	13	6	18
1960	6.3	11.1	2.2	-2	7	10	5	5	11	8	6
1961	6.4	9.1	1.8	7	3	6	8	3	10	7	6
1962	2.8	7.7	-4.3	6	6	5	2	2	4	1	4
1963	5.5	5.9	5.6	10	8	6	7	3	10	-2	12
1964	6.2	8.9	3.3	6	9	5	7	5	12	1	13
1965	5.0	8.4	3.2	—	7	1	7	4.6	9.5	3	3
1966	6.8	7.5	9.2	11	11.6	8.4	7	4.4	9.8	10.7	9
1967				1	9	8	6	5	8	6	9
1968				5	6	5	8	5	7	6	2
1969				13	8	6	4	5	7	7	5
1970				—	7	5	6	5.2	7	5	10
1971				—	8.4	7.5	7.5	4.5	12.5	5.1	8.5

is certainly the case during the take-off period, when an economic infrastructure has to be created out of nothing. Such a situation existed in the U.S.S.R. between 1928 and 1940 when the foundations of the power, iron and steel, and engineering industries were laid. But once growth has begun, it is not only possible but desirable to promote it further by raising the coefficient of capital intensity (capital/labour ratio), without abandoning the principle of priority for department I. We have seen, in fact, that an increase in the ratio c/v is a corollary of the law of priority growth in the capital goods sector.

B. FLUCTUATIONS IN GROWTH RATES DURING THE PERIOD 1951-65

	Variation coefficient in growth rates (a)		
	national income	industrial production	agricultural production
All countries	38.0	22.1	106.4
Balkan countries (b)	58.6	15.1	169.0
Northern countries (c)	31.8	30.1	69.2

(a)   The coefficient is calculated as follows: the arithmetic average of annual growth rates for the period is worked out, then the arithmetic average of divergencies in annual growth rates in relation to the average rate for the period; finally the ratio of the average divergence to the average rate is calculated.

(b)   Bulgaria, Romania, Yugoslavia, Albania.

(c)   G.D.R., Poland, Czechoslovakia, Hungary.

The Soviet Union is at present in the intensive phase of growth. Such at least is the intention of its leaders as outlined in the plans, which insist on the need for a massive diffusion of technical progress in traditional branches and for the further development of growth industries (electronics, chemicals, etc.). The question remains as to whether the socialist countries of Europe, obliged in fact to follow the same line of development, might not have been able to shorten the first stage of development and apply the intensive model of growth more or less immediately. This may have been possible for the most industrialised among them, but probably not for the less developed, for whom the Soviet growth strategy seems to have been the most successful.

The discussion on the extensive or intensive nature of growth shows that it is not enough merely to define the direction of investment. The planning of economic growth requires that the choice of a global strategy should be accompanied by an analysis of the factors underlying that growth.

2. GROWTH FACTORS

An analysis of the factors contributing to growth is of practical as well as theoretical interest in the socialist countries, since it can influence development policy. Recent studies on this subject by socialist economists have much in common with the work of Western economists.[16] These analyses have isolated a certain number of general conditions relevant to growth: natural resources, geographical and climatic conditions (the socialist world is largely situated in the temperate zone), the level of development of productive forces (material and human) and relations of production (including institutional and social structures), and finally subjective conditions (economic policy, its support by the population, the material and moral commitment of workers to development, etc.).

For a more precise analysis factors of growth can be grouped into two categories: the growth of the productive forces, that is to say of the volume of labour and capital engaged in production; an improvement in factor combination, raising output per unit of input. It should be remembered that in Marxist theory labour is the sole creator of value and therefore the only source of growth. Capital is not an autonomous growth factor, since its contribution lies in the fact that it raises the productivity of labour.

On the basis of this analysis it is possible to envisage more scientific planning of economic growth. Using the U.S.S.R. as our example, we shall look at a model of growth employed in planning.

The Growth of Productive Forces: Labour

One of the most significant expressions of economic growth is per capita national income. The rate of growth is the product of two dynamic series, expressing the growth of income on the one hand and of population on the other. If the latter rises at a faster rate than national income, then the country's level of economic development must fall. But it is this same population growth which supplies the economy with the extra labour power necessary for the expansion of production. The ratio between the active population (L) and the total population (P) or L/P, as well as the ratio between the growth of these two magnitudes ($\Delta L / \Delta P$), must be great enough to permit this expansion. However it is not enough merely to increase the number of workers engaged in production. For growth to occur there must also be an increase in production per worker, that is to say in the productivity of labour Q (the ratio between national income Y and the active population, or Y/L).

A RISE IN THE EMPLOYED LABOUR FORCE

At the end of 1971 the total population of the European socialist countries was 373 million inhabitants (*cf.* table 4.4). The distribution of this population was very unequal. Four countries had a population density of over 100 inhabitants to the square kilometre (G.D.R. 158, Czechoslovakia 111, Hungary 112, Poland 105). Four others had densities of between 50 and 100 inhabitants per square kilometre (Romania 86, Yugoslavia 78, Bulgaria 77, Albania 66). The population density of the U.S.S.R. was hardly more than 11 inhabitants per square kilometre (31 in European Russia considered in isolation).

TABLE 4.4[17]

SURFACE AREA AND POPULATION OF THE SOCIALIST COUNTRIES OF EUROPE

	Surface area (1972) (thousands km²)	Population (end 1971) (millions)	Urban population (%)
U.S.S.R.	22,402.2	246.3	57
Albania[1]	28.7	2.0	33
Bulgaria	110.9	8.6	53
Hungary	93.3	10.4	45
Poland	312.7	32.9	54
G.D.R.[1]	108.3	17.1	74
Romania	237.5	20.5	40
Czechoslovakia	127.9	14.4	63
Yugoslavia	255.8	20.5	
Total for all European socialist countries ...	23,677.3	372.7	
Total less U.S.S.R. ...	1.275.1	126.4	
Total less Soviet Asia ...	6,846.1	312.5	

[1]End 1967 (population)

Demographic trends in these countries since World War II have been similar to those in the developed countries. The death rate has declined owing to progress in medicine and hygiene and to rising living standards. At present it is everywhere lower than 10%, except in the G.D.R. where in 1967 it was 13.2% and had been rising since 1959. The exceptional case of the G.D.R. may be explained by the unfavourable age structure of the population resulting from World War II. There has been an even more rapid fall in the birth rate. In 1950 it was everywhere above 20%, except in the G.D.R. where it was then 16.5%. In 1967 it was generally around 15%, with two exceptions. In Yugoslavia the birth rate remains high (around 20% in 1966) and is falling much more slowly than in the other socialist countries. In Romania the birth rate shot up from 14.3% to 27.4% between 1966 and 1967, in conjunction with the ban on abortion introduced at the end of 1966.

The general consequence has been a decline in the rate of natural increase of the population, leading to some slowing down in demographic growth. For example, in Hungary the population increased by 5.2% in the period 1951-5, and by 1.5% in the period 1963-7. In Poland the corresponding figures were 9.9% and 5.7%, in Romania 6.2% and 3.6%, in Czechoslovakia 5.7% and 3.2%, and in the U.S.S.R. 7.0% and 5.5%. Bulgaria is an exception. There the rate of growth of the population has not declined (3.4% from 1951-5,

TABLE 4.5[18]

BIRTH RATE, DEATH RATE AND NATURAL INCREASE IN THIRTEEN EUROPEAN COUNTRIES (average 1963-7)

	Birth rate (%)	Death rate (%)	Natural increase (%)
		Socialist countries	
Bulgaria	15.5	8.3	7.2
Hungary	13.5	10.3	3.2
Poland	17.5	7.5	10.0
G.D.R.	16.4	13.2	3.2
Romania	17.4	8.5	8.9
Czechoslovakia ...	16.2	9.8	6.4
U.S.S.R.	18.9	7.2	11.7
		Capitalist countries	
Great Britain	18.2	11.6	6.6
Belgium	16.3	12.1	4.2
Netherlands	19.9	7.9	12.0
Italy	19.0	9.8	9.2
France	17.7	11.0	6.7
Federal Republic of Germany ...	18.0	11.2	6.8

3.7% from 1963-7). It should be added that for most socialist countries the natural growth of the population differs little from its actual growth, since emigration and immigration are of little significance. This is not the case for Yugoslavia, where economic emigration is important. Nor is it the case for the G.D.R., where political emigration between 1950 and 1961 was considerable and caused an absolute decline in population estimated at 7.1% for the period 1950-67.

Since the socialist countries do not depend on immigration and since they can hardly reckon on any further reduction in the death rate, their main if not exclusive source of demographic growth must be a rising birth rate. But as we have just seen, the trend is towards a fall in this rate. It can be explained in various ways. There is a high economic activity rate among women (in most socialist countries women constitute more than one-third of the total labour force). This is linked with an inadequate development of the service sector and of pre-school institutions. The birth of a child may oblige the mother to interrupt her professional life for several years. Working women are reluctant to do this, in spite of the guarantees they are given. (The woman on leave to bring up a young child usually has her job legally guaranteed for her eventual return. The period of leave itself counts towards total length of service in calculating pension rights.) Equal pay for men and women with the same qualifications and the socialist policy of integrating women into economic life both tend to encourage women to work and therefore to limit child-birth.

Another reason, linked to the first one, is that large families are at an economic disadvantage. A systematic policy of financial assistance to families is only practised in the G.D.R., Czechoslovakia and Hungary, in other words in those countries suffering from a labour shortage. And even there the level of family allowances is not high (*cf.* chapter 6). Tax relief and rent reductions, generally applicable to large families, are of no great advantage in countries where both income tax and rents are usually low. Advantages in kind, such as day-nurseries or boarding-schools, are often theoretical only since there are not enough of them.

The relative growth of the urban population operates in the same direction. The birth rate is always lower in towns than in the country, a phenomenon not peculiar to socialist countries. There are many reasons for this, such as more difficult housing problems or the fact that it is less easy to make children's education fit in with professional commitments.

Finally the general introduction of retirement pensions for the old has a definite and recognisable psychological effect on the propensity to reproduce.

Socialist governments have attempted to counter declining birth rates by appropriate policies. The exception this time is Poland, where the birth rate has remained relatively high (probably due in part to the position of the Church there). Only two states have made abortion illegal: the G.D.R. and Romania. The other states have not abolished it. In the long term such a measure is inefficient, even if abolition does result in an immediate rise in the birth rate (international experience is significant in this field). In the absence of a sufficient quantity of contraceptive devices, abortion remains the principal means for women to avoid giving birth by their own free decision. A socialist regime must guarantee this right. Among the various economic measures which have been introduced to encourage the birth rate, two main categories can be distinguished: family allowances and advantages in kind. The first group tends to raise the standard of living of families with children. To be effective, however, state financial aid must be considerable and must rise at the same rate as the cost of living. In those socialist countries with well-established family allowance systems neither of these conditions has been fulfilled (G.D.R., Hungary, Czechoslovakia). To these should be added Bulgaria, which substantially raised both birth premiums and monthly family allowances in 1968. The precise objective was to encourage the three-child family (from the fourth child there is a sudden fall in the allowance). The philosophy behind the second group of measures is different. The intention is to create such conditions that women will not be forced to choose between professional activity and motherhood. This policy has been applied in the U.S.S.R. for many years, although on an inadequate scale. Interesting too are the series of measures to promote the birth rate adopted in Romania at the same time as the legal prohibition on abortion: expansion of the number of nurseries and parks, priority for the children of large families in holiday camps and hostels, the spread of part-time work for women with children under school age, etc.

Demographic growth is the *sine qua non* of an increase in the labour force. But it is the age structure which defines the proportion of the population able to work. Table 4.6 indicates how once again there is a close resemblance between socialist and capitalist countries. The under fifteen group represents about 25% and the over sixty-five group about 10% of the total population. The anomalous structure of the G.D.R. may be attributed to the war and to emigration during the period 1950-61.

The statistics in the table are not in themselves an adequate basis for establishing a figure for the population of working age, since this depends on the school leaving age (fifteen or sixteen years in most socialist countries) and on retiring age. The latter varies from country to country:

	Men	*Women*
Bulgaria	60	55
Hungary	60	55
Poland	65	60
G.D.R.	65	60
Romania	62	56
Czechoslovakia ...	60	55
U.S.S.R.	60	55

The population of working age, defined according to this juridical criterion, therefore includes for most socialist countries men from 15 (16) to 59 years and women from 15 (16) to 54 years. It comprised nearly 60% of the total population in 1966.

Demographic forecasts up to 1985 reveal a similar trend in all these countries, characterised by an ageing population and a growth in the ratio of the non-active population to that of working age. This presupposes no change in the age of retirement. If retiring age is lowered, the dependency ratio will rise. The same will be true if the school leaving age is raised. Consequently a marked diminution, if not stagnation, in the growth of the population of working age is to be expected.

TABLE 4.6[19]

AGE COMPOSITION OF THE POPULATION IN THE SOCIALIST COUNTRIES AND IN CERTAIN EUROPEAN CAPITALIST COUNTRIES
(as a % of the total population)

		Age groups		
		less than 15 years	16-64 years	over 65 years
		Socialist countries		
Bulgaria	(1965)	25.1	66.1	8.8
Hungary	(1967)	23.8	65.2	11.0
Poland	(1966)	30.2	62.7	7.1
G.D.R.	(1967)	23.8	61.0	15.2
Romania	(1965)	26.4	65.7	7.9
Czechoslovakia	(1967)	26.0	63.4	10.6
U.S.S.R.	(1959)	30.4	60.2[1]	9.4[2]
		Capitalist countries		
Great Britain	(1966)	23.0	64.7	12.3
Italy	(1965)	24.3	65.7	10.0
Federal Republic of Germany	(1965)	21.3	65.5	13.2
France	(1965)	25.6	62.4	12.0

[1] 16-59 years   [2] over 60 years

We can now turn to the active population, which may be defined as that proportion of the population actually exercising a professional activity. In 1970, taking all the socialist countries of Europe, the active population constituted 81% of the population of working age. According to Comecon criteria the active population covers the following categories: everyone employed in public, private, co-operative or State enterprises and organisations, in co-operatives of production (craft), on private agricultural holdings, in public administration. Also included are self-employed craftsmen. Soldiers, full-time students and people exclusively engaged in domestic work in their own home are not included. In its detailed application this methodology raises numerous difficulties. The most serious relates to accounting methods for the category 'members of the family helping the head of the family', which in Comecon countries is included in the active population. The result is that the statistics on the agricultural labour force are artificially swollen, since the effective participation in farming of the members of the peasant family may in fact be very limited. Yet these auxiliary workers in Poland represent 50% of the rural labour force! It is easy to imagine the distortions which such a method of calculation may bring to an analysis of job statistics in Yugoslavia, which does not include 'auxiliary members of the family' in its active population. According to the census the active population in 1967 had reached 3.7 million inhabitants[20] or 18.5% of the total population. This compared with 45.7% in the same year for the member countries of Comecon taken together. The difference between the other countries and Yugoslavia cannot be explained solely in terms of Yugoslav unemployment. Similarly, this particular method of calculation should be borne in mind when considering the ratio of the active population to the population of working age, which in the Comecon countries in recent years has stabilised at around 80%.

Whether one takes the ratio active population/total population (*cf.* table 4.7) or active population/population of working age, the official rate of employment in socialist countries is high. Is this a decisive factor in their economic growth?

TABLE 4.7[21]

DISTRIBUTION OF THE ACTIVE POPULATION (1970)

	Bulgaria	Hungary	Poland	G.D.R.	Romania	Czecho-slovakia	U.S.S.R.
Active population as a percentage of total population ...	50.3	48.2	47.4	46.2	51.7	45.3	42.4
Percentage of workers in the active population employed in:							
industry and construction ...	38.8	43.8	36.9	49.8	30.8	46.2	37.1
agriculture ...	35.8	26.2	35.8	13.0	49.3	18.3	26.8
transport and communications	5.7	6.8	5.7	7.2	4.8	6.8	8.0
commerce ...	6.1	8.0	6.7	10.9	4.3	9.6	7.1
Percentage of workers in the active population employed in:							
the productive sector ...	86.6	84.8	87.0	81.2	89.8	80.9	79.9
the non-productive sector ...	13.4	15.2	13.0	18.8	10.2	19.1	20.1

To reply to this question, it is necessary to understand the initial situation in the socialist countries (i.e. just after the 1917 Revolution in Russia and after World War II in the popular democracies of Europe).

In Soviet Russia the authorities were mainly concerned with eliminating unemployment, especially in the countryside. This was officially achieved in 1931. Given a strategy of growth centred on heavy industry the means adopted were to mobilise the rural labour force for employment in the industrial sector. The percentage of the total active population engaged in agriculture fell from 80% in 1928 to 54% in 1940, while that of the industrial work force rose from 8% to 23%. Urbanisation spread likewise. 33% of the total population lived in towns in 1940 as against 18% in 1920. The scarcity of capital, reserved for priority sectors and within these for the main production processes, stimulated a demand for two distinct types of labour: on the one hand, highly skilled workers using improved modern equipment in short supply; on the other, unskilled workers allocated either to non-priority industrial branches and enterprises operating with out-moded equipment or to auxiliary non-mechanised operations in growth sectors. The intensive utilisation of skilled labour (in short supply in spite of great efforts in the field of professional training) was therefore accompanied by the extensive utilisation of unskilled workers, usually of rural extraction. The co-existence of a scarcity of skilled workers and of a concealed surplus of personnel in individual firms still characterises the Soviet Union today.

Just as she imposed her strategy of growth on the popular democracies the Soviet Union had them adopt her employment policy as well. Its application seemed justified in the case of countries where, as in Russia in the 1920s, a high level of rural unemployment had to be eliminated just after World War II. There were 5 million unemployed peasants in Poland, 3 million in Romania, 1.2 million in Bulgaria, or nearly 20% of the total population of these countries. The objective was achieved, as in Russia, by transferring rural

TABLE 4.8[22]

RATIO OF THE AGRICULTURAL TO THE
INDUSTRIAL LABOUR-FORCE

	1950	1966
Bulgaria	6.6	1.5
Hungary	2.6	1.0
Poland	3.0	1.4
G.D.R.	0.6	0.26
Romania	6.1	2.8
Czechoslovakia ...	1.2	0.4

labour to industry, and is reflected in their present high activity rates. The ratio of the active to the total population is 50.6% in Poland (1967), 51.7% in Romania (1966), and 50.3% in Bulgaria (1966).

Closer examination of the situation in these three countries, however, reveals a continuing high proportion of rural manpower in the active population. This is a clear indication of concealed underemployment in agriculture, given present methods of computing the active population. Moreover urban unemployment is becoming a more serious and open problem. In Bulgaria forced rural depopulation has resulted in an automatic increase in the total urban population without a proportional increase in the active population. Between 1957 and 1967 from 35% to 40% of migrants lost their jobs. In practice this meant that in most cases where a peasant family had moved to the town only the husband found a job while the wife remained at home. Faced with a serious situation, the Bulgarian government introduced a series of measures in 1968 with a view to creating new jobs. They included developing small-scale industry in market and medium-sized towns, an expansion of the tertiary sector to raise the level of employment without having to resort to massive investment, and the redirection of people towards the countryside by establishing agro-industrial units in rural areas. In Poland after 1956 the surplus labour force, particularly marked in the central and eastern regions of the country, led the government to set up an intervention fund. Managed by the municipalities, its purpose was to implement projects of low capital intensity. The 1966-70 five-year plan had as one of its objectives the creation of 1.5 million new jobs, mainly in the processing and service industries, where large quantities of additional capital are unnecessary.

The Soviet Union is at present experiencing problems similar to those of Bulgaria, Poland and Romania. In the U.S.S.R. the political and social will to guarantee work for everyone, and especially to integrate peasants and women into social production, has combined with the economic necessity of extensive employment for an unskilled work-force to produce a high and even excessive activity rate. (Female employment rose especially during the war, growing from 24% of the total labour force in 1928 to 56% in 1945. At present it is stable at around 50%.) Today, in the U.S.S.R. as in the other countries of the same group, there exist local pockets of surplus labour parallel with a shortage of skilled labour in the large towns. From about 1965 a new employment policy has been in operation along the following lines:

1. The systematic organisation of job placements for young people (employment exchanges were created for this purpose at the beginning of 1967 in the Union republics).
2. The retraining of workers displaced by technical progress.
3. The stabilisation of the rural labour-force and its retention in the countryside. The introduction of pensions for all *kolkhozy* members from 1965 helped greatly in slowing down the drift to the towns.
4. An improved regional policy, including the establishment of labour-

intensive industries in small and medium-sized towns and a wages structure designed to attract workers to regions short of labour such as Siberia and the Far East.

It is difficult to estimate the result of this policy. Given that the elimination of unemployment is considered to be one of the greatest social achievements of the regime, no account is kept of unemployed workers. The authorities will just about admit to the existence of temporary and localised surpluses of labour. The magnitude of these surpluses has not been systematically assessed. In 1965 there was a sample survey in 416 medium-sized towns to evaluate their labour reserves, but the results were not made known.

Unlike the group comprising the U.S.S.R., Bulgaria, Romania and Poland, three other countries suffer from an acute shortage of labour. This was the consequence of an economic structure which was initially quite different and of the imposition by the U.S.S.R. of an inappropriate employment policy. In the beginning these three countries had two important advantages: a skilled industrial labour force and an almost fully employed rural labour force. Rural unemployment existed only in Hungary, and then at a much lower rate than in Poland, Romania or Bulgaria. Thus the application to these countries of a strategy of extensive growth led to excessive demands on the labour market, in spite of the mobilisation of all available labour power, including women and pensioners who benefit from considerable advantages when working after retirement age. 83% of the increase in the active population in Czechoslovakia between 1951 and 1966 was due to the integration of women into economic activity. The figure was 93% for Hungary and over 100% in the G.D.R., where the growth in female employment not only accounted for that of the active population as a whole but compensated for the absolute fall in male employment during the same period.

However the activity rate has remained lower than in the previous group of countries: 48.2% in Hungary (1966), 46.2% in the G.D.R., 45.3% in Czechoslovakia. This can be explained by the method used for calculating the active population, since it tends to inflate the figure for the active rural population and consequently raises the activity rate in those countries with a greater rural labour-force.

In such conditions it would probably have been better to apply to the countries of this group a growth policy based not on the Soviet model but on the intensive utilisation of the labour-force. It was a mistake to believe that growth inevitably required an increase in the work-force, even in countries of near full employment.

It might be asked why no encouragement is given within the socialist bloc to the migration of workers between countries with a labour surplus and those with a deficit. Tradition and national sentiment are in this case stronger than economic rationality. The movement of workers from one country to another is rare and limited to the construction of common production units by two or more Comecon countries (*cf.* chapter 7). The 1967 agreement between

Hungary and the G.D.R. is an exception and means that over a period of several years Hungary will send 30,000 young trainees to the G.D.R. for professional training in the most technologically advanced factories. It is interesting that the agreement is between the two countries where full employment has already been achieved. It provides the G.D.R. with an additional though temporary work-force, while it will help raise the productivity of labour in Hungary by improving its quality.

INCREASED LABOUR PRODUCTIVITY

When full employment is reached or there is long-term stabilisation of employment at a lower level, national income can only increase as the result of a rise in the productivity of labour (by definition $Y \equiv QL$). The rise in productivity depends on numerous factors. For the moment we shall ignore factors linked to improvements in production techniques and equipment. These will be studied later when we come to analyse factor combination. There are two other causal factors influencing productivity: the organisation of the labour process and qualitative improvements in the labour-force itself.

Productivity rises as a result of better organisation of the labour process: the intensive use of existing capital (e.g. multiple shift-work on the same equipment), rational maintenance procedures to ensure continuous machine operation, efficient servicing of all operations to avoid lost time through breaks in supply, etc.

Studies on the scientific organisation of the labour process have been developing in the U.S.S.R. since 1959. It was at that time that the annual rate of growth of productivity in industry fell to below 5%. Until then it had been relatively high: an average of 7.6% for 1951-5 and 6.5% for 1956-60. At the same time comparisons of labour productivity between the U.S.S.R. and the United States have shown that in 1959 the productivity of Soviet workers was 49% that of American workers. The disparity could not be explained solely in terms of a higher coefficient of capital intensity in the United States.

Soviet analyses have isolated a number of organisational measures, which, if put into effect, would raise labour productivity without any additional investment.

The first would be a cut in the number of workers employed in enterprises with personnel surplus to requirements. There are many reasons explaining the retention of this surplus labour. Given the opposition of the trade-union factory committee, it is very difficult for the director of a socialist enterprise to dismiss a worker, even where it is justified. Another reason is that even after the economic reform, planning of the wages fund is based on the number of workers employed and any cut in numbers would bring with it a reduction in the total wages fund for the following year. A third reason is that there must be at least an attempt to find laid-off workers alternative employment. At the same time there are certain positive reasons encouraging managers to retain personnel they don't really need. Soviet enterprises do not operate at an even pace throughout the year. At the end of each planning period (quarter, year) there tends to be an increase in the tempo of work to ensure plan fulfilment. At that point it is useful to be able to draw on a supply of reserve labour. Even outside these peak periods, enterprise directors like to have a small reserve supply of labour in order in due course to complete certain constructional operations (plant, workers' flats) with local materials, etc. In rural areas arrangements are often made between enterprises and farms whereby the industrial concern during the dead season will employ agricultural workers who will eventually return to agricultural work. It is interesting to note that although lay-offs by firms are relatively rare, there is in the Soviet Union a very high and voluntary turnover of labour. Workers often change enterprise to improve their wages or working conditions. Sometimes they are attracted to certain regions, such as the Soviet south. Soviet writers have calculated that most Soviet enterprises have a 100% turnover of personnel every three or four years. This situation involves a high loss of man-hours. According to a survey conducted in 1962, a worker changing his job is out of production for twenty days on average and for more than a month if he must at the same time move to another region. It also involves the expense of retraining when the worker changes his job in moving from one enterprise to another. The same survey points out that this occurs in 70% of all cases. The damage done to the economy is more than at first appears, since most of this mobility is attributable to young workers under thirty. This high degree of mobility is a contributory factor in the retention of excess personnel by enterprise directors. Consequently, all other things being equal, the numbers employed in a Soviet factory tend to be higher than in a similar capitalist establishment.

Productivity could be raised by more intensive use of existing equipment. Studies of the engineering industry made by the Central Statistical Department show that equipment is far from being used at full capacity. Counting delays due to repairs to machinery, it appears that machine-tools were not used for more than nine hours a day. The continuous production flow is hardly known in the U.S.S.R. This low rate of employment of productive capacity is due in large part to the antiquity of much of the equipment in use, which makes intensive utilisation impossible.

Substantial gains in productivity could be achieved by rationalising certain auxiliary processes. The proportion of auxiliary workers in the total industrial labour-force is exceptionally high: from 50% to 52% between 1960 and 1965. These workers are employed in maintenance, servicing, the handling of stores, warehousing and technical control. Most of this work is not mechanised. The situation is explained by the history of industrialisation in the U.S.S.R.: because of its scarcity capital was allocated to equipping the productive sector; an abundance of unskilled labour was used in auxiliary work. Large numbers of workers are still required today: to maintain and repair outmoded machines; to machine on the spot numerous parts not produced by specialised factories.

The following figures give some indication of the scale of this makeshift industrial production: 71% of Soviet industrial concerns produce their own castings, 61% their riveting parts, 99% their pinions, 51% their cog-wheels. A better organisation of these auxiliary processes would open up numerous possibilities. However, for effective use to be made of the labour-force thus released, its level of skill would have to be raised.

Productivity also increases as a result of qualitative improvements in the labour-force itself. Such improvements are the effect of lengthening compulsory education, raising the cultural level of the whole population and allocating specific resources to vocational training. In the Soviet Union research in this area has been mainly the work of the economist S. Strumilin. He has attempted to evaluate increases in productivity which may be imputed to investment in education and which are ultimately reflected in a higher national income. Such research requires very careful handling. On the one hand, any increase in national income is the product of several factors. On the other, it is difficult to quantify the yield of any investment in education. Since the product of this investment is in effect the whole of skilled personnel, it is necessary to discover a means of measuring this labour's degree of qualification. For this two methods have been used: the summary but simple method of measuring a particular qualification by the number of years required to obtain it; the more scientific though complicated method of analysing the aptitudes of the skilled labour thus formed, with coefficients attached to these various skills.

According to Strumilin, if Soviet economic growth is analysed over a period of fifty years, technical improvements (expressed by the rise in the capital/ labour ratio) only explain one quarter of the increase in productivity. The rest is due to human investment in the form of research and education.[23]

There are further non-economic factors influencing productivity in socialist countries, such as the level of social consciousness of workers, their spirit of emulation and self-improvement. In the U.S.S.R. the stakhanovite movement before the war and the movement for communist work in recent years led to some remarkable achievements, both individually and collectively. On the other hand, any weakening in the general support of workers for the regime contributes to a fall in productivity as a result of a general relaxation of effort. The point is illustrated by Czechoslovak experience in 1969.

Let us now turn to a consideration of the relative shares of extensive and intensive development (an increase in the labour-force and a rise in productivity respectively) in the total contribution of labour to the growth of the national income.

In their calculations socialist economists begin from the hypothesis that any increase in national income (ΔY) is due entirely to the contribution made by labour. The increase in the labour-force is a known quantity the ratio $\Delta L/\Delta Y \times 100$ expresses the effect of this increase on that of the national income; the residual increase in income is then imputed to the rise in productivity, according to the formula:

$$T = 100 - \frac{\Delta L}{\Delta Y} \times 100$$

In other words, if in a given period national income rises by 5% and employment by 1%, the extensive factor is responsible for 20% of the increase in income, the remaining 80% of the increase being explained by the rise in productivity.

Like any residual method this approach tends to exaggerate the rôle of the second factor. Besides, the statistical data (*cf.* table 4.9) are inadequate for assessing the possibilities of a future rise in either the employed labour force or in productivity. In fact, when $T = 100$ (G.D.R. in 1966, Bulgaria in 1961-5) it means either that full employment has been achieved or that the economy is working at a constant rate of unemployment.

The fact remains that in every country it is the rise in productivity which is the fundamental cause of the rise in national income. Among the factors tending to increase productivity is an expansion of capital employed, to be examined separately.

TABLE 4.9[24]
GROWTH FACTORS IN THE NATIONAL INCOME

Country	Years	Increase in the national income	
		due to a rise in the productivity of labour	due to an increase in employment
Bulgaria	1953-55	95.3	4.7
	1956-60	100.0	—
	1961-65	100.0	—
	1966-70	95.8	4.2
Hungary	1951-55	68.8	31.2
	1956-60	78.6	21.4
	1961-65	100.0	—
	1966-70	85.4	14.6
Poland	1951-55	84.3	15.7
	1956-60	87.8	12.2
	1961-65	72.0	28.0
	1966-70	64.3	35.7
G.D.R.	1951-55	94.2	5.8
	1956-60	100.0	—
	1961-65	100.0	—
Romania	1951-55	87.1	12.9
	1956-60	98.8	1.2
	1961-65	100.0	—
	1966-70	97.9	2.1
Czechoslovakia	1951-55	89.4	10.6
	1956-60	100.0	—
	1961-65	77.0	23.0
	1966-70	84.0	16.0
U.S.S.R.	1951-55	90.0	10.0
	1956-60	77.6	22.4
	1961-65	74.6	25.4
	1966-70	87.0	13.0

Expansion of the Productive Forces: Capital

In the preceding section an attempt was made to evaluate the contribution made by labour to a given increase in the national income. A parallel analysis can be made of the contribution of capital. It may be assumed *a priori* that the growth of the national income will rise with the accumulation and productivity of capital. An analysis of the development of the rate of investment will therefore be followed by an examination of the relationship between capital and production.

THE RATE OF INVESTMENT

The rate of investment expresses the relationship between investment and national income for a given period. In socialist terminology this relationship is called the rate of accumulation, national income Y being divided (from the point of view of its final utilisation) into accumulation (A) and consumption (C).

The statistics give A and Y in current prices. A comprises the whole of net investment, productive and non-productive, in fixed capital and the growth of stocks. Let us look first at the development of the ratio A/Y in socialist countries, and later at the conclusions which may be drawn regarding the effect of investment on the growth of national income.

Since the beginning of the five-year plans, Soviet growth policy has been based on the straightforward idea that economic growth depends directly on the magnitude of investment. Consequently the irreducible minimum of resources was to be allocated to consumption. The remainder would be used for accumulation. In the U.S.S.R. the rate of accumulation rose from 19.5% in 1928-9 to 36.0% in 1929-30. Such a high proportion could not be maintained, but between 1932 and 1960 the real rate hardly ever fell below 25%.[25]

An examination of this rate in the socialist countries (*cf*. table 4.10) reveals considerable differences from country to country, as well as within the same country at different periods.[26] It is only in the long term that a general tendency towards an increase in the rate is observable. Until 1950 the rate of investment was low. The main effort was on raising the standard of living. A reduction in military expenditure made it possible to free resources for social investment without increasing the total rate of investment.

After 1950 there was a sharp increase in A/Y. It was at that point in time that Soviet pressure was at its greatest, imposing a policy of forced industrialisation on every country, with priority given to the development of heavy industry. There was a parallel decrease in the relative and absolute value of consumption. Such an effort could not be maintained for long. From 1954 the rate of consumption began to rise and A/Y fell. For many countries A/Y reached its lowest point for the period 1950-67 in 1956.

Even in Czechoslovakia and the G.D.R. where the fall was less marked, accumulation rose less quickly than consumption. From 1959 A/Y began to

TABLE 4.10[27]

THE DIVISION OF THE NATIONAL INCOME BETWEEN INVESTMENT AND CONSUMPTION (%)

	Investment		Consumption	
	1950	1970	1950	1970
Bulgaria	20.0	29.2	80.0	70.8
Hungary	23.0	27.2	77.0	72.8
Poland	21.0	28.2	79.0	71.8
G.D.R.	9.6	23.1	90.4	76.9
Romania	11.2	30.8*	88.8	69.2*
Czechoslovakia ...	16.9	27.0	83.1	73.0
U.S.S.R.	23.9	29.5	76.1	70.5

*1966-70 (average)

increase again, at a fairly constant rate overall, but more quickly in Bulgaria, Hungary and Poland than in the G.D.R. and Czechoslovakia. The 1966-70 five-year plans continued this trend, emphasising at the same time that it involves no sacrifice of living standards since investment will be used to increase the production of both consumer and capital goods.

The second question is whether a high rate of investment can guarantee a high rate of growth of the national income. The policies adopted in the socialist countries imply a positive answer to this question. It should be noted that investment is here considered to be autonomous, that is to say freely determined by the authorities. There is no causal relationship between an increase in the national income and an increase in investment. Quite simply, the higher the national income, the greater the total mass of investment given the same rate of investment. On the other hand, there is an inverse relationship between investment and national income.

Before analysing this relationship, it is useful to bear in mind that in socialist countries the rate of accumulation is calculated at current prices. But the price index of capital goods does not necessarily evolve in the same way as the general price index. Moreover, in all these countries until the price reforms of the mid-1960s, the capital goods price level was much lower than that of consumer goods (*cf.* chapter 6), even in terms of wholesale prices. Since the national income is calculated in final market prices including turnover tax, there is an even greater distortion between the value of the numerator and denominator in the formula A/Y (A, or accumulation, is composed of capital goods, whose final prices do not generally comprise a turnover tax since this is usually included in the price of consumer goods). Thus the ratio A/Y at current prices, within the same country, may differ substantially from the same ratio at constant prices, especially if a long-term comparison of investment rates is required. On the other hand, the ratio A/Y based on production prices and not on final prices would probably give a much higher ratio of accumulation.

Investment raises national income in two ways: by expanding productive capacity; investment implies expenditure and therefore has an effect on the formation of monetary income. These two effects will be considered separately.

An expansion in productive capacity results in higher production only after a time lapse. In many socialist countries, and especially in the U.S.S.R., this period of capital maturation is excessively long. The norms anticipated for the length of construction work and the bringing into operation of new capital are usually exceeded. For 1959-65 the actual time taken was two or three times greater than the norm. In other words where the plan anticipated two years for the construction and starting up of a factory, from four to six years were in fact required. At the end of 1965, the volume of unfinished construction represented 79% of the total value of investment for the year; in 1967, 87%; in certain sectors (coal, chemicals, mechanical engineering) the percentage was even over 100%. Soviet writers maintain that this is the result of planning errors, of excessive site dispersion and of operational incompetence by construction agencies. In fact the cause goes much deeper. The real problem is permanent over-extension in investment planning. In the U.S.S.R. there is a chronic excess demand for capital goods in relation to supply. Total demand is the aggregate of individual demands made by enterprise directors and transmitted through Gosplan departments, together with the requirements of new construction. This total demand should be adjusted to supply, but in fact it is always planned at too high a level for such adjustment to take place. Excess demand is therefore reflected in a more or less concealed rise in prices, in an increase in constructional estimates, and above all in an extension of construction periods. This situation is not confined to the U.S.S.R. It is to be found also in other socialist countries. In Czechoslovakia, for example, the volume of unfinished construction reached such proportions that the macro-economic plan for 1970 anticipated the allocation of all productive investment to the completion of unfinished projects.

Secondly, the expansion of productive capacity is the result only of productive investment in fixed and circulating capital. However, in the formula A/Y accumulation also includes so-called non-productive investment (housing, hospitals, schools, etc.). The data published on the rate of accumulation in the statistics of the socialist countries do not divide accumulation into productive and non-productive uses. Some idea of this division can be gained from the structure of gross investment (net investment + depreciation) given in table 4.11. Generally speaking, in most socialist countries, the share of productive investment has shown a slight tendency to rise in the long term. According to the country, it has varied from 70% to 85% of total investment.

TABLE 4.11[28]

PRODUCTIVE INVESTMENT AS A PROPORTION OF TOTAL INVESTMENT (%)

Country	1950-55	1956-60	1961-65	1970
Bulgaria	80.1	84.0	86.0	76.0
Hungary	68.5	64.9	70.5	70.9
Poland	74.3	70.3	72.8	76.4
Romania	81.6	75.4	82.2	84.2
Czechoslovakia ...	69.5	72.8	74.4	70.3
U.S.S.R.	76.3	71.4	75.5	69.5

TABLE 4.12[29]

THE COMPOSITION OF INVESTMENT BY CATEGORY (% of total)

Years	Construction and assembly	Machinery, equipment, tools, plant	Diverse
	Bulgaria		
1961-65	53.4	37.2	9.4
1970	50.2	34.1	15.7
	Poland		
1950-55	62.6	32.4	5.0
1956-60	60.6	34.1	5.3
1961-65	55.5	37.8	6.7
1970	52.2	42.0	5.8
	Romania		
1950-55	51.0	33.7	15.3
1956-60	49.8	33.6	16.6
1961-65	44.6	41.4	14.0
1970	48.9	38.3	12.8
	Czechoslovakia		
1950-55	64.0	32.4	3.6
1956-60	60.9	35.8	3.3
1961-65	59.2	37.3	3.6
1970	62.2	34.7	3.1
	U.S.S.R.		
1951-55	66	26	8
1956-60	66	28	6
1961-65	61	32	7
1970	61	31	8

Finally the technological composition of investment must be taken into account. In Comecon classification it is divided into two main groups: construction/assembly and equipment. The share of the first group in investment has shown a tendency to decline in most of the countries concerned (*cf.* table 4.12).

This is a positive characteristic of developed economies already possessing the necessary infrastructure. It contributes to raising the growth rate of the national income, since investment in equipment (machinery, tools, etc.) increases productive capacity much more quickly than great constructional works. This is how one should interpret the latest five-year plans (1966-70) in almost all these countries, where policy is geared in the first instance to the expansion and modernisation of existing enterprises. Such a policy raises the proportion of active investment (in equipment) to passive investment (buildings and installations).

The increase in monetary income as a result of investment expenditure (multiplier effect) is a localised one, since it occurs only in investment sectors. However, in contrast to the expansion of productive capacity, increased income is a product of total investment expenditure, productive or otherwise, and appears with either no operational time-lag at all or after one which is negligible in relation to that for the expansion of productive capacity.

The total increase in national income resulting from investment, through the aggregate effect of these two processes, depends on the productivity of capital.

THE RELATIONSHIP BETWEEN CAPITAL AND PRODUCTION

If the productivity of capital is defined as the ratio of the annual income to the average stock of capital, or as the amount of income obtained in a year per unit of invested capital, it appears clear, as a first approximation, that for a given rate of investment the rate of growth of national income can only rise if the productivity of invested capital increases. On the other hand, where the productivity of capital does not increase, this rate of growth will only be maintained if the rate of investment rises. However there is a limit to an increase in the ratio A/Y since consumption cannot be reduced below a certain level. Is this line of argument justified?

In socialist countries the productivity of capital is calculated as the inverse of the average coefficient of capital, $e=K/Y$, and is therefore considered to be equal to $1/e$. However, the coefficient of capital only expresses a technical relation between capital and production, and it is methodologically incorrect to take its inverse as an indicator of productivity or efficiency (and consequently to interpret any rise in the coefficient as a fall in the efficiency of investment)[30]. Besides, at the macro-economic level it has no real significance on account of the varying composition of capital (type and age) in the different sectors of activity and on account of the great diversity of sectoral coefficients which is the result. Finally, as in all economic systems, an evaluation of the stock of capital poses problems of measurement which are almost insurmountable.

To appreciate developments in the productivity of capital, it is therefore preferable to use the marginal (and not the average) coefficient of capital, or the ratio of the growth of capital ΔK to the growth in national income ΔY. The marginal coefficient has the advantage of avoiding some of the difficulties inherent in measuring the stock of capital. However, it cannot give a definite answer to the question: by how much must productive capital be increased, *ceteris paribus*, if the national income is to be raised by a given amount? In fact, investment is not the only factor in the promotion of economic growth. (The same objection arises in the case of any calculation of the contribution of labour to growth based on the hypothesis that labour alone, apart from capital equipment, determines growth.)

Very generally, all that can be said is that a break in the evolution of the marginal coefficient of capital, when the latter begins to rise after a long period of slow decline, indicates a tendency for the efficiency of investment to fall. Nearly all European socialist countries experienced such a break towards 1960.

However, there are many causes of variation in the coefficient of capital: changes in the distribution of investment between branches or regions (for example, a reorientation of investment towards branches with a high average coefficient of capital will mean a temporary increase at least in the average global coefficient); technical innovation (in the long term technical progress, linked to the use of more efficient equipment, raises labour productivity and leads to a fall in the coefficient of capital;[31] in the short term and during periods of intensive technical innovation, the capital coefficient may rise); the degree of utilisation of equipment (the chronic under-utilisation of productive capacity in socialist countries raises the coefficient of capital); the maturation period of investment.

Thus a rise in the coefficient of capital (average or marginal) does not necessarily mean a fall in economic efficiency, any more than an increase in labour productivity, taken in isolation, means a rise in this efficiency. What matters is the quality of factor combination.

Improvements in Factor Combination

Economic growth results from progress in combining the productive resources of labour and capital.

In the socialist system, the aim of economic policy cannot be simply to achieve the most economic combination of factors possible with a given production objective. The aim of the socialist state is to integrate into economic life the greatest possible proportion of the potential working population, since for the socialist citizen work is both a right and a duty. This assimilation of new labour power requires additional capital expenditure. Since investment funds are limited there may be a conflict between considerations of efficiency implying a rise in productivity, on the one hand, and social policy requiring the allocation of a job to every potential worker, on the other. This must be kept in mind when examining the capital/labour ratio (K/L or the coefficient of capital intensity) and its development.

Table 4.13 shows for the U.S.S.R. the rates of growth of the coefficient of capital intensity K/L, of labour productivity Y/L, and the ratio of these two rates.

TABLE 4.13[32]

THE COEFFICIENT OF CAPITAL INTENSITY AND
LABOUR PRODUCTIVITY IN THE U.S.S.R.

Years	Annual rate of growth of labour productivity	Annual rate of growth of the coefficient of capital intensity	Annual rate of growth of labour productivity attributable to a 1% increase in the coefficient of capital intensity
1927-39	13.2	7.5	1.76
1940-59	6.9	4.7	1.47
1960-63	6.3	4.4	1.43
1927-63	8.2	6.2	1.42
1941-50	4.1	1.2	3.42
1951-55	9.2	8.0	1.15
1956-60	6.5	6.8	0.96
1961-64	4.5	7.9	0.57
1951-60	7.9	7.4	1.07
1941-64	5.7	4.8	1.19
1951-64	6.9	7.5	0.92

The upper section of the table is based on employment data calculated in worker-units, including members of *kolkhoz* families, and workers and employees with auxiliary smallholdings; the lower section is based on data expressed in worker-years, and excludes members of *kolkhoz* families, and workers and employees with auxiliary smallholdings.

It can be seen that there was a rise in the coefficient K/L at two periods in particular, at the beginning of the system of five-year planning (1927-39) and with the resurgence of growth after the post-war reconstruction period (1951-5). It was during these same periods that the annual rate of growth of labour productivity was at its highest. The ratio of the two rates, indicating the annual rate of growth of productivity attributable to a 1% rise in capital intensity, fell constantly over the period.

According to official Soviet sources in the period 1928-38, the U.S.S.R. opted for growth based on a high level of capital intensity. This meant introducing the most modern equipment and borrowing production techniques widely from the developed capitalist countries.

From the viewpoint of the general logic of growth and of the actual situation prevailing in the U.S.S.R. at that time, this type of growth at first appears paradoxical.

In conditions of full employment, and if the rate of demographic growth is low, production can only rise if there is an improvement in capital equipment, that is to say if there is a rise in the coefficient of capital intensity by means of additional productive investment. Given, on the other hand, that the population of working age is increasing rapidly, that at the same time a large part of the active population is under-employed in certain sectors (agriculture in particular) and that capital is scarce, an expansion in production can be obtained by employing more labour together with a relatively slight rise in investment, with priority given to equipping the new jobs created. In this case, labour productivity will remain at a low level, but the national income will grow simply by the addition of new workers to the employed labour force. This second alternative is often considered to be the most appropriate one for developing countries. In such cases investment must be given priority in those branches where the average coefficient of capital is lowest (light industry, agriculture). Such sectors are generally those producing consumer goods.

In fact the U.S.S.R. did not opt for this particular method, even though at the beginning of its industrialisation everything seemed to point in that direction. The high proportion of agricultural workers constituted a large mass of under-employed and unqualified manual labour, creating conditions suited for growth based on capital-saving techniques. But the planners opted for forced industrialisation with absolute priority for heavy industry.

The paradox of Soviet economic growth is explained by a combination of the two types of growth. Investment was centred on a few priority objectives. It was in no way irrational to seek a high coefficient of capital intensity for these. If capital was scarce, skilled labour was no less so, since the abundant flow of labour from agriculture to industry was unusable in modern industrial enterprises. These priority investments were therefore backed up by a high level of investment in human potential, with a view to raising the quality of skilled labour power required in heavy industry. At the same time, as a way of complementing and not contradicting this policy, a further type of growth, of low capital intensity, was promoted in the other sectors. For two reasons: firstly because there was no capital left for these sectors, and secondly to provide work for the under-employed mass of the population[33]. The branches affected were mainly building, agriculture, transport and auxiliary activities serving the main area of production. This historical situation is doubtless partly responsible for the structure of industrial employment still observable today in the U.S.S.R., where there is a large proportion of auxiliary workers in relation to production workers (*cf. supra*).

This type of growth, sectorally unbalanced, was repeated regionally for the same reasons. In the eastern regions of the U.S.S.R. natural resources could only be exploited with a high coefficient of capital intensity, owing to the scarcity of labour. In the European regions capital-saving variants were often preferred.

The European socialist countries adopted similar growth policies. As was seen earlier, this pattern does not seem to have been appropriate for at least two of them: the G.D.R. and Czechoslovakia, where labour was scarce, the reserve of unemployed agricultural workers low, and where the quality of industrial labour would apparently have lent itself to an intensive growth strategy. But only a detailed analysis of prevailing conditions and possibilities for development could indicate whether such a strategy was in fact possible.

Growth Models Used in Soviet Planning

The models used in Soviet planning have a distinctive post-Keynesian flavour. (At the same time they contain theoretical propositions for the construction of a neo-classical type model based on the use of the production function.) This is hardly surprising. Both the general strategy of growth and the analysis of factors increasing the national income emphasise the accumulation of capital as the basis for growth (but not forgetting the rôle of labour as the only source of net additional product). In the socialist economy, the planner can fix the rate of investment directly. This makes it possible to achieve balanced growth, the conditions for which, as defined in post-Keynesian models, are much more difficult to establish in a capitalist system where the rate of investment is determined by decisions taken by individual entrepreneurs.

The main elements of the model may be defined as follows:

X = total social product

Y^1 = final product

Y = national income

These are the fundamental aggregates in Soviet national accounting. It will be remembered that in this material product accounting, common to all socialist countries, the total social product is the sum of the values of gross production, including intermediate consumption, of all branches of material production; the final product and national income are the sum of values added, the difference between the two aggregates being given by depreciation, which is included in the final product.

C = consumption (public and private)

I = gross investment in fixed (Ik) and circulating (Is) capital

A = net investment, or accumulation

R = replacement of capital goods used up in the process of production, in the form of depreciation (Rk) and the reconstitution of stocks (Rs)

t = time

r = annual growth rate of the national income.

We therefore have:

$Y = C + A$ (definitional equality: from the point of

view of its use, national income is divided between consumption and net investment)

$$Y^1 = Rk + C + A$$
$$X = Rs + Rk + C + A = Rs + Y^1 = R + Y$$

(according to the definitions of these aggregates)

$$r = \frac{\Delta Yt + 1}{Yt} \; ;$$

national income at the end of the period can be expressed in the general form:

$$Yt = Yo(1 + r)^t.$$

The determination of r for the planning period will be based on two methods: from an evaluation of labour potential; from an estimate of capital resources.

The first method is based on an evaluation of resources in man-power and on forecasts of the rate of growth of labour productivity.

Demographic growth is first calculated from past birth and death rate coefficients and from the age and sex structure of the population. Then the figure for the active population is calculated, by extrapolating the employment coefficient of the preceding period (active population/total population ratio), with a certain number of modifications relating to labour and employment policy, the general lines of which are known at the beginning of the planning period: any anticipated extension of schooling, the lowering of retirement age, the greater or lesser assimilation of women into economic life, an increase or fall in the work of pensioners, etc. Given the active population it is possible to calculate the number of hours worked in the year, which will generally rise relatively less (through reductions in the working week,[34] longer paid holidays, more part-time work, etc.). Finally the anticipated average number of workers for the year is calculated (taking seasonal variations in employment into account): L. The rate of growth of L is written:

$$l = \frac{\Delta Lt + 1}{Lt} \; .$$

Next the expected growth in productivity is calculated from past trends and from an analysis of factors influencing that growth: technical progress, structural changes tending to increase the share in national income of those branches where productivity is above average, etc. The rate of growth of productivity is written:

$$q = \frac{\Delta Qt + 1}{Qt} \; .$$

Since by definition, $Q = Y/L$, or the ratio of the national income to the average number of workers, $Y = Q.L$.

Similarly, the national income index is the product of the employment index multiplied by the index of productivity:

$$\frac{Yt + 1}{Yt} = \frac{Lt + 1}{Lt} \times \frac{Qt + 1}{Qt} \; ;$$

or $\dfrac{Yt + 1}{Yt} = 1 + r; \quad \dfrac{Lt + 1}{Lt} = 1 + l; \quad \dfrac{Qt + 1}{Qt} = 1 + q.$

We therefore have $(1 + r) = (1 + l) \times (1 + q) = 1 + l + Q + ql$

and by approximation $1 + r = 1 + l + q$

hence $r = l + q.$

The rate of growth of national income is therefore the sum of the rate of growth of productivity and the rate of growth of the number of workers involved in production.

We therefore have $Yt = Yo(1 + l + q)^t$.

This equation makes it possible to define the magnitude of national income for any year of the planned period.

The second method bases the rate of growth of national income on the possible evolution of the stock of capital, of gross and net investment. It comprises two successive stages: the determination of resources available for investment; an analysis of the relationship between capital and production.

The volume of resources available for investment is obtained by calculating the maximum total C (consumption) expected during the planning period. This calculation is based on the following elements: the magnitude of Y obtained by the first method; the ratio between C and A (accumulation) for the reference year; the possible rate of growth of productivity, constituting an upper limit on the growth of C; the definition of standard of living objectives. Let us consider the last two elements.

Cl represents the level of real incomes:

$$Cl = \frac{C}{L},$$

$$cl = \frac{\Delta\, Clt + 1}{Cl}$$

and $1 + cl$ (index of the level of real incomes) $= \dfrac{Clt + 1}{Cl}$.

It will be remembered that q = rate of growth of productivity; a represents the rate of investment: $a = A/Y$.

Consumption will then be: $C = Y(1 - a)$.

If both sides of this equation are divided by L:

$Cl = Q(1 - a)$.

One can write: $\dfrac{Clt + 1}{Cl} = \dfrac{Qt + 1(1 - at + 1)}{Qt(1 - at)}$,

$$1 + cl = 1 + q\,\frac{(1 - at + 1)}{(1 - at)}$$

or $\qquad\qquad cl = q\,\dfrac{(1 - at + 1)}{(1 - at)}$.

If we wish to have $\dfrac{(1 - at + 1)}{(1 - at)} < 1$, that is to say raise the rate of investment or maintain it at the same level during the period in question, it is then necessary for $cl < q$, i.e. the real incomes of workers may increase at most at the same rate as productivity during the planning period. This norm will occur again in incomes policy (chapter 6).

Cl may also be determined on the basis of planned standard of living objectives for the period. These objectives are in turn the product of an analysis of family budgets, of income elasticity of demand coefficients, and of the anticipated structure of consumption.

The relationships between capital and production are also analysed.

K = present fixed capital and k its annual rate of increase;

$$k = \frac{\Delta Kt + 1}{Kt}.$$

$e = \dfrac{Y}{K}$, or the productivity of capital (analogous to $\dfrac{Y}{L}$ expressing the productivity of labour) and $\epsilon = \dfrac{\Delta et + 1}{et}$.

The evolution of e in previous periods is known and can be extrapolated in support of hypotheses about factors influencing the productivity of capital or its inverse, the coefficient of capital:[35] technical progress, variations in the structure of production raising or lowering the total coefficient of capital according to the relative importance in national income of branches with a high capital coefficient; the intensity of exploitation of present capital, etc. (*cf. supra*).

As Y eK

$$(1 + r) = (1 + \epsilon)(1 + k)$$

$$r = k + \epsilon \text{ (by approximation).}$$

The rate of growth of national income is thus the sum of the rate of growth of the stock of capital and the rate of growth of the productivity of capital.

Hence $Yt = Yo(1 + k + \epsilon)^t.$

The rate of growth of the stock of capital itself depends on the rate of investment. It is at this point that the two procedures applied in the second method of evaluating Y meet.

$Y = eK.$

ΔK (increase in the stock of capital) $= I - M$, where M represents the annual value of fixed capital used up in the current process of production; $M = Rk$ if replacement expenditure covered by depreciation coincides with annual wear and tear of equipment.

On the assumption that e is constant:

$$\Delta Y = e \Delta K = eI - eM = e(I - M)$$

Now $I - M = A$ (net investment)

Hence $\Delta Y = eA$

$$\frac{\Delta Y}{Y} = e \frac{A}{Y}, \text{ therefore } r = ea.$$

The rate of growth of national income is equal to the index of capital productivity multiplied by the rate of investment.

$Yt = Yo(1 + ea)^t.$

The magnitude of a still has to be discovered. So far we have only determined the minimum volume of resources available for investment, having calculated the maximum increase in real incomes. Can a (the rate of investment) be increased indefinitely?

Consider again the equation $Y = C + A$

$$a = \frac{A}{Y} \quad c = \frac{C}{Y},$$

$$c = 1 - a \quad \text{and} \quad C = (1 - a)Y.$$

As $\quad Yt = Yo(1 + ea)^t$

$$Ct = Yo(1 + ea)^t(1 - a).$$

It can be seen that consumption C^t rises with ea, and if we take e as constant, with the rate of investment a. But an increase in a reduces the expression $(1 - a)$ and therefore total consumption. What is required is a definition of the optimal rate of investment. Planning has not yet solved this problem.

As we have just seen, the planning of national income growth rates involves the use of two methods or approaches. These are not parallel but convergent and meet in their analysis of the coefficient of capital intensity (ratio K/L).

$$B = \frac{K}{L}; \quad L = \frac{K}{B};$$

if B is constant, $\Delta L = \dfrac{\Delta K}{B}; \quad \dfrac{\Delta L}{L} = \dfrac{\Delta K}{B.L} = \dfrac{\Delta K}{K} = k.$

In other words, if the coefficient of capital intensity is assumed to be constant, the stock of capital and the size of the labour force will grow at the same rate.

But with technical progress B rises: the capital necessary to equip each new job increases. For this expenditure to be efficient, it must raise the productivity of labour.

The productivity of labour is evidently a function of the rate of growth of the coefficient of capital intensity, which is written:

$$b = \frac{\Delta Bt + 1}{Bt}.$$

In its simplest form (actually used in planning) this function is written:

$$q = \mu b.$$

One can have $\quad \mu = 1; \quad \mu > 1; \quad \mu < 1.$

If $\quad \mu = 1, q = b$

In this case:

$$\frac{Qt + 1}{Qt} = \frac{Bt + 1}{Bt}, \quad \text{whence} \quad \frac{Yt + 1}{Lt + 1} \times \frac{Lt}{Yt} = \frac{Kt + 1}{Lt + 1} \times \frac{Lt}{Kt}.$$

$$\frac{Yt + 1}{Yt} = \frac{Kt + 1}{Kt}; \quad \frac{Yt + 1}{Kt + 1} = \frac{Yt}{Kt}; \quad et + 1 = et.$$

Which means that the productivity of capital is constant. It can be shown in the same way that if labour productivity rises at a lower rate than that of the coefficient of capital intensity then the productivity of capital falls, which indicates a decline in investment efficiency.

This growth model is in fact used in the planning of growth. It makes it possible to establish an indicative rate of growth of the national income, but provides no information for the planner on certain essential points. In particular, it says nothing about the magnitude of the rate of investment (on which living standards depend), nor about the proportions of factor combination. Its interest is therefore much reduced.

3. GROWTH AND STRUCTURE OF THE ECONOMY

The strategy of growth followed in the European socialist countries under the aegis of the U.S.S.R. and within the framework of Comecon had the objective of narrowing the economic gaps existing between them. Mutual co-operation between countries was also designed to bring these different levels of economic development closer together.[36] If industrial production and national income per head of the population (table 4.14) are taken as indices of the level of development, it can be seen that in a period of twenty years (1950–70) there was a considerable narrowing of the span between the two extremes. Czechoslovakia and especially the G.D.R. have always had a level considerably higher than the U.S.S.R., while the less developed countries in the group have slowly been making up lost ground (Romania in particular).

TABLE 4.14[37]

PER CAPITA LEVELS OF INDUSTRIAL PRODUCTION AND NATIONAL INCOME

	Industrial production (U.S.S.R.=100)		National income	
	1950	1970	1950	1970
Bulgaria	43	82	60	96
Hungary	78	71	119	81
Poland	70	73	114	81
G.D.R.	136	154	131	135
Romania	31	57	55	70
Czechoslovakia	143	110	172	109

In fact, socialist growth policy has led to greater structural conformity between the states involved rather than to an equalisation of levels of economic development.

Sectoral Structures

Structural development in socialist countries has been characterised by three main features: industrialisation, priority for heavy industry, stagnation of non-productive sectors.

Industrialisation was the first watchword of economic policy in European socialist countries after World War II, just as it had been in the U.S.S.R. twenty years earlier. The greater part of investment was allocated to industry (table 4.15). The effect was a systematic transfer of rural manpower to industry (table 4.16), a much faster increase in industrial than agricultural production (table 4.17) and consequently a rise in industry's share of the national income (table 4.18). As can be seen from table 4.18, this restructuring cut much deeper in countries where agriculture was strongest in the pre-socialist economy (Bulgaria, Poland). In the G.D.R. and Czechoslovakia, already industrialised, the dominance of the industrial sector was extended without structural disruption. For the U.S.S.R. a comparison of 1950 and 1970 reveals no significant change, since the transformation of the main economic structures had been carried out before 1950. In 1928, for example, agriculture accounted for 36.2% of the national income and industry for 33.2%; by 1937 these proportions were already 25.7% and 53%.

TABLE 4.15[38]

COMPARISON OF INDUSTRIAL AND AGRICULTURAL GROWTH

| | Annual average rate of growth of production (1951–65) | | Share of total investment allocated to: | | | |
| | | | Industry | | Agriculture | |
	Industry	Agri-culture	Average 1950–55	Average 1961–65	Average 1950–55	Average 1961–65
Bulgaria	13.8	5.1	44.1	47.2	18.5	25.0
Hungary	9.4	2.1	39.6	37.6	12.5	17.4
Poland	11.4	2.7	44.4	41.7	10.3	13.7
G.D.R.	9.5	7.5	—	—	—	—
Romania ...	13.3	4.4	52.8	46.1	11.4	19.5
Czechoslovakia ...	9.0	1.1	41.7	44.4	11.9	15.0
U.S.S.R.	10.7	4.1	40.4	36.1	15.1	16.2
Yugoslavia ...	10.3	5.7	—	—	—	—

The national income structures of Romania and Yugoslavia seem to indicate exceptions to the general rule. However in both countries and especially in Yugoslavia the agricultural price index has risen much more sharply than the index for industrial products. Consequently, the contribution of agriculture to national income is inflated for recent years when production is evaluated at

TABLE 4.16[39]

SHARE OF INDUSTRY AND AGRICULTURE IN TOTAL EMPLOYMENT IN THESE SECTORS (%)

	Pre-war years*		1955		1965		1970	
	Ind.	Agr.	Ind.	Agr.	Ind.	Agr.	Ind.	Agr.
Bulgaria ...	9.0	91.0	15.2	84.8	37.0	63.0	52.0	48.0
Hungary ...	26.3	73.7	36.7	63.3	51.6	48.4	62.0	38.0
Poland	14.7	85.3	28.6	71.4	35.7	64.3	50.6	49.4
G.D.R.	60.6	39.4	63.9	36.1	73.1	26.9	79.3	20.7
Romania ...	9.3	90.7	15.8	84.2	25.4	74.6	37.5	62.5
Czechoslovakia ...	41.9	58.1	50.1	49.9	66.3	33.7	69.6	30.4
U.S.S.R. ...	29.2	70.8	37.9	62.1	49.6	50.4	56.5	43.5

*Bulgaria, Poland, 1937–9; Hungary, 1949; G.D.R., 1952; Romania, 1930; Czechoslovakia, 1948; U.S.S.R., 1940

TABLE 4.17[40]

A. ANNUAL GROWTH RATES OF GROSS INDUSTRIAL PRODUCTION (%)

	1951–55	1956–60	1961–65	1966–70	1971–75 (plan)
Bulgaria	13.7	15.9	11.7	10.9	9.2 – 9.9
Hungary	13.2	7.5	7.5	6.0	5.7 – 6.0
Poland	16.2	9.9	8.5	8.4	8.2 – 8.5
G.D.R.	13.8	9.2	6.0	6.5	6.0 – 6.4
Romania	15.1	10.9	13.8	11.8	11.0 – 12.2
Czechoslovakia ...	10.9	10.5	5.2	6.8	6.0 – 6.4
U.S.S.R.	13.2	10.4	8.6	8.5	7.3 – 7.9
Yugoslavia ...	7.0	13.3	10.7		

B. ANNUAL GROWTH RATES OF AGRICULTURAL PRODUCTION (%)

	1951–65	1961–65	1966–70	1971–75 (plan)
Bulgaria	5.1	3.2	3.4	3.2 – 3.7
Hungary	2.1	1.7	2.8	2.8 – 3.0
Poland	2.7	2.8	1.8	3.4 – 3.9
G.D.R.	7.5	1.3	1.5	3.2
Romania	4.4	2.4	1.9	6.3 – 8.3
Czechoslovakia	1.1	– 0.5	4.9	2.7
U.S.S.R.	4.1	2.4	3.9	3.7 – 4.0
Yugoslavia	5.7	2.5		

current prices. An evaluation in constant prices would reveal different proportions (for Romania, 69.5% and 11.1% in 1966 for industry and agriculture respectively). In Hungary the 1968 price reform led to a more than proportionate rise in commercial and transport prices and therefore to a fall in the share of industry and agriculture in the national income for 1970.

TABLE 4.18[41]

SECTORAL STRUCTURE OF THE NATIONAL INCOME

(%, national economy, total = 100; current prices)

	Industry			Construction			Agriculture		
	1950	1966	1970	1950	1966	1970	1950	1966	1970
Bulgaria ...	36.8	44.8	49.1	6.6	7.8	8.7	42.1	33.6	21.9
Hungary ...	49.1	57.1	43.6	6.8	10.0	12.5	24.4	21.1	17.7
Poland	37.1	51.5	57.5	7.9	8.9	9.8	40.1	20.3	13.1
G.D.R.	55.9	63.9	60.9	5.1	5.2	8.2	12.3	11.9	11.7
Romania ...	44.0	49.2	59.3	6.0	8.3	10.3	28.0	28.8	19.0
Czechoslovakia ...	62.5	65.8	62.1	8.7	9.4	11.3	16.2	12.6	10.1
U.S.S.R. ...	57.5	52.4	51.1	6.1	9.0	10.4	21.8	22.0	21.8
Yugoslavia ...	52.0	45.9		7.4	8.3		25.4	26.3	

In industrial development priority has been given to heavy industry,[42] in accordance with the law of faster growth in the production of capital than of consumption goods (groups A and B respectively). The table below gives the average annual rate of growth of production in these two groups between 1951 and 1970, for all the socialist countries taken together.[42]

TABLE 4.19[43]

AVERAGE ANNUAL GROWTH RATES OF GROUPS A AND B

	1951–66	1951–55	1956–60	1961–65	1966–70
Group A	12.0	15.0	14.0	9.0	8.8
Group B	9.1	13.0	9.0	6.5	7.7

The above are averages and the relationship of the rates to each other varies in time from country to country. In the U.S.S.R. the annual growth rate of group A exceeded that of group B by 70% between 1925 and 1940, and by 60% between 1959 and 1965. Since 1966 the two rates have drawn closer together. Only in 1968, and for the first time ever, did production in group

B rise more than in A (8.3% and 8.0% respectively in relation to 1967). In almost every other country there has been at some time a more rapid growth of group B in spite of a long-term trend in the opposite direction: Czechoslovakia in 1955-8, Bulgaria (1953, 1957, 1961), Poland (1957-8), Romania (1954-5), Hungary (1966-9).

The structure of industry has therefore been modified everywhere. Table 4.20 shows that in 1970 the share of group A in gross industrial production was in every socialist country except Bulgaria above 60% (the proportion it usually reaches in developed capitalist countries).

TABLE 4.20[44]

SHARE OF THE CAPITAL GOODS SECTOR (GROUP A)
IN GROSS INDUSTRIAL PRODUCTION (%)

	Year preceding the war	1950	1960	1970
U.S.S.R.	33.3[1]	68.8	72.5	73.4
Bulgaria	22.6	38.2	49.9	54.7
Hungary	44.8	—	66.0	63.9
Poland	47.1	52.6	59.4	63.6
G.D.R.	—	66.6	66.5	70.2
Romania	45.5	52.9	62.8	69.2
Czechoslovakia	49.3	52.9	60.1	61.6

[1] 1913

It is generally considered that this particular trend has now drawn to a close. We saw earlier that some socialist countries would have preferred to bring it to an end much sooner. Excessive growth in group A carries the risk of over-investment in that sector and inhibits the growth of consumption. Consequently most of the 1966-70 five-year plans anticipated a slackening of growth rates in group A in favour of higher production in group B. This trend is confirmed in the 1971-5 plans, although group A maintains a slight lead over group B.[45]

The internal structure of group A is not necessarily the same between countries. Similar proportions in gross industrial production by A groups may correspond to traditional structures (with the extractive and metallurgical industries predominating) or to modern structures (where a significant percentage of total production is accounted for by the chemical, electrical and electronic industries, and by mechanical engineering). In socialist industry three branches were given priority: the production of electric power, mechanical engineering and later the chemical industry (table 4.21). These three account for between one-third and one-half of total industrial production, according to the country, and taken together have an annual growth rate above the industrial average. On the other hand, the extractive industries (with a few exceptions: coal in Poland, oil in Romania) and steel (except in Romania) have expanded at a lower than average rate for industry as a whole. These developments are linked to the international division of labour within Comecon.

TABLE 4.21[46]

GROWTH OF PRODUCTION OF ELECTRIC POWER, MECHANICAL ENGINEERING AND CHEMICAL INDUSTRY 1951-66

	Increase for 1951-66 (1950=1)			Ratio of growth rates (whole of industry=1)			Share of the three branches in total industrial production (%)	
	Electric power	Mechanical engineering	Chemical industry	Electric power	Mechanical engineering	Chemical industry	1950	1966
Bulgaria ...	12.5	19.8	21.4	1.9	2.6	2.8	13.7	25.2
Hungary ...	3.9	5.8	9.8	0.96	1.4	2.4	32.3	39.6
Poland ...	5.0	15.6	10.6	0.9	2.9	1.9	13.6	38.2
G.D.R. ...	2.9	6.0	4.6	0.7	1.4	1.1	45.3	52.3
Romania ...	9.8	14.2	21.4	1.4	2.0	3.5	18.3	32.2
Czechoslovakia	3.9	6.9	8.0	1.03	1.8	2.1	27.6	35.8
U.S.S.R. ...	6.0	8.6	8.9	1.2	1.7	1.8	27.0[1]	35.0
Yugoslavia ...	7.0	6.0	11.3	1.6	1.4	2.5		

[1] 1960

The third structural characteristic of socialist countries is the concentration of investment on those sectors producing material goods (*cf.* table 4.9). As far as living standards were concerned, this policy only aggravated the consequences of the priority given to group A within the productive sector. To an inadequate supply of agricultural or industrial consumer goods was added an inadequate supply of services of all kinds. It is doubtless true that all these countries, keen on implementing a socialist policy in the main areas of public health and education, have allocated an important part of their annual budget (between one-fifth and two-fifths) to financing social and cultural measures, so that everywhere medical attention and education are now free (*cf.* chapter 6). Moreover, the standard of living (particularly of workers and other employees as table 4.20 shows) has risen regularly. Basic consumer needs (food, clothing) may be taken as satisfied in all these countries. But certain other needs are very imperfectly covered. This applies especially to housing, where investment has lagged behind requirements. What the socialist countries have achieved in this area is justice in the distribution of scarcity. Norms of living-space are applied in every town, so that every family is supplied with a minimum and scandalous contrasts between the badly and sumptuously housed are unknown. But everyone is cramped for room. In addition, the expansion of leisure activities resulting from a reduction in weekly hours of work, an extension of paid holidays and a reorganisation of the working week (the five-day week is more or less general)[47] has brought with it an increased demand for services as yet inadequately satisfied. Such services could be provided with relatively little investment. An extension of the tertiary sector would have the further advantage of providing employment for the labour surplus existing in certain countries. In the others, the flexibility of this sector would make it possible to employ women or retired people. The 1966-70 five-year plans often antici-pated such a move: Czechoslovakia, for example, expected an increase of 7.2% in the labour-force employed in non-productive activities (as against 1.3% for productive workers), so that in 1970 this sector would account for 21.1% of total employment (16.7% in 1960). In Hungary the number of employees in the non-productive sector was to increase by 8.3% in the same period, as compared with 4.9% for productive workers. In Bulgaria the corresponding rates were 13.4% and 5.7%. Planning results did in fact tend to conform to these forecasts, although the increase in employment in the non-productive sector as a proportion of the total was slightly less than expected. It is through an expansion of the non-productive sector that it is hoped to solve the problem of under-employment which has recently appeared in small Soviet towns. This same problem is linked also to regional economic structures, which will be examined next.

TABLE 4.22[48]

STANDARD OF LIVING INDICES OF WORKERS AND EMPLOYEES 1970

	Bulgaria 1952=100	Hungary 1950=100	G.D.R. 1955=100	Poland 1955=100	Romania 1950=100	Czecho-slovakia 1955=100
Money income	218	343	173.6	218	392	161.4
Cost of living	78	174	90.5	137	—	101.8
Real income	262	198	191.8	159	271	158.5

Regional Structures

This section will be confined to an analysis of the regional policies of socialist countries.[49] Given its size and the unequal distribution of resources on its territory, it is in the Soviet Union that the problems of regional development can be most clearly seen (Siberia covers 50% of Soviet territory, possesses 80% of its fuel and energy reserves, and yet only 11% of the total population live there). However the same problems can be found in other countries. It could be said that the objectives of regional policy are to ensure the most rational localisation of production from the point of view of economic efficiency, while at the same time raising levels of economic development in traditionally backward areas up to the national average. There may be a conflict between these two objectives. That being the case it seems that a socialist policy should give priority to the second of the two.

In Soviet regional policy the principle of equalising regional levels of development has for a long time been subordinated to the rational localisation of productive activity. During the first five-year plans, regional growth was centred essentially on the needs of the European part of the U.S.S.R. The construction of the Ural-Kutnetsk combine during the second five-year plan of 1933-7 does not really constitute an exception, since the objective was to supply the Ural metallurgical industries with Siberian coal and not to establish manufacturing industry in Siberia. A number of enterprises were transferred to the east during the war, but this movement was not systematised until much later. It was the Twentieth Party Congress in 1956 which floated the idea of a third metallurgical base in Siberia on the Kutnetsk coalfield. The Twenty-second Party Congress in 1961 included long-term expansion for Central Asia and Siberia in its programme, including the Siberian Far East, where a fourth metallurgical base was projected.

The problem was how to accelerate industrial development east of the Urals, given the shortage of labour and transport costs. Given the enormous energy potential of Siberia, it is now thought desirable to establish industries there requiring a great deal of power and little labour: aluminium, heavy chemicals, a section of the iron and steel industry. Production would then be re-exported to the west, transport costs being more than counterbalanced by economies in energy and fuel. The recent discovery of immense oil reserves in Siberia seems to confirm this analysis. The main obstacle remains attracting and keeping a labour-force, even in the present situation of concealed unemployment. The annual number of workers returning from Siberia continues to exceed the number going there, in spite of the advantages offered to potential migrants to the east: travel and accommodation allowances, high wages. The truth is that economic and social conditions in Siberia and the Great North are not good enough to compensate for the rigours of the climate and distance from a civilised environment. The cost of living is high, the service sector underdeveloped and problems of accommodation considerable. So at most workers do no more than respect their contract (three years) and usually return to the European regions of the U.S.S.R. The cost to the country is about two milliard roubles a year, or more than 1% of the annual budget.

Equally rich in raw materials but poor in manpower,[50] Kazakhstan has had to face similar problems. This Soviet republic came into the limelight round about 1953 as a result of the Virgin Lands project. The scheme was supported by heavy investments and organised immigration. Within ten years the cultivated area under cereals had been tripled. But its overall development under the Soviet regime has been mainly characterised since 1928 by systematic industrialisation. The aim was to exploit raw materials to satisfy the needs of the European regions of the U.S.S.R.

The degree of success of regional equalisation policy in the U.S.S.R. can be gauged from its application in Central Asia, whose four republics cover 5.8% of Soviet territory and account for 7% of the population. These republics still have a per capita national income well below the Soviet average. Agriculture continues to occupy a dominant position in the economic structure, constituting more than a third of the region's national income. The maintenance of this traditional structure rests on certain features typical of underdeveloped areas: the climate (lack of water especially, only partially remedied by irrigation), shortage of a skilled local work-force, and bureaucracy in the administration of general and economic policy.

The rational localisation of production principle links regional development to macro-economic considerations. There are two complementary aspects to this principle: specialisation and diversification.

According to the specialisation principle, each region should have a particular vocation: power, coal-mining, manufacturing, etc. Industries corresponding to this vocation must be given priority and will constitute the growth point of the region. The Ural region, for example, is centred on metallurgy, which in turn is linked to the engineering and chemical industries; eastern Siberia is based on power; the Centre on manufacturing industry. Others are more difficult to classify. Kazakhstan, for example, has a mixed vocation.

Numerous analyses have been made of regional specialisation. The most common indices used are: absolute volume of production in the various branches of the region's economy; the share of exports in the total regional production of a given branch of activity; the share of the branch in total regional production.

The principle of specialisation is tempered by that of diversification: a region must not rely too much on a unilateral approach to problems of development; ancillary activities must support the main one. The development of central Siberia before the war, for example, entirely geared to the production of power, ran counter to the principle of diversification.

This second principle also means that the establishment of a particular industry in a particular region must involve not only the solution of purely technical or economic problems, but the tackling of all the other factors involved: urbanisation, the development of social services, etc. This concern for a co-ordinated policy of regional development is recent in the U.S.S.R. The implementation of such a policy is hindered by administrative barriers (since urbanisation, commercial organisation, control of the labour market and industrial administration all depend on different authorities).

The other socialist countries have also had difficulties in introducing balanced regional policies. These problems are still most acute in Yugoslavia. Marked regional inequalities persist, in spite of a heavy programme of federal investment. In 1963 the index of per capita national income in the Kossovo-Metohie region was 30.9, and 63.6 in the republic of Montenegro, against an average index of 100. The index for the most economically advanced of the republics, Slovenia, was 191.4.[51]

Regional inequalities still hamper economic growth in the countries where they are most pronounced. Among other structural impediments to growth the most frequently quoted is agriculture, in every socialist country. It is politically the least reliable sector, whether collectivisation has succeeded or not. It remains economically backward, because of inadequate investment in modern production methods and the fact that the most productive workers have tended to leave the land for urban industry, and because a discriminatory prices and incomes policy is hardly calculated to supply the necessary economic incentives (*cf*. chapter 2).

Having made these reservations, can it still be said that economic growth in the socialist countries of Europe has been a success? Declining rates of expansion since 1960 can be explained by the relative degree of maturity which these countries have now reached. The main cause, however, is to be found in poor planning and management methods. It was to improve these that economic reforms were introduced. They do not appear to have been an unqualified success, particularly where bureaucratic resistance to reform was strong, as in the U.S.S.R.

In any case it is difficult to judge economic performance on quantitative results alone. The growth of production must not be identified with social progress. One essential conquest of socialism needs to be reiterated: the right to work is effectively guaranteed. Wherever and whenever signs of regional or sectoral under-employment have appeared, they have immediately been seen as the most urgent social problem. Perhaps the greatest weakness of Yugoslavia has been to rely on emigration as a means of eliminating unemployment. Seen in this perspective, the fact that the application of the constitutional right to work has often resulted in an inefficient use of labour is of secondary importance.

Appendix

THE MEASUREMENT OF RESULTS: THE VALUE OF SOVIET STATISTICS

There are two possible attitudes to the reliability of Soviet statistics. They may be taken in their entirety as incorrect, or even as deliberately mendacious. In this case an attempt may be made to reconstitute whole series of 'true' statistics by means of corrections and cross-checking. The second possibility is to use Soviet sources as they stand, but to take account of their undeniable defects, to disclose what these are and to rely on the safest data available.

The first attitude is widespread among American specialists of the Soviet economy (*cf*. table 4.23). It is motivated not only by a concern for scientific rigour, but also by political considerations. It can hardly be coincidental that the most important reconstructions of statistical indices have been undertaken at the request of United States government institutions (*cf.* the work of the Joint Economic Committee of the Congress of the United States, *Dimensions of Soviet Economic Power,* Washington, 1962, since supplemented by an annual review, and the voluminous study sponsored by the National Bureau of Economic Research, *The Growth of Industrial Production in the Soviet Union,* edited by G. Warren Nutter in 1962). The date of these two works, 1962, is as significant as the circumstances of their preparation: it was in 1961 that the new programme of the Communist Party of the Soviet Union challenged the United States in the following terms: 'During the course of the next ten years (1961-71) the Soviet Union . . . will overtake the richest and most powerful capitalist country in per capita production: the U.S.A.'

Without denying the value of such detailed work on Soviet statistics, employing large teams of U.S. researchers, it is questionable whether it is really worth the trouble, especially in view of the divergency of results obtained. It might be preferable to give reasoned credence to Soviet sources. This is the view of most French specialists, and in Great Britain is upheld by the economist Alec Nove. It is the one we shall adopt.

TABLE 4.23[52]

A COMPARISON OF SOVIET DATA AND CERTAIN
AMERICAN ESTIMATES

INDICES OF NATIONAL INCOME GROWTH IN THE SOVIET UNION
(1937 = 100)

	Soviet data	Estimate of A. Bergson (1937 weighting)	Estimate of N. Jasny (1926-27 weighting)	Estimate of G. Warren Nutter (1937 weighting)
1928	25.9	59.7	46.2	54.1
1937	100.0	100.0	100.0	100.0
1940	133.1	117.0	122.0	117.3
1945	110.7	—	—	—
1948	154.0	—	115.0	—
1950	218.5	144.0	—	135.7
1955	373.9	204.0	—	188.1
1960	582.6	—	—	255.2

INDUSTRIAL PRODUCTION INDICES   (1928 = 100)

	Soviet data	Estimate of N. Jasny	Estimate of G. W. Nutter	Estimate of D. Hodgman	Estimate of N. Kaplan and R. Moorsteen
1928	100	100	100	100	100
1932	202	165	140	172	154
1937	446	287	279	371	249
1940	646	350	312	430	263
1946	494	236	183	304	168
1950	1,118	470	385	646	385
1955	2,067	—	608	—	583

When using Soviet statistics the following points should be kept in mind:
1. The reliability of official statistics, computed and published by the Central Board of Statistics of the U.S.S.R., is increasing as time passes. The data published during the last fifteen years are undoubtedly of better quality than before.
2. Present defects in these statistics proceed from methodological mistakes rather than from a conscious desire to mislead.
3. Comparisons between Soviet and Western results cannot always be relied upon for the simple reason that certain aggregates are subject to different definitions in the various national accounting systems (e.g. national income, gross social product, production by branch).

Let us consider these three points in more detail:
1. Until 1953-5 the volume of data published by Soviet statistical agencies was very limited. Much information was kept secret, even in areas which appeared to have nothing at all to do with national defence or State security. Published data were incomplete, and above all incorrect or deliberately exaggerated. Why, and how?

The reply to the first question is obvious. Because the Soviet government wished to give the impression that the Soviet economy was more prosperous than was really the case. Two observations need to be made in this connection. In the first place, this type of exaggeration does not necessarily falsify estimates of growth rates, provided the degree of exaggeration remains constant. This is what Alec Nove calls 'the law of equal cheating'. Of course, the degree still has to be evaluated. In the second place the Central Board of Statistics was not alone responsible for the exaggeration. Statistics of production were (and still are) calculated from information provided by enterprises. We have already seen that in the economic system prior to the 1965 reform, the main criterion of success, and the one determining the allocation of bonuses, was overfulfilment of production plans. In effect, enterprises were indirectly prompted to overvalue their results. The situation was certainly known to the statistical departments. On the other hand, it was not encouraged, since the falsification of statistics was and remains an indictable offence under criminal law. The situation was made even more confusing by the fact that enterprises were also tempted to undervalue certain data. This applied particularly to stocks (so as to be able to build up hidden reserves) and even to production figures when it was feared that an excess of output might lead the authorities to impose too rigorous a plan on them for the following year. Cheating was even more significant in agriculture, both in the collectivised and private sectors. Even now production figures for the private sector are only approximations. To voluntary distortion of the facts must be added the effects of the so-called biological method of calculating crop production, based on an evaluation of standing corn and ignoring harvest losses. In 1952 it was officially announced that the cereal crop was 130 million tons—brought down a few years later to 92 million tons in statistical publications! This biological criterion was abandoned in 1953.

The second question is more difficult to answer: how did the statistical departments manage to inflate the results? The simplest reply is that they invented them. This hypothesis is very rarely advanced by specialists, even by those least favourably disposed towards the Soviet Union. It is, in fact, extremely difficult to continue to cook the books over a long period of time and for a large number of items. It should not be forgotten, either, that

Soviet statistics are not merely (or even essentially) instruments of propaganda. They are also a means of drafting plans, and to this end they must be as coherent and precise as possible. So other means have been used to embellish the statistics. For a long time unfavourable data were simply not published immediately, although the information would be released a few years later.

Secondly, until 1950 the general growth indices of the national income were statistically inflated by a valuation in 1926-7 prices. This weighting is perhaps the fundamental cause of distortion at the top end of the data. These prices corresponded to the high point of inflation which had developed during the N.E.P. Later, wholesale industrial prices had fallen, and by evaluating production in 1926-7 prices there appeared to have been more growth than would have been the case with a different weighting. At the same time the base period referred to an early stage in the process of industrialisation. Later on numerous new products appeared and were included in the index on the basis of the cost of their first year of mass production. This cost was usually higher than in following years and was expressed in the purely nominal prices of 1926-7.

From 1951 to 1955 weighting was based on 1951 prices, on 1956 prices for 1956-8, and on 1958 prices for 1958-65. 1965 prices have been used since 1966. The corresponding series of indices were merely appended to each other, without any modification. The result has been a considerable inflation of the global index of national income since 1928. Evidently the more recent series are the more reliable.

2.   That is not to say that present Soviet statistics are perfect. The main tool of the researcher is the statistical year-book, *The Economy of the U.S.S.R. in* . . . published by the Central Board of Statistics from eighteen months to two years after the end of the year concerned. To this are added partial statistics (on an industrial branch or sector of activity) published in no particular order by the Board's journal the *Statistical Bulletin*. These publications can be criticised on various counts: explanatory notes are inadequate; the presentation changes in detail from year to year, so that it is almost impossible to trace the development of the same index over a period of several years; from one edition to another of the year-book figures relating to the same facts are modified without explanation; comparisons are often made impossible by the absence of homogeneous data (for example, in agriculture, different notions are used for total production and state purchases; wool is calculated in the first case according to gross weight and in the second case according to a conventional weight based on coefficients of quality—but the size of the coefficients is not given).

3.   The defects of presentation just mentioned make it difficult to compare data within the Soviet system of statistics. Comparisons between countries are still more difficult to achieve. Even within Comecon the data are not homogeneous, although the standing committee on statistics is attempting to work out a standard methodology and system of classification. As far as comparisons with Western countries are concerned, there are two major problems:

Firstly, the structure of production and consumption is different from country to country, either for historical or economic reasons, or because the criteria of classification are not the same. One of the main difficulties is due to the fact that in Soviet practice many services are not included in the productive sector, whereas in capitalist national accounting systems services come under production. Moreover, the definitions of the various industrial branches do not always coincide with each other. Soviet statisticians therefore use 'consistency tables' for converting foreign data into statistics comparable with Soviet figures.

Secondly, statistics on the value of production are not established in the same way. For example, Soviet production statistics are based on the gross production of the different sectors, whereas American statistics refer to value added.

In addition, comparisons of value can only be made after converting national estimates into a common monetary unit. This implies choosing a particular rate of exchange. It is impossible to use the official exchange rates of international commerce for this purpose. The method at present recommended by the Central Board of Statistics for comparing the national income of two countries consists of recalculating the national income of one country in the prices of the other, and vice versa. From this is deduced a conversion rate for the two corresponding currencies.

Chapter 5

PLANNING METHODS

In definitions of the socialist economic system, the terms socialist economy and planned economy are often used synonymously. This definition has already been rejected (*cf.* Introduction). Planning alone cannot define the socialist economy. It does, however, constitute the basic method of economic policy within such a system. The nature of the system itself, characterised by social ownership of the main means of production, determines how it will be applied. Planning methods in the U.S.S.R. will be the main subject of analysis in this chapter.

Socialist planning may be defined as a set of techniques for determining what future economic action is required to achieve predetermined objectives, with a maximum of coherence and efficiency.[1]

The planner is neither politician nor administrator. His function is to formulate, improve and apply techniques which, on the basis of scientifically drafted plans, will make possible a coherent and efficient economic policy. These techniques have become gradually more refined since the beginning of the planning era, and especially since it has been possible to computerise the drafting of plans. However Soviet planning continues in large measure to use routine methods (for example, the forward extension of plans designed for the previous year, with more or less arbitrary coefficients of variation: this is called in the U.S.S.R. 'planning from the level achieved').

Every plan is naturally oriented towards the future. But at any point in time the implementation of present plans and the drafting of future ones are closely connected and mutually interactive. Planning is a continuous process of implementing, controlling and elaborating a multiplicity of plans. That is why the instruments of planning always have two aspects, the planned aspect and the accounting aspect. Thus the enterprise plan indicators, described above (chapter 2), are at one and the same time forecasts of future results, targets to be fulfilled and data showing what the enterprise has actually accomplished. For example, the output sold indicator is calculated before the planning period and imposed as an objective of production. Output actually sold is compared at the end of the planning period to the planned indicator. Balances, the planner's main tool, have similarly both a planning and accounting function.

The plan involves economic intervention and volumes of documentation running to several thousand pages in the case of the detailed macro-economic plan. Its aim is to cover the whole of economic activity. In this, socialist planning is clearly distinguishable from indicative capitalist planning: the plan imposes a specific line of action on a large number of executive bodies (enterprises, administrative departments, etc): it is a mandatory document whose implementation is subject to control and judicial sanction.

The plan has objectives which are determined by the political authorities (Party, organs of State power) with a limited degree of participation by social organisations (trade unions, etc.). The planner has no personal power of decision, although he may, for example, draw the attention of the authorities to the incompatibility of two objectives or to the over-ambitious nature of some of them.

Finally the plan must aim at both coherence and efficiency. These two factors require some comment.

1.   COHERENCE

Coherence must be achieved both spatially and in time. In the case of the first, planning objectives must be formulated at every level in such a way that no contradiction exists between them (general, regional, branch and enterprise objectives). For the second, there must be harmonisation of short-, medium- and long-term plans.

A.   Spatial Coherence

The following will be examined in turn:
Formulation procedures in macro-economic plans (with specific reference to the annual plan, which is the operational or working plan of the economy);
Data adjustment methods.

PLAN FORMULATION

Plan formulation passes through several stages, during which objectives are established and translated into indicators or orders for the various economic agencies. At the end of this process the complete structure of the plan emerges with its sectoral, functional and regional divisions.

The Stages

The planning departments draft the plan according to certain established objectives, by calculating available resources and allocating them to different uses. This is done by a process of adjustment which becomes increasingly precise during the period of formulation.

The various stages succeed each other in the following manner:
An analysis of the initial economic situation;
Determination of the rates and proportions of development;
Detailed formulation of the plan.

The analysis of the initial economic situation expresses the very simple requirement that the plan must be realistic and based on the present state of the economy. This principle may appear to be rather trite, but two things can be said about it:

Firstly its implementation requires a reliable statistical apparatus able to isolate either mistakes or conscious deception by production units and to communicate results quickly to planning departments. In fact Soviet statistics are not absolutely comprehensive (economic sectors such as collectivised agriculture and part of commerce are left out); although they reflect the quantitative aspects of information well enough, the qualitative aspects of productive activity are almost totally ignored; nor are they particularly quick in obtaining results (hence the slowness of plan formulation, especially in details: productive units at the base often receive the plan after the planning period has begun).

Secondly if this principle is interpreted bureaucratically, it can become a factor of mere routine. This defect in Soviet planning is well known. Planners may do no more than take the initial data, not worry about the real-world situation to which they correspond, and endow them with an arbitrary rate of growth: production and productivity will be raised by so many per cent, etc.

The rates and proportions of development are based on the long-term orientation of economic growth as defined in current five-year plans or on even longer-term directives such as those established by the Twenty-second Party Congress in 1961 for the period up to 1980. Such programmes usually define one or more sectors as pilot sectors in the economy. In the early years of Soviet planning, a single pilot sector corresponded to each planning period (electric power in 1928-32, metallurgy in 1933-7). At present the policy is one of priority diversification. Growth sectors are chemicals, electronics and agriculture, and have priority in investment and labour.

Two sorts of proportion in the economy determine the future balance of development: general proportions (between agriculture and industry; between production and transport; in the distribution of resources between consumption and investment); particular proportions (equilibrium between branches, between

188 The Socialist Economies of the Soviet Union and Europe

regions). Often infringed, the principle of proportionality has consequently been the cause of distortions seizing up the whole planning mechanism. For example, in 1961 it was decided to increase investment and production in the chemical industry. However those elements of mechanical engineering related to chemicals were not encouraged to the same extent. The result was a bottle-neck at that point. Another example: a new and modern enterprise was set up in a certain region but it was unable to function since no provision had been made to supply it with raw materials and labour. The nature of the planned system, unlike the market economy, is such that it cannot react automatically to such situations.

Rates are fixed according to two principles: high rates of investment must ensure high growth rates for the economy as a whole; group A (capital goods) must grow more quickly than group B (consumption goods). In fact growth rates tend to be planned rather empirically. It is felt that investment should be maintained at around 25% of national income. In recent years the growth of industrial production has been planned at an annual rate of 7%-8%. At the same time there has been a tendency for the growth rates of groups A and B to draw closer together, with a higher rate for group B since 1968 (1968: an increase of 8.1% in industrial production, comprising 8% for group A and 8.3% for group B; 1969: 7.0%, 6.9% and 7.2% respectively; 1970: 8.5%, 8.2% and 8.9%; 1971: 7.8%, 7.7% and 7.9%). The same trend is observable in the 1971-5 five-year plan (total industrial production: +47% in 1975 in relation to 1970, A: +46.3%, B: +48.6%). However the annual results for 1972 (6.5%, 6.8% and 6.0%), as well as anticipated annual production in the 1973 plan (5.8%, 6.3% and 4.5%), tend to contradict the hypothesis. This is doubtless not so much a sign of a conscious change in policy as the effect of poor agricultural production in 1972, which influenced progress in both food and light industries.

The end of this second stage makes possible an overall outline of the plan, known as the control figures.

The third stage involves the detailed formulation of the plan. Each ministry and administrative department communicates directives to the enterprises within its jurisdiction, these directives having been established on the basis of the control figures. The enterprises then present their own draft plans, accompanied by their demands for equipment, finance and labour. At that point the ministry establishes the plan for its branch, which is transmitted to the Gosplan departments. Having received all the drafts, Gosplan can proceed to establish the overall economic plan. During its initial analysis of the drafts it has received, Gosplan makes sure that they have made the fullest possible regional use of resources, checks that resources correspond to requirements, and studies the sectoral structure of production and any possibilities of specialisation. In establishing the final overall plan, the essential task of Gosplan is to ensure that it forms a coherent whole and that federal interests are put before the particular interest of branch or region.

The draft plan is submitted to the Council of Ministers of the U.S.S.R. and then approved by the Supreme Soviet. It is then transmitted once more to the ministries, who finalise their own plans and establish a final plan for each enterprise.

The Indicators

The indicators are a quantitative statement of the targets to be fulfilled during the planning period. At the end of the period, actual results are compared with the planned indicators: the indicator is therefore both a means of planning and of control. The number of indicators was reduced as a result of the economic reform (chapter 2). At the level of the macro-economic plan they can be grouped under the following heads:

Compulsory and auxiliary indicators: In a well-planned system there should be few compulsory indicators at the centre. At the same time the administrative agencies should be in a position of relative freedom in allocating tasks to the enterprises under their control. In fact indicators in the macro-economic plan are still very numerous, although their number diminished after 1958, and especially after 1965. They are essentially production indicators. In industry the number of goods whose production is established in the macro-economic plan fell from 1,250 in 1966 to 615 in 1968. It should be observed that planned distribution, on the other hand, covers a much larger volume of products (about 2000 items in 1968).

Among auxiliary indicators not included in the overall plan, and which the ministries may draw up themselves, are indicators of productive capacity and raw material use, etc.

Quantitative and qualitative indicators: The first are the most numerous. They may be sub-divided into:

(a)   volume indicators (quantity of production, level of investment);

(b)   distribution indicators (figures relating to the labour force, the number and dimensions of enterprises).

The so-called qualitative indicators are either economic (measuring the degree of efficiency in the use of financial resources and labour) or technical (quantity of steel used up in the manufacture of a machine, daily coal output per working face); the latter are usually planned within a sectoral framework.

Indicators in kind (physical quantities) and in value: For a long time the most important value indicator in Soviet planning has been gross production. The 1965 economic reform replaced it by the output sold indicator for planning at enterprise level (chapter 2). However, for three years after that there was no co-ordination between micro-economic planning (for enterprises transferred to the reformed system) and macro-economic planning, where the gross production indicator continued to be applied. Since 1968 the output sold indicator has been employed at every level, based on both current and constant prices (1 July 1967).

Structure of the Plan

The macro-economic plan covers every aspect of economic activity (regional, sectoral, functional).

Soviet planning has always stressed the sectoral aspect, even when economic administration was organised according to the territorial principle. From the beginning, particular pilot sectors have been given priority in the allocation of resources. From the point of view of coherence, sectoral planning has long been badly co-ordinated. Until the publication at the end of 1968 of *New Instructions in Methodology for the Formulation of State Plans,* there existed a number of different classifications of industrial sectors and branches. There were 54 divisions for the plan of production, 150 for the investment plan, and 240 for statistical purposes. The new instructions require a single system of classification into 17 sectors and 260 branches.

In theory the co-ordination of regional and sectoral planning requires two organically linked divisions within the macro-economic plan. One would deal with the development of economic branches, and the other with the co-ordination of those branches within a given territory. In practice things are different.

Regional planning is one of the functions of the Gosplan system, whose organisation runs parallel to that of the territorial administration. Each of the fifteen Union republics has a republican Gosplan, which is subordinate to both the federal Gosplan and the Council of Ministers of the republic in question. Its primary allegiance, however, is to the federal Gosplan. Within the Union republics there is a planning board for each of the 20 autonomous republics, the 113 regions or territories, and the 2,976 districts. These boards, like the republican Gosplans, tend to refer to the planning authority immediately above them rather than to the local executive. In addition, for the sole purpose of planning, the U.S.S.R. is divided into eighteen large economic regions which have no administrative existence as such.[2] These regions are autonomous entities and operate on the principle of diversification. Each region has a planning board, composed of from five to ten people, and has the function of defining the general direction of regional policy.

In theory, the real regional plan is drafted at Union republic level. It should cover not only problems of sectoral development within the competence of the republics, but also those related to sectors controlled by the federal departments. The republican Gosplans should therefore examine the draft plans devised by federal ministries for their own enterprises operating within the Union republic, and should subsequently propose any necessary amendments. In most cases these drafts are not even sent. At the same time, the republican authorities should be able to scrutinise draft plans for the whole of the republic before they are transmitted to the federal Gosplan. Again these authorities are often short-circuited. Territorial planning at lower levels is practically non-existent. It is limited to questions of purely local interest (industries using local raw materials, development of commerce and services, housing construction, etc.).

It is evident that the annual operational plan is not structured to include specific regional divisions. Each territorial unit certainly has a plan, but it is nothing more than the aggregate of sectoral and functional plans applying to that particular zone. At the same time, non-directive schemes of probable long-term development in the future are drawn up: a general project of industrial localisation, projects for the development of new regions and industrial complexes. These are purely indicative forecasts.

From the functional viewpoint, the plan structure has the following divisions:

The industrial and agricultural production plan. This is central to the macro-economic plan.

The productive and non-productive investment plan. This covers new construction, of both infrastructure and productive units; the expansion of existing capacity; the financial sources of investment; the supply of raw materials and equipment to projects of great importance. The 1968 instructions on methodology introduced a rubric which, in the light of economic reform, assumes considerable importance. It was seen in chapter 2 that enterprises obtained much greater scope in accumulating incentive funds for the financing of social and productive investment. However they found it extremely difficult to put these funds to effective use. This was because the corresponding material resources had not been catered for in the general plan of investment and were therefore unobtainable. As from 1970 the investment plan was to include an estimate of material resources corresponding to the decentralised investments of enterprise. Enterprises will nevertheless remain free to determine these investments as before. Also part of the investment plan, but itemised as specific sections, are technical research and research department activities, and the special plan for geological work as the basis of development in the extractive industries.

Labour and employment plan. This shows the regional and sectoral distribution of labour, productivity objectives, planned growth of wages, and the plan for the general and vocational training of workers.

Plan of material and technical supply; this covers raw materials and equipment earmarked for industry.

Plan for domestic trade and services.

Plan for the development of the non-productive sector (national education, public health, culture).

Standard-of-living plan; until 1968 this division of the plan had a residual character. The different items of private and collective consumption could be deduced from the other plans (production of consumption goods, wages, housing construction, expansion of the non-productive sector, etc.). The 1968 methodological instructions outline the methods for formulating synthetic standard-of-living indices: real incomes by social group, the structure of consumption, standard budgets by population group, living-wage budgets, etc.

Finally, there are a certain number of plans, co-ordinated with the macro-economic plan, but formulated separately, which fall into the category of functional plans. They are the foreign trade plan, the financial plan and budget, the financial and credit plan of the State Bank, and the planning of price changes.

The vast number of data in the macro-economic plan are adjusted by a method which is specific to Soviet planning and which is known as the balance method.

PLANNING ADJUSTMENTS: THE BALANCE METHOD

On the one hand, a balance presents in table form the resources to be mobilised for implementing the plan, and on the other needs or uses implied in the fulfilment of planning objectives. The two sides of the balance are necessarily in equilibrium.

The balance system traditionally employed in planning has been recognised as inadequate for some years, in so far as it gives insufficient attention to inter-branch relationships. Since 1960 there has been considerable research into the possible formulation of a production and distribution inter-branch balance revealing the relationship of the various sectors with each other. The classical and inter-branch balances will be studied in turn.

The Classical Balances

In the practice of planning, three groups of balances are used:

1. Material balances; these are the most numerous and are established for the main branches of industrial and agricultural production. Examples are the fuel-energy balance or the balance for metals. All balances underline the objectives of production (by zone and enterprise group) and the destination of the products. The balances are generally expressed in kind (in physical units or conventional physical units: for example, in the fuel balance fuels other than coal are converted into coal equivalents).

(Simplified) scheme of balances:

Resources	Uses
1. Initial stocks	1. Productive consumption
2. Production	2. Investment
3. Imports	3. Transaction funds
4. Other	4. Exports
	5. Other (including reserves)
	6. End-of-period stocks
Total	Total

They formerly included several thousand denominations (there were 18,000 material balances in 1963). Economic reform led to a reduction in their number, so that at present there are about 2000.

2. Labour balances show the sectoral distribution of the labour force and the

allocation of workers just entering the production process.

3. The synthetic balances are expressed in monetary units and are intended to ensure equilibrium between income and expenditure in the economy, and between the objectives of production, construction and services on the one hand, and their financing on the other. Within the synthetic balance category, we have the production and distribution of the gross social product balance. This is a value synthesis of all the material balances (see table 5.1). It shows the production and distribution of the total product by material composition (capital goods, consumer goods) and by sector (industry, agriculture, transport, etc.). The national income balance also comes in this category. The national income is equal to the gross social product after deducting the value of capital goods used up in the production period: raw materials, depreciation. The balance presents the national income in the form of three equivalent aggregates: net product, the sum of final incomes, the sum of accumulation and consump-

TABLE 5.1 [3]

SCHEME OF THE GROSS SOCIAL PRODUCT BALANCE

	Production* (wholesale prices)	Increase in the value of production added by commerce and transport	Production (final prices)	Imports	Total resources	Productive consumption*	Non-productive consumption including personal, social	Accumulation	Losses	Exports	Total uses
Gross social product											
1. by material composition:											
(a) capital goods (by type)											
(b) consumer goods (by type)											
2. by branches: industry agriculture forestry construction communications other											

* by branch and sector (state, co-operative, private)

TABLE 5.2 [4]

SCHEME OF THE NATIONAL INCOME BALANCE

Balance divisions	State enterprises	Kolkhoz farms and co-operatives	Kolkhozy	Private farms of citizens	Total productive sector	Non-productive sector	Population	Workers and employees	Total
I. PRODUCTION (product perspective)									
1. Gross social product									
2. Depreciation									
3. National income (net national product)=(1)−(2)									
II. DISTRIBUTION (income perspective)									
4. Primary income of workers in the productive sector of which: wages and salaries other income									
5. Primary income of enterprises									
6. Transferred by enterprises (—), received by the population as primary income (+)									
7. Transferred by enterprises (—), received by the population as social consumption (+)									
8. Received by enterprises and the population (+), transferred from the non-productive sector from social funds (−)									
9. Balance from the creation and utilisation of social funds and service payments									
10. Final incomes									
III. UTILISATION (expenditure perspective)									
11. Accumulation (productive)									
12. Accumulation (non-productive)									
13. Increase in reserves									
14. Total accumulation and reserves									
15. Consumption									
16. Total utilisation									

tion (*cf.* table 5.2). Still within the category of synthetic balances is an array of financial balances, including the State budget, the balance of income and expenditure for the population as a whole, the plan of foreign financial operations or the balance of payments, the financial and credit plans of the State Bank.

These balances are established at federal level. Similar balances are of course also formulated by republics and regions. In addition, indicative inter-sectoral balances are worked out for each branch. Finally the enterprises themselves formulate balances, including enterprise income and expenditure.

The series of balances described above are crowned by the total balance for the economy, known as the general synthetic balance (see table 5.3). It provides information on all aspects of the employment of human and material resources in the planned programme of production, consumption and accumulation. It is calculated in value terms (except for manpower). The form of the table corresponds to the structure of the economy: *A* units of production (according to legal forms of organisation: state units, co-operatives, auxiliary smallholdings of peasants, workers and craftsmen; also by sector); *B* non-productive sector; *C* population, including household consumption.

The columns show the material and human resources available at the beginning and end of the year and the main elements relating to economic growth during the planning period. Thus columns 1 and 24 give the figures for manpower and its distribution between economic branches. Column 2 gives the time worked in the year for the productive sector. On the basis of columns 2 and 5 (gross production) it is possible to calculate daily production per worker in each branch. Columns 3 and 4, 22 and 23, give the material resources of the economy at the beginning and end of the year.

Columns 5-10 and 12-16 provide information on the production and circulation of the social product. There is only one figure for column 11: the foreign trade balance. Columns 17-21 are an indicator of the final use made of the product: replacement of means of production, consumption, investment and losses.

The balance is based essentially on the production side of economic life. From the viewpoint of product allocation, the non-productive sector and households are covered by column 15 (sales), column 19 (consumption) and column 20 (investment for expansion in the sector; an attempt is made to isolate the investment by individuals in consumer durables).

Within the scheme as a whole, the material balances are the most important, reflecting a planning system for long dominated by the priority given to a restricted number of basic sectors. The hierarchy of balances therefore attaches primary importance to the objectives and resources of priority sectors. If equilibrium cannot be achieved in a given sector, that is to say if available resources prove unequal to the task of reaching the planned target, the planner will first check technological coefficients to make sure that the use of existing resources cannot be improved. His next step will be either to reduce the final

TABLE 5.3[5]   SCHEME OF THE SY...

	Labour force		Material resources at beginning of year		Production and primary distribution of social product				
					total production	Distribution of product			
							National income		
	figure at beginning of year	average time worked in the year	fixed capital	working capital	total production	value of capital goods used	workers' incomes	net product	total 7 + 8
A. Units of production:	1	2	3	4	5	6	7	8	9
1. By form of property:									
(a) State									
(b) Co-operatives, of which *Kolkhozy*									
(c) Private (peasants)									
(d) Private (workers and employees)									
(e) Craftsmen									
Total									
2. By branch:									
(a) Industry									
(b) Agriculture									
(c) Forestry									
(d) Construction									
(e) Transport									
(f) Commerce and supplies									
B. Non-productive sector:									
1. Social and cultural administration									
2. Scientific research establishments									
3. Public administration and defence									
Total									
C. Population, total:									
1. Workers									
2. Peasants									
Imports from various sources									
Total									

Circulation of the social product				balance of redistribution	Final use of the product					Material resources at year-end		number of workers at year-end
stock variation	non-marketed part of product	products for sale	products sold		total	of which				fixed capital	stocks and reserves	
						replacement	consumption	investment	losses			
12	13	14	15	16	17	18	19	20	21	22	23	24

TABLE 5.4   SYSTEM OF BALANCES USED IN PLANNING

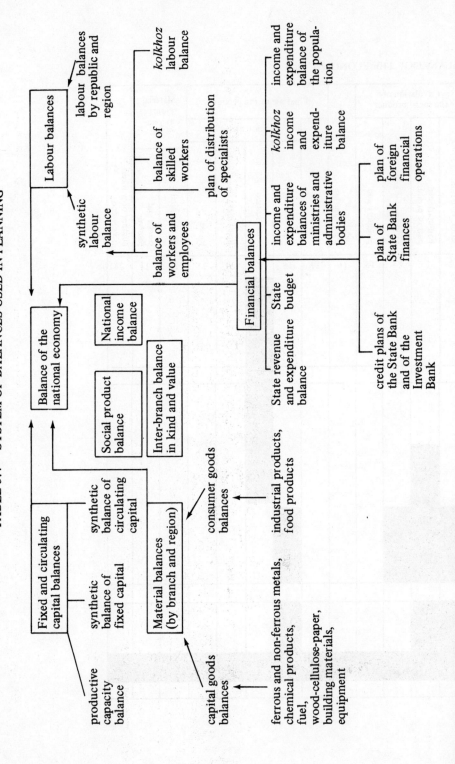

demand for the product if it is not a priority, or else to increase resource allocations to the branch in question. The second option would certainly affect balances lower down the hierarchy of priorities. This sort of adjustment was made easier by the fact that priority sectors were usually situated at an early point in the production process (heavy industry).

This method, which does not require a very complicated administration for making the necessary calculations, suffers from the great disadvantage of leaving out inter-sectoral movements. Apart from approximations, no account is taken of the effects which modifications to a production programme in one sector may have on other sectors. Consequently, from 1958, work already undertaken in the U.S.S.R. in the 1920s on the formulation of an inter-branch balance of production and distribution was taken up again and developed further.

The Inter-Branch Balance

This is a sort of input-output table showing what each productive branch supplies to and receives from the rest of the economy. Methodologically it is extremely important: for general planning; as a point of departure for the application of mathematics to planning; as an instrument of price formation.

Let us examine the problems raised in the formulation of the inter-branch balance and the use that can be made of it.

The formulation of the first inter-branch balance, for 1959, was inspired by research undertaken in the U.S.S.R. even before planning began and which resulted in an inter-sectoral economic balance for 1923–4.[6] The balance was drafted in accounting form by the departments of the Central Statistical Board.

The 1959 balance was structured in the following way:
1. In kind for the 157 most important industrial products (there have never been more than 600 products in this category, since to retain some idea of inter-sectoral flows the balance must remain within manageable proportions).
2. In value; this is the category we shall concentrate on.

The inter-branch balance by value was based on dividing the whole into 83 sectors: 73 for industry, 2 for agriculture, and 1 for each of the following sectors: construction, forestry, transport, post and communications, commerce, agricultural supplies, material and technical supplies, other.

The balance is a double-entry table. If the balance is read by line, horizontally, one sees the distribution of production for the sector in question between internal consumption, supplies to other sectors, accumulation and consumption. The costs of production in each sector are in the vertical columns; purchases from other sectors, reserves, wages paid, taxes, net profit.

The balance is divided into four quadrants.

The first quadrant contains the flow of means of production between the sectors of material production. The second quadrant shows the distribution of national income between consumption (personal and public) and investment (increase in fixed productive capital, stocks and circulating capital). The third

TABLE 5.5
SCHEME OF THE INTER-BRANCH BALANCE OF THE PRODUCTION
AND DISTRIBUTION OF THE SOCIAL PRODUCT FOR 1959,
IN VALUE

Branches of production	Depreciation (production expenditure) 1, 2, 8, 15, n, total, etc.	Replacement of obsolete equipment and large scale repairs	National income					Export—Import balance
			Accumulation		Consumption			
			Increase fixed capital	Increase circulating capital	Private	Public (health, education, etc.)		
			productive	non-productive				
Industry								
1 Ferrous minerals								
2 Ferrous metals								
3 Carbo-chemicals								
....								
8 Coal								
....								
15 Electric and thermal power								
....								
....								
etc.								
73 Other								
Total for industry	QUADRANT I		QUADRANT II					
74 Construction								
75 Agriculture								
76 Stockbreeding								
etc.								
83 Other sectors								
Total material costs of production								
Reserve fund								
Wages and pay Profits Turnover tax Other elements in net income	QUADRANT III		QUADRANT IV					
TOTAL								

quadrant gives the structure of the national income (industrial and agricultural wages, profit of State enterprises, net income of *kolkhozy* and co-operatives, interest, etc.). The fourth quadrant gives an indication of the redistribution of income: wages distributed in the non-productive sectors, etc.

This particular balance raised numerous methodological problems. Significant among these were:

The definition of net branch activity; this problem arose because in any given sector, metallurgy for example, not all production is comprised of metallurgical products. It will also contain ancillary products going to other sectors. When primary information is collected from enterprises it is therefore necessary to apportion their production, if it is heterogeneous, between the different sectors involved.

Reserves; the 1959 balance placed reserves in the third quadrant and large-scale repairs and replacement of obsolete equipment in the second quadrant. This decision was the result of practical difficulties in the calculation of reserves by sector, but it is not logical since depreciation reserves are part of material costs of production and should be situated in the first quadrant.[7]

Valuation of production; for 1959 current prices for that year were used. For balances drawn up subsequently there was the problem of comparability with 1959. It was found necessary to establish two versions of the balance, one in 1959 prices and the other in current prices. The 1967 price reform aggravated these difficulties. Another problem of valuation concerns the choice between valuation at final consumer prices or at production prices. For convenience, since it is a convention of Soviet national accounting (*cf.* note to table 5.2), the first solution was adopted. Methodologically this choice was justified for the 1959 balance which was an accounting balance (*a posteriori*); for planned balances, production prices would be preferable (excluding turn-over tax), although until now final consumer prices have always been used even in these cases.

The 1959 accounting balance was followed by several estimated balances drafted by Gosplan. For 1962 an experimental balance in kind and value was formulated on the basis of plan data for the same year. For 1963 a balance in kind was drawn up with two variants (one for 372 and the other for 435 products). Finally Gosplan prepared an estimated balance for 1970 with two variants, one in value (125 branches) and the other in kind (584 branches).

The methodology of estimated balances is not yet firmly established, and so far they constitute auxiliary tools of verification rather than methods of plan adjustment.

Research into the calculation of accounting balances is much more advanced, since statistical data are more reliable. Final adjustments to the 1966 inter-branch balance were made in 1968, the second balance after 1959. It was formulated in both value (for 110 branches) and kind (for 237 branches). It was also sub-divided by Union republic. A comparison of the two balances, which are based on the same methodology, makes it possible to analyse the development of the structure of the social product, of input-output coefficients, etc.

All these balances are established for the whole of the Soviet Union. A tentative regional accounting balance, in value, was made for 1961 for the Baltic economic region, covering the three Baltic republics. An attempt was also made to translate the financial–technical–industrial plan into a planned value balance. This work remains at the experimental stage.

The balances, whether accounting or planned, are static. In other words, they include investment as an autonomous factor independent of production. That is why there has been a switch towards the construction of dynamic balances in which investment is a function of the growth of production during the period of the plan. In the models now being formulated (notably the 1971–80 balance for 600 products) marginal coefficients of investment are used expressing the volume of investment necessary for a given increase in unit capacity.

The balance may be used in several ways. The first use of the inter-branch balance is to define inter-sectoral flows. If 'supply' branches are called i (lines in the balance) and 'consumer' branches j (columns), a series of co-efficients of type a_{ij} (or input–output coefficient) can be established. This will show the quantity of product i expended for one unit-product j. For example, if the total supply of conventional fuel for power production is 117.5 million tons and if power production is 250 milliard kwh, the coefficient of conventional fuel expenditure in power production will be $117.5 : 250 = 0.47$ or 470 kg for 1000 kwh.

From these coefficients of direct expenditure it is possible to establish coefficients of indirect expenditure, still on the basis of the balance. For example, the indirect expenditure of coal in car production can be calculated from the amount of coal necessary in the production of metal used in manufacturing cars. By going back the whole length of the manufacturing process, it would be possible to establish for each product the direct and indirect expenditure of intermediate goods.

The situation may be represented diagrammatically in the following way:

	consumer sectors				
supply sectors	1	2	...n	final demand (consumption + investment)	total production
1	x_{11}	x_{12}	x_{1n}	Y_1	X_1
2	x_{21}	x_{22}	x_{2n}	Y_2	X_2
n	x_{n1}	x_{n2}	x_{nn}	Y_n	X_n
wages (v)					
+ net income (m)	D_1	D_2	D_n		
Total production	X_1	X_2	X_n		

From the table of intermediate consumption (upper left) one can deduce the coefficients of direct expenditure. The 'exports' of each branch (its sales to other sectors) can be seen on the horizontal lines and the 'imports' (purchases from other sectors) in the vertical columns. The intersection of line and column gives the consumption by one branch, j, of the production of another branch, i (in the form of a value x_{ij}). Since the total production of the branch is known (X_j) it is possible to calculate the coefficient aij expressing the quantity of i expended to obtain one unit of j: $a_{ij} = \dfrac{x_{ij}}{X_j}$.

Total costs can now be looked at, including indirect expenditure. This particular calculation is of great interest from both the accounting (analysis of inter-sectoral flows in a given period) and planning point of view. It makes it possible to calculate the total consumption of intermediate goods from different branches in the production of a given branch. The planner must be aware of the implications of establishing a particular production figure for a given product, since total production (X_i) will have to satisfy the requirements of all other branches $(\sum_j a_{ij} X_j)$ and final demand (Y_i) itself. The planner will also have to take account of the fact that this particular branch of production will use specific quantities of product from other sectors, either directly or indirectly.

There are two ways of calculating total expenditure: by successive approximation, calculating direct expenditure to the 1st degree (on the basis of coefficients a_{ij}) then to the 2nd degree, etc. (in practice this is done electronically); or by using matrix methods of calculation. Referring to the table above, we have:

$$X_i = \sum_{j=1}^{n} a_{ij} X_j + Y_i.$$

If it is assumed that Y_i is known (final demand), X_i may be determined (total production) taking account of total intermediate consumption of product i. But for that it is necessary to work out the coefficients of total expenditure of type A_{ij}. In matrix calculation this problem is solved by inverting the matrix of the direct coefficients a_{ij}[8].

The calculation of input–output coefficients can be extremely useful in general planning. They make possible a more coherent plan. At the same time a comparison of coefficients over time, and a comparison between average coefficients taken from the balance and the employment norms of particular capital goods provide information on the efficiency of production.

A recent development has been the attempt to convert all direct and indirect expenditure in the production of a particular commodity into total labour expenditure. This is being done from the inter-branch balance of labour expenditure (based in turn on the inter-branch balance of production and distribution).

The inter-branch balance of labour expenditure is based on the principle that the value of the social product in a given period is composed of the

TABLE 5.6

SCHEME OF THE INTER-BRANCH BALANCE OF LABOUR EXPENDITURE (IN ANNUAL WORKERS)

Types of expenditure \ Consumption of labour	Ferrous metal minerals and non-mineral raw materials for iron and steel	Ferrous metals	Carbo-chemical products	etc.	Total productive consumption	Non-productive consumption — Personal	Non-productive consumption — Social (by branch)	Accumulation — In fixed capital	Accumulation — In circulating capital	Exports and other expenditure	Total
A. Expenditure of materialised labour											
1. Ferrous metal minerals and non-mineral raw materials for iron and steel	QUADRANT I					QUADRANT II					
2. Ferrous metals											
3. Carbo-chemical products											
....											
Total productive material expenditure											
Depreciation											
Total material expenditure (including depreciation)											
B. Expenditure of living labour											
1. for the creation of the wages replacement fund (a) of workers and employees (b) of kolkhoz workers	QUADRANT III					QUADRANT IV					
2. For the production of the net additional product, in: (a) state and co-operative enterprises (excluding kolkhozy)											

aggregate expenditure of living labour and of labour incorporated in the means of production.

Like the production and distribution balance, the first labour expenditure balance (for 1959) isolates eighty-three branches. The expenditure of labour is expressed in terms of the average annual employment figure. The balance takes the form of a double-entry table. The same branches appear horizontally and vertically in quadrant 1, considered as suppliers (horizontally) and consumers (vertically). The labour expenditure of each branch is divided among the others in proportion to the distribution of the product of the branch in question among them. For example, assuming that 1,250,000 workers are occupied in coal-mining, this figure is divided among productive and non-productive sectors in the same proportions as their consumption of coal.

The balance is divided into four quadrants (*cf.* table 5.6). The first reflects production relations between branches of production according to labour expended in the products consumed by these branches. The second shows the proportion of labour expenditure going to the formation of the product allocated to the non-productive sphere, to accumulation, and to other uses. The third indicates the expenditure of labour in material production, and the fourth in the non-productive sphere.

An examination of each horizontal line of the balance shows the distribution of the direct expenditure of living labour of each branch among all productive and non-productive branches. A consideration of the vertical columns reveals this same expenditure of labour in terms of past labour incorporated in the products used by the branches of material production as capital goods and by the non-productive sphere as consumer goods. The total of each column of the branches of material production therefore shows the sum of production costs for the manufacture of each product (expenditure on past labour in the form of means of production supplied to a particular branch by the others [quadrant I], and expenditure on living labour [quadrant III]).[9] But at this stage expenditure is still direct (for example, labour expended on the production of metal used in making machines only includes the labour used in the metallurgical industry, but not that used up in mining).

The first stage in the formulation of the inter-branch balance of labour expenditure, therefore, provides a table where the columns express the proportions of living and past labour used in the production of articles in each branch, and where the lines reveal the direct expenditure of the living labour of each branch distributed among the other branches as a function of the allocation of its products among them.

A more detailed formulation of the balance makes it possible to obtain the total expenditure of labour on each product (that is to say, all the labour accumulated in the manufacture of the product from the extraction of the raw material onwards). This can only be calculated electronically.

In ascending order of complexity it is therefore possible to establish: firstly, the direct expenditure of living labour in obtaining each product; secondly, synthetic labour expenditure (sum of living labour expenditure in the branch under consideration) and direct expenditure of materialised labour (raw materials and depreciation); thirdly, total labour expenditure, including the whole of direct and indirect costs in the production of the commodity in question.

This conversion of production costs into labour is methodologically very important, since it makes possible the planning of prices based on labour-value without ignoring material costs of production (*cf.* chapter 6). That is why, parallel with price reform, Gosplan researchers have attempted to evaluate different commodities in terms of labour. However, the results have not been used directly in establishing new prices.

On examining the utilisation of inter-branch balances one is struck by the contrast between the possibilities of inter-sectoral analysis in a planned economy, where it can be exploited much more profitably than in a market system, and the feebleness of its actual application. One Soviet writer has remarked that the inter-branch balance of production and distribution played no part in establishing annual and long-term plans. There are several reasons for that. In the first place, the balance is based too much on aggregates, and although successive versions include a growing number of branches the balance is still far from the detailed break-down of the classic material balances. Secondly, since it is founded on the principle of net branches, it cannot be linked up with specific administrative departments. Finally, aggregates such as the final product, accumulation and consumption, depreciation, and the balance of foreign trade are included in the model of the planned balance either as variants chosen arbitrarily or on the basis of the provisional calculations of planning departments, whereas data concerning production are co-ordinated with the corresponding production plan.

Techniques of inter-branch analysis have not therefore substantially modified traditional methods of planning based on the addition of branch plans, more or less crudely co-ordinated by the material balances. The formulation of inter-sectoral plans starting from final demand is still very far away.

Up to this point we have examined only problems raised by coherence in the drafting of the annual macro-economic plan. It is now relevant to turn to the problem of coherence over time.

Coherence over Time

At any given moment the Soviet economy is subject to several plans of different duration. In any particular year (let us take 1970), the U.S.S.R. will have four plans:

1.   The general perspective 1961–80, which is an objective, an horizon rather than a real plan, indicating the general programme of Party policy. This plan was submitted to the Twenty-second Party Congress in 1961. Its main features

are as follows: to develop production from 1961 to 1970 so as to reach the economic level of the United States in 1970, particularly through accelerating expansion in pilot branches with a high level of technical progress such as chemicals, mechanical engineering and power; to ensure a general abundance of consumer goods between 1971 and 1980. This general perspective has certain features akin to planning: there is a breakdown by republic, region and branch.

2. The perspective plan. Apart from the 1959-65 plan, the U.S.S.R. has known only five-year plans since the beginning of imperative planning in 1928. Even the 1959–65 plan was in fact an extended five-year plan, since a 1964–5 plan was drafted at the end of 1963 to conclude a seven-year period. What happened was that the Soviet authorities realised in 1963 that the objectives of the seven-year period would not be achieved with any degree of precision (some would be exceeded and some remain unfulfilled). It was therefore found necessary to correct all the indicators for 1964–5. The five-year plan is prepared two years before the beginning of the five-year period itself. The 1971–5 plan was thus studied from the end of 1968. It fixes the objectives to be achieved by the end of the planning period, as well as those for the intervening years, for the whole of the U.S.S.R., for the regions and for the different branches. Before being finalised, the perspective plan is first drafted as a series of directives, with a general orientation, just like the annual plan. Unlike the annual plan it is not compulsory for production units. However since 1965 enterprises have been required to prepare their own indicative five-year plan into which the annual plans can be inserted.

3. The continuous five-year plan is a sort of sliding plan, and has been in operation since 1963. The Soviet authorities decided that perspective planning needed more continuity. The innovation was intended to avoid a situation where the data of the perspective plan are realistic enough at the beginning of the five-year plan, but where there is a considerable divergence between real data and five-year plan objectives during the final year of the period. Consequently a decree of 11 January 1963 on better economic planning insisted on the principle of continuity. It was decided that without drafting a five-year plan each year the main objectives for the end of the fifth year would be calculated (for example, in 1969 for 1973). This would make possible the conclusion of contracts for periods in excess of one year and the anticipation of successive stages in investment projects.

4. The annual plan is the operational economic plan. This plan is formulated annually for all indicators on the basis of the five-year plan. To ensure continuity in planning, the annual plan is not newly formulated each year but constitutes a correction or adjustment of the five-year planning indicators for the year in question. Similarly the general lines of the plan for the following year are defined at the same time as the annual plan, though more sketchily. Thus at the end of 1968 the 1969 operational plan and the 1970 indicative plan were both formulated at the same time; a further innovation introduced

by the decree of 1963.

Of all these plans, it is the long-term general perspective which is the most frequently sacrificed. The authorities have a certain concealed mistrust of it. In the U.S.S.R. only two plans of this type have ever been officially approved: the Goelro electrification plan of Russia and the 1961–80 perspective. Other socialist countries, particularly Czechoslovakia and the G.D.R., are much more advanced in the formulation of long-term plans. In the U.S.S.R. the authorities have confined themselves to defining hypotheses of development based on demographic forecasts, estimates of available natural resources, the extrapolation of growth rates of production, and the evaluation of needs. To these are added hypotheses of structural change (in production and consumption). They have hardly begun to establish long-term projection models: models of criteria and objectives making possible the definition of the strategy and methods of growth; models related to alternative growth patterns with a view to optimum efficiency (macro-economic and sector models, etc.).

2. EFFICIENCY

This is the key planning problem which is always raised in any judgement on the value of the socialist economic system. Is it possible in such a system to allocate existing resources in such a way as to ensure the maximum development of production and the optimum satisfaction of needs, in the absence of a market mechanism such as regulates the 'liberal' economy?

This problem will come up again in connection with price formation. The existence of a rational price system is in fact a necessary condition of rationality in the choices made by planners.

Criteria of efficiency are used openly in the present planning of investment to determine which choice of variants should be employed to achieve predetermined planning objectives. Some economists of the mathematical school would like to go further and construct optimal functional models of the economy. However this research is still highly theoretical and for practical and political reasons has no influence on planning.

Criteria of Efficiency in Investment

For a long time Soviet planning dispensed with any criteria of investment efficiency. This bias reflected official dogmatism and was viable within the context of growth at any cost, centred on the development of a few priority sectors into which the limited resources available for investment were poured. But even at that time the engineers and technical experts responsible for implementing projects (especially in power and transport) often calculated the comparative economic effects of different operations, unofficially of course.

With economic diversification and a multiplication of investment alternatives, it became necessary to determine rationally and systematically the possible effects of any given expansion in productive capacity.

Such calculations were officially reintroduced from 1954, at a very modest level, with the establishment of medium-term credit (three years maximum) which could be granted by the State Bank to industrial enterprises wishing to make investments on a small scale (modernisation, technical improvements, etc. The Bank found itself in the position of having to operate a selective credit policy according to economic criteria. It granted preferential credit to projects permitting the earliest repayment of the principal advanced. To this end it employed the criterion of the pay-off period, well-known to capitalist entrepreneurs, which will be discussed later.

A few years later, in 1958, a debate developed among economists on the efficiency of investment, which ran parallel to the discussion on prices and which was just as important. As a result of these discussions several institutes of the Academy of Sciences formulated a standard method for determining investment efficiency. A first version, in 1960, was redrafted several times and given greater precision. At present a standard method introduced in September 1969 is used and is mandatory on all planning departments. Before looking at the criteria which have to be applied, they must be put in the context of general investment policy.

Problems of Principle

At present investment policy is dominated by three principles:
  The plan establishes the total sum and the general orientation of investment;
  Planning must take account of the efficiency of capital expenditure;
  The efficiency criteria used for this purpose only apply to a part of invest-
    ment planning.
Let us examine these principles.

THE PLAN MUST ESTABLISH THE TOTAL SUM AND GENERAL ORIENTATION OF INVESTMENT

We saw in chapter 2 that the reform of Soviet enterprise, although conferring greater flexibility on management, gave it no more freedom than before in the field of investment. An investment indicator is imposed on the enterprise, deriving from the centralised plan of investment drafted at macro-economic level. The question is whether in the near future there will perhaps be some decentralisation of investment decisions in favour of the individual enterprise. Within the framework of a planned socialist economy such a development is hardly possible, for two reasons.

The first is that in this system private property in the means of production no longer exists. The means of production are State property and are managed by autonomous units of production. These cannot take the initiative in creating new productive units in other regions, nor can they promote the development of new branches of production. The very basis of socialism (socialist, State property in the means of production) inevitably means that a central authority must determine the sectoral and regional orientation of investment.

Secondly, it might be thought that existing enterprises, since they cannot establish new units, might be freer to take decisions on their own expansion beyond the mere modernisation of workshops or the introduction of new techniques. An enterprise director, for example, might wish to double his productive capacity. He would have to be in a position to evaluate the general effect of his investment and to ensure the existence of outlets for the additional production of his enterprise. Unable to do this, he could only take decisions on the basis of the profitability of the project for his own individual firm, assuming a given price for its product and that any additional product would be sold at that price. But it is clear that if all enterprises had this freedom, the advantage of the socialist system would be discarded. This advantage, assuming particular investment priorities, is the advantage of planned rather than anarchic growth. At the same time, socialism implies a number of social aims which can only be achieved through centralised planning (balanced regional development, investment to improve the material and cultural standards of the population, etc.).

That is why planned and centralised investment decisions are necessary. Four other points need to be made in this connection:

1.   Centralised planning should not be confused with centralised financing. The centralisation of investment decisions can be accompanied by decentralised sources of finance (the substitution for budgetary investment grants of long-term credit or enterprise profit). That in no way means greater autonomy for enterprises, which are still required to adhere to the investment indicator imposed in the plan. It merely simplifies the financial system.

2.   Centralised investment planning is not contrary to greater flexibility in the regulation of enterprise supplies. On the contrary, the greater the precision of the investment plan the greater the potential freedom of enterprises in choosing their suppliers (machinery, building materials, etc.). There can be no serious economic dislocation if the investment plan has paid close attention to available resources and if it has established by region, branch and enterprise the corresponding limits of investment. The distributive mechanism would certainly be much simplified.

3.   The plan may leave the enterprise a certain margin of freedom in matters of small-scale investment which have little effect on total productive capacity

but which may improve enterprise organisation and productivity. ¬
be in the field of limited but effective internal financing (given greate
in the supply situation).

4. The reorganisation envisaged in the economic reform, involving the creation of associations of production bringing together enterprises in the same branch (*cf*. chapter 2), should not change the general data of the problem. The association would be responsible for the implementation of the investment plan by its constituent enterprises. It would be in a position to find an operational solution to the corresponding problems of finance and suppliers.

INVESTMENT EFFICIENCY CRITERIA MUST BE USED IN PLANNING

Doctrinal objections to the use of such criteria have now largely disappeared. Indeed, contrary to the theses dominant in the Stalinist period, most Soviet economists no longer consider that their use contradicts the Marxist theory of value.

When it is said that an investment has a certain efficiency, it does not imply that in addition to labour there is a second factor of production able to create value. The work of Gosplan in this area is of great methodological importance: the attempt to evaluate total labour expenditure by converting into labour costs the whole of production costs; in other words, by estimating in terms of living labour the past labour incorporated in the means of production. In fact, the incorporated labour is unproductive unless associated with living labour. It is the combination of direct and indirect labour whose efficiency can be measured.

A measure of investment efficiency is necessary because of the scarcity of capital goods and is linked to an economic estimate of the time involved. Scarcity of resources makes it necessary to choose between various possible uses, since their employment in one branch means that they cannot be utilised in another. A comparison of investment projects presupposes a criterion which will make it possible to reduce to a common measure items of expenditure which are unequally distributed over time, and results materialising at different dates. Thus the recovery period of capital investment is variable (generally longer in extractive than in manufacturing industry); the time elapsing between the introduction of a new investment and the functioning of the new unit at full capacity is equally variable (the maturation period of the investment).

EFFICIENCY CRITERIA WILL NOT APPLY TO THE WHOLE OF INVESTMENT PLANNING

In the first place, the choice of the rate of investment is a political choice. The authorities determine what portion of the national income will have to be allocated to investment in view of the objectives of economic growth. The choice implies renouncing the present satisfaction of needs in favour of higher consumption in the future. During the early period of Soviet economic development, from 1928 to the end of the post-war reconstruction period, the sacrifice of present consumption was a heavy burden on the population – but without it the U.S.S.R. would certainly not have reached its present level of development.

In the second place, as we have already seen, the allocation of investment between regions or branches largely escapes the criteria of efficiency. The development of new regions or investment in heavy industry mean the tying up of considerable resources for long periods. The application of uniform criteria of efficiency would put them in an unfavourable light in relation to projects immobilising fewer resources for less time. That does not mean that the planner is entitled to ignore the comparative cost of such projects. On the contrary, he must be clear about the implications of the policy he recommends. But efficiency criteria will in this case have a purely indicative value.

These criteria will be decisive, however, where the possibilities of choice are less wide-ranging, for example:

efficiency of enterprise concentration;

comparison between the extension of an existing enterprise and the construction of a new one;

comparison of investment schemes raising productive capacity in substitute
goods (e.g. cotton and synthetic fibres);

effects of improved quality;

effect of enterprise location in different regions;

choice between two technical variants in implementing the same project, etc.

The Application of Efficiency Criteria

The 1969 standard method for determining the efficiency of investment contains two criteria, one measuring absolute and the other relative efficiency.

The first is indicative and is applied within the framework of the economy as a whole to the formulation of general investment plans (annual, five-year and longer-term plans) at sectoral, regional and even enterprise level. Its purpose is to determine the distribution of productive resources. In relation to enterprises it can be used as a planning indicator to forecast and later to evaluate the results of an increase in fixed capital.

This particular criterion is defined as the relation between an increase in national income at constant prices (or net production for the enterprise) and the investment bringing about this increase. It can be expressed by the symbol

E appears as the inverse of the marginal coefficient of capital.

The introduction of this coefficient into investment planning, made official by the 1969 standard method, is explained by the concern of Soviet planners at the rise in the coefficient of capital after 1958. (The gross marginal coefficient of capital, or the relation of gross investment to the increase in national income, i.e. the ratio $I/\Delta Y$, rose from 1.27 in 1958 to 2.9 in 1965 for the economy as a whole, and from 0.85 to 0.96 for industry.) It is questionable whether the choice of this indicator is the best one: the meaning of the term coefficient of capital is itself ambiguous, varying according to whether reference is made to total or sectoral coefficients, gross or net, average or marginal; it raises problems of measurement (particularly in the U.S.S.R. with its inadequate statistical apparatus); the multiplicity of factors influencing its size is a further difficulty. It is especially dubious to take the inverse of the coefficient of capital (which only expresses a relation between capital and production) as an index of the productivity of capital. How, at the macro-economic level, can one define the investment permitting the annual increase in national income? Can one take the ratio of investment I of year t to the increase (ΔY) in national income for the same year t? But ΔYt does not necessarily result from It. It would be more exact to impute it to It—1 or It—2. Account must be taken of the maturation period of capital, which is variable according to economic branches and types of investment. At the same time, the formula leaves out of consideration the length of life of the invested capital. In fact, for any given enterprise, the significance of the ratio $\Delta Y/I$ (ΔY here equals the annual increase in net production), as a measure of capital productivity, will be different if I has to be redeemed in five years rather than ten. Finally, for $\Delta Y/I$ to have any significance at all, certain minimal norms of productivity must be established. Hitherto such norms have only been fixed for particular sectors (for example, the minimal increase per rouble of investment has been calculated for the net production of electric power, measured in kwh).

The absolute efficiency criterion still remains essentially informative. The criterion of relative efficiency is operational.

This criterion must make it possible to choose between two solutions which, from a production viewpoint, lead to the same result. Examples: the choice between building a hydro-electric or thermal power station to obtain a given output of electricity; the choice between laying a double-track or a single-track line which can be doubled later to take a given volume of traffic.

These are classical problems of investment choice: In the first case there is a choice between high capital costs leading to low working costs once the project is finished, and the opposite situation. Problems of external economies or diseconomies must also be reckoned with. (The building of a dam may involve submerging a whole area, so that the rebuilding of flooded villages and agricultural losses have to be costed. Conversely, dam building may be accompanied by the regulation of waterways and the development of irrigation networks, etc. In the case of thermal power stations the eventual consequences of air pollution will have to be considered.)

In the second case the choice is between heavy simultaneous investment and investment staggered over time.

The basic criterion recommended in the standard method is the **pay-off** period. This has been used in the U.S.S.R. for a long time. Before World War II engineers in the power industry made (secret) use of it in comparing investment variants in their sector. It was applied from 1954 by the State Bank in medium-term selective credit operations.

Take two projects (1) and (2). In relation to the second the first project has high capital costs K_1 and low annual working costs C_1 so that $K_1 > K_2$ and $C_1 < C_2$. It is assumed that the two projects will have the same annual output. Each solution is related to a given variant (with parameters K_0 and C_0 and one deduces for which project the total initial capital will be recovered first, according to the formula:

$$\frac{K_1 - K_0}{C_0 - C_1} = T_1 \quad \text{and} \quad \frac{K_2 - K_0}{C_0 - C_2} = T_2$$

where T_1 and T_2 are the pay-off periods (in years). They show in what period of time total investments necessary for the completion of each project will be 'recovered' through annual economies in production costs (in relation to the variant C_0). That variant will be chosen where T is lowest. The inverse of T, or $1/T = E$, will be the criterion of the relative efficiency of investment.

When there are a large number of variants to be compared, the pay-off period formula can be represented more generally, and more practically, as $C + EK =$ minimum. Once again $\frac{K_1 - K_0}{C_0 - C_1} = T_1$; T_1 must be less than the base pay-off period T_0, where $\frac{K_1 - K_0}{C_0 - C_1} < T_0$.   If we multiply the two sides of this inequality by $C_0 - C_1$ and divide them by T_0, $C_1 + 1/T_0 \cdot K_1 < C_0 + 1/T_0 \cdot K^0$. If the inequality is not satisfied, project K_1 will have to be abandoned in favour of project K_2 whose capital and working costs together will be lower. If $1/T_0$ is replaced by the efficiency norm coefficient E, the general condition which must be fulfilled by the variant retained will be $C + EK =$ minimum.

The standard method provides specific instructions containing a series of base coefficients E by branch of activity (since we are not concerned here with calculating the absolute efficiency of investment but with its effects within a particular branch). The coefficients worked out for the investments whose efficiency is being measured must be at least equal to the base coefficients. A norm-coefficient of general orientation was also established. The way in which these coefficients were calculated is not clear. They constitute a compromise between routine coefficients used by the research and planning departments in the various branches (often lower than the official recommended coefficients, since each department wishes to be able to justify the greatest possible number of projects) and coefficients derived from the rate of profit (profit/productive capital ratio) outlined for each branch in the 1967 price reform (*cf.* chapter 6).

Two other fundamental criticisms may be levelled at this criterion. Firstly it takes no account of the staggering of investment over time and of its results, since it consists of a comparison of total investment expenditure, hypothetically considered as a single act at the beginning of the project, and the average annual cost economies of the operation.

Secondly it is concerned only with the direct investment necessary for a given project, without taking account of complementary investments subsequently required in other branches.

To reply to these criticisms two additions were made to the standard method:
1. The use of the coefficient E' as a rate of conversion to evaluate expenditure staggered over a period of time.

Let us assume that to complete variant I it is necessary to invest 9 million roubles: 5 million the first year, 2 the seventh year and 2 the tenth year. Variant II requires 8 million roubles, to be invested entirely in the first year (*cf*. the example of the railway given earlier, or another practical case, the construction of a large factory: variant I assumes that construction will be in several stages, the first stage leading to partial use of the factory after five to six years, the following stages leading gradually to full-capacity operation; variant II, on the other hand, assumes immediate full-capacity utilisation of all plant and buildings). Let us assume for arithmetical convenience that both variants will have the same flow of production after ten years, with the same annual working costs: if the pay-off period criterion is applied in its simplified form, variant II is preferable.

However, as from the first year, in variant II 3 million roubles more than in variant I are tied up. If variant I is chosen the 3 million roubles would be available for some other investment. In other words, they would increase the total investment fund of the initial year.

To compare the two variants, therefore, it is necessary to determine the present value of the staggered investment of variant I. This can be calculated by applying the general conversion formula

$$K_0 = \frac{Kt}{(1 + E')^t}$$

where K_0 = converted value of investment K.

Kt = value of the investment which by definition was to be effected in year t.

E' = the conversion coefficient.

In effect a given investment is less expensive if it is made in time t rather than in time o, since the capital not used in this time o is available for some other use; its conversion value will therefore be lower.

According to this formula, the expenditure of 2 million roubles in the seventh year in variant I, if we take a conversion value of $E' = 0.1$, represents:

$$2 \text{ millions} \times \frac{1}{(1 + E')^t} = 2 \times \frac{1}{(1 + 0.1)^7} = 2 \times 0.51 = 1.02 \text{ million roubles.}$$

Similarly, the 2 million roubles spent in the tenth year represent a conversion value of $2 \times 0.38 = 0.76$ million.

The total conversion value of the investment in variant I will therefore be equal to $5 + 1.02 + 0.76 = 6.78$ million roubles. Variant II, requiring 8 million roubles, will be less worthwhile.

The same method will be adopted where current working costs vary over time.

Next, to evaluate the total efficiency of the project the formula given earlier will be applied: $C + EK = \text{min}$. The purpose is to minimise the total conversion cost of the operation.

It is interesting that similar formulae are used in the West in selecting investment priorities, especially in the nationalised sector.[10] In a market economy the conversion rate for such decisions is decided by reference to the interest rate on the money market (but not necessarily at the same level). In a socialist economy, where there is no money market, the rate will be a fictitious one fixed purely as a matter of economic policy. The standard method is not very explicit on this point. It lays down that given 'existing procedures for depreciation' the conversion norm E' will be 8%. It seems that no attempt has been made to calculate an equilibrium rate of conversion equalising investment demand and supply. The standard method also insists that this figure must only be used for choosing between technical variants for the same project, so that its field of application is very limited.

2. The calculation of complementary expenditure required by a given investment.

According to the standard method, any evaluation of investment efficiency must take into account complementary expenditure implicit in the project, such as:

eventual expansion of the productive capacity of building firms;

costs of future road development;

investment necessary to provide a new factory with water, electric power, etc.;

expenditure related to the importation of additional labour if there is a shortage in the area in relation to project requirements: transport, housing, commercial and sanitary facilities, etc.;

raw material or finished product transport costs, depending on whether the enterprise is located near consumers or raw materials.

Conversely, certain economies may result from the project in hand, and these too have to be calculated (fuller use of local resources, etc.).

In practice, complementary investments are determined by planning departments according to the formula:

$$K_p = K + K_1 + K_2$$

where K_p = total investment

K = direct investment in the variant

K_1 = investment in the branch supplying the project with raw materials (for example: for a thermal power station, investments in coal-mining)

K_2 = investment in the branch supplying the project with equipment.

The calculations do not exceed more than one or two degrees of complementarity; otherwise they would become too complex. For example, in the above hypothesis account would be taken of the investment (in timber for pit-props, etc.) implied by an increase in coal production, but this would be the outer limit of such calculations.

The general formula would then be:

$$K_s = \sum_{j=1}^{m} \sum_{i=1}^{n} A_{ij} K_j$$

where K_s = total joint investment

A_{ij} = total quantity of raw materials or equipment i in the degree of complementarity chosen, for product j

K_j = investment per unit of product j

n = quantity of materials or equipment (by type)

m = number of degrees of complementarity

These formulae are used to calculate efficiency in introducing new techniques and in formulating projects within a given sector.

Enterprises making investments out of their own funds within the framework of reform (relatively few cases in practice) use the criterion of profitability (anticipated profit related to capital expenditure) where the base coefficient of efficiency is the rate of the charge on productive capital, at present equal to 6% in most branches.

It can be seen from the above that the criteria of efficiency used in the U.S.S.R. at micro- and macro-economic level are fragmentary. This is a natural consequence of the principles on which these calculations are based, since they do not cover the general distribution of investment.

That is why a group of mathematical economists have criticised the limited and approximate nature of the methods (at present in use) for selecting projects, and recommend that the whole planning process should be based on the calculation of an optimal plan.

Definition of the Optimal Plan

The initial impulse to do research on the application of mathematics to planning was given by academician Nemtchinov. In May 1959 he proposed to the economic science section of the Academy of Sciences that a conference should be convened on this question. The conference took place in April 1960 and was the starting point of work on the mathematical analysis of growth, the mathematical formulation of the inter-branch balance, linear programming, the application of mathematics to transport, and mathematical statistics.

These researches were not completely new in the U.S.S.R. As early as 1939 the economist Kantorovitch had published fragments of his work on linear programming,[11] edited in their final form in 1960. Analogous studies by Novojilov appeared between 1939 and 1946.[12] However during the Stalinist period, and even until 1960, these researches were looked upon with some suspicion in the U.S.S.R. as tainted with heterodoxy. This was largely due to the fact that the mathematical economists used the methods of marginal calculation, a symbol of the marginalist theory rejected outright by Marxists.

This resistance has still not been entirely overcome. Following on Kantorovitch and Novojilov, Nemtchinov argued that Soviet economists, whilst using the techniques of marginal theory, in no way subscribe to the bourgeois marginalist or neo-marginalist doctrine as such. It is simply a question of putting the most advanced mathematical techniques at the service of planning.

Since the death of Nemtchinov in 1964 mathematical economics has been developed principally within the Institute of Mathematical Economics, in the Academy of Sciences, founded by Nemtchinov. The latter was succeeded by Fedorenko who is today the most authoritative representative of the mathematical school. Research on optimal planning constitutes the main work of this institute.

The objective is to construct a planning model in which non-reproducible natural resources, reproducible resources and labour will be used in such a way as to achieve the optimal result. The optimal situation is defined as the one obtaining when the transfer of one unit of a factor of production from one use to another cannot increase the satisfaction of an individual without reducing the total satisfaction of needs. This is clearly the optimum as defined by the mathematical branch of the marginalist school.

The successful application of the theory to a planned economy requires the presence of certain conditions:

1.   A definition of the criterion of optimalisation: this will be the maximal satisfaction of the total needs of society (individual and collective). This point of departure constitutes one of the main difficulties in optimal planning, on account of the political and methodological implications (definition of aims, evaluation of social needs).

2.   The planner must have an adequate system of information at his disposal. In the U.S.S.R. at present the compilation and processing of statistical information are still very much rule-of-thumb. The creation of a unified system of electronic computer centres is still in its very early stages. There is a centre dependent on the Central Board of Statistics, to which the other centres will be gradually linked in the formation of a single three-tier system. The lower tier will comprise the statistical centres of large enterprises, centres servicing groups of small enterprises, and centres for the collection and primary processing of information. At the second level will be several dozen centres located at concentration points in the flow of information. The third level will be the operational control centre for the network as a whole. This will also service federal State agencies. The function of the system will be to collect information, but above all (from the second level) to undertake optimisation calculations for current and perspective plans and to compute investment efficiency on the basis of existing criteria. The general lines of this unified system were defined in a decree of 1966. However various obstacles have so far prevented its completion: political obstacles, since every administration wishes to retain control of its own present network (Gosplan, State Committee for Material and Technical Supplies, State Bank, ministries); technical

difficulties, due to scarcity of computers, electronic equipment, servicing and programmers. It is perhaps significant that although the production of computers has been increasing at a rate of 30% per year since 1959, the U.S.S.R. still lags behind in this area, even in relation to such countries as the G.D.R. and Czechoslovakia. And yet the general computerisation of information is vital for the U.S.S.R. In 1965 a Soviet academician maintained that if there was not a rapid and general diffusion of electronic techniques between then and 1980, nearly 100 million people would be engaged in processing economic/statistical data before the end of the period. The concern of the academician becomes clearer when it is realised that many departments in the U.S.S.R. are not even equipped with the most elementary mechanical apparatus, and that the abacus is still one of the most common calculating machines in use.
3. Optimal planning requires appropriate mathematical methods. Research in this field is going ahead in the U.S.S.R.:

Research on optimal planning; the main objective is to construct planning models reconstituting the basic elements of reality, which will make it possible to study the repercussions of controlled variations. A further aim is model optimisation: an attempt to employ existing resources with a view to optimal satisfaction of social needs at the lowest total cost. These models may be either informative (planning preparation) or cybernetic. They should make possible the self-regulation of economic systems. The techniques of matrix mathematics are widely used in this research

The inter-branch balances are of course models themselves. The attempt to optimise them by allocating resources according to given criteria would in fact result in optimal planning schemes. The work of the U.S.S.R. Gosplan on the optimisation of the power-fuel balance for 1965 and 1970 and of the 1970 inter-branch balance comes within this context.

Inter-sectoral and inter-regional problems are the most characteristic of optimal planning. More specific problems are those relating to the rational structure of material and technical supplies, to the planning of transport, to the relationship of financial investment with material resources, and to the establishment of new enterprises.

Statistical research; the Central Board of Statistics is developing the study of mathematical statistics (until now confined mainly to demography). At the same time it is working on an automated system of statistical and accounting information. This research is still in the early stage of studying an algorithmic terminology (system of terms and symbols for the description of information and methods of processing information, and which may be used on different types of electronic computer). In this field a great deal of importance is attached to work done in the United States.

Research on operational planning (in the Soviet Union this expression is preferred to 'operational research'); here the objective is to perfect automatic control mechanisms, at enterprise level, for example. At present and at best automation is to be found only in accounting departments (usually they are only mechanised). Planning departments are not yet automated: theoretical research is in progress on the formulation of cybernetic models of the financial-technical plan for enterprises, but it has not yet reached the operational stage. What is required here is the development of simple, flexible cybernetic machines able to transmit information which has been collected and systematically processed directly to other control apparatus. It is hoped that in this way it will be found possible to automate completely the economic-technical standardisation of enterprises.

4. Units of production must be left sufficient autonomy and incentive to pursue optimal economic results themselves. This is a basic condition, and explains why mathematical economists have always been the first to press for greater freedom of enterprise management.

In fact, a complex economic system cannot be simply regulated by some computerised centre of control. This has been clearly demonstrated by a Soviet mathematician; a simple problem involving 2 objectives and 2 variants for each will have 4 solutions; with 5 objectives and 3 variants we already have $3^5 = 243$ solutions; 500 objectives and 10 variants (still a very simplified economic mechanism) would give 10^{500} solutions, when even the number of atoms in the universe is 'only' 10^{73}! Enterprises must therefore be in a position to determine, within certain fixed limits, their volume and methods of production. This implies: a degree of freedom in choosing suppliers and customers (greater than under the present economic reform), linked to relative price flexibility; an effective stimulus to the maximisation of net profit by enterprises, and of course more extensive enterprise rights over the use of a part of these profits; a price system taking account of the profitability of invested capital, so that the enterprise does not over-extend its use.

In such conditions, central planning, relying on the mathematical determination of the optimum, could concentrate on the essential problems of development and could eventually confine itself to adjusting those choices made by production units.

Appendix

SOVIET PLANS

We have seen how the plan is formulated, according to methods and techniques which have been improved a great deal since planning began. How is it implemented? The history of Soviet planning is full of examples of unfulfilled plans, revised and adjusted during the course of their implementation. This is true even if we exclude agricultural plans, whose objectives have never been achieved.

The idea of a single plan covering the whole economy was first mooted in 1920, in connection with the project for establishing a network of electric power throughout Russia. In that year a commission of the Supreme Economic Council drafted a plan defining the stages of electrification over the next ten to fifteen years, the so-called Goelro plan. It went well beyond the technical and economic problems of electrification. Already making use of the balance method, it constituted in effect the first Soviet perspective plan. The State Economic Planning Commission (Gosplan) was set up in February 1921. However the N.E.P. period was not favourable to an extension of planning. During War Communism the idea of planning had been linked to the notion of centralised economic control, and the partial return to a market system permitted only indicative methods in the general orientation of development.

There is a close relationship between the end of the N.E.P. and the beginning of five-year planning. The launching of the 1928-32 plan at the end of 1927 might appear to be the *coup de grâce* of the N.E.P. and the point of departure for a restructuring of the economy based on systematic industrialisation. In fact the first really operational annual plan was not introduced until 1931.

The plan for 1928-32 concentrated on heavy industry and especially on power. The 1933-37 plan was centred on iron and steel; nearly one-quarter of all investment for this plan went to the construction of the Ural-Kouznetsk complex, which was based on exploiting Ural iron-ore resources and the coal of the Kuzbas, linked by a railway line 2000 km in length. The third plan, 1938–42, disrupted by the war, was intended to develop the engineering industry. The fourth plan, 1946-50, was mainly concerned with post-war reconstruction. Implementation of the 1951-5 plan was partly interrupted by the death of Stalin; it was characterised by the vast scale of the projects anticipated: powerful hydro-electric stations in both European and Siberian regions of the U.S.S.R., and the establishment of a new metallurgical base in Siberia. Soviet data on the sixth plan (1956-60) are rather vague. It is probable that the plan was never completed in its original form. From 1959 it was replaced by the 1959–65 seven-year plan, the only one of its type in the U.S.S.R. Its aim was the diversification of objectives and greater emphasis on the development of consumer goods industries, trends which were to continue in the plan for 1966-70.[13]

From the viewpoint of plan fulfilment, the Soviet system has two main characteristics.

Firstly, the annual plan is the most important for economic life and the direction of the activity of productive units, even if the medium-term plan is of greater significance as a political programme. Thus the non-fulfilment of the five-year plan is of relatively secondary importance, since economic agencies do not work on this basis.

Secondly, the annual plan was traditionally both 'extended' and 'minimal'. In other words, the use of resources had to be organised in the fullest possible way and plan targets had to be exceeded. This meant encouraging the overfulfilment of production plans by giving prominence to such phenomena as the stakhanovite movement. This clearly involved a contradiction. If the plan was extended and if it had been correctly calculated, it could not possibly be exceeded (otherwise factor combination was not optimal). As a matter of fact the preceding analysis of planning methods shows that given existing planning procedures it was impossible to draft an optimal plan. The extended plan therefore referred to a much more empirical notion. The planner evidently assumed *a priori* that the data on productive capacity and resources supplied by enterprises were an under-estimation. He then more or less subjectively increased the evaluation of productive potential, counting on the existence of resources in addition to those indicated. In such circumstances the plan might remain below productive potential; in that case systematic encouragement to exceed it was the remedy. On the other hand, the plan might be too ambitious in relation to resources. It could not then be realised, even if it appeared coherent on paper.

That is why one of the aims of the economic reform of 1965 was to eliminate the silent struggle between production units and planning departments. This was to be achieved by creating a system which would encourage the enterprise to formulate an extended plan on its own initiative and which would dispense with traditional stimulants of plan overfulfilment. This system does not seem to be operating satisfactorily. It compels enterprise to make precise adjustments so as to execute the plan exactly, since neither overfulfilment nor underfulfilment are now desirable.

Above all the system rests on a cardinal principle of Soviet planning: the State plan must express the maximum global output obtainable given existing resources. Increased production should not be an aim in itself but an objective subordinated to the social need for a given product, quantitatively defined. Soviet planners have not been particularly sensitive to this requirement, since for a long time the scarcity of goods amply justified the principle of increasing production without limit. The appearance of relative over-production in certain lines will doubtless change this frame of mind.

THE TOOLS OF ECONOMIC INTERVENTION

The means used by the socialist state to influence economic activity, in addition to the planned direction of production and distribution, include certain economic tools superficially very similar to those employed by a modern capitalist state: prices and incomes policy, monetary policy, financial policy.

For the capitalist state, however, they are methods of intervention used with a view to correcting an economic situation which has come about naturally (prices and incomes policies) and influencing the activity of economic units (monetary and financial policy).

In the socialist state the use of economic instruments (monetary categories) completes the planning process to which it is subordinate. These categories themselves are a product of the plan and not of the free interaction of economic units: prices and wages are planned; credit and financial plans are nothing more than the translation into monetary terms of balances and adjustments previously defined in physical quantities in the plan.

Economic reform in the socialist countries has for some years been attaching greater importance to these tools of economic intervention. In this connection the problem of combining plan and market is an ever sharper focal point of discussion: can market mechanisms be used as the auxiliary tools of planning, do they tend to rationalise the operation of the planned economy or do they lead to disorganisation and a radical transformation of the socialist system? We shall meet these problems again in the Conclusion to this book. However to pose the problems correctly one must first know how, in concrete terms, the socialist state fixes prices, plans incomes and defines its monetary and financial policy; how, in socialist terminology, it organises money-commodity relations.

What characterises these economic tools of intervention is that they necessarily imply the use of money.

At present no socialist country has abandoned the use of money, nor does any socialist country envisage the possibility of doing so. And yet the question of planning entirely in kind, with the maintenance of certain forms of market exchange, did arise under the early Soviet socialist system.

Immediately after the Revolution Lenin drew up a plan for building socialism in Russia in which he mentions the possibility of using monetary and market relations. However with War Communism (1918) there appeared a current of thought which denied the necessity of using money at all and affirmed the possibility of measuring all expenditure directly in terms of social labour. At the time the disappearance of money seemed so imminent that no attempt was made to create a monetary and financial system.

On the contrary, in conformity with the doctrine of Marx himself, an effort was made to develop a stable unit of account for the economy and budget based on the unit of labour. A commission, led by the economist Strumilin, was given the task of establishing the basis of this system.

Strumilin's propositions may be summarised in the following way: it is possible to conceive of a non-monetary economy in which it would be feasible to resolve at one and the same time the macro-economic problem of allocating scarce resources between different uses, the micro-economic problem of the rational combination of factors of production within the enterprise, and in which at the same time each member of society would be free to choose consumer goods in conditions of relative scarcity. As unit of value Strumilin proposed to take the value of a product manufactured during a normal day by a worker performing his task 100% according to accepted norms = unit of normal labour corresponding to labour of 100,000 kgm, or *tred* (abbreviation for *trudovaja edinica,* labour unit). The value of the product is thus measured not by the quantity of time expended in its production but by the quantity of physical labour supplied. But to take account of the social utility of goods requires at the same time a second unit of measure, representing the minimal needs in food of an average man in one day, or 2000 calories: this was the *dov* (unit of satisfaction, *dovolstvija*), with its subdivisions (for example, the *centidov* or 1/100 of a *dov,* the *kilodov* or 1000 *dov*). Strumilin's project, like others of the same type, was soon forgotten as the New Economic Policy brought a provisional restoration of the 'capitalist' market.

Circumstances thus dictated the reintroduction of money into the Soviet economy. It was not to disappear, even after the abolition of the N.E.P. and the inauguration of integral economic planning. The birth of socialist-type economies after World War II did not lead to any further projects for the abolition of money. The experiences of Soviet War Communism had been enough. Money continues to exist under socialism because it is useful in the building of communism, because it still has certain functions to fulfil; money serves planning.

What are these functions? According to Marxist theory there are four:

1. Its most basic function is as a measure of value. It was precisely to replace it as the universal equivalent that the theoreticians of War Communism had formulated a complex system reducing to a common non-monetary unit the valuation of goods produced in the economy. It is as a measure of value that it is used by planners in price formation and in determination of wages and pay.

2. Money is a means of circulation. It makes possible the conversion of producers' pay into consumer goods.

3. It is a means of payment. It enables enterprises to pay their workers and to obtain the goods necessary for productive activity with the money they receive from the sale of their product.

In functions 2 and 3 money appears as a means of exchange in the spheres of consumption and production. In Marxist theory, however, they are two quite different functions, as we shall see in our analysis of monetary policy.

4. Money is a means of accumulation and saving. Through state financial policy it makes possible the creation of mobilisable reserves.

The employment by the socialist state of tools of economic action implies the use of money in its various aspects. We shall examine this problem mainly in the light of Soviet experience, with a few examples drawn from the European socialist countries.

1. MONEY AS A MEASURE OF VALUE: PRICE FORMATION

The problem of price formation in the U.S.S.R. has already been referred to in connection with enterprise reform. Reform was made necessary by the more or less permanent financial deficit of a large part of industry. This was the result not only of a poor system of planning and management, but also of defective methods of price determination. Price revision was an essential element in economic reform.

The mere existence of goods valued in money does not necessarily constitute an economically meaningful price system; for that, price formation must be based on some degree of rationality. However for a long time in the U.S.S.R. prices were fixed arbitrarily as a function of the objectives of economic policy. For example the prices of capital goods were deliberately fixed at a low level to reduce the costs of their users. In the period 1956-8 there began a series of discussions on economic theory and practice which culminated in recognition of the fact that prices would have to be based on the law of value as outlined by Marx.

The Marxist Theory of Value

Point of departure: the exchange value of a commodity reflects the quantity of labour expended in its production.[1]

Remarks

It is not the concrete labour expended in a particular enterprise or by a particular individual which matters, but the average quantity of labour socially necessary at a given moment in time for the production of the commodity in question (i.e. under historically determined technical and working conditions). The quantity of labour is measured most easily in labour time, but account must be taken of differences in skill and labour intensity. This raises the problem of the reduction of skilled to unskilled or simple labour. The problem is solved in practice by the ratio between hourly wages paid for labour of different skill and intensity, which expresses the conversion rate of skilled into unskilled labour.

It is not only a question of the present living labour of the workers directly engaged in producing the commodity, but also of the past labour embodied in the means of production. In the case of capital goods, past labour is incorporated in the value of the new commodity gradually, as the equipment wears out. As far as the raw materials are concerned, the past labour they represent is transferred completely and immediately into the value of the finished product.

The value of a commodity may therefore be represented by the formula
$W = c + v + m,$
where c = value of the capital expended in the form of the partial consumption of equipment and the use of raw materials (constant capital)

v = wages paid by the capitalist (variable capital)

m = surplus value, created by labour alone; it derives from the fact that wages represent the cost of the upkeep and reproduction of labour power and not the whole of the new value created by labour; it constitutes the product of the exploitation of wage-labour by the capitalist.

Value thus defined is the basis of price. The price of a given product expresses the socially necessary labour cost required for the production of that commodity. However it is possible that a particular product may command a higher (or lower) price than another incorporating the same expenditure of labour. Whatever the case may be, for the economy as a whole the total price of national production is necessarily equal to the amount of productive labour supplied by the members of society (sum of prices = sum of exchange values). This means that if one product is sold at a higher price than is justified by its labour cost, another product is necessarily sold at a lower price.

Up to this point we have summarised the elements of value theory as given by Marx in Book I of *Capital*.

But in Book III Marx completes his analysis of price formation by explaining how, in the capitalist system, the normal price of a commodity is not determined solely by the labour cost required for its production. Why? Because the capitalist attempts to maximise the rate of profit, or the ratio of surplus value to the total of capital advanced (constant and variable), and because the ratio of constant capital c to variable capital v is not the same in all branches (c/v or the 'organic composition of capital'). Competition tends to equalise rates of profit in the different sectors of production. For each commodity there is then an average price equal to the magnitude obtained from adding to the cost of production the average annual rate of profit on total invested capital: $P = C + V + m/K$ (K being capital invested per entrepreneur). P is the 'modified form of value' or 'price of production' (to use Marx's own terminology).[2]

Soviet economists have always admitted that the Marxist theory of value was intended to serve as a basis for analysing the capitalist economy. But there has been considerable controversy over the application of the theory to socialist conditions. The evolution of theory has run parallel to the practical development of planning.

Application of the Law of Value to Price Formation in the Socialist System

There have been two periods in the development of both the theory and economic policy. The first went up to 1958–60 and was characterised at the theoretical level by a denial that it was possible to apply the law of value to socialist conditions. At the practical level, it meant the determination of prices by voluntarist methods, so that they were fixed as a function of the immediate objectives of economic policy. In the second period, since 1960, there has been a remarkable renewal of economic science, and a confrontation of several schools of thought in the attempt to work out a rational solution to the problem of prices. At the same time the methods employed by planners in fixing prices have been challenged.

THE STALINIST PERIOD

The definitive version of the Stalinist conception is to be found in the brochure which Stalin published in 1952, *Economic Problems of Socialism in the U.S.S.R.*: Marx's law of value, according to which commodities exchange at prices proportional to the quantity of labour socially necessary for their production, is applicable to a market economy. It cannot govern a socialist economy, since private ownership of the means of production has been abolished.

However within socialism there exists a market for consumer goods, and even in the productive sector itself, side by side with socialist, state ownership of the means of production we find collective, co-operative ownership in agriculture. Thus market categories still exist in the consumption sector and in *kolkhoz* production. This partial and temporary persistence of the market justifies the subordinate rôle which the law of value continues to play in a socialist economy.

The economy is therefore divided into two spheres according to the legal criteria of the mode of property. They are rigorously separated, so as to avoid any contamination of the completely socialised sector by the one still subject to market conditions:

In the case of consumption goods, the planner will take account of the value relationship of products in determining prices (as well as supply and demand).

On the other hand, the law of value will not influence the distribution of capital goods: book-keeping, the allocation of these goods to different uses and the measurement of the results obtained with their use will be effected mainly in kind. For convenience capital goods will be evaluated in money terms, but this evaluation will be for purely accounting purposes.

In the first sector, then, the law of value will in principle be respected in price formation. Of course, it can be partially ignored if economic policy so requires. In the second case, however, it will in no way dictate to the planner.

Such was the dogmatic Stalinist conception of the law of value. It led to a completely arbitrary policy *vis-à-vis* prices as a whole, since it is obviously impossible to divide the economy into two sectors in this way. How, for example, is it possible to evaluate consumer goods accurately if the value of the intermediate goods going into their production is unknown? But it was above all the irrational determination of prices for capital goods which had the most disastrous effects on the economy, both at macro-economic and enterprise level. Why? Because these goods are scarce, and even if theoretically they have no value, they have to be allocated by choosing between their various possible uses. Of course at national level the choice will have a political character (determined by the priority attaching to different sectors, if the first Soviet five-year plans are anything to go by). But this in no way solves the concrete problems of resource allocation.

At macro-economic level the application of official doctrine made it impossible to calculate investment efficiency. To take account of the existing scarcity of equipment and raw materials, experts and engineers, in choosing between investment variants within a particular field of resource allocation, resorted to technico-economic calculations which dissimulated their use of a rate of scarcity. For example, transport engineers had the official responsibility of establishing which particular project involved the lowest operational cost (cost price per *t/km*) for a given volume of transport. However, they would first include in the project a secret rate of interest equal to about 10% of the total investment, so as to minimise not only the operational cost but also total cost including a capital charge. As early as 1938 engineers in the power industry applied that same pay-off period criterion which is today the official criterion for selecting investment.

At enterprise level the absence of a rational valuation of capital goods had equally deleterious effects. The theory that these goods had no value led to the fixing of the prices of equipment and raw materials at deliberately low levels. But enterprises could not buy these goods freely. Consequently their scarcity led to the imposition of a cumbersome and ramified system of distribution.

This prices policy, constant during the so-called Stalinist period, was justified by an apparently logical argument: the wholesale prices of capital goods and raw materials determine industrial costs as a whole. In a socialist system these costs must be as low as possible, since in the last analysis they determine the price of consumption goods sold to the population. To this end the prices of capital goods will be kept as low as possible. What will be the result? Heavy industry will not be profitable. But in an economic system in which profit is not an index of enterprise success, as was the case in the U.S.S.R. until recently, the absence of profit presents no inconvenience. It may be objected that if heavy industry operates at a loss the State will have to subsidise it through budgetary grants. The answer to this is that although the State may lose as a creditor to heavy industry, it will recover its costs in the consumer goods sector: light industry, making cheap purchases of raw materials and machinery, will make a profit even if the price of its product is fixed at a relatively low level, since its costs are correspondingly low.

This argument was first challenged in 1956–7 (beginning of the great Soviet debate on the principle of price formation), and was implicitly repudiated by a Party decision in July 1960, which recommended a revision of wholesale prices.

There were two flaws in this argument. In the first place, heavy industry enterprises had become accustomed to their deficit and reliance on State subsidies. Consequently they made no effort to improve their economic management. Secondly, in industry as a whole, a tendency to waste capital goods and raw materials had become firmly established, since, although they were difficult to acquire on account of their scarcity, they cost enterprises practically nothing.

Hence a double paradox:

Heavy industry, which had received priority treatment and investment during the Stalinist period, had the worst results in economic and financial terms;

The price system led indirectly to the wastage of capital equipment which was scarce in relation to requirements.

Just after the war, the deficit in heavy industry was so great that in 1949 the Soviet government had to raise wholesale prices. Prices as a whole were increased by 80%, so that industry could have a rate of profit of 3% to 4% (in relation to costs). The prices of certain goods were raised much more (three times in the case of coal). But this rise had been forced on the government. The previous low-price policy was resumed in 1950.

Results of this policy: in 1959 20% of Soviet industrial enterprises were operating at a loss. Whereas industry as a whole had a profit rate of 12% (26% in the processing of oil products, 8.5% in iron and steel, 3.8% in building materials), certain branches, especially in the extractive industries, were in deficit: coal 18%, iron ore 14.5%.

The decision taken in 1960 was fundamental. It meant abandoning the previous principle of price formation and substituting a new one. In future all enterprises, in average operational conditions, would have to earn a 'normal' profit. This decision was preceded from the end of the Stalinist period by important theoretical debates which underlined the necessity of providing a rational basis for prices.

EVOLUTION TOWARDS A RATIONAL PRICE SYSTEM

Theoretical Discussions

The first great debate on the principles of price formation began in 1957. Criticism of the practical determination of prices by planners had been made before, but the critics were very often isolated and found it difficult to operate openly. This was the case with the mathematical economists, Kantorovitch and Novojilov, who outlined their ideas in works of limited circulation just before and during World War II. From 1957 public discussion revealed a fertile body of propositions, some of which had already been published but not widely distributed on account of Stalinist censorship; others were more recent.

Apart from a small number of conservatives who maintained that the planners' pricing policy was correct and merely required more systematic implementation, there were three theoretical positions all based on an application of the Marxist law of value to socialist conditions.[3]

The first school of thought was led by Strumilin and proposed that prices should be established in strict proportion to labour costs (i.e. to wages), according to the principle that labour is the sole source of value. In this case the price formula would be $P = c + v + m$, in which m no longer represents capitalist surplus value, but the net additional product or new net value created by labour. In practice the planner would have to calculate at macro-economic level the rate of accumulation M/V (the absolute magnitude of M being the difference between national income D and total wages V since $D = V + M$). The price of each product would then be determined by adding to the cost of production $c + v$ the rate of accumulation M/V—proportionately to v, according to the formula $P = c + v + v \, (M/V)$.

The second school advocates the price of production theory. According to this prices should be fixed by adding to the cost of production a supplement (rate of profit) proportional to the total capital invested in productive enterprises. What in effect is being suggested is that one should apply to the planned formation of prices under socialism, the price of production formula which appears in the capitalist system from the equalisation of profit rates between branches (as demonstrated by Marx in Book III of *Capital*). The contention is that to apply Strumilin's formula is to imply that the same quantity of labour (abstract labour, *cf. supra*) represents the same net contribution to society. According to this second school such a position is untenable, since it takes no account of the total capital invested in the different branches, and more particularly of the organic composition of capital or c/v, the ratio of capital to expenditure on labour (coefficient of capital intensity). Now the capital invested in a branch or enterprise represents a cost for society, rising with the length of the production cycle and the consequent period of immobilisation of productive capital (fixed and circulating).

Therefore, in the practical determination of prices, to the average branch cost $(c+v)$ must be added magnitude m representing the net additional product, no longer in proportion to living labour costs alone (v) but to the fixed and circulating capital invested.

The average norm of the net additional product, the socialist version of the average rate of profit, must be determined at macro-economic level by the formula: $M=P-(C+V)$ (value of the gross national product minus production costs), M being the total value of the net additional product.

If K=total capital invested in the economy, the average norm of the net additional product will be: $r=M/K$.

The price of each product will then be equal to: $P=c+v+m$ where $m=rK'$ (K' being the average total capital invested in the production of one unit of the commodity in question).

A third school, led by mathematical economists Kantorovitch and Novojilov, maintains that the prices of means of production must be proportional to their marginal productivity.

These economists analyse the problems of price formation in the wider context of optimal planning. They are interested in the choice of production methods which minimise the total quantity of labour (direct, living, or indirect, incorporated in capital goods) expended in obtaining a given product.

Using different terminology, they show that this optimum can only be realised if the marginal rates of profit of different investments are equalised in their various uses. Kantorovitch uses the notion of objectively determined valuations of factors of production corresponding to the idea of marginal productivity in Western theory. Novojilov uses the expression 'differential expenditure', which comprises the sum of production costs and scarcity costs due to the fact that, to produce a given commodity, scarce means of production must be attracted away from other branches of production.[4]

For a long time these theses were opposed by the majority of Soviet economists who held the view that the very use of the marginal concept in a socialist economy was contrary to Marxism. However this prejudice has gradually though not entirely been overcome, with the wide application of modern methods of mathematical analysis to planning. The basic problem remains: is it possible to reconcile the labour theory of value with the laws governing the optimal use of invested capital, implying that prices should equal marginal costs of production? (We met this problem earlier, in connection with the determination of investment efficiency in chapter 5). Mathematical economists believe it is possible, but their point of view in no way involves recognising that capital creates value of itself; the net product created in the economy must always be imputed to total labour costs in a given period (the combination of direct labour and indirect labour embodied in the means of production).

We have just examined the three main schools of thought concerning the application of the law of value under socialism. What influence have they had in practice?

The theses of the Strumilin school have not played a significant part in price formation, but they have served as a basis for Gosplan calculations of the conversion into labour time of direct and indirect production costs.

The procedure is as follows. Direct labour costs per unit of a given product are known. To obtain total labour costs (quantity of labour required to produce the raw materials and equipment necessary for manufacturing the commodity in question) the technological coefficients of the inter-branch balance are used (*cf.* chapter 5). For a relatively small number of products it is therefore possible to determine total labour cost coefficients per monetary unit. From this information one can extend the calculation to other products, using the coefficients established in the first stage as initial data.

The price of production theory has likewise had no direct influence on price formation. However it has had very important practical repercussions. One of its exponents, Liberman, as early as 1962 formulated a criterion for evaluating enterprise results. This was the rate of profit or profit/productive capital ratio, which is simply the average norm of the net additional product m/K. Liberman was careful to emphasise that he did not recommend the price of production formula for determining prices. It is nevertheless true that this particular theory was at the origin of both the profitability indicator introduced with the economic reforms and the introduction of a charge on productive capital.

Finally Soviet marginalist theories are at the root of research in mathematical economics on optimal planning. Their present influence on planning is zero, but they will doubtless exercise a fruitful influence in the long term.

Is the conclusion that these debates served no real purpose? Certainly not. The theoretical economists were involved in preparing the price reform which was decided on in 1960 and completed in July 1967. Their proposals were synthesised and regrouped in the form of a programme for the concrete determination of prices, which was presented several times by Diatchenko, president of the prices council at the Economic Institute of the Academy of Sciences.

The Principles of Price Planning

The principles underlying the planning of prices as recommended by Diatchenko are the following:

Price formation must take as its basis the socially necessary expenditure of labour in the production of goods, that is to say, their value. But the planner will not be able to use value directly; he will employ the usual categories of cost and profit. He will therefore have to be informed, in practice, what profit margin to add to cost in order to establish a price, and to what the rate of profit will apply.

The prices system must take account of both labour and capital costs. A profit margin will therefore be added to cost. The profit margin will be obtained from a rate of profit calculated with a view to ensuring a certain level of profitability to every enterprise operating under normal conditions. This rate of profit will be applied partly to wages and partly to productive capital. The planner will also have to establish provisional or localised margins between prices and value, according to the requirements of economic policy.

The end result is a complex system of different types of prices. Industrial wholesale prices would be the base and in principle would represent the addition of average branch cost and a branch rate of profit. However in sectors with highly variable natural or technical conditions of production, as in the extractive industries, there would be area prices. These would be wholesale prices (to enterprises in the case of capital goods, to retail shops in the case of consumer goods). The wholesale prices actually received by the producing firms might differ from these to stimulate management; to compensate for any consequent fluctuations a price regularisation fund could be established. Agricultural prices would be fixed according to the special conditions prevailing in this sector (effect of climatic variations, existence of differential rent). Finally retail prices might be subject to considerable manipulation by the authorities. In this case planners would have to be well aware of the possible repercussions of any such measures if the market was not to be disorganised. The power of planners would therefore be discretionary but not arbitrary: any action to influence retail prices would be based on a serious study of demand and market conditions (still embryonic in the U.S.S.R.).

This system has not substantially modified existing practice, since the basic method of planning prices has been retained: a profit margin added to average cost. However it has rationalised procedure, by giving a more scientific definition to the content of the rate of profit (the total of this rate being linked to general economic policy).

The formula for these propositions is the following:

$$P = Ci + Wi\,(1+r) + ek\,Fi + D$$

where P = price of product I;
  Ci = material costs of production of one unit of i (raw materials, depreciation);
  Wi = wages imputable to the production of one unit of i;

r =fraction of the rate of profit related to wages; this fraction calculated as a function of the rates of social security contributions made by enterprises (from 4% to 9% at present);

e =fraction of the rate of profit related to the value of productive capital;

k =coefficient of sectoral differentiation of norm e (which is consequently not uniform throughout the economy);

Fi =productive capital employed in the production of i;

D =turnover tax (usually $D = 0$, since the tax is not normally included in the wholesale price).

The planner must not only take account of the exchange value of commodities, determined by the process of production, but also of their use value, so as to reflect their different properties for consumers. This is particularly important for capital goods if prices are to stimulate innovation and quality in manufacture. Coefficients measuring use values will therefore have to be developed (the productivity or length of life of machinery, for example).

The economists have clearly gone quite a long way in their search for a formula reconciling practical requirements and theoretical coherence. What repercussions has this had?

The Planned Determination of Prices

The agency responsible for determining prices is the U.S.S.R. Gosplan, under the general aegis of the Council of Ministers of the U.S.S.R. and with the participation of the Central Board of Statistics (basic data) and the Ministry of Finance of the U.S.S.R. (possible fiscal effects of price formation).

A prices bureau was set up in 1957 as a subdivision of the U.S.S.R. Gosplan. In 1965 it was replaced by a State committee on prices, which in 1970 was attached directly to the Council of Ministers of the U.S.S.R. Wholesale prices are established almost entirely by Gosplan and the committee on prices. In this area, republican agencies have very little power, and unlike the retail price situation, must accept the price scales established at federal level.

THE PRICE STRUCTURE

The price of an industrial product may be represented diagrammatically:

Total cost of product	Profit	Wholesale distributive margin	Turnover tax	Retail distributive margin
Enterprise wholesale price				
Industrial wholesale price				
Retail price				

Factory cost (1) .... 92 roubles

Non-productive expenditure (workers' flats, nurseries, etc.) (2) .... 8 „

Total cost (3) = (1) + (2) .... 100 roubles

Profit (4) .... 5 „

Enterprise wholesale price (5) = (3) + (4) .... 105 roubles

Margin of wholesale distributive agency (6) .... 5 „

Turnover tax (7) .... 20 „

Industrial wholesale price (8) = (5) + (6) + (7) .... 130 roubles

Commercial margin of retail distributive agency (9) .... 10 „

Retail price (10) = (8) + (9) .... 140 roubles

This outline is not sufficient by itself to explain how prices are established. We also need to know which elements are given and which are derived. The Soviet price system includes two distinct categories, each with its own policy and planning methods: wholesale and retail prices. Retail prices for goods and services are fixed so as to establish an equilibrium between supply and demand and so as to influence the latter in the direction required by the authorities, given a particular level of purchasing power. Wholesale prices are the aggregate of production costs and the normal profit margin. The difference between retail and wholesale prices, ignoring distribution costs, is composed of the turnover tax, which is at one and the same time a net revenue for the State and a means of establishing a flexible link between wholesale and retail prices. If the State raises the enterprise wholesale price to stimulate production of a particular commodity, the retail price will not necessarily increase; in this case the yield of the turnover tax will fall and the profit of the producing firm will rise. Conversely, the State may decide to increase or diminish retail price so as to reduce or stimulate consumption without changing wholesale price: only the tax yield will rise or fall.[5]

It is noteworthy that the turnover tax is virtually not levied on capital goods (with a few exceptions: oil, gas). It is as if the Soviet State had chosen to collect its net income—representing its own participation in productive activity—at the stage of distribution of final goods. But that does not change the economic nature of this tax. Through the price mechanism the total profit from the sale of final goods is in effect divided into two parts: one part, included in enterprise wholesale price, goes to the enterprise; the other part goes to the State in the shape of the turnover tax (which explains why this tax is not considered to be an indirect tax in Soviet financial theory).

The basic planned price is the enterprise wholesale price. When the planner has to fix the price of a new product, he proceeds in the following manner: he adds to total cost a rate of profit which is generally low (3% to 5% of cost); since the reference cost is the cost price of the first year of manufacture, it is anticipated that the cost will fall progressively and that the real manufacturing rate of profit will stabilise at the normal level. Evidently this method does not encourage the manufacture of new products, since profitability is at its lowest point in the initial stages of production. Various ways have been tried to get round this inconvenience, notably the establishment of higher provisional wholesale prices. But experience has shown that it is very difficult to lower prices once the period for assimilating new products is passed.

We shall not return here to the special problems of agricultural prices, which are still mainly political (*cf.* chapter 3).

Let us now turn to the reform of industrial wholesale prices, introduced on 1 July 1967 as part of the general economic reform. How did it integrate the theoretical propositions examined above?

THE 1967 REFORM OF WHOLESALE PRICES

The principle of reform had been decided in 1960. The preparatory work before 1965 retained the basic formula traditionally applied in planning:

Price = cost of production + margin of profit proportional to this cost.

It was therefore necessary first to determine the average cost of production for each product. At first (1961) the intention was to take the cost indices of 1961. However since the structure of costs was modified by the implementation of new rates of depreciation on 1 January 1963, the initial data had to be rectified.

The data for the calculation of costs, supplied by enterprises, were collected by the Central Board of Statistics, which then worked out average branch costs. This calculation was difficult, since the Central Board was not equipped with a sufficiently precise methodology and because the data supplied by enterprises were incomplete and even deliberately falsified (enterprises having raised their costs so as to obtain better prices for their products).

Some idea of the preliminary work involved can be gained from the fact that in 1965 draft lists of prices covered 38,400 printed pages; every branch had its price schedules (the electronics industry, for example, has twelve schedules covering *in toto* more than 50,000 price items!).

Next the chain reactions resulting from price .changes were calculated. Suppose, for example, that the planner estimates that for coal-mining to be sufficiently profitable it is necessary to raise the present price of coal by an average of 40%. At the same time it may be felt necessary to lower the price of engineering and metal industry products by about 20% on account of high profits in these branches. But if the price of coal is increased, costs in the metal and electric power (thermal) industries will rise. To guarantee them a normal rate of profit, their prices will have to go up, with obvious consequences for costs in engineering. Consequently the price reduction in this branch will have to be less than was originally anticipated if the initial profit/cost ratio is to be maintained.

To resolve this problem, use was made of the inter-branch balance for production and distribution (*cf*. chapter 5). With this it is possible to ascertain the distribution of the product of a given branch between various uses, and conversely the consumption by each branch of the products of other branches. One can deduce the repercussions of a price change in a given sector on the costs of other sectors, and the return effects of these repercussions themselves (what the Soviets call ricochet effects).

A revision of prices in this form was practically complete when the 1965 reform intervened. The work had to begin again and had to be completed quickly since the introduction of new prices was a *sine qua non* of reform in the greater part of heavy industry, hitherto in deficit.

In these conditions the first objective of the planner was to ensure that every branch was sufficiently profitable for each enterprise, given normal management, to make a profit adequate for paying the charge on productive capital and for building up its stimulation funds. For this reason it seemed impossible to keep the previous formula (the addition to cost of a profit margin proportional to cost), since the adoption of a more or less uniform rate of profit/costs (fixed before 1965 at about 12%) would give an unfair advantage to enterprises with a low capital coefficient. It was therefore proposed that a profit margin should be calculated which was proportional to productive capital, and which would be added to costs. In fact the planner showed no inclination to abandon the traditional method: the new prices were established according to the old formula, but account was taken of the capital intensity of production. In practice the methodological instructions for price revision involved the following procedure: definition of the rate of profitability (profit/productive capital ratio) at branch level; calculation of the mass of profit (M) obtained by applying this branch rate; calculation of the rate of profit (M/branch total cost); determination of the price of each product, by adding to average unit cost the profit margin proportional to cost. It seems that in fact the planning departments often economised on the first stages of this calculation, and quite simply took the rate of profit obtaining before reform after applying a corrective coefficient chosen empirically.

Whatever the case may be, the reform did achieve one of its aims: it has reduced the number of firms with a planned deficit. But they still account for 6% of total production, as against 20% before reform. The extractive sector of industry remains in deficit. To make all coal mining profitable, for example, the price of coal would have had to be quadrupled and not merely increased by 78%. Reform was also supposed to lead to a certain equalisation of profitability rates. However the authorities have deliberately chosen to maintain different levels of profitability in different branches: for a rate of 15% in industry as a whole, prices were fixed so as to give an average rate of profitability of 13.5% in heavy industry and 20% in light industry. What has been the result in reality? The following are the real rates (profit/productive capital ratios) prevailing in industry after the new prices had been introduced:

	1967	1968
Industry, total	17.1	20.1
of which:		
electric power	7.2	10.6
oil, extraction and primary processing	18.6	25.5
coal	—5.3	8.2
iron and steel	14.2	19.2
chemicals	16.0	16.2
petro-chemicals	27.1	30.3
engineering	20.1	21.2
light industry	38.3	39.6
food industry	21.0	22.4

The variation in profitability rates has therefore been wider than was anticipated in the reform.

Overall, prices were considerably increased: 8% for the whole of industry, 15% in heavy industry. Where the rise would have led to excessive profits, one of two methods was applied by way of counteraction. The first was to pay the producer a lower price than that paid by the purchaser, the difference being pocketed by the material and technical supplies department for subsequent payment into the budget (the so-called account price technique). The second method was a special tax called rent payment, levied on enterprises making very high profits.

Certain enterprises or branches may in fact earn high profits because prices must take into account the fact that some products can be substituted for others. This is especially true of fuels. The equalisation of profit-earning capacity in this sector would lead to much higher prices for coal than for oil and gas. But in order not to discourage firms from using coal as a fuel, prices had to be harmonised. The present prices for calorific equivalents of coal, oil and gas are fixed at indices of 100, 103 and 93 respectively. Consequently enterprises producing oil and gas have above-average profitability, which is equalised by the methods described above.

Finally, it must be remembered that retail prices were not modified in the reform.

Soviet price policy can be characterised in the following way:

In the first place, it remains highly centralised and authoritarian. Prices are determined centrally. They are imposed on the enterprise without discussion. The enterprise is only involved at the beginning of the procedure, in communicating its production costs.

Secondly, it has no rational basis. Of course, in principle the planner uses the synthetic price formula given above (the Diatchenko formula), which has been approved officially. But there is a great difference between this formula and the methodological instructions given to pricing authorities, and a similar gap between these instructions and the old routine which is still apparently applied.

Thirdly, the best methods for calculating prices are not in use. One might think that authoritarian planning would at least profit from modern techniques (computerisation, etc.). To judge from the slowness of reform, it would seem that these techniques are very little utilised. Consequently just as one general price revision has been completed it is already almost time to begin again.

Does price planning in the other socialist countries escape these defects?

Before economic reform, prices were generally determined in much the same way as in the U.S.S.R. The reforms were everywhere accompanied by a revision of prices (*cf.* table 6.1): to ensure adequate enterprise profits with a view to covering costs, and to building up incentive funds and margins for budgetary payments. From that point onwards, however, the methods of price determination used in the socialist countries are very different from Soviet practice, and in three ways in particular:

Firstly, the price base has been more precisely defined. In Czechoslovakia and Hungary, for example, the price of production formula was chosen, with a single rate of profit for the economy as a whole.

Secondly, prices planning is more scientific: price models are established and calculated by modern techniques. The evolution of the price structure is planned in such a way as to avoid any revision of prices *en bloc*.

The third and main difference between the U.S.S.R. and the other socialist countries is that the procedure for determining prices is less authoritarian and less centralised. There is greater freedom in this area for enterprises or groups of enterprises (*cf.* chapter 2). But as we have already seen, it would be wrong to conclude that prices are formed freely on the market; prices are always imposed for essential products.

Given the way in which prices are formed in socialist countries, it is easier to understand the purposes for which they may and may not be used.

Prices are an instrument for measuring value. When they depart from values they cannot fulfil this role. They are then considered to be a means of economic action in the service of a particular incomes policy. This is the case for retail prices which orientate individual consumption, and for agricultural prices in a general sense (the purchase price of agricultural produce, and of machinery and industrial products needed in agriculture). This action through prices is closely linked to financial policy. In the U.S.S.R. the turnover tax makes it possible to vary retail prices without affecting wholesale prices. Conversely, when the prices of agricultural machinery and fertilisers were raised after the general reform of industrial wholesale prices in July 1967, the prices paid by farms were not changed and were in fact below wholesale prices. The difference was made good by budgetary grants.

Industrial wholesale prices are in theory the closest possible expression of values. They could therefore be used by planners at macro-economic level for checking the coherence of adjustments in value and in kind. But we have seen that Soviet planning is based on the system of material balances, which are established in kind. Parallel value balances are certainly calculated, but they

TABLE 6.1[6]

PRICES IN SOCIALIST COUNTRIES

	Bulgaria	Hungary	Poland	G.D.R.	Romania	Czechoslovakia
Dates of wholesale price reform	1 January 1962 1 January 1969 1 January 1971	1 January 1959 1 January 1965 1 January 1968	1 June 1960 1966 (lower chemical product prices) 1967 (engineering) 1 January 1971	1 January 1964 (raw materials, power) 1 July 1964 (chemical products, textiles) 1 January 1965 (other intermediate products) 1 January 1967 (engineering)	1963	1 April 1964 (raw materials, semi-finished products: average rise of 34%) 1966 (average rise of 3%) 1967 (average rise of 25%) 30 August 1969 (price freeze)
Degree of price flexibility	Fixed prices for essential products + contractual and ceiling prices, price brackets	Fixed prices (30% of raw materials, 1% of finished products, 20% of retailed products) Ceiling prices (40, 10, 30%) Price brackets (2, 4, 27%) Free or contractual prices (28, 85, 23%)	Fixed prices in general Negotiated prices for goods made to order	Fixed prices (for most products) Ceiling prices Negotiated or calculated prices Considerable price differentiation according to quality	Fixed prices	Fixed prices (64% of products in 1967) Price brackets (29%) Free prices Since 1970: fixed prices
Influence of foreign trade prices on domestic prices	Export taxes or subsidies	Partial harmonisation of domestic prices with foreign prices	Partial harmonisation of domestic prices with foreign prices	Export taxes or subsidies	Limited	Partial harmonisation of domestic prices with foreign prices

only constitute for the planner supplementary means of verification, or else, in the case of macro-economic balances (national income, gross social product), very general models of the development of the main aggregates during the planning period. If planners resort so infrequently to value calculations, it is because they have no confidence in prices as a measure. Given the rule-of-thumb methods used in fixing prices, they are probably right. At the level of macro-economic planning, prices are used in assessing investment efficiency and the choice of the main methods of production. But even since the 1967 reform prices cannot constitute a safe indicator of scarcity, especially since the principle of a single profit rate equalising the return on capital in all branches has been ignored.

Even at the micro-economic level, as the mathematical economist Novojilov pointed out in an article published after the price reform, prices do not provide sufficient information. They do not tell the enterprise what to produce, what sort of quality is desirable, nor what the upper limit should be on socially necessary production costs, nor do they provide information on optimal factor combination. If prices do not give the information required for making economic decisions, then this information has to come through administrative orders and sanctions: hence the maintenance of a bureaucracy and the impossibility of abandoning the authoritarian distribution of the means of production.

According to this author and the school of Soviet marginalists as a whole, prices can certainly be rationalised, but even more systematic reform would not really get to the root of the problem. Prices should not first be fixed and then used to determine the orientation of production. The procedure should be reversed. The optimal plan must first be calculated, defining the maximum output possible with available resources; the general structure of production would be determined by the authorities in view of final consumer demand; optimal corresponding prices could then be established.[7] Novojilov would proceed to calculate this optimal plan–optimal prices scheme by branches. It would be necessary to formulate plan variants approximating as closely as possible to what he calls 'demand price' (reflecting the maximum labour which society is willing to allow for the production of one more unit of a given product) and 'supply price' (minimum price covering production costs of the product in question on the assumption that producers are using the most efficient production methods).

Such proposals are not feasible in practice. But it does not follow that an attempt should not be made to rationalise the process of price formation, so as to make of prices a more efficient tool in the measurement of values. This can be done by: a more precise calculation of production costs; by frequent and partial revisions of the price structure so as to avoid a situation, such as exists in the Soviet Union, where immediately after a mammoth reform of prices their internal structure is already out of line with the relationship between costs and profit; by a more systematic application of the planner's price formula (cost + profit margin proportional to productive capital). Two reasons explain why the socialist countries of Europe seem to have 'better' prices from this point of view than the Soviet Union. Firstly, they tend to have better organisation in their planning departments. In the second place, the smaller scale of their economies makes possible a more rapid and better co-ordinated calculation of a more limited number of prices. At the time of price reform in Czechoslovakia, for example, about 1.5 million concrete prices were dealt with by electronic computer. In the Soviet Union an addition of the items on the sectoral price scales would give a figure of several millions.

A more rational prices structure would make it possible to avoid not the central planning of production and investment, but the establishment in detail by planners of the required supply of products by enterprises and their purchases of intermediate goods. If the enterprise is induced to maximise profits by means of an effective incentive system, and if it is left a certain freedom of choice in determining the volume of its production and its supplies, the global proportions of the plan will not be disturbed provided that prices have been correctly established. For example, if the prices of intermediate goods are below value, the liberalisation of exchange will cause enterprises to rush to buy these products, with a consequent hyper-extension of demand. It will then be necessary to revert to some form of authoritarian distribution. If, on the other hand, prices correspond approximately to values, there will certainly be local distortions (a greater demand for a particular product than was planned for), but the plan will be able to correct them precisely on the basis of the information being communicated by the market mechanism. Such a procedure could be accompanied by a degree of price flexibility (within specific limits). It is possible to conceive of a system in which prices would be fixed for product groups, and in which the enterprises themselves would establish the selling prices of goods falling within a particular category. This would certainly make future price revision easier.

Up to this point we have examined prices as the monetary expression of value, taking the valuation of labour itself as given by the wages structure. In Marxist theory the value of a commodity is created by labour. It is therefore essential that wages and other forms of pay should be a correct measure of labour.

2. MONEY AS A MEASURE OF LABOUR: INCOME FORMATION

The question is complicated by the fact that wages appear on the one hand as a measure of labour supplied and on the other as an element in incomes policy.

The principle of distribution according to the labour contributed is the basic principle of socialism: from each according to his ability, to each according to his work. The coming of communism, in Marxist theory, will bring with it a higher principle: from each according to his ability, to each according to his need (this in a society of affluence some time in the distant future: 1961 programme of the Communist Party of the Soviet Union). But from the beginning of socialism, in addition to distribution according to the criterion of work, other forms of distribution according to need have had to be introduced. In other words it was found necessary to satisfy certain collective and individual needs, both material and cultural, regardless of the specific work contribution of the beneficiaries. Consequently, the total income of workers in the socialist system is made up of pay plus the advantages accruing from the social consumption funds.

The Determination of Wages and Pay

After the Revolution, during the period of War Communism, different forms of pay in kind were employed in the U.S.S.R., including food rations, a procedure which conformed to the idea of abolishing monetary categories altogether under socialism. But money payments were soon reintroduced into industry. This was not the case with agriculture, where certain forms of payment in kind persisted until 1966. At present it can be said that in general all Soviet workers are paid in money.

We shall not return here to the question of *kolkhoz* pay (*cf. supra,* chapter 3). This is subject to special regulations, especially since the income of *kolkhoz* members is derived from two sources: pay from the co-operative itself and income from the sale on the free market of produce from their private plots of land. In the case of *sovkhoz* workers, their wages are fixed in much the same way as those of the industrial labour force. And how are these established?

The Stalinist period was characterised in this area, as in others, by a voluntarist policy comprising several elements:

The basic form of pay was the efficiency wage or payment by results. This wage was completed by a system of bonuses linked to overfulfilment of production plans and constituting from 45% to 60% of total pay.

Wage differences between equivalent jobs were considerable: according to branch (priority for heavy industry meant higher wages in coal-mining, iron and steel, power and engineering than in light industry); according to working conditions (work underground was better paid than surface work, etc.). On the other hand, wage differentials between regions were low, since the forced recruitment of labour meant that where necessary workers could be sent 'administratively' into regions with a harsh natural environment (Siberia, Far East).

Wage differentials based on skill were also substantial, and the theses of War Communism preaching the levelling out of wages were attacked.

After the death of Stalin, the Twentieth Party Congress stated in 1956 that priority should be given to revising the system of wages and salaries. A series of decrees followed between 1956 and 1960. Present policy has two main features:

Firstly, to rationalise wage determination with a view to ensuring equivalence between wage and work done;

Secondly, to make sure that at the macro-economic level there is equivalence between the mass of distributed wages and the results of the labour process; in other words, the right proportions must be established between the growth of wages and labour productivity.

Wages are fixed by the economic authorities. At present that means by the State committee on labour and wages, with the participation of the trade unions. In theory wages cannot be determined by the individual enterprise, but in spite of the absence of a legal labour market firms have always attempted, by devious means, to attract or retain the work-force they thought necessary (particularly skilled labour). The situation was in no way changed by the economic reform of 1965.

The Fixing of Individual Wages

The wages system established between 1956 and 1960 comprises the following elements:

1.   Increased predominance of time-wages. Payment by results covered 76% of workers in 1936, 77.5% in 1956; by 1960 it had fallen to 58%, and the proportion continues to decline. This development is due to a greater concern for rationality and justice. Formerly payment by results was calculated by means of a large number of different formulae (progressive piece-rates, indirect piece-rates for white-collar workers, collective piece-rates for team production). The system was also based on output norms which were arbitrarily established, rarely revised and often unco-ordinated. The basic wage is at present completed by bonuses. But as a result of economic reform, they are no longer essentially linked to individual output, but to the total output of the enterprise collectively (since they are paid out of the incentive fund derived from profits).

2.   A narrowing of wages dispersion. Before the 1956–60 reform there were more than 2000 wage scales. For the whole of industry there are now ten. Each scale is divided into categories (six to ten) corresponding to qualifications. The qualifications themselves are outlined in professional schedules, which define the work required of a worker with a particular skill and the knowledge necessary to fill the corresponding job. The ratio of the lowest to the highest wage category within each scale stands at present at a minimum of 1 to 2 and

a maximum of 1 to 3.75 (coal-mining). The average is 1 to 2.6. The general minimum wage was raised to 60 roubles a month on 1 January 1968, and is to be further increased to 70 roubles a month in the period 1972–75.

3. A reduction of the disparity existing between branches of the productive sector by selective wage increases; the 1971–5 plan has fixed a timetable for these increases: 1971 for railway workers and agricultural mechanics, 1972 for doctors and teachers, 1974–5 for employees in the health services and commercial sector.

4. On the other hand greater regional differentiation to attract labour to the Great North, Siberia and the Far East will be linked to the abolition of the various forms of constraint used in the past to supply these underdeveloped regions with labour power. A resolution of 26 September 1967 made it easier for workers in such remote areas to benefit from the various advantages attaching to employment there: a three-year instead of a five-year labour contract; all activities are now covered, not only the previous beneficiaries in heavy industry, building and transport; the advantages themselves consist of increases in wages (10% every six months or every year up to a ceiling of 100% of the initial wage or 300 roubles a month), various benefits (payment of a grant equal to 50% of the average wage when the contract is renewed; removal expenses), lower retirement age (fifty-five and fifty years for men and women respectively).

In the other socialist countries, wage determination has generally followed the lines of Soviet development. The main difference is the absence in these countries of regional wage differentiation. That is easily explained. The smaller size of the countries of Central Europe and a more even distribution of the population makes it possible for them to dispense both with organised recruitment and economic incentives to attract labour to distant or under-populated regions. Yugoslavia is an exception. Taking 1966 as the base year (100) for the whole of the country, the wage index was 84.9 for Macedonia, 92.5 for Montenegro, 92.7 for Bosnia-Hercegovina, 98.2 for Serbia, 102.6 for Croatia, 116.3 for Slovenia. This shows considerable wage dispersion regionally. The pattern, however, is the reverse of that prevailing in the Soviet Union, since it is in the least developed regions that wages are at their lowest, a situation which accentuates the tendency for labour to migrate to the most industrialised areas. The position in Yugoslavia is due to the fact that wages are not planned but are fixed at enterprise level by the organs of self-management. It is in fact the practical application of the principle of self-management which reinforces initial inequalities in this area.

Apart from regional wages policy, the socialist countries followed the Soviet pattern very closely in reforming their wages and salaries system. There has been in every case a rise in the proportion of time-wages to payment by results. Before 1960 the latter brought the same inconveniences as in the U.S.S.R., and especially an uncontrolled rise in wages, since an automatic increase in pay could be achieved simply by lowering output norms. Similarly there has been a rise in the share of the basic wage in total pay, accompanied by a more rational organisation of the bonus system. Sectoral differentials (*cf.* table 6.2) are tending to narrow, but follow the same general principles: relative advantage of productive sectors over so-called non-

TABLE 6.2[8]

AVERAGE MONTHLY WAGE DIFFERENTIALS BY SECTOR IN SIX SOCIALIST COUNTRIES (INDUSTRY=100)

	Bulgaria		Hungary		Poland		G.D.R.		Czechoslovakia		U.S.S.R.	
	1950	1964	1950	1964	1950	1964	1950	1964	1950	1964	1950	1964
Productive sectors												
building	+18	+19	−7	+3	+16	+8	−3	+4	+6	+7	0	+5
agriculture (State)	−22	−15	−44	−16	−36	−24	−22	−13	−34	−18	−39	−30
transport	+17	+9	−14	−1	−10	−6	−6	+3	−1	+7	−5	+2
commerce	−7	−14	−7	−12	−19	−24	−20	−18	−30	−22	−33	−35
Non-productive sectors												
municipal services	−12	−18	−5	−1	−21	−13			−24	−30	−36	−36
public health	−14	−17			−41	−26			−18	−23	−32	−35
teaching	+7	−10			−20	−15			−18	−17	−20	−22
banking and insurance	+17	−10			−10	−13					−17	−21
administration	+1	+5			−11	+3					+2	−5

productive sectors (administration, services), and within the productive sector the advantage of heavy industry (the average wage is everywhere higher in mining, metallurgy, oil industry, etc., than in industry as a whole). Finally, as in the U.S.S.R., the period of high wage dispersion due to qualifications has been followed by a levelling tendency varying from country to country. In Czechoslovakia, for example, wage differentials due to qualification are extremely narrow. An inquiry carried out in 1968 in three engineering factories revealed that the highest grade technician earned an average wage 20% above that of the unskilled worker (and higher than that of the engineer coming straight from university). According to U.N.O. estimates, the average difference in socialist countries between the industrial wages of engineering and technical staff on the one hand and workers on the other was 40%–50% (with a maximum of 65% in Poland and a minimum of 30% in Czechoslovakia).[9] This development is dangerous in that it is hardly an incentive to acquire knowledge and skill.

From the viewpoint of wage differentiation Yugoslavia again occupies a peculiar position. There was a marked levelling tendency until 1956. Since then differentials have grown due to the free play of market mechanisms and the autonomy of enterprise. Within firms wage ratios according to different qualifications and jobs are on average 1 to 4, 1 to 2.5 at a minimum, and 1 to 10 at a maximum. The differentials between enterprises in the same branch are often considerable, and are the outcome of the relative prosperity of productive units. Although between industrial branches differentiation follows the same pattern as in other socialist countries (relative advantage of heavy industry: electricity, oil, chemicals), the reverse is true of the relationship between sectors. Commerce, services, public administration and especially the banking sector all offer higher pay than the industrial average (*cf.* table 6.3).

TABLE 6.3[10]

INDICES OF DIFFERENTIAL PAY IN YUGOSLAVIA BY SECTOR

			1963	1964	1965	1966	1967
Economy (as a whole)	...	...	100	100	100	100	100
Industry ...	...	...	102.9	103.7	103.5	101.8	99.5
Agriculture, fishing	...	...	80.1	79.4	82.4	87.1	90.1
Building ...	...	...	95.6	94.0	91.1	93.8	98.2
Transport	...	...	115.4	115.2	114.9	112.9	110.1
Commerce, hotel trade	...	...	107.4	107.4	107.0	107.4	108.2
Craft workers	...	...	98.2	96.0	93.0	92.6	95.5
Banking and insurance	...	...	145.6	139.2	138.0	140.2	150.5
Non-economic activities	...	...	132.4	126.1	123.1	117.4	122.1
Ibid.=100	...	...	100	100	100	100	100
Public administration	...	...	102.5	104.2	102.5	106.2	107.3
Teaching ...	...	...	100.5	98.4	97.3	94.9	95.5
Research ...	...	...	118.0	119.5	112.9	116.6	116.7

The experience of the socialist countries shows the difficulty of planning individual wages and especially of fixing the ratios between different wage categories. It is clear from the example of Yugoslavia that a free market mechanism in this area will result in pay levels and ratios quite different from those desired by the authorities. The difficulty is exacerbated by the existence of a labour market in these countries. Labour mobility is no longer limited by administrative regulations. Even in the Soviet Union the only restrictions now operative concern the following groups: young people leaving higher or technical education, who must work for three years in their profession in the enterprise or service to which they are sent; demobilised soldiers; young Komsomols sent to work in remote areas. Freedom to choose one's occupation is also guaranteed, assuming the necessary qualifications have been acquired. Access to higher education, the gateway to some professions, is by examination. But nothing prevents a failed candidate from entering employment straightaway and making use of the many forms of promotion available by following some educational course or other. In theory this freedom in the supply of labour is not balanced by a corresponding freedom of demand, at least in the U.S.S.R. and those countries which, in spite of economic reform, have retained planning control over the total enterprise wages fund. Given a fixed total fund as well as the wage rates which may be paid to different categories of worker, it is obvious that employment in the firm can only vary within very narrow limits. Nevertheless enterprises have always managed to retain a certain latitude in this area, twisting wage regulations by various methods of deception such as up-grading, multiplication of bonuses (politeness bonus, sobriety bonus, etc.). But hidden wage increases are not the only means used to attract a work-force, since wages are not the only factor in the labour market exercising an influence on the labour supply. The chance of an enterprise flat, for example, or particular social advantages offered by the firm play an important part.

In fixing wages the planner must consequently take account of the labour market. At the same time, like prices, wages constitute a tool of economic policy. Also like product prices, the price of labour has a theoretical basis, expressed in the formula 'to each according to his work'. Is this formula adequate?

If the formula is interpreted as meaning that each worker must be paid according to the quantity of work performed, one immediately comes up against the problem of the heterogeneity of labour, which was discussed earlier in connection with the theory of socially necessary labour time and prices. On that occasion it was seen that qualitative differences between different types of labour (due to labour intensity or workers' skills) were measured in practice by wage ratios. A given type of labour is considered to be more complex than another according to the wage attaching to each job. The labour of the worker on the basic wage being taken as unity, the labour performed by more skilled workers will be weighted by appropriate wage coefficients. But does the wage express these differences correctly? Given the present state of wage determination, the reply must be in the negative. That is why researchers (especially in the G.D.R., Czechoslovakia and the U.S.S.R.) have attempted to make direct calculations, without using wages, of conversion coefficients of skilled into unskilled labour, paying particular attention to the length and cost of previous professional training. So far this work has not influenced wage planning.

The principle of pay according to work can also be interpreted as meaning the need to pay each worker according to the results of his work, that is to say according to his contribution to society. But how can this contribution be calculated before the value of the goods produced has been determined? And how can their value be assessed before labour costs have been evaluated, that is to say before wages have been rationally defined? This is a vicious circle which has often been referred to and which makes the first interpretation preferable.

If we accept the first interpretation, along with the fact that the law of distribution according to labour means equal pay for equal work, wages will vary as a function of the quantity and quality of labour supplied.[11] But this principle gives no indication of the absolute level of the basic wage, nor of the wage ratios between different types of labour. That is why Soviet writers have recently developed another theory. According to this the law of distribution according to work is inadequate for fixing wages since wages must also be established as a function of the reproduction costs of labour power. The law of value does not of course apply to labour, which is not a commodity. But to determine the level of the basic wage it is necessary to calculate the minimum cost of reconstituting labour power. This cost will comprise minimum subsistence plus the expenditure socially necessary at any given historical period for the upkeep of the worker and his family, including expenses for education, leisure, etc. This would constitute a floor to wages and would be used by planners as a point of reference in fixing the guaranteed minimum wage. A wages ceiling would have to be calculated within the framework of the general incomes policy and would be linked to the growth of labour productivity.

General Wages Policy

For some years, socialist policies have been based on the principle that wage rises must not exceed increases in the productivity of labour. Incomes policies in the capitalist system are regulated according to the same principle.

The theoretical justification of this principle has been elaborated by several writers, but especially by the Soviet economist Bor,[12] whose argument runs as follows. The average wage is the ratio of the total mass of wages to the number of workers in the State sector; the average productivity of labour is the ratio of the national income of the State sector to the number of workers. The national income may be expressed as the sum of wages and primary incomes (before tax) in State enterprises; these primary incomes are used for investment (productive and non-productive), the maintenance of workers and establishments in the non-productive sector, and the complementary incomes of productive workers. The total monetary fund of productive workers' wages can therefore only increase by: a fall in investment; a fall in expenditure on the maintenance of the non-productive sector; a fall in the complementary income of productive workers, which means in practice a fall in the value of bonuses paid out of enterprise profits. If the State wishes to maintain a given rate of accumulation (share of national income allocated to investment) and if consumption in the non-productive sector must also be maintained as a given proportion of national income, a rise in the monetary wages fund must not exceed the rise in national income at constant prices. That means that the maximum rate of growth of average wages cannot exceed that of labour productivity.

In the Soviet Union this principle has been the official basis of wages policy since 1954, when State Bank control over enterprise wage payments was recognised and strengthened. This control was not weakened by the economic reform of 1965. The wages fund indicator is still imposed on firms, and the Bank will not release the sums necessary for paying workers until it has checked that they correspond with the wages plan. Between 1954 and 1967 the average annual rate of growth of labour productivity was stable at between 7% and 5%; the growth of the average industrial wage varied from 3.4% to 4.5% per year (table 6.4).

TABLE 6.4[13]

DEVELOPMENT OF THE PRODUCTIVITY/AVERAGE WAGE RATIO
IN THE U.S.S.R. (1951–75)

Years	Annual growth rate of productivity (1)	Annual growth rate of the average wage (2)	Ratio (2)/(1)
1951–55	8.3	2.2	0.26
1956–60	6.5	3.1	0.47
1961–65	4.6	2.5	0.54
1966–70	5.8	4.5	0.77
1971–75 (plan)	6.8	4.2	0.60

It cannot be said without reservation that the basic principle has been adhered to. There are a number of reasons for this.

In the first place labour productivity is calculated both too generally and by methods which are too rough and ready for wage determination to be really adapted to developments in productivity. The productivity index used in planning is the ratio between total production and the number of workers (by enterprise, by branch and at the macro-economic level). But since total production includes all intermediate consumption, the use of this index artificially raises productivity in processing industries. That is why theorists have recommended using the concept of gross domestic product. But this aggregate is not at present calculated in Soviet national accounting.

Secondly, at present there is considerable upward pressure on wages in the Soviet Union. In 1967 the minimum wage was increased from 40–45 roubles a month to 60 roubles, a rise of from 33% to 50% for the categories affected, with repercussions on the grades immediately above and on all benefits and allowances linked to the minimum wage. Taking other increases into account in the same year (notably a rise of 15% for 1.5 million workers in the machine-tool industry), the increase in the average monthly salary in 1968 was 7.5%, whereas productivity in industry rose by only 5%.

Thirdly, even if such wage increases are episodic (in 1969 the average industrial wage rose by 3.9% and labour productivity by 4.8%), the effects of economic reform should not be forgotten. Reform did not really modify the power of production units in wage determination, but it did open up new possibilities for enterprise to increase workers' total income (basic wage + bonuses). In so far as bonuses are paid out of profit, a residual factor which it is difficult to plan in advance, there is the possibility of an uncontrolled increase in total pay. That is why an experimental bonus scheme was introduced in 1962 for 102 textile firms and was later extended to a few enterprises in the food industry. According to this scheme, stimulation funds for the payment of bonuses vary as a function of the increase in labour productivity planned by the enterprise. If the enterprise proposes an indicator above the one calculated by its ministry, it can increase the bonuses paid to its personnel. This experiment will probably be extended to every branch where profitability is high and where enterprises are therefore tempted to distribute large bonuses to their employees.

Productivity may be improved at enterprise level by cutting down on the number of workers employed. However the economic reforms do not encourage the contraction of employment. Enterprises have a wages fund imposed on them and are tempted to use all of it. Since they must also adhere to current wage rates, the numbers they employ are largely predetermined. To stimulate a more rational employment policy in enterprises, a new and experimental method of wage planning was introduced into a chemical firm at Chekino (south of Moscow). The annual wages fund was fixed until 1970 at the 1967 level. Wage economies resulting from the dismissal of surplus personnel were left at the disposal of the enterprise for increasing the wages of workers and middle management. Within three years the enterprise had dismissed nearly 15% of its personnel, raised the average wage by 8.8% a year, and productivity even more. In 1969 the experiment was applied to petro-chemical and metallurgical enterprises as well. However in view of the potential technological unemployment it might bring, the experiment is unlikely to be extended to the economy as a whole. In 1972 it was operating in a total of 300 firms.

Finally, the upward trend of the average wage is limited by the rate of increase of productivity. The planner must keep well within this limit, for he must take account not only of nominal wages but of real wages. This means he must consider the influence of tax reductions (progressively downwards since 1960), the fall in retail prices (considerable between 1947 and 1954, slow since

1955), the shortening of the work period with no corresponding cut in wages, and especially the importance of the share of social consumption funds in workers' total incomes.

The difficulties inherent in an incomes policy are no less in a socialist than a capitalist system, in spite of the means at the planner's disposal. The reason is that decisions do not merely have to be imposed. They have to be taken rationally in the first place, and many of the factors involved escape the attention of the planner.

TABLE 6.5[14]

DEVELOPMENT OF NOMINAL (A) AND REAL (B) WAGES PER WORKER
(average annual %)

		1961–65	1966–70
Bulgaria	A	3.2	4.6
	B	1.9	3.9
Hungary	A	2.3	4.4
	B	1.7	3.4
Poland	A	3.7	3.7
	B	1.6	1.9
G.D.R.	A	2.7	3.5
	B	2.7	3.5
Romania	A	5.6	5.2
	B	4.1	3.7
Czechoslovakia	A	1.7	5.2
	B	1.2	3.5

Since economic reform, every socialist country has experienced an accelerated rate of growth of wages (table 6.5), accompanied in general by a decline in the rate of increase of labour productivity (table 6.6). In countries where the wages fund is still planned (U.S.S.R., G.D.R., Poland, Romania), the authorities have managed to keep wage growth within acceptable proportions by direct control. On the other hand in Hungary, Czecho-

TABLE 6.6[15]

AVERAGE ANNUAL RATES OF GROWTH OF LABOUR PRODUCTIVITY
IN INDUSTRY (%)

	1951–55	1956–60	1961–65	1966–70
Bulgaria	7.4	4.4	6.8	7.2
Hungary	3.7	3.7	4.9	3.5
Poland	9.6	7.0	5.1	5.1
G.D.R.	9.1	7.6	5.6	5.5
Romania	8.3	8.0	7.7	7.3
Czechoslovakia ...	8.4	7.1	3.5	5.2
U.S.S.R.	8.3	6.5	4.6	5.8

slovakia and Bulgaria the authorities have had to use the whole arsenal of financial and monetary policy, but without achieving the desired results.

An immediate consequence of economic reform in Czechoslovakia was a rise in wages: 8% in 1968, 10% in the first six months of 1969. And yet severe restrictive measures had been taken. Enterprises were obliged to pay a tax of 18% of their gross income (including the pay fund), and a so-called stabilisation tax representing 30% of the difference between the mass of wages actually paid in the year and 90% of the 1966 planned annual wages fund (last year of authoritarian wage planning). The local authorities were also empowered to levy a supplementary local tax not exceeding 2% of the wages fund. This heavy taxation did not prevent enterprises from allocating part of their gross income to wage increases. The credit restrictions imposed in 1968 had no more effect than increased taxation, since the financial position of enterprises was particularly sound, thanks to the rise in wholesale prices decided in January 1967 (an average of nearly 30%). Wage rises have therefore been subject to direct control since 1970 and limited to an average of 2.9% per year in industry.

Following economic reform in Hungary, enterprises were able in 1968 to dispose of nearly 40% of their profits, as against 15% in 1967. To prevent them from allocating too great a proportion to the payment of bonuses, various controls were imposed: in the building up of stimulation funds (expansion of production and profit-sharing) payment norms out of profit were calculated in such a way as to favour the first of these. Similarly in 1969 the creation of a reserve fund, which in 1968 was optional, was made compulsory. This fund, paid out of profit, must amount to at least 8% of annually distributed wages and 1.5% of the value of fixed productive capital. Its purpose is to cover any eventual deficit. Finally, still with a view to limiting the share of profit going to the profit-sharing fund, this share has been subjected to a progressive tax linked to the ratio of the fund to total wages.

Like Czechoslovakia, Hungary was obliged to re-establish direct control over increases in the average wage. In 1969 the limit was 4%. From 1 January 1971 there was a return to indirect control by means of a special and highly progressive tax on increases in the average wage (*cf*. chapter 2). There has been a similar move in Bulgaria, where a maximum ratio has been fixed between the wages fund and total enterprise production.

Social Consumption Funds

Up to this point in our examination of socialist incomes policy we have looked at the application of the principle 'from each according to his ability, to each according to his work'. The existence of social consumption funds, or what Marx refers to in his *Critique of the Gotha Programme* as funds for the collective satisfaction of needs, corresponds to the second stage of incomes policy, 'to each according to need'. In a socialist society, anticipating a future communist society, a certain number of consumer needs must be satisfied independently of the work contribution of individuals. That does not mean that social parasites are to be encouraged. Socialist law prohibits activity designed to appropriate income which is not the product of work: speculation, illegal sub-letting of flats, etc. The social funds are used by the State (or collectivities) to cover needs which would be incompletely or unequally satisfied. Their share in the population's total income varies from 20% to 30%, according to the country (table 6.7).

The principle of distribution according to work, even rigorously applied, cannot eliminate inequality in levels of consumption. In the first place, it applies by definition only to those in work. But society must care equally for people who are unable to work on account of their age or health. It might be objected that retirement or disability pensions are calculated as a function of the wage earned when active, that is to say as a function of the work actually done by the beneficiary. But a distinction must be drawn between the way the pension is calculated and the fact that it is allocated at all. The fact of its existence proceeds from a sense of social justice which is independent of the pay attached to any particular type of work. In the second place, the income from work is generally used for satisfying priority needs: food, clothing, housing. Consumption in the form of culture, leisure and even medical services tends to come second. If the goods and services in this second category have to be paid for, they will not be consumed by the worst-paid workers. To inequality of consumption due to inequality of pay must be added inequalities arising from different family situations. Large families are at an automatic disadvantage if income is not supplemented by allowances; again it is non-priority consumption which is sacrificed.

TABLE 6.7[16]

INCOME COMPOSITION OF THE POPULATION

	Bulgaria (1962)	Hungary (1963)	Poland (1964)	G.D.R. (1960)	Czecho-slovakia (1963)	U.S.S.R. (1960)
Total income	100	100	100	100	100	100
From work of which:	81	77	79	71 (c. 70)	—	77
wages and salaries	45	49	53	—	—	54
agricultural incomes (excluding wages paid by State farms)	33	22	21	—	—	21
of which in kind	—	14	10	4	5	—
private income and other	—	5	5	—		2
Social consumption funds of which:	19	23	18	29 (c. 30)	—	23
social advantages	9	8	7	14	14	—
transfers in kind	10	15	11	15	16	—
Other income	—	—	3	—	—	—

The collective satisfaction of social needs has made considerable headway in the capitalist system as well. The real difference between the two systems in this area is to be found in the underlying philosophy and application of social policy.

Using the U.S.S.R. as our example, the basic features of the social consumption funds can be outlined in the following way:

1.   The origin of these funds is social. In other words the resources for paying or allocating different types of benefit derive from the collectivity, that is to say from the State (budgetary resources), enterprises or co-operative farms. In 1965 the relative proportions of these three sources were 85.9% from the State budget, 10.7% from enterprise and State department funds, 3.4% from *kolkhoz* funds. Social policy is therefore essentially financed by the State. However it would be incorrect to say that since State budgetary resources come from taxation the beneficiaries of this policy also, in the last analysis, finance it. There are several reasons for this: in 1967 taxes accounted for only 7.9% of budgetary resources, whereas social and cultural expenditure reached 37.8% of total budgetary expenditure. It should be added that the lowest paid workers, who benefit relatively more from social services, are exempt from taxation. The second reason is that social security contributions, covering less than one-fifth of social and cultural expenditure, are paid into the State budget entirely by enterprises without deductions from workers' wages, and are therefore counted as part of cost price (representing anything from 4.4% to 9% of wages). The enterprise and *kolkhoz* funds are an ancillary source of finance of the social funds. They are constituted from payments out of profit. Enterprises use their fund for paying for extra holidays over and above the legal period, for building workers' flats, nurseries, play-parks, leisure clubs, etc. The *kolkhozy* finance a wider range of social measures, since in spite of a trend towards equality in this area between town and country the State still only covers 80% of the social needs of *kolkhoz* members (as against 90% for workers and employees). For example, the budget covers only two-thirds of *kolkhoz* retirement pensions, the rest being taken care of by the complementary *kolkhoz* retirement fund, whereas it finances the whole of workers' and employees' pensions.

The social origin of the consumption funds is in part paralleled by social management. Since 1933 the trade unions have managed the social security budget. Trade union agencies calculate and pay social security pensions and benefits, and distribute travel and rest home vouchers as well as running these homes.

2.   The social consumption funds constitute free allowances for the beneficiaries once certain conditions are fulfilled. For example, to qualify for a retirement pension one must have reached a certain age (fifty-five for women, sixty for men) and completed a certain length of service (which varies from sector to sector) in one's occupation. To qualify for a higher education grant the student must pass his examinations (76% of students receive a grant; family

circumstances are taken into account in their allocation). Free benefits pose no problem in their monetary form. Benefits in kind (goods and services) are more complicated. Some are free: children's general education, medical care. Others are so moderately priced as to be half free: parents must make a contribution to their child's nursery, playground, boarding-school, etc.; the same applies to people staying in rest homes (these are more like family boarding houses than medical establishments and are run by the trade unions; the worker may obtain a travel and residence voucher to take his family to a rest home for their holiday but he must pay part of the expense). Finally we come to a category on the dividing line between social benefits and goods which are simply very cheap. We shall classify them in the social consumption funds, since in the not too distant future many will doubtless be completely free, and already the price paid by the user is more like a statistical tax than a price reflecting the value of the goods or service in question. Housing comes into this category. 65% of the population (the proportion is higher in the town than in the country) live in accommodation belonging to the State or local collectivities, and pay a very low rent bearing no relationship to either maintenance or replacement cost. Certain other charges have to be added to rent. These are very low and fixed as a lump sum (water, gas, electricity and telephones are paid for in the form of fixed rates which are independent of use). Canteen meals and medical supplies are sold at very moderate prices (that is medical supplies bought directly by the user or on prescription from chemists' shops; in surgeries and medical establishments they are free). Urban transport is extremely cheap, as is entry to museums. Theatre and cinema seats might almost be put in this category, given the low prices everywhere, whatever the performance or accommodation.

The extension of free benefits comes within the logic of every socialist system and long-term action programmes usually anticipate it, as in the case of the 1961 C.P.S.U. programme. In the future there should be a reduction or abolition of contributions made by the beneficiaries of certain goods and services. Apart from the cost of such a policy, it might be asked whether the free supply of goods and services might not cause waste. It is unlikely that free meals will make canteen users eat twice as much or that free transport will generate a new race of compulsive travellers. However certain problems have already arisen as a result of this policy. Since electricity costs the domestic consumer practically nothing, he tends to leave his flat without switching off the light—although street posters tell him how irresponsible such an attitude is and urge him to turn it off before going out. As for cultural consumption, the present cheapness results in an unsatisfied demand. Since not everyone can see the best plays or listen to the best concerts, selection is no longer according to one's purse, but according to a system of toadying and recommendation which leads to the same inequality.

The policy nevertheless continues, especially for all forms of collective consumption. A characteristic of the social funds is that they are collective not only in origin but also in their use.

3. In the allocation of social consumption funds preference is given to collective uses. This is so for all services financed from the public health and physical education budget, for most cultural and educational services and for State housing. It is true that in all these areas the user benefits from a service individually, but the can only do so within a collective framework. Social security benefits are quite different. 97% are composed of individual allowances which can be isolated as such in the family budget (pensions, various allowances). The importance attached to collective consumption explains why in the U.S.S.R. family allowances are so little developed. Only unmarried mothers receive a monthly allowance to raise their children (up to the age of twelve years); mothers of large families (more than three children) also have a monthly allowance, but in 1965 the average was very low—7 roubles per month per qualifying mother. Benefits for large families are usually of the collective sort: nursery or boarding-school facilities, holidays, etc. The idea that an additional child might bring in money for the parents is felt to be repugnant. However, the 1971-5 plan contains a new measure which goes back on traditional social policy. It introduces family allowances for low-income families. As from 1974 regular allowances will be paid for every child where family income is less than 50 roubles monthly for each of its members.

In the other socialist countries, the policy of monetary aid to families is much more developed than in the U.S.S.R. Monthly family allowances are paid from the birth of the first child, especially in those states (Czechoslovakia, Hungary, G.D.R.) where a scarcity of labour has pushed governments into encouraging the birth rate. For example, in Czechoslovakia in recent years from 6.5% to 7% of the national income has gone into various family assistance schemes. These include not only family allowances as such (maternity allowances; monthly child allowances, from the first child for low-income groups and second or third child for higher income brackets) but also tax concessions and rent reductions for large families (up to 50% of average rent for a family with four children). In the G.D.R. families benefit from income tax reductions, allowances for the birth of each child, and monthly payments from the first child onwards, with special advantages for families with more than four children. The allowances are paid until the child is fifteen years old. In calculating old-age pension rights, women who have borne and raised children benefit from increased allowances. In Hungary alongside family allowances an original form of assistance for mothers was introduced in 1967. After maternity leave working women may request special leave until their child is two and a half years old and receive a monthly allowance equal to one-third of the average monthly wage of their profession. The measure applies equally to peasant women in the agricultural co-operatives.[17]

4. Almost half the social consumption funds take the form of monetary benefits; the share of benefits in kind must increase. The two tend to balance each other out: advantages in kind are consumed collectively; monetary benefits

can only be used individually, since the beneficiary is free to employ his pension, grant, etc., for whatever purpose he wishes.

5.   The social funds can also be grouped into benefits linked to pay (44% in 1965) and independent of pay (56%). In conformity with the principle of distribution according to need, the second is tending to grow as a proportion of the whole. Benefits in kind and in money are to be found in both categories. For example, the following monetary allowances are linked to pay: all types of pension, the total varying as a function of the wage; social security benefits for pregnancy and child-birth; holidays with pay. On the other hand family allowances are paid independently of the wages earned by beneficiaries. Most benefits in kind are allocated independently of pay, but pay is taken into account in placing children in boarding-schools, holiday camps, in distributing rest-home vouchers (and in calculating the personal contribution of the beneficiary).

An analysis of the present features of the social consumption funds shows clearly that they are still an imperfect reflection of the communist principle 'to each according to need'.

It is true that the share of these funds in total consumption rose from 9.6% in 1928, to 29.5% in 1965, and to 31.6% in 1968. But these proportions are not uniform throughout all social groups and the countryside is less well favoured than the towns. The *kolkhoz* peasants have less extensive medical and cultural facilities than State workers and employees, and their social security system is not so well developed.

Even if these inequalities were attenuated or abolished, the general problem posed by the extension of the social funds would not be solved. What should the optimal proportion be between these funds and individual pay for work in the total income of worker or consumer? And since the goods and services supplied through the social funds stand outside the market mechanism, how is it possible to evaluate the economic efficiency of investment in this area?

The first question was put previously in connection with the general incomes policy. This is based on the principle that the average wage must not rise faster than the rate of increase in labour productivity, precisely because the workers' total income includes social fund benefits in addition to his pay. But is it possible to go further and quantify the optimal relationship between pay and social benefits from which one might deduce a growth norm for them? In conformity with a socialist incomes policy, the Soviet authorities favour a faster growth of the social funds than of the total wages fund. The social funds may in fact be divided into two general categories: pensions and grants paid to members of society who do not work, and medico-cultural services supplied to the whole population. The first category is bound to increase at a slightly faster rate than the wages fund, since earlier retirement, increased longevity and the growing numbers of young people in higher education tend to increase the proportion of those benefiting from these allowances in the population as a whole. The second category of social benefits must also increase, since social progress implies a faster increase of medical and cultural than of basic material needs. An examination of recent Soviet plans reveals that for the period 1959-65 the social consumption fund rose by 74%, with a 53% growth in the national income actually consumed. The social consumption funds therefore expanded more quickly than nominal wages. For 1966-70, the two parts of total income (wages fund and social funds) were to grow at about the same rate, without any theoretical justification being given for this ratio. It seems that at present the social consumption funds are planned independently of income from work, and that this planning is based on a more or less stable proportion of socio-cultural expenditure in the State budget (between 37% and 38%) which is maintained from year to year.

Is there any attempt to evaluate the efficiency with which these resources are deployed, with a view to the maximum satisfaction of collective needs? Theoretical studies are made of the efficiency of expenditure on education, health and housing investment, particularly from the point of view of its effect on labour productivity, which tends to rise as a result of better qualifications, higher levels of culture, lower death rates and better living conditions. One particular feature of this research is the attempt to determine by how much better collective services increase the female labour supply. Practically speaking little use has been made of this work, and the efficiency of social expenditure is studied mainly from an organisational point of view: the better use of the educational and medical network, the more rational maintenance of flats, etc.

What criterion is used then to fix a limit to the satisfaction of needs through the social funds? At present this limit is imposed by available resources. However once affluence has been achieved under communism the planner will have to organise distribution according to needs which will have to be evaluated. How will he go about this, especially for non-material needs once basic consumption requirements have been met? How will he take account of individual preferences in matters of culture and leisure? The concept of a communist society implies an ideal citizen possessing simple if not austere and uniform tastes: this is a condition of totally free consumption, and reflects the Utopian character of such a society.

In the meantime, even with a systematic expansion of the social funds, it is doubtful whether perfect social justice and equality can be achieved. Inequality will inevitably continue to exist as long as a double principle is applied to income distribution: 'to each according to his work' and 'to each according to his needs'. Even if the free satisfaction of needs is expanded much more than at present, collectively and in kind, the person who earns more from his work will still be able to consume more. Luxury will then mean the purchase of those goods and services which are not distributed freely, or the possibility of opting for individual rather than for collective forms of culture and entertainment: collecting works of art for oneself, having one's own car instead of relying on free collective transport, etc. It could only be otherwise if payment in money were abolished. But the elimination of money as a universal equivalent seems to have been put off to a very distant future.

3. MONEY AS A MEANS OF EXCHANGE

We have so far examined the function of money in a socialist economy as a measure of the value of goods and of labour. In other words we have analysed the criteria used in planning for fixing prices and incomes.

The monetary income obtained by individuals serves to acquire goods and services at fixed prices. Money thus circulates in the economy as an instrument of exchange. How can the planner control the exchange circuit so as to obviate the build-up of pressures characterised by an excess or scarcity of money in relation to commercial needs; how can such pressures be detected and corrected?

A preliminary question must be answered first: can capitalist and socialist monetary mechanisms be compared from this point of view? In capitalist economies monetary disequilibrium is a reflection of macro-economic imbalance in growth. Inflation, for example, proceeds from an excess of total monetary demand in relation to supply at full employment level. Corrective action by governments in the monetary sphere is therefore a means of acting indirectly on economic growth. In socialist economies, on the other hand, economic growth is planned directly in 'real' terms (*cf.* chapter 4); the problem is to make sure that money, oiling the wheels of the economic machine, does not disturb the real equilibrium defined by the planning process.

In developed Western economies government policy attempts to ensure economic growth which is rapid (with the fullest possible utilisation of the human and material means of production), stable (without excessive price fluctuations), and equitable (with the greatest possible justice in income distribution—the criteria of 'justice' being subject to varying interpretations). At present all these economies are subject to an inflationary drift, or a more or less chronic upward trend in prices. Monetary policy (linked to other methods of intervention, such as incomes and financial policies) aims to contain this rise within reasonable limits, so as to avoid open inflation on the one hand or deflation accompanied by a contraction of economic activity and under-employment on the other.[18]

In a socialist economy the planner obviously has no need to worry about the eventual repercussions of variations in the general price level on the level of employment and the rate of growth. The resources of society are directly distributed by the plan between investment and consumption so as to maintain a high rate of growth of the national product. The plan guarantees full employment. Consumer goods are distributed in such a way as to absorb all resources available for this purpose, to avoid social inequality and to ensure a gradually rising standard of living.

What then is the field of application of socialist monetary policy? Within the productive sector money plays an essentially passive rôle: its purpose is to translate into financial terms the real data of production.

Within a classical frame of reference unchanged in the U.S.S.R. by economic reform, the plan imposes on enterprise the prices of its product, total distributed wages, the cost of supplies in intermediate goods, and its total investment. Money is an accounting instrument. It enables the State Bank to control the implementation of enterprise plans, since their transactions must still be effected through the bank. On the other hand at the level of exchange in the consumer sector money appears in an active rôle and could disturb the equilibrium anticipated in the plan between the production of goods on offer to the population, the level of incomes and the level of prices. This is because individuals are free to use their income as they wish.

Socialist monetary policy as traditionally practised is therefore only concerned with monetary circulation in the sector of consumption, adapting the quantity of money to transaction requirements in this area. If correspondence between the two is not achieved, if there is an excess quantity of money held by the population in relation to these needs, equilibrium will have to be re-established by action on prices, on incomes and on the supply of goods and services.

This classical conception was somewhat shaken by economic reform, but continues to exist in the U.S.S.R. and in those countries retaining close control over the activity of economic units. However, increased enterprise autonomy, particularly in their mutual transactions and in their wages policy, has brought about a certain activisation of money within the productive sector. This development has raised fresh problems for the banking and monetary authorities. The same conception is seriously questioned in those countries which have effected a more radical economic reform and which are now confronted by a monetary inflation in the productive sector.

Before examining the instruments and methods of monetary planning, we shall first look at the institution responsible for making use of them: the State Bank.

Monetary Issue: the State Bank

In every socialist country the issue of money and the overall control of monetary policy are in the hands of a central bank,[19] the State or National Bank. Usually there are also specialised banks (investment, agriculture, foreign trade, etc.), with subordinate and strictly circumscribed functions. They cannot operate an active banking or monetary policy. The Soviet State Bank will be used by way of illustration, since it served as a model to the other countries when they established their own banking systems after World War II.[20]

One of the first measures taken by the Bolsheviks was the nationalisation of the private banks, on 14 (27) December 1917. The State Bank was established four years later, on 12 October 1921, as a department of the People's Commissariat of Finance. It did not become totally independent of the Ministry of Finance until August 1954. However in the meantime it had acquired increasing power in the Soviet economy, especially as a result of the credit reform of 1931. This gave it a monopoly of short-term credit, by preventing enterprises in the future from granting credit to each other directly without going through the Bank. A further reason for its enhanced rôle was the gradual liquidation of the other banks.

During the N.E.P. period, there was a whole network of banks, including the industrial bank, the electricity bank, the bank for foreign trade, the bank for the Far East and Central Asia, the agricultural bank, and the co-operative and communal banks.

Between 1927 and 1932 this network was gradually simplified, and by the end of that period, apart from the State Bank and the Foreign Trade Bank, there remained only four long-term credit and investment banks: *Prombank* (industry), *Selkhozbank* (agriculture), *Torgbank* (state commerce), *Tsekombank* (communal services). Moreover these establishments were more like offices for distributing budgetary funds allocated to investment. In April 1959 a single bank for investment was set up. This was *Strojbank*, which, like the four establishments it replaced, is a fund for economic development rather than a bank, since long-term investment credit remains very limited in practice (even since the 1965 economic reform).

The State Bank of the U.S.S.R. or *Gosbank* is exchequer to the State and to the economy; it is the centre of credit to the economy; and finally it is the bank of issue. Let us look first at this last function.

As under the Tsars the Soviet monetary unit is the rouble. After the Revolution and until 1922 the old roubles ceased to be tender and were replaced by a kind of forced currency assignat, the *sovznaki*. In 1922, after the introduction of the N.E.P. and to put an end to the galloping depreciation of the *sovznaki* by reintroducing a real currency, bank notes or *tchervonets* were issued. These were worth 10 tsarist roubles or 7.74234 grm. of gold. The issue was 25% guaranteed by the gold and foreign currency reserves of the State Bank. For two years *sovznaki* and *tchervontsy* circulated together. In 1924 monetary reform abolished them both and reintroduced the traditional rouble. The *sovznaki* were exchanged on the basis of 1 rouble for 50,000 *sovznaki*; 1 *tchervonets* was valued at 10 new roubles (scrupulous care was taken to maintain equivalence with tsarist currency).

In 1926 it was forbidden to export the rouble, and in 1928 to import it. Since then there have been two dissociated Soviet currencies, the domestic rouble and the rouble of international exchange (since January 1964 there have in fact been two international roubles, following the creation of the transferable rouble for exchanges within the framework of Comecon). This dissociation is essential, since it makes internal monetary circulation totally independent of the state of the balance of payments.

THE DOMESTIC ROUBLE

The value of the domestic rouble depends on the value of the goods produced in the economy (once the standard of value has been chosen for the determination of prices). In order to ensure stability in the value of the currency, that is to say its purchasing power, the State Bank in its capacity as the bank of issue must maintain the right balance between the quantity of money in circulation and the real currency needs of the transactions of individuals (since transactions between firms are directly planned in kind).

The tools used for this purpose, which will be examined later, have not always protected the U.S.S.R. from inflationary pressures, reflected in excessive monetary circulation and a rise in retail prices. This was particularly true of two periods: 1929-32 (corresponding to the launching of the first five-year plan) and 1941-7 (war and reconstruction). Both had similar causes: the monetary financing of public expenditure (a deliberately inflationary policy of issue); inadequate control over nominal wages, which rose faster than productivity; stagnation in the supply of commodities on the retail market (due in the first period to a deliberate policy of priority for heavy industry, and in the second to the burden of military expenditure). In both cases the effects of inflation were an increase in retail prices on the State market, a measure which the planning authorities were forced to take in view of the dizzy rise of prices on the free market.

The 1947 monetary reform, the first in the Soviet Union since 1922-4, was intended to mop up war inflation. Notes in circulation were retired and exchanged at the rate of 10 old roubles for 1 new. The operation was overtly directed against speculators, especially *kolkhoz* peasants who were suspected of having enriched themselves by means of sales on the free market at excessively high prices. In fact 30% of the total volume of notes in circulation were not presented for exchange, the holders of excess liquidity rightly fearing that they would be subjected to investigation and sanctions.

There was a very different operation in 1961: on 1 January the unitary value of the rouble was multiplied by ten, that is to say all prices and incomes were divided by ten. In Soviet literature, the operation was referred to as a 'modification of the prices scale'. It was emphasised that contrary to the reform of 1947 the aim of the operation was neither to soak up inflation, which was non-existent in 1961, nor to control speculative incomes. At the same time, the gold value of the foreign rouble was multiplied by four. Some commentators concluded from this that there had been a *de facto* devaluation of the rouble. But in a system where a solid screen is placed between domestic currency and the currency used in international transactions, comparisons between the domestic purchasing power of the rouble and its international rate are meaningless.

THE INTERNATIONAL ROUBLE

Between 1928 and 1950 the rouble was not officially linked to gold. Its rate was fixed in relation to foreign currencies; but this was hardly more than a gesture, since the U.S.S.R. used—and continues to use—its gold and foreign currency reserves for foreign transactions, at international prices. The State monopoly of foreign trade, blocking access by Soviet enterprises to international markets and conferring on specialised agencies the responsibility for all foreign transactions, only reinforced the symbolical character of the international rouble. Until 1933 the rate of the rouble *vis-à-vis* the dollar was fixed at 1 rouble = 0.52 dollars. On 31 January 1934 the devaluation of the dollar led to a new official rate of 1 rouble = 0.87 dollars. At that time the normal rate for the franc was 1 rouble = 13.1 francs. From 1 January 1936 a more advantageous rate of 3 francs to the rouble was established for tourists. This rate was made official on 1 April 1936—an implicit devaluation which brought the rouble down to 23% of its previous value. This hidden devaluation was made possible by the absence of defined rates between 1934 and 1936, and by the substitution of the franc for the dollar as a reference currency. The procedure, however naive, is a clear indication of how careful the authorities are to conceal any depreciation of the national currency. From 1937 the instability of the franc meant that the rouble was once again linked to the dollar, 1 dollar = 5.30 roubles, which corresponded to 1 rouble = 0.167674 grms. of gold.

In 1950 the rouble was officially linked to gold (1 rouble = 0.222168 grms.). This meant that 1 dollar was now worth 4 roubles, a revaluation which the financial authorities justified by the fall in Soviet domestic prices of 29% since the 1947 reform. As part of the 1961 monetary reform referred to earlier the value of the rouble was raised to 1 rouble = 0.987412 grms. of gold = 1.11 dollars. It was in fact a devaluation, disguised as in 1936, but in such a way as to create the illusion of an appreciation of the rouble. The operation was necessary because the official rate established in 1950 had considerably overvalued the rouble. For that reason some Soviet economists had disapproved of the 1950 measures, but to no avail. Their stand was justified eleven years later. Appearances were safeguarded, however, and the prestige of the rouble maintained, since it was worth a little more than the dollar—a fine example of monetary vanity.

It might be wondered what use a devaluation or a revaluation is to a currency which is not used in international trade. The most common argument advanced in Soviet literature is the following: a long-term overvaluation (or, more rarely, an undervaluation) conceals the real efficiency of foreign trade.

When the currency is overvalued the federal foreign trade agencies lose on exports, since they must pay national currency to the exporting firms whose sales they are guaranteeing abroad at higher prices than they would obtain on domestic markets. On the other hand, the agencies gain on imports from the profits in national currency which they make on selling imported products to Soviet firms or organisations requesting them. It may be objected that these gains and losses cancel each other out, but in the long term the economic calculations of the foreign trade agencies are disturbed, and there develops an artificial impression of the cheapness of imports and the disadvantage of exports. From this point of view devaluation has positive consequences, since its first effect is to make imports dearer and exports a more profitable operation.

As far as everyday life is concerned, the official rate only affects tourists, since it is at this rate that they can buy roubles in the U.S.S.R. It is also interesting that they pay for most tourist services directly through Intourist (one of the foreign trade agencies), which invoices them at international prices bearing no relation to the price of the same services for Soviet citizens. Similarly, numerous products can be obtained by foreign tourists using foreign currency from currency shops at prices which are again very different from domestic prices. Table 6.7 gives socialist exchange rates against the rouble.

TABLE 6.7[21]

EXCHANGE RATES OF SOCIALIST CURRENCIES

Monetary unit	Rate in roubles on 1 January 1973		Gold content of the monetary unit
	official	for non-commercial transactions	
100 Albanian leks ...	18.0	11.94	not fixed
100 Bulgarian levs ...	76.92	128.21	0.759548
100 Hungarian forints ...	7.67	7.63	0.075696
100 dongs of the Democratic Republic of Vietnam...	30.60	52.08	not fixed
100 G.D.R. marks ...	40.50	31.25	0.399902
100 yuen of the People's Republic of China ...	45.00	77.52	not fixed
100 von of the People's Republic of Korea ...	74.93	69.44	not fixed
1 Cuban peso ...	0.90	—	0.888671
100 Mongolian tugriks ...	22.50	23.92	0.222168
100 Polish zloty ...	22.50	6.54	0.222168
100 Romanian leu ...	15.00	12.05	0.148112
1 Soviet rouble ...	—	—	0.987412
100 Czech crowns ...	12.50	10.36	0.123426
100 Yugoslav dinars ...	4.39	—	—

The creation on 1 January 1964 of a sort of second international rouble with the same gold value (0.987412 grms.), that is to say the transferable rouble used as a means of settlement within Comecon, has not changed the basic facts of the problem for the time being. This is because the second international rouble is not convertible and serves basically as a common unit of account within the socialist bloc.

It can thus be seen that the money issued by the Soviet State Bank has characteristics which are very different from capitalist money. The inconvertibility of the rouble and the State monopoly of foreign trade completely isolate the domestic monetary circuit from foreign influences. Even inside the country the concept of monetary circulation has a quite different sense from the one it assumes in a market economy.

The Planning of Monetary Circulation

As we saw at the beginning of this chapter, Marxist monetary theory distinguishes between two different functions of money: the function of circulation and the function of payment. In this way it dissociates a function which Western theory, both classical and Keynesian, has always considered to be unitary: the function of exchange.

This distinction, made by Marx and translated into socialist conditions by Soviet writers, is based on the division of the economy into two sectors which we encountered in relation to price formation: the productive sector in which relations are based on the socialist ownership of the means of production (industry, State agriculture, transport); the consumption sector based on personal property in which market relations continue to exist (collectivised agriculture, only imperfectly socialist, stands at the junction of these two sectors). There is a consequent dichotomy in the monetary circuit: in the socialist sector exchanges, even expressed in roubles, are not truly monetary; in the non-socialist sector, money circulates with all its concomitant dangers.

To these two functions of money correspond two types of money: fiduciary (notes and coin) and representative (bank money—credit balances in current accounts). Fiduciary money has the exclusive function of circulation and is confined to exchanges involving individuals. Representative or bank money fulfils the payment function. It does not circulate in the true sense of the word. It serves as a means of settlement between State production units, and between these and units of distribution. There are certain curious practical consequences. Individuals cannot utilise representative bank money. They have no account with the State Bank. They can open an account at the savings bank and even deposit part of their wages automatically (though this is rare). But there are no savings bank cheque books, and for the purchase of a car or flat the consumer must deliver a packet of roubles which may sometimes represent several months' wages. A short time ago the automatic deduction of rents and other charges from savings accounts made its first tentative appearance in some Soviet towns. With the exception of the G.D.R., cheque books for individuals are unknown in the socialist countries.

Conversely, State units of production and distribution must deposit all their liquid assets with the State Bank. Their own funds are almost non-existent. Sums for the cash payment of wages are delivered by the State Bank as required, on the basis of the wages fund plan imposed on the enterprise or commercial organisation.

To sum up, exchanges in money represent on the one hand flows of representative bank money between State units of production and distribution, and on the other hand flows of fiduciary money between these units and individuals, or between private individuals. Monetary planning does not concern the first type of flow, since this corresponds to planned movements in real terms (purchases and sales by firms). The present system of enterprise direction excludes all uncontrolled monetary movements by enterprise: payments reflect transactions anticipated in the investment or material and technical supply plans. In principle, they cannot obtain credit outside the Bank, and the procedure for the short-term credit it does grant is very complex, always ensuring the allocation of the credit to a particular use. The only danger is to be found in overfulfilment of the wages plan. That is the main reason that the wages fund remains under strict planning control, in spite of economic reform.

The planning of monetary circulation therefore concerns only fiduciary money flows. The following diagram gives a summary picture of these flows.

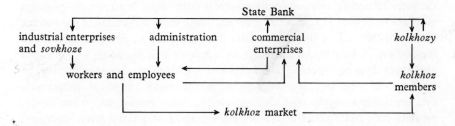

It can be seen how wages paid by enterprises and administrative agencies, together with *kolkhoz* pay, are used to purchase consumer goods and services on State and *kolkhoz* markets, the corresponding sums returning to the State Bank (paying in of commercial enterprise receipts, *kolkhoz* deposits).

In spite of the dichotomy of the two sorts of money, there is a degree of permeability between the circulation of fiduciary money and the circuit of bank money payments at every point where bank money is transformed into fiduciary money. That is why some economists have recommended overall planning of monetary flows. They emphasise that a liberal credit policy, reflected in swollen current accounts, is by no means neutral from the viewpoint of monetary circulation and can exercise an influence on the mass of fiduciary money. As yet these ideas have had no practical application, and both the instruments and methods of monetary planning relate primarily to fiduciary money.

THE INSTRUMENTS

In every socialist country since 1950-1, and in the U.S.S.R. since the introduction of planning, the main tool used by the State Bank is the population's estimated balance of income and expenditure.

An outline of this for the U.S.S.R. is given in table 6.8. Most of the items in this balance are worked out within the framework of general planning. Monetary income consists mainly of wages and salaries from work, used essentially for purchasing goods and services on the State market, where the volume of supply is planned and retail prices are fixed. Other items can easily be deduced from the plan: transport expenditure, various municipal charges, incomes from grants, retirement and disability pensions. There are other sources of income and expenditure which largely escape the planning authorities: *kolkhoz* pay, *kolkhoz* income from the sale of produce on the free market (and corresponding expenditure by the urban population). The pay disbursed by the *kolkhozy* is a function of their monetary receipts, which come mainly (85.5% in 1964) from the sales of agricultural produce to the State, the approximate total of which can be anticipated. Soviet government policy, aiming at a regular and guaranteed monetary income for *kolkhoz* members (*cf.* chapter 3), is doubtless linked to the desire to exercise greater control over the movement of incomes in the co-operative sector. A similar interpretation must be put on the introduction in 1966 of credit granted by the State Bank for the payment of wages on farms. This measure gives the Bank some knowledge of the volume of pay distributed in the countryside. The monetary movements over which the authorities have least control are in fact those corresponding to unplanned exchanges between *kolkhoz* members and the rest of the population. The existence of this free market constitutes the main threat of inflationary pressure: when supply is inadequate on the State market and when money incomes rise, State retail prices being maintained at a fixed level, there will inevitably be a rise in prizes on the *kolkhoz* market where supply is relatively inelastic. But this threat, considerable in periods of scarce supply on the State market (as is shown by past Soviet experience), diminishes as supply increases. and as the share of the *kolkhoz* market in the totality of agricultural produce sold decreases (a fall in fact from 18.1% to 9.5% between 1950 and 1965).

The population income and expenditure balance is therefore a synthetic table establishing a correspondence between the indicators of different plans: of production, of the sale of commodities and services, and of pay in different sectors. As table 6.8 shows, the balance is divided into two parts, A (corresponding to monetary movements in the socialised sector, or 90% of total monetary circulation) and B (exchanges on the *kolkhoz* market plus a few private transactions: payment for the services of a housekeeper, etc.). This global balance is completed by territorial balances (republics and regions), and by balances according to social group.

What happens when the two sides of the balance are not in equilibrium? If

TABLE 6.8

THE POPULATION'S BALANCE OF MONETARY INCOME
AND EXPENDITURE

Monetary incomes	total	workers employees	peasants	Monetary expenditure and saving	total	workers employees	peasants
A. From State and co-operative enterprises and organisations:				A. Expenditure in State and co-operative enterprises and organisations:			
1 Wages				1 Purchase of goods			
2 *Kolkhoz* pay				(a) From State and co-operative concerns			
3 Receipts from the sale of agricultural produce				(b) From the *kolkhozy*			
4 Pensions and allowances				(c) From consumer co-operatives at local market prices			
5 Grants				2 Payment for services (municipal charges, cultural expenditure, etc.)			
6 Payments from the financial system (e.g. loans, national lottery, interest on deposits, insurance compensation, building grants, etc.)				3 Taxes and rates, insurance premiums, repayment of loans, purchase of State bonds, etc.			
7 Other income (bonuses, business expenses, etc.)							
B. Receipts from the sale of goods and the supply of services to the population:				B. Expenditure on the purchase of goods and services from individuals:			
1 Income from the *kolkhoz* market				1 Purchase of food on the *kolkhoz* market			
2 Income from services				2 Payment for individual services, etc.			
Total A + B Fall in the liquidity balance of the population (difference expenditure-income)				Total A + B Rise in the liquidity balance of the population (difference income-expenditure)			

in preparing the balance there appears, for example, an excess of income over expenditure, the planning departments will have to take measures to increase the supply of commodities and eventually to raise certain prices. In the opposite case, the Bank will recommend either a lowering of retail prices or a rise in wages.

The population income and expenditure balance serves as a basis for establishing the cash plan of the Bank: under receipts, the paying in of takings from the sale of goods and services (90% of the total), and under payments, withdrawals from enterprise accounts for wage payments and other remuneration (about 80%):

TABLE 6.9

CASH PLAN OF THE STATE BANK

Receipts	Payments
Takings from commercial establishments, transport services, etc.	Outgoings for the payment of wages and other forms of remuneration
Other returns (taxes and rates paid by the population in cash, savings banks payments)	Withdrawals from *kolkhoz* accounts
	Payment of pensions and other allowances
	Other payments
Total	Total
Strengthening of bank finances from reserve funds	Payment of Bank cash surplus into its reserve funds

The cash plan of the Bank is necessarily in balance. If receipts exceed payments, excess cash is transferred to the reserve funds of the Bank. Conversely, if payments exceed receipts, the reserve funds are used to increase Bank finances. It is the second situation which is most often encountered and means in concrete terms an increase in distributed incomes which will not be precisely compensated for by anticipated monetary expenditure (purchase of goods and services, payment of taxes, savings bank deposits). The macro-economic plan will then have to make the necessary adjustments. Only then will the cash plan of the State Bank be approved, followed in due course by an authorisation of issue.

This brings us to a fundamental aspect of monetary policy: issue, or the injection of additional fiduciary money into circulation, can only be accomplished through a credit operation of the Bank.

Every credit operation does not *ipso facto* create fiduciary money. When the Bank grants credit to an enterprise or commercial organisation, it makes available means of payment out of the Bank's resources (deposits of other enterprises and organisations, its own funds, budgetary resources). These means may be used to pay other State units for supplies and services. In this case they remain in the circuit of representative bank money. At the same time they may be used to pay wages: in this case, credit oils the economic circuit with fiduciary money.

It is a function of the plan to calculate how much credit should be created throughout the economy as a whole, bearing in mind the requirements of economic growth and the avoidance of monetary disequilibrium. Over-generous loans to enterprises may encourage them to request the Bank to unfreeze cash for the payment of additional wages ('justified' by the requirements of production), and may lead to the creation of excess purchasing power and open inflation (hidden if prices are fixed).

The credit plan of the Bank, the third instrument of monetary planning, is therefore designed to indicate the possibilities of monetary creation, as a function of the needs of circulation and on the basis of Bank resources (*cf.* table 6.10). The approach of the planning authorities might be summarised in the following way: firstly, calculation of the monetary mass in circulation for the planned period by means of the population income and expenditure balance; secondly, establishment of the cash plan of the Bank, which determines the amount of liquidity to be fed into the economic circuit; thirdly, adjustment of the short-term credit plan.

TABLE 6.10

CREDIT PLAN OF THE STATE BANK

Resources	Uses
Funds (statutory, reserve)	Loans for temporary needs of enterprises
Deposits in settlement accounts (of State enterprises)	Loans against documents in circulation
	Settlement credits
Deposits in current accounts (of *kolkhozy*, trade unions, etc.)	Loans for wage payments
Deposits with savings banks	Loans to cover temporary shortage of working capital
Deposits of credit establishments	
	Other loans
Local budget deposits, republican and federal	Reserves of the Bank Committee
Money in circulation	Other assets
Other liabilities	

Where will the Bank obtain the resources necessary for an extension of credit and ultimately of the money issue without provoking inflation? It will utilise the permanent reserve built up from the annual surpluses of State budgetary expenditure. The rôle of the Soviet budgetary surplus in State financial policy as a safety reserve and counterpart of new Bank credit has often been underlined. The same is true of the other socialist countries.[22]

It is therefore essential for the State Bank, the only centre of credit in the economy, to exercise very close control over loans made to enterprise by its agencies and thereby over the money issue. An examination of practice in different socialist countries shows that in Hungary and Czechoslovakia the local agencies of the Bank have much more autonomy in this area than is the case in the U.S.S.R. This autonomy, together with the greater initiative of banking institutions in operating a selective credit policy (*cf.* chapter 2), contains a potential risk of inflation.

This last term was banned for a long time from socialist terminology, which preferred the expression 'excess money in circulation' and reserved the words inflation and inflationary pressure for the capitalist system. However a few years ago the word began to circulate freely in socialist literature, first of all in Europe and then in the U.S.S.R. It is now admitted that even apart from the serious historic inflations such as were experienced in the socialist countries after World War II, inflationary pressures may build up, in spite of rigorous planning of monetary circulation. What means are used to remove such pressure?

TRADITIONAL ADJUSTMENTS

These will be examined with reference to Soviet practice. To prevent the creation of an excess money supply, the planning authorities must control the expansion of the population's monetary income. In other words it must ensure the implementation of macro-economic policy on pay and the wages plan of enterprises. However, if an unplanned increase in wages should produce an excess of money in circulation, what will the immediate and spontaneous effect be?

Nothing in the productive sector (at least in the short term): a rise in labour costs does not mean that firms can increase prices, since these are immutably fixed. Similarly an increase in demand resulting from higher incomes cannot directly elicit a greater supply of consumer goods since the enterprises producing these goods have a plan determining a given volume of production. In the consumption sector individuals holding a quantity of money in excess of the possibilities of purchase on the State market have a number of alternatives. They can increase their deposits in the savings bank; or they can simply hoard their money. This amounts to forced saving in both cases. On the other hand they may decide to buy more on the free market and push prices up there: this mechanism was at the root of Soviet historic inflations.

To remove these pressures, the planner will have to take measures to re-establish equilibrium voluntarily. There are several possibilities:

1.   An increase in retail prices on the State market. This policy runs the risk of generating an inflationary drift, which, according to Soviet writers, is characteristic of capitalist economies. At the same time it would be contrary to traditional Soviet policy on retail prices which is to sell products of prime

necessity cheaply, even if supply is inadequate in relation to demand; the same applies to a certain number of social or cultural goods (books, mèdical supplies, records, etc.); a further element in this policy is to maintain the general trend of lower retail prices. The price index did in fact fall from 100 in 1950 to 74 in 1960. Since then there has been a slight upward trend due to a regular though moderate increase in food prices. Large increases have been applied only to luxury goods. On 1 April 1969 for example the prices of gold and platinum articles and of furs were increased at rates of from 60% to 75%. Retail price policy is based more on social considerations than on a concern for monetary equilibrium, and is often contrary to the latter. In 1964 the prices of transistor radios were reduced. This caused an even greater increase in an already inflated demand, in excess of supply possibilities.

2. An increase in the supply of goods. Obviously this increase cannot be automatic under conditions of Soviet planning (even since economic reform, which gives enterprise an interest in increasing sales, but does not provide the means for them to respond autonomously to a rise in demand for their products). The plan itself must anticipate an increase in supply when it creates additional purchasing power. The 1968 plan for example, anticipating an increase of 8.6% in the money incomes of the population, also fixed on a rise of 8.6% in the production of consumer goods. It goes without saying that an increase in the supply of commodities can only re-establish equilibrium if these particular commodities are in demand. Far from re-establishing equilibrium, planning policy can accentuate imbalance if there is an increase in the supply of goods with which the market is already saturated, and similarly if a shortage of scarce but much-sought-after goods is maintained. Then the planner will find himself both with stocks to be reabsorbed and liquid cash to mop up.

Soviet planning has hitherto concentrated more or less exclusively on the supply of current consumer goods. It has tended to neglect the supply of services and durable consumer goods, where demand has been buoyant for several years. From the point of view of monetary and financial policy for example it would be an advantage to develop the construction of flats in co-ownership (nearly 9% of total building in 1968). This would reduce State budgetary expenditure on housing and would at the same time absorb a part of the population's liquidity. But it would be contrary to present social policy in this area.

3. Recourse to financial instruments—taxation or borrowing. Both these tools have been used in the past, notably in the post-war anti-inflationary struggle in the U.S.S.R. Until 1957 State loans were imposed on wage-earners, and were more like taxation than a subscription in the usual sense of the word. This type of loan was terminated in 1957, redemption being staggered until 1967. At present there is only an optional lottery loan at 3%, which is hardly an effective weapon in the counter-inflation armoury. Similarly the rôle of household income tax is declining both as a source of budgetary revenue (*cf. infra*) and as a tool in the struggle against inflation (the planned industrial wage

increases of 1967 were accompanied by a reduction and not a rise in income tax rates).

4.　The mobilisation of household liquidity via saving. This is now the main tool of monetary policy. Private individuals are no longer forced to save administratively as in the past; they do so freely, since deposits earn interest (2% on current account deposits, 3% on fixed deposits), since they can reckon on reasonable price stability and since economic expansion means that in the near future they will be able to transform their accumulated savings into durable consumer goods. The significance of saving is confirmed by the following figures: in 1965 deposit balances at the end of the year were equal to the total value of non-food commodity stocks in the retail trade, or two and a half months' wages of all workers and employees; since 1965 deposit balances have been increasing at an annual average of 20%.

New Problems in Monetary Policy

This increase in saving indicates on the one hand the success of anti-inflationary policy and on the other the fact that latent inflationary tendencies exist but cannot express themselves as overt price rises.

The 1965 economic reform could reinforce these tendencies in three ways:
An increase in incomes beyond plan targets;
An expansion of short-term credit linked to greater enterprise autonomy in financial management;
The development of internal or self-financing.

These three factors threaten monetary equilibrium not only in the U.S.S.R. but in every socialist country, and particularly where the liberalisation of economic mechanisms has been most pronounced.

THE INCREASE IN MONEY INCOMES

This phenomenon was analysed earlier. It will be remembered that whereas in the U.S.S.R. and countries which have retained the planning of enterprise wage funds the inflationary risk due to increased pay can only at the moment occur through the bonus system, the same is not true of countries where reform abolished the compulsory wages indicator formerly imposed on enterprises. This is particularly the case in Czechoslovakia.

THE EXTENSION OF CREDIT

Before Soviet economic reform, short-term credit was secured on the material values of the enterprise. At the same time it was allocated to specific needs. A decree of April 1967 anticipated more flexible procedures. According to this enterprises will in future be able to ask the Bank for a global credit to cover the whole of their working capital needs. There is of course no question of introducing a money market into the U.S.S.R. Interest has no rôle as an instrument of economic action. It is a sort of charge paid by firms for the services of the Bank, whose interest rate variations have no connection with the demand and supply of credit. Interest rates are very low: 1% to 2% per annum in general, 6% at the most. But more flexible credit conditions do mean a relaxing of the Bank's control over the financial management of firms. If, as a later development, enterprise acquires more power in the organisation of its sales and supplies, the State Bank will doubtless have to return to its traditional position where the circulation of representative bank money does not contain within itself the seeds of inflation. Moreover, some experts demand the reintroduction of commercial credit, which would imply a regime of bills of exchange and State Bank control similar to that existing in the capitalist system.

In most other socialist countries, action through short-term credit is already in use to influence economic activity. In Hungary for example the interest rate varies from 0.5% to 18%. It is very low in the case of credit required by enterprises working for export, and high for credit needed to build up stocks. Interest is paid on enterprise deposits, varying from 3% to 7% according to the length of the deposit.

Two countries, Hungary and Czechoslovakia, have begun to experience the difficulties inherent in a policy of medium-term credit.

In Hungary the medium-term interest rate of 8% (5% for branches where expansion was to be encouraged) was not sufficient to contain the demand for investment capital by enterprises, which was very high from the beginning of reform. During the early months of 1968 construction work prices rose by 16% to 17%, and in spite of a highly restrictive credit policy (maximum repayment period reduced from three to two years in June 1968, requirement of an annual profit rate of 20% on the capital invested as against 7% initially) the demand did not slacken. Consequently in 1969 the credit plan of the banks was frozen at the 1968 level. From 1971 it was found possible to return to indirect regulation (through the rate of interest and the profit rate required from any given project).

In Czechoslovakia too the Bank had become the instrument of investment allocation. The managers of the banking agencies were unprepared for this change. Before reform, as in the other socialist countries, they had been mainly concerned with the distribution of short-term credit within the framework of planning. Now, apart from the general priorities defined at macro-economic level, they had no imperative plan to guide them. Decisions had to be based upon the profitability of different projects and profitability criteria worked out. It seems that in 1967-8 the Bank was unsuccessful in its attempts to orientate enterprise demand via the manipulation of interest rates. In 1969, as in Hungary, the government was obliged to freeze credit. Later the procedure whereby different units directly competed for credit was suppressed. It was replaced by budgetary financing linked to authorised mobilisation of internal resources within the framework of the branch.

This increased demand for credit is linked to the greater freedom enjoyed by enterprises in most socialist countries in the financing of their investment. They have in effect been invited to employ sources of capital other than the State budget.

THE DEVELOPMENT OF INTERNAL FINANCING

We saw in our analysis of Soviet reform that enterprises were encouraged to finance certain productive and non-productive investments from internal sources (from the fund for the expansion of production or the socio-cultural fund). It was also seen that these possibilities were gravely hampered by the centralised planning of material and technical supplies, which tended to prevent firms from finding unplanned supplies of equipment or raw materials. Even if self-financing by enterprise did develop, implying a liberalisation of the exchange of capital goods, the fact that these are often in short supply would result in either price rises or, if prices were frozen, a serious dislocation of that particular sector. In fact in those socialist countries where the centralised planning of investment was abandoned there was an immediate rise in enterprise demand for capital goods. Eventually, in view of the short supply, the demand had to be brought under control by authoritarian methods.

It may be said in conclusion that under present planning conditions monetary policy remains rather crude, and boils down to the adjustment of the quantity of money to transaction requirements on the retail market, given price, wage, employment and production levels. However there can be little doubt that further development of the potentialities of economic reform will oblige the planning authorities to widen the scope of monetary policy in order to combat inflationary pressures.

4. MONEY AS A MEANS OF ACCUMULATION

This section will not analyse the rôle of money as a means of accumulation at the individual level (hoarding or saving), but as an instrument in the creation of reserves at State level. This will lead to a study of financial policy in a socialist state which must have at its disposal financial resources sufficient to cover its general operational expenses (national defence, administration) and to finance economic growth (since it owns most means of production) and social policy (education, public health, etc.).

The object of financial planning is to define what resources are necessary for these different uses. The State budget is the instrument for mobilising and distributing these resources. These two points will be examined with particular reference to the Soviet model.

The Principles of Financial Planning

Financial planning co-ordinates macro-economic planning in volume and corresponding monetary movements. Its objectives are the following:

To isolate the resources necessary (after determining their total and origin) for investment, for the current financing of the economy, and for expenditure in the non-productive sphere;

To distribute these resources by economic branch and region so as to maintain a basic equilibrium between the development of branches, and between the productive and non-productive sectors;

To look for ways of eliciting further resources, especially by mobilising enterprise reserves.

The main difficulty in financial planning is to obviate distortions between monetary and real flows. For example, if investment funds are allocated to a branch or region without being backed up by existing means of production, the result will be a sterilisation of these same funds. On the other hand if the investment plan in kind represents a volume of funds higher than those actually allotted, the result will be either non-fulfilment of the investment plan or serious financial difficulties for the economic units concerned.

Given these requirements and objectives, financial planning is realised through the drafting and implementation of a series of financial plans (enterprise and administration plans; State budget; social security budget; Bank and savings bank plans), leading to a single financial plan for the whole country.

At the base are the financial plans of socialist enterprises, comprising three elements: receipts and returns in general; expenditure and payments; budgetary balance (positive or negative according to the relationship of receipts and expenditure). This structure of the financial plan of the enterprise shows that there is a clear separation of its own finances and those of the State. The financial plans of enterprises are subsequently aggregated within the framework of the sectoral ministries. This provides the basis for forming the financial plan of the branch, which comprises further specific elements (estimated future branch expenditure: research, training of skilled staff, etc.; calculation of resources for this purpose to be obtained from enterprises or budgetary sources).

Kolkhoz financial plans concentrate essentially on relations with the State budget.

The financial plans of social, educational and cultural establishments and of the administrative network are financed exclusively from budgetary resources. They take the form of estimates of the total volume of expenditure and of its allocation to particular purposes in the maintenance of the institution in question.

All these plans serve as a basis in drafting the State budget, which is thus the fundamental financial plan of the socialist state.

But the budget does not give a picture of the totality of financial relationships at the level of the economy as a whole. This is because it only records net results, or the balances of the relationships of the different entities of economic activity with the budget. Consequently the budget is completed by another instrument, the synthetic financial plan. This is the financial resources/State expenditure balance and constitutes a financial duplicate of the macro-economic plan. Unlike the budget it is subject to approval by neither the Supreme Soviet nor the Council of Ministers. It remains a document for internal use by Gosplan, and its main purpose is to verify how far the objectives outlined in the state plan are compatible with existing financial resources. Its interest is essentially methodological.

Table 6.11 reproduces the synthetic financial plan in outline. In the form of a balance, it indicates all the income of enterprises and State economic organisations, independently of its distribution (total profit is not divided as between its allocation to the budget or to enterprise expenditure). At the same time all their financial sources are shown, whether they come from the budget or not. In the case of the *kolkhozy* and co-operative organisations only the total income tax is indicated, financial movements in this sector thus escaping from the global financial plan.

The resources shown derive essentially from the following sources: net income of socialist enterprises; net income of enterprises and services in the non-productive sphere; depreciation of the fixed capital of enterprises; a proportion of the net income of the population (taxes and voluntary contributions).

Enterprise net income is the difference between sales receipts and production costs, after subtracting social security payments and interest on credit. Depreciation on enterprise fixed capital also appears on the receipts side of the balance, replacement cost of productive fixed capital being entered on the side of expenditure. Social security revenue is entered separately (payments by enterprise as a percentage of the wages fund). The item 'other income deriving from the economy' comprises trade union payments for financing social and cultural activities or training schemes. The anticipated tax yields are based on budgetary data. Increases in savings deposits and other returns are calculated from the results of the preceding year (voluntary or compulsory insurance, receipts from the national lottery, subscriptions to diverse organisations).

Only planned monetary receipts are entered in the balance. The financial plan takes no account of that share of the net income of society which does not appear in monetary form – increased stocks of commodities or raw materials.

Expenditure is distributed in the following way: economic investment and capital maintenance, increase in working capital; cultural, educational, public health and social security expenditure; administration and defence.

Expenditure on financing the economy includes expenditure itemised in the

TABLE 6.11

OUTLINE OF THE SYNTHETIC FINANCIAL PLAN

Income	Expenditure
1. Monetary accumulation of State enterprises and organisations: (a) profit (total and by branch) (b) turnover tax	1. Financing of the economy: investment capital maintenance and replacement increase in circulating capital other
2. Depreciation	
3. State social security funds	2. Increase in State reserves
4. Income from foreign trade	3. Financing of social and cultural measures: investment current expenditure of firms grants, allowances, pensions
5. Other State revenue (local tax, forest tax, etc.)	
6. Other returns from the economy	
7. Income tax on *kolkhozy* and co-operative organisations	4. Administrative and defence expenditure: investment current expenditure of administrative and defence departments
8. Receipts from the population: taxes increased savings bank deposits other receipts	5. Reserve funds of the Council of Ministers of the U.S.S.R. and Councils of Ministers of the Union republics
	6. Other budgetary expenditure
Total	Total

plan as well as some enterprise expenditure and special outlays which are not (training programmes, finance of enterprise research). The item 'increase in State reserves' comes in this category.

In fact the expenditure side of the synthetic financial plan includes almost the whole of the accumulated portion of the national income (including the creation of reserves) as well as public consumption and the replacement of fixed capital.

In this way the financial plan shows the distribution and redistribution of monetary income between the productive and non-productive spheres, and between the socialised funds and the private incomes and expenditure of citizens. Distribution within the productive sphere is reflected not in the synthetic financial plan but in the financial plans of firms and branches.

There are three main reasons for the importance of the synthetic financial plan:

1. Based on the general economic plan, it harmonises material and money flows at the planning stage.

2. It co-ordinates material and money flows at the stage of implementation of the economic plan. However, since the financial plan is not compulsory its efficiency is limited in this respect.

3. It makes it possible to check the cohesion of the various financial plans, the main one being the State budget.

The Budget

The State budget of the U.S.S.R. represents a little more than 50% of national income (53.2% in 1960, 52% in 1964, 52.5% in 1967, 50.8% in 1973). This is a much higher proportion than in capitalist countries (one-third of national income on average).

It is in effect the State centralised fund, and is necessarily more important in a planned economic system than in a market economy, since the State intervenes directly in economic life. It is therefore not surprising that in recent years more than 40% of budgetary expenditure has been earmarked for financing the economy. The economy in turn constitutes the main source of budgetary revenue: more than 90%. However the 1965 economic reform will undoubtedly affect these proportions since it anticipates greater financing of the economy from its own resources, especially in the field of investment. The network of relations between budget and economy, built up between 1930 and 1933 and hardly modified until 1965, was based on a sort of osmosis of State and enterprise income. The State creamed off enterprise income and the enterprise counted on State financial assistance in case of difficulty. The reform is intended to draw a clearer line between State and enterprise funds.

The State budget is complex, being a synthesis of the federal budget and nearly 50,000 other budgets: of the Union republics, autonomous republics, territories, regions, districts, towns, urban localities and villages.

The budgetary system consists of three elements: the federal budget; the republican budgets of the Union republics; the republican budgets of the autonomous republics and local budgets. The first of these accounts for nearly one-half of total budgetary resources, and finances that part of the economy within federal jurisdiction, a part of social and cultural expenditure, the expenses of general administration and the whole of military expenditure. The Union republic budgets finance about 70% of economic and socio-cultural expenditure. The autonomous republic and local budgets concentrate essentially on social and cultural investment.

The State budget is voted every December by the Supreme Soviet and always shows a slight surplus. This is paid into the State Bank and constitutes the reserve underlying its monetary issue.

Budgetary Expenditure (table 6.12)

This is divided into four categories: economic expenditure; socio-cultural expenditure; national defence; civil expenditure (public administration).

ECONOMIC EXPENDITURE

Although its share in total budgetary expenditure has remained at 43% to 45% for some years, as far as the productive sphere is concerned the budget appears as a supplementary source of finance. The principle is that productive enterprises cover current expenditure with receipts, investment alone being financed from the budget. To the extent that economic reform leads to an extension of internal financing and greater recourse to bank credit for investment, the future rôle of the budget should diminish in importance. Budgetary financing should increasingly concern only the creation of new enterprise and heavy investments in infrastructure. However, for those enterprises actually transferred to the reformed system, the credit financing of investment in 1966 and 1967 did not exceed 9% of finance from all sources. Again, internal financing is necessarily restricted in a system where the firm cannot obtain unplanned capital goods.

If we look at the statistics, it is true that for 1973 for example centralised investment (i.e. included in the plan) will reach 70.5 milliard roubles, of which 33.7 milliard (47.8%) will be financed from the budget, 11.3 milliard (16.1%) from enterprise profit, and 16.1 milliard (23.0%) from depreciation. This seems to indicate that 39.1% of investment will derive from internal resources. But since it is always a case of centralised investment imposed on the enterprise in its plan, finance from the firm's own resources means quite simply that from their profits and depreciation they make payments into the centralised fund of each ministry, which is used for capital expenditure. This is not self-financing in the true sense of the word.

Industry represents nearly 40% of total economic expenditure. The division between investment and current economic expenditure gives a slight edge to the latter (56% of total economic expenditure in 1969, 58% in 1970). Current economic expenditure includes the working capital of new enterprise, increases in the working capital of industrial and commercial firms (exceptionally), special grants to enterprises whose selling prices are fixed at such a level that costs cannot be covered by sales receipts and, especially, the mass of subsidies to agriculture.

SOCIAL AND CULTURAL EXPENDITURE

Its share in budgetary expenditure has been increasing regularly and now represents about 38%. Most is allocated to the finance of national education (a little under one-half). About one-sixth goes to finance public health and sport, and the rest to social security and State insurance.

TABLE 6.12

THE STRUCTURE OF BUDGETARY EXPENDITURE IN THE U.S.S.R.
(as a % of total expenditure)

	1960	1965	1973 (forecast)
Not itemised	3.0	4.3	4.9
	1.0 (a)		
Administrative expenditure	1.5	1.3	1.0
Military expenditure	12.7	12.6	9.8
Public health	6.6	6.6	5.5
Social security and State insurance	14.4	13.8	15.0
Social and cultural expenditure — National education and scientific research	14.1	17.2	16.5
Economic expenditure	46.7	44.2	47.6

(a) Servicing of the public debt: negligible the following years (0.1%).

The financing of national education covers the following objectives: national education in the strict sense (primary, secondary, higher education, pre-school institutions); professional training and adult education; culture (libraries, clubs, museums, etc.); scientific research, periodical publications and publishing; artistic activities (theatres, concerts, radio, television, building of cinemas; the production of films however is considered an economic activity).

In the field of public health, the budget finances the cost of health units (hospitals, welfare centres, clinics, sanatoria, nurseries) and prophylactic and counter-epidemic measures.

Finally social expenditure covers the finance of social security (self-financed in the sense that enterprises and administrative agencies pay into the central social security fund a sum calculated on the basis of distributed wages). 70% of social security expenditure goes on retirement pensions. The rest covers sickness, pregnancy and maternity benefits. The social security budget is managed by the trade unions.

In cases where social security only applies to workers and employees it is completed by other forms of assistance known as State insurance: for artistes, war invalids and since 1965 for *kolkhoz* members for whom a special fund of 1.4 milliard roubles was established that year, one-third of the sum coming from the State budget.

MILITARY EXPENDITURE

Officially the national defence budget is relatively small (in recent years an average of 13% of expenditure, whereas in most developed countries from 15% to 20% is normal). But as in every country, in the U.S.S.R. only a part of military expenditure comes under the head 'national defence'. It also appears in other categories: economic expenditure to finance defence industries; social and cultural expenditure covers military research and pensions; military aid to foreign countries also falls outside the item military expenditure.

ADMINISTRATIVE EXPENDITURE

This item represents a little more than 1% of total expenditure.

Budgetary Receipts (table 6.13)

The State budget resources of the U.S.S.R. are based essentially on taxation. Some revenue is derived from borrowing (0.1% of budgetary receipts), and some from payments made into the social security fund by enterprises and administrative agencies on the basis of wages and salaries (an average of 5% of budgetary receipts).

More than 90% of budget revenue comes from economic activity. The share

TABLE 6.13[23]

THE STRUCTURE OF BUDGETARY RECEIPTS IN THE U.S.S.R.
(as a % of total receipts)

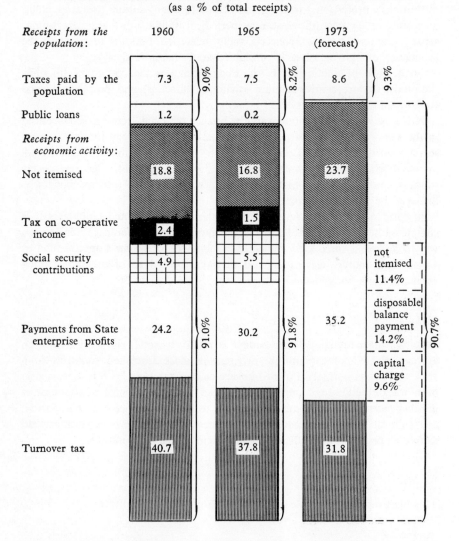

of taxes paid by the population diminished rapidly until 1967 and has tended to rise slightly since then.

TAXES ON ECONOMIC ACTIVITY

These are payments into the budget made by State economic enterprises and organisations (industrial enterprises, commercial organisations, State farms) and by co-operative units (*kolkhozy,* consumer co-operatives).

For a long time in Soviet fiscal theory it was considered that budgetary payments made by this first category were not really of a fiscal nature. That is easily understood in a situation where no clear division is made between State revenue and State enterprise revenue. Given such a conception of the fiscal system, it is just possible that the enterprise should be obliged to transfer almost all its net profit to the State. In return it would receive all funds necessary for investment and sometimes to cover its deficit. Recently, since the 1965 reform reaffirmed the financial autonomy of the enterprise, the separation of enterprise and State revenue has been made more evident. However enterprise payments into the budget still look very much like a redistribution of income between State and enterprise. The fiscal character of co-operative payments is much more obvious.

The taxes paid by the co-operative sector represent a negligible fraction of budgetary resources (1.1% since 1966). Payments made by State enterprises and organisations make up the greater part (about 70%).

Payments into the budget made by State units are effected on the basis of the 'two forms of mobilisation of net revenue created in the economy', as defined by the fiscal reform of 1930 and still in force. These two forms are turnover tax and payments made out of profit.

According to Soviet financial theory, the net revenue formed in the economy may be divided into two parts: centralised State revenue or net product for society, entirely absorbed into the budget; net enterprise revenue or profit, partially appropriated by fiscal means and partially retained by enterprise by virtue of its managerial autonomy.

It is through the price mechanism that the State determines the size of its own net revenue and that of the enterprise. As was seen in connection with price determination, the planning authorities establish the wholesale prices at which firms sell their products. The level of wholesale prices should permit firms to cover their costs and earn a normal profit under average conditions of management. But normal profit only represents a fraction of the net additional product. The other fraction, State net revenue, appears in retail prices. These are fixed by the planning authorities as a function of the general equilibrium which must be achieved between supply and demand (consumer incomes), and according to the objectives of economic and social policy. Retail price determination is independent of that for wholesale prices, with no interaction between the two.

The difference between retail and wholesale price therefore constitutes a primary revenue for the State, which is appropriated directly. It is this part of the net additional product which, in Soviet financial terminology, 'is mobilised for the State budget' in the form of the turnover tax. That is why, for Soviet fiscal experts, the turnover tax is not an indirect tax (although levied at the stage of distribution) but a real income, the size of which is determined by the planning authorities operating through prices policy and whose economic character is identical with that of enterprise profit.

The second channel devised by the 1930 fiscal reform for mobilising the net additional product for the budget was appropriation from profits. According to the principle of financial autonomy, enterprise income should be taxed at a definite rate (proportional or progressive), the rest remaining at the disposal of the enterprise. The way in which appropriation from profits had been organised shows clearly that in spite of appearances there was until 1965 a confusion in practice between the finances of the State and of enterprise. This was quite contrary to the principle of financial autonomy. The appropriation from profit was in fact a distribution tax. It was planned as an overall total for the financial year, and was calculated on the basis of estimates of expected profit, after deducting a minimal proportion (4% to 5% on average) which was to be left to the enterprises, and a proportion to be allocated to the reserve funds of the agencies of economic administration. This overall total could be increased during the year if the profits plan was exceeded. The tax burden was then distributed arbitrarily between tax-paying enterprises by the economic administration. It is easy to see that the situation was hardly designed to encourage enterprises to augment their profits. If profits exceeded the plan, the budget swallowed them up. On the other hand if a firm found itself in deficit it could always count on a subsidy to make it good. It is true that the pre-1965 system made provision for the accumulation of enterprise funds out of profit, but they were surrounded by so many conditions that enterprises usually found it impossible to build them up. In any case, the stake was so paltry that there was hardly any incentive to do so.

The 1965 fiscal reform replaced the appropriation from profits by three new taxes: a 6% charge on fixed and circulating capital; payment into the budget of the disposable profit balance; and, for certain enterprises, rent payments.

The charge was originally intended to become the main tax paid out of net enterprise income. It was based on capital so as to encourage enterprise to maximise profits by means of better management of productive assets. The two-channel principle for mobilising net income was not abandoned. The turnover tax remained, although its share in budgetary resources was to decline. This was inevitable since the rise in wholesale prices meant that the global distribution of the net additional product would lead to a reduction in the net revenue of the State and a concomitant increase in the total profit of enterprise. Secondly, the charge replaced the appropriation from profits as the form of taxation on net income. The State did not lose by it. The base of the charge guaranteed a stable revenue, independent of variations in enterprise profit; the yield would in fact rise with the expansion of productive potential. At the same time enterprise autonomy was guaranteed, since it had the possibility of disposing of its profit more freely once its obligations to the State were acquitted. It could now establish the total of its obligations in advance, and with certainty.

This ideal set-up was soon impaired. In the first place, side by side with the charge, rent payments were instituted, also paid out of profit. This is a very special tax, paid by certain enterprises only. Firms falling into this category are those earning a 'rent' due to advantageous natural conditions or favourable locality, or those with a higher than average rate of profit in their branch for reasons outside their own control. For example the use of cheap raw materials does not depend on the choice of the firms using them, since supplies are planned. Similarly the wholesale price of a product may be fixed at a level well above cost in order to harmonise with the price of a substitute good. In practice these payments affect enterprises in the extractive industry (oil, gas) and, exceptionally, manufacturing firms. They are in effect profit-rate equalisation taxes.

Much more serious is the way disposable profit balance for payment into the budget is calculated and collected. In theory, this balance was to represent a mere fraction of profit (10% according to proposals made at the time of reform). Above all, it was intended to be nothing more than a residue, to be paid by an enterprise after financing its own stimulation funds. This implied that where actual profits were less than planned the enterprise could nevertheless build up its own funds (at lower rates than predicted since the profits plan would not have been fulfilled), and that the balance going to the budget would be correspondingly reduced. It also meant that in the case of higher profits due to improved management the enterprise would reap the full fruits of its labour. In fact the exact opposite has been the case. The finance departments have made no distinction between the disposable balance and the former appropriation. They have continued to determine the yield of this tax *a priori*, which since the beginning of the new system has absorbed 60% of enterprise profits. If the enterprise makes less profit than anticipated in its plan, it must nevertheless pay the whole of the planned balance. If it makes more, the supplement is shared between the reserve fund of its ministry, centralised investment contributions and increases in the balance. The final additional profit remaining at the disposal of the enterprise is either negligible or nil.

Consequently the fiscal reform announced by the introduction of the charge on productive capital has proved to be of little significance. The charge was originally supposed to constitute from 30% to 35% of budgetary receipts. In 1967 it was 2%, in 1968 4.5%. The 1970 budget, by which year the reform had been fully implemented, anticipated a proportion of 9% (less than one-third of all enterprise budgetary payments from profit). The turnover tax has changed relatively little as a share of budget revenue: 37% in 1966, 32% in 1970.

In a rational and equitable fiscal system the present profit balance payment would have to be entirely abandoned. It would have to be replaced by a method of fiscal appropriation from enterprise income guaranteeing both a stable revenue for the State and the retention by enterprise of a fraction of its profit which would be clearly defined in advance. Two Soviet fiscal experts, Jakob Liberman (not to be confused with his namesake Evsei Liberman who inspired enterprise reform) and B. Rakitskij, have proposed a system of consolidated payments. These would be based on the resources of the enterprise at fixed rates for several years: fixed and circulating capital (the present charge), natural resources, labour (tax on wages). Eventually, if it seems indispensable to lower exceptionally high profit rates, payments into a price regulation fund could be introduced. The total of such payments should not be more than 50% of profit. In these conditions the enterprise would obviously become much more responsible for its management, and would not be able to count on the budget for contributions to cover deficits or finance investment. The scheme would undoubtedly reduce total budgetary resources, but it would diminish expenditure at the same time (at present 20% of budget funds merely circulate through the budget: enterprises make payments into the budget, but then receive funds for the budgetary financing of certain expenditure[24]).

The fiscal system in some socialist countries, following economic reform, resembles this scheme, especially in Hungary and Czechoslovakia where firms pay taxes from profit which are based on the value of productive assets and outlay on wages.

TAXES ON THE POPULATION

Their low proportion in budget revenue does not necessarily mean their ultimate disappearance (8.5% in 1950, 7.3% in 1960, 7.9% in 1967, 8.6% in 1973). The law of May 1960 on the gradual liquidation of income tax has been partly implemented. It led notably to the exemption of all incomes below 60 roubles a month. However in September 1962 any further exemptions were postponed. Then a decree of September 1967 lowered tax rates on wages in the 61-80 roubles bracket by 25% (they were already very low: 0.45% to 4.5% for the 61-70 roubles bracket, 12% for 71-80 roubles; the tax on wages never exceeds 13%). The 1971-5 plan anticipates progressive tax exemption, to be completed in 1975, for incomes below 70 roubles, and reduced rates for the 71-90 roubles bracket.

Incomes apart from wages are taxed more heavily. The rate may be as much as 81% on the income of craft workers above 7000 roubles per annum. The tax is also highly progressive on the income of people in the liberal professions (writers earning royalties, etc.).

The financial systems of the U.S.S.R. and the other socialist countries are on the whole very similar. That goes for the significant share of the budget in national income as well as for the general structure of revenue and expenditure (the former deriving mainly from the economic sector).

There are important differences in detail, however, particularly in the organisation of budget revenue. With the exception of Romania, turnover tax is lower than in the U.S.S.R. In some countries (such as Hungary) it is considered to be an indirect tax and not merely a means of mobilising the net income of the State. As a result of economic reform, there have been developments everywhere in the nature of payments out of profit. The G.D.R., Poland and Romania have maintained the same conception of it as in the U.S.S.R.: total payments are planned, both globally and by enterprise; they may vary as a function of enterprise results; the actual rates to be paid are determined by enterprise group in the form of norms differentiated by sector and variable over time. In the G.D.R. and Poland, the arbitrary element in this system as it affects enterprise has been attenuated by the creation of associations. In the G.D.R. the associations are responsible for budgetary payments and distribute the tax burden between their constituent units. These make payments corresponding to their net income after acquitting the charge on productive assets. The enterprises then add to their stimulation funds according to norms defined by the association. Since 1969 any remaining balance no longer goes to the State budget but is shared between association and enterprise (to finance investment, increase circulating capital, repay loans, etc.). In Poland payments into the budget are made from the global profit balance of each association, after the financing of stimulation funds by enterprises (and not before as in the G.D.R.).

TABLE 6.14

THE TAX ON ASSETS IN THE SOCIALIST COUNTRIES OF EUROPE

	Rate	Basis	Date of introduction	Observations
Bulgaria	3% to 6% of assets	balance sheet or replacement value, according to branch	1964-5	
Hungary	5% of assets; 1% in certain branches	balance sheet value	1 January 1964; generalised in 1968	included in the cost of production
Poland	5% of fixed assets (may be lowered to 2.5%)	balance sheet value since 1970	1 January 1966	
G.D.R.	6% (may be lowered to 1.4%)	balance sheet value	1 July 1964	
Czechoslovakia	5% (3% exceptionally)	balance sheet value since 1971	1966	
Yugoslavia	3.5% (may be lowered to 1.7%)	balance sheet value	1950-4 (reform on 1 January 1967)	

Bulgaria, Hungary and Czechoslovakia have replaced the payments system by a real profits tax. The planning of budget payments from profit in absolute terms has consequently been abandoned. Tax rates are either proportional or progressive. In these three countries there is also a wages tax paid by the enterprise, used as an instrument of incomes policy.

Finally, every socialist state except Romania has introduced the charge on productive assets (table 6.14).

Yugoslavia stands apart. Its budget constitutes a lower and shrinking proportion of the national income (31.4% in 1961, 21.3% in 1967). Income tax supplies 43% of budget revenue and indirect taxation 39.4%. There is no tax on enterprise income (except where there is a foreign holding). On the side of expenditure, defence and administration costs are considerable (26.4% and 16.6% respectively in 1967). On the other hand economic expenditure is relatively unimportant (10.7%), since in general enterprises must cover all their costs from their own resources or from borrowing. Budgetary investment in the economy consists mainly of grants to underdeveloped regions and the financing of economic infrastructures.

Part 3

SOCIALIST ECONOMIES AND INTERNATIONAL RELATIONS

Chapter 7　　　　　**1. The Structure of Comecon**
　　2. The Functions and Activities of Comecon

ECONOMIC RELATIONS BETWEEN SOCIALIST STATES

Economic relations between European socialist states develop within an international organisation generally known in the West as Comecon (Council for Mutual Economic Assistance). It was set up in 1949 to provide an institutional framework for exchanges between socialist countries in Eastern Europe, and in the longer term to co-ordinate the internal planning of the countries involved. It was a first step in the direction of international economic integration.

There have so far been two phases in the organisational development of Comecon. The first period, from 1949 to 1962, covered the establishment of its basic structures; Council policy at this time was dominated by a concern for developing the exchange of commodities. The more recent period is characterised by a new type of international relations within the framework of a stable administrative structure.

The member countries have not remained the same as the first six signatories of the communiqué of 25 January 1949 announcing the creation of the organisation (Bulgaria, Hungary, Poland, Romania, Czechoslovakia, U.S.S.R.). Albania joined in 1949 and the G.D.R. in 1950. Other countries were admitted as observers: Yugoslavia, Mongolia, China, North Korea, North Vietnam (1956-8). The deterioration in the relations of certain communist parties in the socialist bloc led from 1961 to the *de facto* withdrawal of Albania, while China, Korea and Vietnam abstained from participating in Comecon meetings. On the other hand, Mongolia became a full member in 1962 and Yugoslavia an associate member in 1964. Cuba, an observer since 1965, was admitted to membership in July 1972.

1.　THE STRUCTURE OF COMECON

Until 1959 Comecon rested on a series of agreements concluded between the member countries on the aims, principles and organisations of the institution. The drafting of its charter took several years and the agreement signed on 14 December 1959 came into operation on 13 April 1960.

The general aims of the Council for Mutual Economic Assistance are defined in article 1 of its charter. These are, by co-ordinating the efforts of member countries, to contribute to balanced economic development, to an accelerated rate of technical and economic growth, to a higher level of industrialisation in the less developed countries, to a continuous increase in labour productivity and to constant progress in the welfare of member countries.

The Council must respect the principles of absolute equality in rights, of national sovereignty and interests and of mutual advantage and assistance. Juridically speaking the acts of Comecon ('recommendations' and 'decisions', article 4 of the charter) are only mandatory on those countries which have given their assent. The principle of national sovereignty is thus clearly expressed and sanctioned. It has sometimes been considered an obstacle to the co-ordination of economic plans and policies, and was invoked by Romania in June 1964 against the development of Comecon as a supra-national body. But the dominant position of the Soviet Union, strengthened by the fact that the Council has its headquarters in Moscow, gives it the power in fact if not in theory to initiate and advance policies of co-ordination.

At present Comecon comprises the following organs: the Session of the Council for Mutual Economic Assistance, the Executive Committee (established in 1962), the Committees of the Council, Standing Commissions, the Secretariat. There are other organs formally independent of Comecon, but connected with it in the area of economic relations between socialist states.

The Session of the Council for Mutual Economic Assistance

This is the highest organ of Comecon. It can discuss any question relating to the Council's functions, and has the power to adopt recommendations or decisions. Recommendations are made on questions relating to economic and technico-scientific co-operation; these recommendations are implemented by the member countries as a result of decisions taken by their governments or competent organs. Decisions are made on questions of organisation and procedure; they are normally operative from the time the relevant report is signed.

The Council Session is composed of delegations from every member country.

Each national delegation, whose composition is defined by its government, has one vote. It meets at least once a year, in the capital of each member country in turn, under the presidency of the head of the delegation of the host country. An extraordinary Session of the Council may be convened at the request or with the agreement of at least one-third of the member countries. This has happened twice: the Sixteenth Session (June 1962 in Moscow) and the Twenty-third (April 1969 in Moscow).

The Session of the Council examines the report of the Secretariat on the activity of the Council and proposals relating to economic and technico-scientific co-operation made by the Secretariat, the Executive Committee, the standing commissions and member countries. It defines the orientation of the activity of the other organs of the Council, and sets up any new organs necessary for exercising the Council's functions.

The Executive Committee of the Council

The second organ of Comecon in order of importance, the Committee was established in 1962 and is composed of representatives of member countries. There is at least one representative per country, at the level of vice-president of the Council of Ministers. Whereas the Session has the function of initiating policy, the Committee is responsible for directing its execution and meets at least once every two months. The establishment of the Executive Committee conferred on Comecon a means of effective action going beyond the organisation of foreign trade between member countries.

The Committee implements the decisions of the Session of the Council, and directs work on the co-ordination of plans, on specialisation and co-operation between member countries and on trends towards a rational division of labour. It co-ordinates the overall activity of Comecon, creates any new organs which appear necessary and makes recommendations and decisions.

In July 1971, two Council committees were instituted to co-ordinate the activity of members in two essential areas: the committee for co-operation in planning, where countries are represented by the directors of national planning departments; the committee for economic and technical co-operation.

The Standing Commissions

These are organs created by the Session of the Council to study specialised questions and to prepare the decisions and recommendations which will be adopted ultimately by the higher organs of the institution. Within certain limits they have the right to make recommendations and decisions themselves. In principle standing commission meetings take place at their permanent head-quarters, which are decided on by the Session of the Council in view of the balance which has to be maintained between states and of the specialisation or priority of a particular country in a given economic sector. Each standing commission is serviced by a secretariat, whose functioning depends in terms of administration and budgeting on the Council Secretariat.

Standing commissions can be divided into two groups: general economic commissions and sectoral commissions.

To the first group belong the commissions for standardisation (centred in Berlin), for statistics (Moscow) and for financial and monetary problems (Moscow).

In the second group are to be found standing commissions for electric power (Moscow), the coal industry (Warsaw), the use of atomic power for peaceful ends (Moscow), the oil and gas industry (Bucharest), iron and steel (Moscow), non-ferrous metallurgy (Budapest), mechanical engineering (Prague), chemicals (Berlin), light industry (Prague), the food industry (Sofia), building (Berlin), agriculture (Sofia), transport (Warsaw), foreign trade (Moscow), geology (Ulan Bator) and electronics (Budapest).

Recently these standing commissions, comprising all member countries, have been supplemented by inter-governmental committees for economic co-operation, usually on a bilateral basis. The first were established in 1964 (the Soviet-Czech and Soviet-Hungarian inter-governmental committees). The standing commissions are also empowered to establish their own auxiliary agencies.

The Council Secretariat

This comprises the secretary to the Council, together with his assistants and staff who are in effect international civil servants recruited from the various member countries. They must have a satisfactory knowledge of Russian, which is the working language of Comecon (the languages of every member country of the Council being official languages). The seat of the Secretariat is in Moscow. The same language rule applies to the staff of the standing commission secretariats centred in other capitals.

The secretary of the Council, assisted by vice-secretaries representing all member countries, is the highest functionary of Comecon, which he represents at the various organisations of the member countries as well as at other international organisations. With these organisations the Council can establish and maintain links which are more continuous than is generally believed. In 1967-8 for example the Comecon Secretariat participated in conferences organised by the Secretariat of the Economic Committee of the Common Market on statistics, agriculture and waterways economy. The two secretariats are involved in joint work on national accounting in planned and market economies. Representatives of each organisation often take part in commission or standing committee meetings of the other. Similarly the Comecon Secretariat has contacts with U.N. economic organisations (such as the International Atomic

Energy Agency, the International Labour Organisation and the Social and Economic Council). These contacts take the form of participation in the sessions and general conferences of the organisations, and are more diplomatic and formal than in the case of E.E.C. organs.

The Secretariat is responsible for ensuring the execution of Council decisions. It prepares the sessions and meetings of those organs which meet periodically, and presents to the ordinary Session of the Council a report on their activity. In addition it drafts documents relating to the economic situation of the socialist bloc.

Related Organs

The Council for Mutual Economic Assistance is not the only form of international economic co-operation in the socialist countries. They have been led progressively to the establishment of specialised international organisations, which are not formally dependent on Comecon but which are in fact controlled by it through its standing commissions.

THE INTERNATIONAL BANK OF ECONOMIC CO-OPERATION (IBEC)

This is the archetype of such organisations. An international financial establishment created by the eight fully accredited socialist members of Comecon, it constitutes the institutional framework for the agreement on multilateral payments in transferable roubles which was concluded between them on 22 October 1963. It began operations in 1964 and has never been juridically dependent on any organ of Comecon. But it was set up on the initiative of the Executive Committee, and its articles were drafted by the standing commission for monetary and financial problems (which, like the Bank, has its headquarters in Moscow). In theory, the organisation is open to countries which are not members of Comecon. However there have been no new members so far.

I.B.E.C. began its work with a capital of 300 million transferable roubles. Each country's quota was proportional to the volume of its exports in relation to total exchanges within Comecon. These deposits may be in transferable roubles, gold or freely convertible foreign exchange. I.B.E.C. also has a reserve capital and special funds created with the agreement of member countries. The initial capital of 300 million roubles was divided as follows:

Bulgaria	17
Hungary	21
G.D.R.	55
Mongolia	3
Poland	27

Romania	16
U.S.S.R.	116
Czechoslovakia	45

40% of this capital had been paid up by 31 December 1972.

The highest organ of the Bank is its council; its executive body is the board.

The council of I.B.E.C. comprises representatives from every member country. It is presided over in turn by the representative of each country. Independently of its holding in the bank, each country has one vote in the council. Decisions must be reached unanimously. The council orientates the activity of the bank, draws up its credit plan, approves its annual accounts, and issues instructions.

The board is composed of representatives of the central banks of member countries (one per country). As executive organ, it is appointed for five years by the council and represents the interests of the bank before all national or international authorities.

The administrative organs of the bank include:

An economic and exchange department, which keeps an eye on the economic situation and credit system of each country, and analyses the activity of international economic, financial and banking institutions, as well as exchange rates on the main world markets, the conditions of purchase and sale of gold, etc.
A credit and planning department, concerned with all credit operations in transferable roubles, which are quite different in technique from domestic transactions of the same sort.
A general department concerned with operational management in the bank: credit and payment procedures, accounting and statistics.

THE INTERNATIONAL INVESTMENT BANK (I.I.B.)

The Twenty-third Session of the Council in May 1969 recommended the creation of a joint long-term credit establishment. This was set up in May 1970. Romania joined the seven founder states in January 1971. The aim of I.I.B. is to concentrate medium- and long-term financial resources for investment in projects outlined in agreements on multilateral co-operation. I.I.B. therefore completes the bilateral credit mechanisms for economic co-operation which will be examined later.

The initial capital of 1 milliard transferable roubles, subsequently augmented by the Romanian contribution, was divided as follows:

Bulgaria	85.1
Hungary	83.7
G.D.R.	176.1
Mongolia	4.5
Poland	121.4

Romania	52.6
U.S.S.R.	399.3
Czechoslovakia	129.9
	1,052.6

35% of this capital had been paid up on 31 December 1972, 30% of it in gold and convertible foreign exchange.

The administrative structure of I.I.B. is similar to that of I.B.E.C. (council, board, specialised departments). The two banks are linked by an agreement on co-operation which was signed at the end of 1970.

'Ad hoc' Organs to Facilitate Co-operation between Socialist Countries

Responsible for specific operations or covering particular branches, these agencies were mainly set up or developed after 1962. This date was a turning point in the evolution of Comecon towards closer co-operation in economic activity. The most important organisations are listed below.

IN THE FIELD OF PRODUCTION

Intermetal, an international organisation for the joint planning of iron and steel production, was established by an agreement of July 1964 between Hungary, Poland and Czechoslovakia. Its functions are to keep statistics of joint capacity and of plan implementation, to propose measures of resource distribution and to recommend specialisation in products where demand is restricted and which it would be irrational to produce in every country. Thus Hungary has specialised in the production of rails for overhead railways, and Czechoslovakia in heavy steels. Bulgaria, the G.D.R. and the U.S.S.R. joined Intermetal in 1965. It has its centre in Budapest.

An organisation for co-operation in the production of ball-bearings was also created in 1964. With its head office in Warsaw, it aims at the rational utilisation of productive capacity in satisfying the needs of member countries in bearings of different types.

Interchim was founded in 1969 to cover the requirements of member countries in parachemical products (synthetic dyes, chemical products for protecting crops, substances for use in the textile and paper industries, etc.). It is based in Halle in the G.D.R. It studies the co-ordination of plans, proposes the conclusion of specialisation contracts, analyses world market developments and examines the possibilities of harmonising research.

To these inter-state organisations should be added bilateral enterprises, such as the Polish-Hungarian company Haldex, which was established in 1959 for the complementary extraction of coal and the recovery of building materials from Polish slag-heaps. The Hungro-Bulgarian companies Intransmach and Agromach were set up in 1964 for the production of handling and lifting machines in the first case, and the development of agricultural machinery in the second. The G.D.R. joined both of these in 1972. The U.S.S.R. had entered Agromach in 1969. Of these three enterprises only Haldex can be considered to be a truly international firm.

Interatominstrument was founded in 1972 with the participation of enterprises and organisations from six countries (the European members of Comecon minus Romania). This was the first international management organisation, with financial autonomy and operational as well as co-ordinating functions. Its purpose is to develop and organise the production and sale of nuclear apparatus and equipment.

IN THE FIELD OF POWER

Two organisations are responsible for co-operation in the distribution of fuel and power:

The Central Board of the joint power networks of the socialist countries, whose function is to manage the distribution of high tension electricity. 1200 km of this network were constructed between 1962 and 1964 to link the power systems of the seven European countries of Comecon. The whole system, called Mir or 'Peace', is controlled by the Board which was established in Prague in 1962 where it began operating the following year. This organisation operates according to bilateral or multilateral agreements on the supply and exchange of electric power, and the joint exploitation of certain sections of the power network. It may propose the joint construction of electric power-stations in the different countries.

The oil pipeline 'Friendship' (Droujba): this was built between 1959 and 1963 as a result of the collective effort of the Soviet Union, Poland, Czechoslovakia, the German Democratic Republic and Hungary.

IN THE FIELD OF TRANSPORT AND TELECOMMUNICATIONS

Here there are five organisations, some of which range beyond the confines of Comecon:

The Organisation for Railway Co-operation was founded in 1956 to standardise transport regulations and charges, to study the possibilities of co-ordinating railway reconstruction and the rational utilisation of rolling stock and to organise technical co-operation in the production of railway equipment. Like the standing commission on transport created in 1958, it has its centre in Warsaw.

The Common Stock of Goods Waggons (1963) organises a rational rotation of waggons in international traffic, so as to avoid unloaded trips and bottlenecks in marshalling yards. A pool of waggons has been built up, each member country putting a certain number of standardised waggons at the disposal of the pool, though retaining ownership over them. In 1972 there were about 200,000 such waggons.

The Danube Commission was set up in 1948. Initially it comprised all the socialist river states, but since 1957 the German Federal Republic has been admitted as an observer and Austria as a full member (1960). With its head-quarters in Galati (Romania), it is in touch with the standing commission of Comecon on transport. Various joint international projects are either being studied or implemented in connection with the multiple use of the Danube: river development to permit large ships to pass from the Black Sea to Belgrade, irrigation plans and the building of hydro-electric stations.

The Organisation for Co-operation in the field of postal and telecommunications (1957) groups all Comecon members except Yugoslavia. It has no fixed headquarters and has only one organ, the conference of ministers for postal and telecommunications. This meets at irregular intervals to examine questions linked to improving the telephone and telegraph networks, the exchange of radio and television programmes, the harmonisation of postal charges and the co-ordination of research.

Intersputnik (1971) operates an international transmission system via artificial satellites. It is based in Moscow.

IN THE FIELD OF RESEARCH

There are five co-ordinating agencies, mainly in the area of fundamental or theoretical research.

The Joint Institute for nuclear research was established in 1956 in the Moscow region (Dubna). Its object is a common programme of research in nuclear physics with a view to developing the peaceful use of atomic power. Most of the financial burden is borne by the U.S.S.R. which in effect also determines the programme of research.

The International Laboratory for the study of heavy magnetic fields and low temperatures, founded in 1968 by the academies of science of the U.S.S.R., Poland, the G.D.R., and Bulgaria, is situated in Wroclaw, Poland.

The International Centre for scientific and technical information (Moscow 1969) is a vast common department for documentation.

The Standardisation Institute (Moscow 1962) has its plan of work drafted by the standing commission on standardisation.

The International Institute for studying problems of the world socialist system (Moscow 1970) analyses the theoretical and practical problems posed by co-operation among Comecon members (commercial, financial, organisational).

Agreements between national State committees for science and technology or between national academies of science complete the activity of these organisations.

2. THE FUNCTIONS AND ACTIVITIES OF COMECON

The first objective of Comecon was to facilitate exchanges between member countries. From a quantitative viewpoint Comecon has certainly succeeded. From 1951 to 1971, the volume of trade between member countries rose by an annual average of 8.5%. More than 60% of the total volume of foreign trade of member countries takes place within the bloc. But the organisation of trade, the fixing of prices and the payments mechanism pose many unsolved problems.

Since 1962 Comecon has aimed at co-ordinating national economic plans and creating real international planning based on the international socialist division of labour, the principles of which were adopted by the Sixteenth Session of Comecon held on 6-7 June 1962. On this basis a degree of co-operation between the various countries for the co-ordinated development of their economies was introduced. There has been considerable specialisation of production in certain fields, as well as mutual assistance in various forms (credit, technical aid).

Recent developments in international relations between socialist countries have raised questions about their future evolution. In particular military intervention in Czechoslovakia in August 1968 by the Warsaw Pact powers caused speculation as to whether the U.S.S.R. intended to transpose the idea of limited sovereignty into the economic field and to encourage her partners to strengthen trends towards economic integration. This would be a final stage in the co-ordination of plans.

In July 1971, after more than two years' preparation, a programme of economic co-operation and integration was adopted at the Twenty-fifth Session of the Council in Bucharest. Is economic integration the final stage of plan co-ordination, as the 1962 principles would seem to indicate? Perhaps—in the very distant future, but certainly not in the short term, if we go by the 1971 programme mentioned above. This is mainly concerned with ensuring efficient and operational co-operation between member countries, and not with enforcing perfect unanimity of action at any price, which would have no chance of success in any case.

Foreign Trade between Comecon Countries

Before the existence of Comecon, trade between the European socialist economies was very limited. All these countries were going through a period of reconstruction and economic recovery after the war and (with the exception of the U.S.S.R.) socialist revolution. Trade was based on bilateral treaties between the U.S.S.R. and each of the socialist countries. Typical was the 1948 treaty between Poland and the U.S.S.R., dealing with mutual deliveries of goods and Soviet supplies of equipment to Poland on credit. The creation of Comecon did not greatly alter the existing channels of exchange. In 1950-1 a series of long-term commercial treaties on a bilateral basis was concluded between the U.S.S.R. and its Comecon partners, as well as among the latter as a group. From 1954, parallel with the development of specialisation and co-operation within Comecon, foreign trade between member countries was increasingly linked to the co-ordination of national economic plans. In 1955, for example, the Sixth Session of the Council for Mutual Economic Assistance recommended member countries to draw up treaties in 1956 for the period 1956-60, and at the same time to bear in mind Council suggestions with regard to the specialisation of production by country (especially machinery and equipment). To this end a number of *ad hoc* committees were set up in Comecon to examine the possibilities of adjusting member countries' main branches of production to each other through foreign trade, for the period 1956-60. The principal sectoral commissions of Comecon were created in 1956: iron and steel, non-ferrous metal, gas, oil, chemical industry, engineering, agriculture. That same year the Council adopted recommendations for special-isation in more than 600 groups and types of machinery.

The first test of the efficiency of a foreign trade policy linked to the co-ordination of domestic plans came in 1957. Within the framework of specialisation projects Poland had been given the job of becoming the main supplier of coal in Comecon. At the end of 1956 and the beginning of 1957 Poland cut back her coal supplies because of internal difficulties. This threatened economic equilibrium in other countries (particularly in the G.D.R.). The U.S.S.R. could only very inadequately supplement Polish supplies. Therefore in June 1957 the Eighth Session of the Council (in Warsaw) decided to take measures to raise Polish coal production so as to guarantee exports: other countries would participate in the financing and opening of coal-fields in Poland.

Several important institutional measures for the organisation of foreign trade were adopted in 1958:

The decision to adopt world prices as a basis for intra-bloc trade;

The adoption of certain general conditions for the delivery of goods between the foreign trade organisations of Comecon countries;[1] this created a uniform international commercial law for these countries (procedure in the conclusion of contracts, delivery dates, procedure for receiving goods, organisation of technical documentation, conditions of payment, claims procedures, sanctions for non-fulfilment of contracts, arbitration);

the signing of an agreement on multilateral clearing; this was of no great practical importance in the immediate future, but did anticipate the 1963 agreement and the creation of the Comecon Bank in 1964.

From this date foreign trade centred increasingly on specialisation agreements. The period 1959-62 was characterised by an annual 14% rate of growth in this type of exchange. At the same time commercial agreements gave concrete expression to policies of specialisation, by guaranteeing long-term outlets for national production as outlined in the basic principles of the international socialist division of labour adopted in 1962: 'The international socialist division of labour is the basis of the exchange of goods between socialist countries, which is founded on the principle of equivalence . . . The practical application of recommendations on international specialisation and co-operation adopted by the competent organs of member countries implies the conclusion of bi- and multilateral long-term commercial agreements.'

To put foreign trade on a truly multilateral footing, a multilateral payments system had to be organised. This was accomplished in October 1963.

Without any shadow of doubt the development of Comecon foreign trade has been positive. In 1971 the volume of foreign trade of member countries was eight times as great as in 1950. About 67% of this exchange is with the socialist bloc, and a little more than 60% between members of Comecon (*cf.* tables 7.1 and 7.2).

TABLE 7.1[2]

DEVELOPMENT OF THE VOLUME OF TOTAL FOREIGN TRADE AND OF MUTUAL TRADE OF COMECON COUNTRIES (1950 = 100)

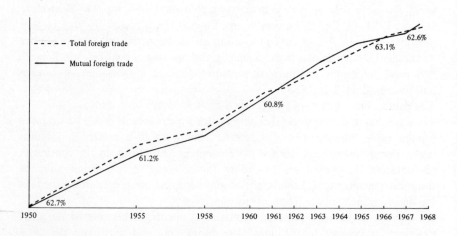

The figures show the volume of mutual trade as a proportion of total foreign trade in 1950, 1955, 1960, 1965 and 1968.

TABLE 7.2[3]

THE VOLUME OF FOREIGN TRADE OF COMECON MEMBERS
(milliard roubles; the figures show mutual trade as a proportion of total trade)

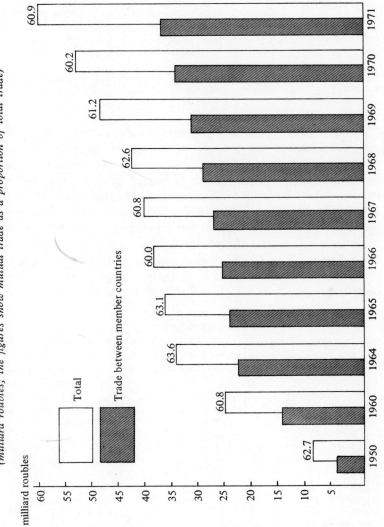

TABLE 7.3[4]

THE SHARE OF EACH MEMBER COUNTRY IN MUTUAL
FOREIGN TRADE IN 1968 (%)

U.S.S.R.	...	...	...	36.5
G.D.R.	...	...	...	16.7
Czechoslovakia	...	...	...	13.0
Poland	...	...	...	12.1
Hungary	...	...	...	8.3
Bulgaria	...	...	...	8.0
Romania	...	...	...	4.9
Mongolia	...	...	...	0.5
Total	...	...	...	100

About one-third of total trade between member countries is represented by the foreign trade of the U.S.S.R. (table 7.3). At the same time, the Soviet Union is far less dependent on foreign markets than its socialist partners. This is shown by the per capita volume of foreign trade, which in 1971 was 530 roubles in the G.D.R., 508 in Czechoslovakia, 472 in Hungary, 451 in Bulgaria, 217 in Poland, 185 in Romania, 96 in the U.S.S.R. The dominant position of the Soviet Union both as importer and exporter within Comecon should not be forgotten in any examination of the problems of this organisation (table 7.4). From 30% to 45% of the foreign trade of each member country is with the U.S.S.R., while nearly 60% of Soviet foreign trade is with Comecon countries (table 7.5).

TABLE 7.4[5]

TRADE BETWEEN THE U.S.S.R. AND MEMBER COUNTRIES
OF COMECON

Country		Share of the U.S.S.R. in the foreign trade of Comecon countries (%)				Share of Comecon countries in in the foreign trade of the U.S.S.R. (%)			
		1950	1955	1960	1971	1950	1955	1960	1971
Albania	...	50	40	54	—	0.5	0.3	0.6	—
Bulgaria	...	52	47	53	54	5.1	3.8	5.6	8.7
Hungary	...	27	22	31	34	6.5	4.0	5.0	7.0
Poland	...	27	32	30	35	13.9	11.1	7.8	10.7
G.D.R.	...	40	38	43	38	10.6	15.2	17.7	14.6
Romania	...	52	45	40	25	7.8	7.4	4.8	4.0
Czechoslovakia	...	28	35	34	33	13.0	11.5	11.5	10.2
Whole of Comecon (including Mongolia)						60	56	54	56

From the point of view of the composition of trade, the share of machinery and equipment has tended to rise, both in imports (26.2% in 1960, 35.1% in 1970) and in exports (30% and 32.7% respectively), with a parallel fall in the

TABLE 7.5[6]

THE SHARE OF DIFFERENT COUNTRIES IN SOVIET FOREIGN TRADE (1971)

	%
COMECON COUNTRIES	56.2
German Democratic Republic	14.6
Poland	10.7
Czechoslovakia	10.2
Bulgaria	8.7
Hungary	7.0
Romania	4.0
Mongolia	1.0
OTHER SOCIALIST COUNTRIES	9.2
Cuba	3.8
Yugoslavia	2.3
Korea	1.9
Vietnam	0.6
China	0.6
INDUSTRIALISED CAPITALIST COUNTRIES	21.5
Japan	3.1
German Federal Republic	2.8
Great Britain	2.6
Finland	2.4
Italy	2.1
France	2.0
DEVELOPING COUNTRIES	13.1
United Arab Republic	2.7
India	1.6

TABLE 7.6[7]

COMPOSITION OF THE FOREIGN TRADE OF COMECON COUNTRIES 1970

EXPORTS		IMPORTS	
Machinery and equipment ...	32.7%	Machinery and equipment ...	35.1%
Industrial raw materials ...	25.3%	Industrial raw materials	21.1%
Food products	22.6%	Food products	23.7%
Industrial consumer goods ...	10.0%	Industrial consumer goods ...	11.0%
Other	9.2%	Other	9.1%

share of industrial raw materials (from 26.7% to 21.1% for imports, 28.0% to 25.3% for exports) (*cf*. table 7.6). The composition of exports and imports for countries taken individually departs quite a way from the average. For example, the U.S.S.R. appears as an important supplier of industrial raw materials and of agricultural produce. These two items taken together represented 57.7% of its sales in 1970, as against 47.9% for Comecon as a whole. The

U.S.S.R. supplies its partners with between 47% and 84% of their iron-ore consumption, almost all their oil, and 70% of their timber. On the other hand the U.S.S.R. is an important purchaser of machinery, equipment and industrial consumer goods (53.8% of its purchases, compared with 46.1% for the group as a whole). The contrast is striking in a country like the G.D.R., where machinery and industrial products constitute 71.9% of sales, and raw materials and food products 55.6% of purchases. The difficulties of price formation for exchanges within Comecon are closely linked to these structural disparities.

The main economic problems posed at present by the organisation of foreign trade in socialist countries are the planning of the volume of exchange, price formation, and methods of payment.

PLANNING THE VOLUME OF EXCHANGE

In an idealised vision of the functioning of Comecon, and given the effort which has been expended within the organisation to place foreign trade on a multilateral basis, one might suppose that decisions on what commodities to exchange would be the result of recommendations made by Comecon specialisation and co-operation agencies. Such is the theory.

However an examination of the socialist planning of foreign trade reveals that this principle is imperfectly applied. Otherwise exchanges between member countries would be much more developed than they are. Of course, *vis-à-vis* the outside world, the seven European members of Comecon form a bloc tending towards self-sufficiency and a policy of autarky. But within the bloc each country does the same. Foreign trade is seen basically as a means of obtaining essential imports. Each country exports to pay for imports. The effects of exports on domestic activity (on the level of employment, for example) are neglected. This is due to domestic planning methods and the priority given to them. What is more each country tries to balance its trade with each of the other members of Comecon in kind, and not with the bloc as a whole. This barter mentality can only be explained by routine, political considerations and the tradition of planning in kind.

The organisation of foreign trade in socialist countries has two main characteristics: it comes within the competence of the State, since foreign trade is a State monopoly; it is a segment of general domestic planning.

To take the first characteristic, every socialist country has instituted a State monopoly in foreign trade. This is now applied in absolute fashion only in the U.S.S.R., by the Federal Foreign Trade Ministry which draws up import and export plans and controls the activity of fifty-two federal associations for foreign trade. These associations direct import and export operations for a specific group of products. They are an obligatory intermediary between national units of production and foreign buyers or sellers. This system of associations was introduced gradually after 1930. The most well-known is Intourist, through which are channelled all foreign tourists visiting the U.S.S.R. (from either capitalist or socialist countries). In addition there are two regional agencies: Lenfintorg for commerce between the Leningrad region and Finland, and Dalintorg for trade between the Far East and Japan.

It seems that the foreign trade monopoly, excluding direct access by Soviet enterprise to foreign markets, is not becoming more flexible. There have been a number of proposals in support of some relaxation, but only in connection with socialist countries and still under the control of federal associations.

The Foreign Trade Ministry delegates part of its responsibilities to the State Committee for foreign economic relations, established in 1957 to develop exchanges with non-capitalist countries (i.e. the socialist countries and the Third World). The main function of this committee is to organise the methods of economic and technical co-operation which either accompany or follow foreign trade operations.

In the other socialist countries the principle of State monopoly is combined with the organisation of foreign trade along commercial lines and no longer along administrative ones (*cf.* chapter 2). Economic reforms have given direct access to foreign trade to enterprises or groups of enterprises, and have involved them in the results of their operations on the international market. But that does not mean that enterprises are free to fix the volume of purchases and sales abroad at their own discretion. Even where reform has gone furthest (Bulgaria, Hungary, Czechoslovakia) foreign trade indicators are still centrally planned.

The second characteristic is that the foreign trade plan remains a subdivision of the general economic plan. This plan, in the other socialist countries as in the U.S.S.R., is drawn up by the balance method (*cf.* chapter 4). The most important balances in the organisation of foreign trade are the material balances, showing for each product the origin of resources and their destination. These balances include foreign trade, by showing either imports as a source of supply for the product in question or exports as one of its uses.

In the early period of Comecon, trade between member countries was based on bilateral agreements generally concluded for one year. These agreements enumerated most of the content of mutual trade (quantities and price). The mutual adjustment of domestic planning and foreign trade was extremely difficult. On the one hand socialist country A might sign the annual commercial agreement with partner B before its domestic plan had been drafted in its entirety. In this case country A ran the risk of internal bottlenecks, either because it had committed itself to exporting more than it could produce, or because anticipated imports were inadequate to cover domestic needs. On the other hand, if the agreement was signed after the plan had been drafted, country A could be led into commercial exchanges on unfavourable terms, or even find itself in a position where it was unable to market the whole of its exportable product.

Consequently Comecon recommended that from 1956 its members should draw up long-term bilateral agreements, broken down into annual agreements and submitted for approval to the planning committees of the countries concerned before any negotiation between foreign trade ministers took place. This would permit effective co-ordination of domestic and foreign trade plans. The procedure was brought into full use for the agreements covering 1961-5 which were to be renewed at the end of 1965 for the period 1966-70.

Such a procedure can be criticised on two counts. First of all it is still based on bilateral agreements. The very existence of Comecon implies that foreign trade agreements should be the logical culminating point of plan co-ordination between member countries with concrete policies of specialisation. When, as a result of a recommendation by Comecon, a country specialises in a given line of production (for example Hungary in buses, the G.D.R. in diesel motors) which it expands well beyond its own needs, it is entitled to expect its partners to buy this product in the requisite quantities. This is especially true as the recommendation itself was adopted after an assessment of the needs of each member country for this product. This mechanism has broken down on numerous occasions. A Soviet writer has commented that there should be a material as well as a moral responsibility on countries for non-fulfilment of obligations resulting from the international division of labour. The U.S.S.R. is less affected by these difficulties than the other socialist countries, since it specialises in a much wider range of products and its domestic market is vast in relation to the foreign market, but some countries have accumulated considerable unsold surpluses (Czechoslovakia, for example, in certain types of machine-tool).

At the same time foreign trade agreements are long-term. For example a particular country will agree to supply its partner with semi-finished products of given quality and quantity six years in advance if the beginning of negotiations and the last year of the agreement are taken into account. This system may put a brake on technical innovation, or it may encourage the exporter to market out-moded or poor quality products at the end of the period. If we go by the reciprocal complaints of different countries concerning the quality and technical level of their imports deriving from the socialist bloc, it would seem that at least until 1965 such cases were not rare. Two new factors may change this situation: the expansion of production itself will give a wider choice to buyers; economic reform in most socialist countries (except the U.S.S.R.) involves enterprises in the results of their foreign transactions and should make commercial partners more exacting.

The fact remains that in the organisation of trade between member countries of Comecon, national sovereignty is the dominant factor. Since Comecon is not a supra-national body, it cannot impose true multilateralism in international commerce (the same applies to payments). Nor can it breach the monopoly of foreign trade of each individual state.

Comecon is therefore far from being a Common Market within which commodities circulate freely, duty free and with a common customs tariff applicable to the outside world. It is true that goods are not subject to customs duties between socialist countries. But quotas are in fact imposed owing to the very nature of the planning of foreign trade. There are also domestic taxes of a para-customs type on imported goods. For a limited range of goods, some bilateral agreements do anticipate trade without quotas. An example of this is the Czech-Hungarian agreement of 1968 introducing the free circulation of a small number of consumer goods between the two countries. The Comecon Programme for 1971 gives no indication of a decisive change in policy. No reference is made to customs problems. Socialist countries will continue to practice an individual policy with regard to imports from capitalist markets. Within the community quotas in value or quantity will remain. The residual category of goods circulating freely will comprise a short list of commodities of secondary importance agreed on in bilateral negotiations (section 6 of the programme).

FOREIGN TRADE PRICES BETWEEN SOCIALIST COUNTRIES

Two questions need to be answered: are these prices discriminatory and can they be rational?

1. The problem of discrimination through prices has been the subject of numerous Western publications.[8] The most usual interpretation has been that the prices in operation in Comecon discriminate against the socialist countries, since the U.S.S.R. sells to them at higher prices and buys from them at lower prices than it does for the same commodities in its relations with non-socialist countries.

There have in fact been several stages in the evolution of price determination on the socialist market:

Until 1951 commercial agreements were based on the application of average world prices prevailing at the time of the agreement.

From 1951 to 1956, given the instability of world prices due to the Korean War, 1949-50 world prices were used.

For 1958 to 1962, Comecon recommended average world prices for 1957 as a basis (with possible adjustments).

Since then prices established between Comecon countries have been systematically based on corresponding world prices, corrected to eliminate trade cycle variations and stabilised over the long term in bilateral agreements. At present average world prices for 1965-9 are in use. These can be actualised if necessary when agreements are renewed, one function of price being to guarantee equality in exchange[9] as far as possible. According to Hungarian calculations, prices for commodities exchanged within Comecon differ by at least 25% from world prices, and in the case of raw materials by a least 15%.[10]

To what extent do these prices favour the Soviet Union in her exchanges with her Comecon partners? It is almost certain that for the first ten years of

Comecon's life such discrimination did exist. At present the situation is more complicated. The U.S.S.R. often practices dumping in the West. But so do the other socialist countries. Bulgaria sells her preserved foods to the U.S.S.R. (and to other socialist countries) at a higher price than to Western countries. Moreover many products are only sold within the socialist bloc. Finally comparisons of Soviet imports from the West or from Comecon countries are suspect, since they may concern products of different quality.

This theme could be debated indefinitely, since here political arguments have more force than economic considerations. Statistical proof is impossible since the data are incomplete, often misleading and hardly ever comparable. With reservations, one can perhaps say this: the conditions of supply and demand on the intra-Comecon market tend to operate in favour of the exporter of raw materials and to the relative disadvantage of the exporter of machinery and manufactured industrial products. The U.S.S.R. is certainly a large supplier of raw materials. In this respect she benefits from intra-bloc prices, which are usually above world prices. Soviet economists maintain that this differential should be even greater and justify their argument in the following way: to honour its Comecon commitments, the U.S.S.R. is obliged to invest in the research and exploitation of new reserves, which are increasingly distant and decreasingly profitable. It is therefore only right that purchasers should bear a part of these costs. At the same time it should not be forgotten that the U.S.S.R. is also a purchaser of raw materials and a seller of industrial products. From this, the British economist, P. Wiles, concludes that it would be wrong to concentrate one's attention only on the U.S.S.R.; in fact given the composition of their foreign trade, two countries are at an absolute disadvantage within Comecon, the G.D.R. and Czechoslovakia, and one country derives an absolute advantage, Bulgaria.[11] The same author adds that if the U.S.S.R. is guilty of exploitation, it is not through prices but through quantities: by obliging her partners to supply certain products in quantities above those implied by a rational allocation of resources in the exporting country, the exporting country is compelled to restrict its domestic demand for those products or prevented from exporting them on better terms to other countries. An interesting thesis, but again difficult to prove.

2.   Even if we reserve judgement on the discriminatory nature of these prices, it must be recognised that they are at least arbitrary. They correspond neither to world market prices nor to the conditions of production and exchange in the socialist market. Especially in socialist countries outside the U.S.S.R., increasing pressure is being brought to bear for a revision of socialist international prices, abandoning fictitious world prices and creating a price basis suited to the socialist market.[12] In fact in all socialist countries economic reform has been accompanied by a revision of wholesale prices. The progressive standardisation of methods of domestic price formation makes it possible to envisage the establishment of rational international prices. It might even be said that domestic price revisions have made a solution to the problem all the more

urgent: these have led in general to a considerable rise in the price of raw materials and fuels which is steeper than for manufactured goods. The domestic price ratios for these groups of products will therefore diverge considerably from world price ratios (even 'corrected').

The Soviet authorities are generally hostile to any modification of the price system. For them, any reform would have to be very gradual and would at first be confined to goods exchanged exclusively within Comecon. For these goods prices would be based (as in domestic planning) on socially necessary labour time calculated within the Comecon framework (expenditure of living labour and of that incorporated in the means of production, plus transport costs). Account would also have to be taken of supply and demand, that is to say of the scarcity or relative abundance of goods on the socialist market. The Soviet authorities place great stress on this final condition, since at present the socialist market is characterised by a relative abundance of machinery and manufactured industrial products and by a relative scarcity of raw materials. For goods exchanged both within Comecon and on outside markets, it is felt that the existing system should be retained. From a Soviet viewpoint, fictitious world prices do have the advantage of stability; the determination of prices as a function of socialist market conditions could entail price fluctuations.

There is an echo of these debates in attenuated form in the 1971 Programme. In the immediate future the status quo is to be maintained. Problems relating to improvements in the price system will however be studied as a joint project (articles 28 and 29 of section 6).

Any improvement in the price system is closely linked to improved monetary and financial relationships between countries. Present exchange rates are no guarantee of a coherent link between domestic and international prices in the socialist community. They are an inaccurate reflection of relative price levels and make it impossible to determine the efficiency of foreign trade transactions in a rational way. It is clear that the socialist system of international payments is also in need of revision.

INTERNATIONAL PAYMENTS

Since 1964 payments between socialist countries have been made through the International Bank for Economic Co-operation, which is the institutional framework for the agreement on multilateral payments in transferable roubles concluded between the countries of Comecon in 1963.

Until then payments between socialist countries had been on a bilateral clearing basis. This was organised on the principle of an annual equality in the supply of goods and in payments between pairs of countries. These countries had therefore to deliver to each other goods of equivalent value. In cases of disequilibrium the debtor had to repay his debt the following year by means of additional supplies of goods. This system had become an obstacle to the further expansion of trade between Comecon countries. Permanent debtor and creditor countries had emerged, without any satisfactory means of payment.

That is why, from the moment when the Council for Mutual Economic Assistance turned decisively towards the close co-ordination of economic policies, it appeared necessary to put an end to bilateral payments. Such bilateralism could in fact check the progress of co-operation and specialisation policies. Let us assume, for example, that country A is responsible for specialising in a given type of engineering product. If it is in the position of permanent creditor *vis-à-vis* country B, it will obviously not wish to deliver to B more articles than are represented by imports coming from B. Otherwise A's credit would grow even more. If B does not obtain enough engineering products from A to satisfy its needs, it will have to manufacture them itself. The principle of specialisation will have been compromised.

However a multilateral system of payments would not solve all problems. In fact, every country would in theory have to balance its payments with seven others taken as a group. If one (or several) countries develop into permanent creditors of the rest of the group as a whole, they will have a positive foreign exchange balance which sooner or later they will have to spend on their partners' products. Assuming that they do not wish to increase their purchases, they will be led to restrict their sales, a limiting factor therefore on intra-bloc trade.

Before the introduction of a multilateral system, the socialist countries resolved concrete difficulties by concluding trilateral trade or payment agreements. At the end of 1962 the standing commission of Comecon on financial and monetary problems began work on an improved system of payments. This led in 1963 to the introduction of a multilateral clearing system, which began operations in January 1964.

Payments between Comecon countries were henceforth made in a conventional monetary unit, the transferable rouble (1 rouble = 0.987412 grammes of pure gold). The fact that the currency chosen is the rouble gives no special advantage to the U.S.S.R., since, like the other countries, she can acquire transferable roubles only through exporting goods and services to countries party to the agreement (besides, before 1964 the rouble was already the currency for settlements in the bilateral clearing system). The rouble is transferable (between countries party to the 1963 agreement), but not convertible. Socialist countries cannot use surplus transferable roubles to obtain foreign exchange from countries outside the bloc. That is why the introduction of the transferable rouble appeared above all as a psychological operation. Basically it was not really necessary, since payments between socialist countries merely overlie bilateral exchange agreements which are planned in kind.

There seemed to be a step towards convertibility in October 1965, when countries which were members of the Bank decided to subscribe a part of its capital (10%) in gold and convertible foreign currencies. A further 10% was freed in the same way in 1970. Operations in Western currencies rapidly became an important part of total transactions, passing from 9% to 30% of the total between 1966 and 1971. Contrary to what might be expected, these transactions consist far less of credits granted to member countries in foreign exchange for the settlement of some of their transactions abroad, than of short-term operations, highly profitable for the Bank, on international money markets through the intermediary of foreign banks with which I.B.E.C. has an account. Until 1971 operations mainly took the form of very short-term loans in Euro-dollars. Since 1972 I.B.E.C. has on several occasions borrowed considerable sums in Euro-money (nearly 200 million dollars in 1972-3). The Bank's activity on the capitalist money market appears to be autonomous, separate from its rôle as a central clearing bank for intra-Comecon payments. Its foreign currency holdings seem in no way destined to serve as exchange reserves for eventual convertibility.

The main resistance to convertibility for socialist currencies comes from the U.S.S.R., pointing to the instability of the world monetary system and to the predominance of mutual exchanges in the foreign trade of Comecon countries. The most resolute supporters of convertibility are Poland and Hungary, whose Comecon representatives have been defending this position since 1964.[13] Permanent creditor nations certainly have an interest in being able to convert their surplus transferable roubles into strong foreign currencies. But is it in the interest of Comecon? The Soviet thesis is not without substance: a socialist common market has been instituted precisely to create an area of preferential trade and to reduce purchases by member countries on outside markets as much as possible. Would convertibility contribute to greater multilateral trade within the bloc? There is no reason to believe that it would. Finally, there are other means available for encouraging permanent debtors to reduce their debt. In particular the International Bank for Economic Co-operation could raise its interest rate on credit. Until 1969 this was 2% for payment credits, which was hardly calculated to encourage the beneficiaries to temper their demands. To have any real dissuasive effect a rise in rates would have to be significant. In 1970 the rates were increased, but without ever exceeding 5%, even in cases of non-repayment on due date. Consequently debtor countries did not substantially modify their *modus operandi*.

Nevertheless the possibility of limited convertibility has been discussed by Comecon organs, especially at the Twenty-third Session of the Council in April 1969. It is not envisaged that Comecon should follow a similar evolution to that of the European Payments Union, which led to the liquidation of that organisation once its aim had been achieved: the transferable rouble as a unit of payment could not be displaced by gold and foreign currency.

The Soviet press merely mentions the possibility of extending the converti-bility of the rouble within the socialist market, and eventually to the outside world for certain types of transaction. Trade in consumer goods would be freed entirely, but in stages. Quotas and imposed prices would be abolished. Socialist countries would make mutual payments in national currencies at market rates.

The balance would be converted into transferable roubles. By this mechanism a single rate for each socialist currency would appear in relation to the transferable rouble. This would make it possible to establish a single rate for the socialist monetary unit *vis-à-vis* world currencies: but only on the basis of transactions in consumer goods. There is no question of involving trade in capital goods.

The Comecon Programme devotes a substantial part of its seventh section to this question, which deals with international monetary and financial relations. It adopts a restrictive position. It envisages the convertibility of socialist currencies mutually and with the transferable rouble, but not general convertibility with capitalist currencies. Even this limited reform would have to be prepared over several years. A decision, not necessarily positive, will be taken in 1980 after the completion of a two-stage procedure. First of all realistic exchange rates (or conversion coefficients) will have to be defined. In other words, rates will correspond to actual relationships of purchasing power between the different countries. Secondly regional convertibility will eventually be introduced, according to forms and for fields of application to be agreed on between the countries concerned. There would be a single rate for each national currency, which implies that the present multiplicity of rates would be abandoned (official, tourist, for non-commercial payments, and the whole gamut of unofficial conversion rates or foreign trade multipliers, as they are called in Hungary, which are used to determine the efficiency of foreign trade and the real profitability of exports by product and zone).

The Co-ordination of Plans in Comecon

If, in spite of the efforts of the Council for Mutual Economic Assistance, the socialist countries have not yet got beyond the stage of bilateral commercial relations, how can they co-ordinate the economic policies of member countries? This was the aim which Comecon assigned itself in 1962. Was the co-ordination of national plans a reasonable objective? At least three factors tend to justify such an aim:

The first is the geographical unity of the socialist bloc. Comecon certainly has a world-wide commitment, but in spite of the presence of Mongolia and Cuba in the organisation the association of Yugoslavia in 1964 underlines its essentially European character.

The second factor is that an identity of economic system remains a unifying factor among socialist countries. This system is founded on socialist (state) ownership of the means of production, even if socialisation is not conceived of in the same way everywhere (chapter 1). The fact that Poland has preserved private holdings in agriculture, where the socialist sector only supplies 10% of gross production, and that in the G.D.R. only 26% of industrial enterprises are entirely state-owned, does not fundamentally threaten the unity of the system. Similarly, differences in the economic reforms introduced into all these countries since 1964–5, both in the management of production units and the structures and functioning of the economic administration, are only variants in the organisation of a planned economy, for the time being at least.

Thirdly, Marxism-Leninism constitutes a common ideological base in socialist countries. Conferences of representatives of communist and workers' parties (1958, 1960, 1962), as well as of government and party leaders of member countries (1963, 1966, 1967) have adopted resolutions defining common economic policies running parallel to the decisions and recommendations of Comecon organs. Ideological unity has certainly been shaken on several occasions. Even if we ignore the Moscow-Peking dispute and the consequent *de facto* withdrawal of Albania (still a legal member of Comecon), other serious differences have become apparent in the last few years, most conspicuously in the Czechoslovak events of August 1968. Nevertheless no country has ever questioned its attachment to Marxist-Leninist principles, even indirectly, and this is the common touchstone which is clearly underlined at every session of the Council.

The economic and political community of the socialist countries, creating between them international relations of a new type, nevertheless has limitations which prevent plan co-ordination from leading to supra-national planning:

In the first place the legal foundations of relations between socialist states, confirmed in the Comecon charter of 1960, are the principles of sovereignty, non-interference in internal affairs and free consent. The Council for Mutual Economic Assistance can only take decisions on organisational and procedural matters. In matters relating to economic co-operation it adopts recommendations, and these are mandatory only on those states accepting them. Existing political relations between socialist countries make it improbable that there will be any modification of the institution in the short term. At present, the organs of Comecon do not have the right to plan the economic activity of member states directly without their agreement.

Secondly, the inequality of size between the U.S.S.R. and the other members of Comecon confers a dominant position on the Soviet Union, which is reinforced by its seniority in the socialist system. This inequality of size is accompanied by disparities in levels of development. Without counting the U.S.S.R., there is a clear division between developed industralised countries (G.D.R., Czechoslovakia) and less developed countries (Romania, Bulgaria), Hungary and Poland occupying an intermediate position (*cf.* chapter 4).

Within the framework of domestic planning it is possible to proceed to redistributive measures to finance the development of underdeveloped regions from the resources of the developed areas, or to have enterprises with a planned deficit maintained by the rest of the economy (as in the Soviet coal industry). At the international level it is more difficult to use that sort of compensation, even if it is justified from an economic point of view. As is indicated in the second section of the 1971 Programme, the most that can be done is to recommend preferential development for the least industrialised countries of the bloc and to insist on the principle of collective assistance for the most backward country—Mongolia. But it is politically unacceptable to define a policy of regional development which would establish the regional priorities of different states in the name of some collective optimum. It is the reluctance of certain countries to be assigned the rôle of suppliers of raw materials to the rest of the bloc (Poland for coal, Romania for oil) which is at the bottom of the main conflicts within Comecon.

If favourable conditions exist for the extension of socialist international planning, it will certainly differ from domestic planning both in its methods and instruments of implementation.

METHODS OF PLAN CO-ORDINATION

Plan co-ordination between socialist countries was adopted as official policy in the basic principles of the socialist international division of labour of 1962. In fact it began as early as 1956, with bilateral consultation between the planning organs of Comecon countries in connection with the joint development of certain lines of production for the period 1956–60. It was then that common balances for deficit products were first drawn up (coal, coke, iron-ore, oil and oil products, rolled steels, non-ferrous metals). Later certain chemical products were added to the list. This procedure ran parallel to the annual recommendations of Comecon.

In 1958 the Council recommended member countries to co-ordinate their perspective plans until 1965. In 1963 a conference of party and government leaders requested member countries to begin preparing the general co-ordination of plans for 1966–70, and in particular to plan for the co-ordination of energy policies by working out production schedules as far ahead as 1980. Work on plan co-ordination for 1976–80 began in 1973. This procedure has three main aspects.

Firstly it only concerns perspective plans, in conformity with point 2 of the basic principles of the international division of labour adopted in 1962. However in all socialist economies the operational plan governing economic activity is the annual plan. There is no question of co-ordinating annual draft plans between countries. At present the emphasis is on the joint prospective forecasting of the development of the main lines of production, basic investment (from the viewpoint of the community), international transport and scientific research over periods of ten to fifteen years.

Secondly it covers only certain key sectors of the economy (power, metallurgy, chemicals, mechanical engineering, transport). For these sectors it concerns only production (traffic for transport). Between the socialist countries there is no concerted policy on employment, investment and monetary and financial matters. That is easily explained. Only commodities circulate within the socialist bloc (hence the emphasis on co-ordinating production and transport plans so as to provide a more stable and coherent base for foreign trade); labour and capital movements between countries are negligible. Finally one important sector is more or less totally absent from co-ordination: agriculture —in this area the example of capitalist countries is certainly no encouragement.

Thirdly, in spite of Comecon papers insisting on the importance of multi-lateral procedures, co-ordination is essentially bilateral. States discuss the harmonisation of planning in pairs, since their objective is above all to establish the nature and quantity of reciprocal supplies so as to conclude an agreement on trade and payments. These bilateral consultations between planning departments lead on the one hand to a series of commercial agreements, and on the other to a synthesis submitted to the organs of Comecon before the beginning of the period to be planned. There is therefore no continuity either between the bilateral consultations undertaken when it is time to renew commercial contracts, or between the multilateral discussions within Comecon organised to debate the reports on possible synthesis. The drafting of co-ordinated plans for 1971–5 does not seem to have improved this procedure very much, although countries have been invited to conclude final contracts after the synthesis plan has been prepared by the organs of Comecon.

It is hardly surprising that in these conditions the methodology of co-ordination remains rudimentary. If Comecon countries were to commit them-selves to real international planning (and they are far from it), Comecon planning departments would have to solve all the problems raised by domestic planning (the search for coherence in adjustments and for maximal efficiency in international specialisation). A solution would also have to be found to the problem of data comparability. In all these fields, present methods are crude.
1. A necessary condition for the co-ordination of economic plans is the knowledge and comparability of data in different countries on the national income and sectoral structure of their economies, etc.

The comparison of indices of the volume of industrial output between socialist countries is simplified by the fact that they all have the same basic classification for planning and statistics (industrial and non-industrial activities). In addition since 1958 there has been a standardised classification of industrial branches in member countries, which is used by the standing commission on statistics. However this classification has only sixteen divisions; a further breakdown into sub-branches and aggregate product groups is necessary.

Comparisons of national income pose the problem of evaluation. An appreciation of the value indices of two or more countries cannot be achieved by multiplying physical quantities by the monetary unit of reference (since products are not identical from the point of view of their use-values). Nor can it be achieved by comparing evaluations in national wholesale prices converted into the same currency at the official rate of exchange, given the great differences in price ratios from country to country. Price revisions in socialist countries since 1965 have done something to reduce these differences, but price structure remains variable (as was seen in chapter 6, there is no uniformity in the proportions between the component elements of price, especially for the rate of profit included in it).

What is more the socialist countries have no common methodology for calculating costs, labour productivity and the value of industrial production. This is almost virgin territory.

2.   The result is that in the search for coherence in adjustments in international planning, to which the balance method of internal planning will be applied, only volume data can be used. Even at this modest level numerous elements necessary for the preparation of the correct balances are lacking: norms of raw-material or labour-power consumption by country, variations in technological processes, the size of reserves.

In practice Comecon has been able to establish material balances for a few products only, on the basis of the general orientation of technical policies. How can they be improved?

In the first place if they are to serve as a basis for a common policy they must be drafted in an organic relationship with the corresponding plans for the development of the branch in question in all the socialist countries. In effect if any one of the national balances for a given product (such as coal) is incorrectly established and if the country in question (A), having contracted to supply country B with coal, cannot do so at the end of the day for lack of exportable surpluses, A and B will both be in difficulty. What is more the whole policy based on the international balance will have to be revised.

Secondly, the different, partial international balances will themselves have to be co-ordinated and linked to the balances of trade and payments. That is why they should be established in both kind (physical quantities) and value (transferable roubles). However, given the present state of methodology and the lack of a rational prices system, estimates in value are meaningless.

3.   It is therefore almost impossible to determine the international division of labour necessary for the optimal co-ordination of plans.

The different socialist countries have devised individual criteria of the profitability of foreign trade, which allow them to calculate the advantages to be derived from exports and imports.[14]

How can the effect of the division of labour, i.e. of specialisation, be calculated at the international level? It must be studied from the viewpoint of the interest both of each individual socialist country and of Comecon as a whole, since a satisfactory solution for the community of countries could not be imposed if it harmed the interests of a particular member.

In 1963 the Comecon standing commission on economic questions publicised 'a method of comparing the economic efficiency of investment in the member countries of Comecon'. One section deals with the efficiency of inter-state specialisation. Similarly certain sectoral commissions are studying the efficiency of specialisation; thus in 1967 the standing commission on mechanical engineering submitted to the Executive Committee of Comecon a number of proposals on measures for improving international specialisation and co-operation. The different possible criteria for optimisation are:

The productivity of labour. But it is difficult to apply this criterion at the international level. For example the fact that labour productivity in the manufacture of machines of a particular type is greater in the G.D.R. than in Poland does not mean that production of these machines for both countries should be concentrated in the G.D.R. Account must still be taken of the productivity of labour in branches serving the engineering sector (metallurgical industry, power, fuel). The criterion of productivity is only useful for precise and clearly defined purposes (as in the choice of setting up a specialised factory in one country or another).

The cost of production. This is a surer index for comparing the efficiency of production of an article in two or more countries. But it has several defects: it takes no account of investment; the method of calculating cost price is not identical in all socialist countries.

The macro-economic cost. This further criterion is the one recommended by the Comecon standing commission on economic questions. The macro-economic cost of a good is the addition of production costs at every stage of manufacture (from raw material to finished product), removing from cost price at each stage the elements of net income which it contains. It amounts to calculating the whole of the expenditure of living and past labour incorporated in a given product. Macro-economic cost can therefore be expressed in value (which poses the usual problems of comparing national valuations) or in labour time. This makes direct comparison much easier. But this is not a satisfactory criterion since, like the others, it takes no account of investment or of the capital intensity of the specialisation variants.

The 1963 method for comparing the economic efficiency of investment in Comecon countries therefore recommends as a criterion of the efficiency of international specialisation the formula of actualised expenditure $C + EoK$, which is employed in socialist countries for determining the effect of investment (*cf.* chapter 4): the investment variants taken into consideration (K) will be the investments implied by the existence or absence of international specialisation in a given product; annual working costs (C) will be calculated according to the same hypotheses, Eo being the coefficient-norm of investment efficiency.[15]

On the basis of this criterion it is theoretically possible to calculate by product the most advantageous specialisation variant for all the countries, and to draw up a scheme of specialisation satisfying the total needs of Comecon countries at lowest cost and with the minimum of investment. A concrete policy of specialisation could then be developed by choosing first those products whose actual distribution is furthest from the optimal scheme.

However what is optimal for the whole may not necessarily be so for particular individual countries. What interests country A is to know whether there will be a real economy in buying a particular product from country B, specialised in that line of production, rather than in manufacturing it itself. If the general scheme of specialisation has been based on the minimisation of actualised expenditure, country A will certainly have a *direct* advantage in purchasing its specialised product from B, since by definition it is in B that total actualised production costs are at their lowest. But will it have an *absolute* advantage in such specialisation?

It might be objected that the minimisation of total actualised expenditure would tend to concentrate the production of the main industrial goods in the most developed countries of Comecon. The argument loses its force if it is conducted in terms of relative and not absolute magnitudes (countries special-ising in products where their comparative advantage is at its greatest).

Other factors must be taken into consideration:

The effect of the concentration of production in each country, resulting from specialisation in a given product and from the corresponding decline in the variety of production which is linked to specialisation in other countries;

The difference between the domestic costs of production of the goods which a given country no longer manufactures as a result of the agreements on speciali-sation and which it must therefore import, and the domestic costs of production of the specialised product exported;

The gains (or losses) in foreign exchange resulting from the expansion of foreign trade (exports and imports) brought about by greater specialisation.

The economists of the socialist countries have devised different methods for calculating the overall effect of these factors, but they have not yet got beyond the stage of experimental research. Concrete recommendations for specialisa-tion, made by the sectoral commissions of Comecon, are based on far less refined techniques and are rarely adhered to. In fact their practical application can only be effected through bilateral agreements on specialisation or through foreign trade contracts for the delivery of specialised articles, buyers often requesting modifications to the contract.

The 1971 Programme does not reveal any really new elements in the general concept of plan co-ordination. It is dealt with in the section called 'co-operation in the field of planning'. It brings out the inadequacies of existing mechanisms and recommends that they should be eliminated by establishing closer links between plan co-ordination and commercial procedures and agreements, at the same time increasing State responsibility in the field of specialisation. Multilateralism is established in principle as an objective, with bilateral procedures being maintained in the meantime. Side by side with traditional methods, such as the co-ordination of five-year plans, the Programme advocates the co-ordination of ten- to twenty-year investment plans. But the real innovation is the introduction, experimentally for the time being, of joint planning. In this the interested countries will decide to draft a joint programme of production after a study in depth of the community's long-term needs for the product in question, of export possibilities outside the bloc, of technical questions of manufacture and of after-sales service, and after the precise determination of each country's contribution to the investment required by the project. This procedure will respect the independence of domestic planning and national ownership of productive capacity (article 25 of section 4), and in its first phase will be restricted to the most up-to-date branches. The first agreements signed concern the joint planning of the manufacture of machine-tools and the development of a unified system of international container transport (1972). What we have, then, is a promising formula for future action, but one whose practical application is still very limited and specific.

If specialisation were really extended, it would become the most powerful instrument in the co-ordination of economic policies. It still occupies a minor place, side by side with looser forms of co-ordination, such as co-operation in production, mutual credit and technical assistance.

The Instruments of Plan Co-ordination

SPECIALISATION

As we have just seen, the international division of labour inevitably leads to specialisation, since its aim is to release each country from the necessity of producing domestically all the goods required for its existence.

The branch in which specialisation is most developed is mechanical engineering. Its products cover more than 30% of trade between Comecon countries. At the beginning of 1969 specialisation extended to more than 4000 items of machinery or equipment. For example the production of metallurgical equipment is concentrated in the U.S.S.R., Poland and Czechoslovakia; coal-mining equipment in the U.S.S.R., the G.D.R., Poland and Czechoslovakia; machinery for the aluminium industry in the U.S.S.R and Hungary (*cf.* table 7.7).

Traditionally this specialisation covers finished products. Specialisation in sub-sections and semi-finished products, as well as sub-contracting, are not particularly advanced in the socialist countries, and this is reflected in their international trade. But some progress has been made. An example is the co-operation since 1972 between the U.S.S.R. and its partners in manufacturing the car Jigouli, which is produced in the Togliattigrad factory on the Volga, delivered to the U.S.S.R. by Fiat in 1966. The U.S.S.R. supplies its partners with finished cars, in exchange for parts delivered by her partners specialising in the production of forty-one different items. This type of co-operation, widespread in the West, is beginning to develop in bilateral and trilateral agreements for the engineering and chemical industry.

In the chemical industry there are specialisation agreements covering fifteen branches and 2000 types of product.

In metallurgy the G.D.R. and Hungary have agreed not to push investment since they lack iron-ore and coking-coal. On the other hand, the Kremikovtsy combine under construction in Bulgaria with Soviet assistance will supply the whole bloc in certain specialised sectional steels.

TABLE 7.7[16]

MAIN EXPORTERS OF MACHINERY, EQUIPMENT AND CHEMICAL
PRODUCTS; FROM THE AGREEMENTS ON SPECIALISATION
FOR 1966-70

	Bulgaria	Hungary	G.D.R.	Poland	Romania	Czecho-slovakia
Equipment for electric power stations						x
Equipment for the production of rolled steels	x					x
Machine-tools for the metal industry	x	x	x			
Pressing and forging machines						x
Machinery for the chemical industry				x		x
Drilling equipment					x	
Textile machinery						x
Machines for the food industry	x			x		
Agricultural machinery	x					
Diesel motors		x				
Electric locomotives						x
Goods waggons	x			x		
Ships			x	x		
Buses	x					
Motor cycles						x
Electric motors	x				x	
Precision apparatus		x				
Chemical products	x		x		x	
Medicines	x			x		
Paints				x		

There has also been some development of specialisation in the production of raw materials, although to a lesser extent. All Comecon countries are in effect trying to develop their raw material base, usually with the organisation's assistance: new coal deposits have been discovered in the G.D.R., Poland and Bulgaria, sulphur and copper in Poland, iron and non-ferrous metals in Bulgaria, oil and gas in the G.D.R., Poland and Bulgaria.

One example of co-operation through specialisation is the Soviet-Hungarian agreement of November 1962 in the aluminium industry. Hungary although rich in bauxite does not possess sufficient electric power for the production of aluminium; at the same time the share of power in the total cost of aluminium production in Hungary is 53%, whereas in the U.S.S.R. it is 15% to 20%. The agreement means that Hungary will supply the U.S.S.R. with alumina: 30,000 tons in 1967, 330,000 tons in 1980; for her part the U.S.S.R. will supply aluminium to Hungary, the costs of transporting alumina to the U.S.S.R. and aluminium to Hungary being from three to four times lower than the cost economies derived from producing aluminium in the U.S.S.R rather than in Hungary.

Questions relating to specialisation are studied within the Comecon framework by the International Institute on Standardisation set up in 1962, and by the Comecon standing commission on standardisation.

One of the problems of international specialisation is the cost of transport. Greater specialisation means that transport costs will constitute an increasing share of the total value of foreign trade. They are already quite high, varying from 0.4% to 24% depending on the product (according to estimates made in 1964 on the basis of the single transit rate operating between socialist countries).

CO-OPERATION IN PRODUCTION THROUGH JOINT INVESTMENT

This type of co-operation involves two or more Comecon countries in a joint investment project. Its aim is:

to promote better use of the member countries' material and labour resources;

to share among several countries the burden of heavy investment projects which it would be difficult for one country to bear alone;

if the investment is made in one of the less developed countries of the bloc, to contribute to equalising levels of development. This is particularly characteristic of Soviet aid, which has resulted in the construction of 98 industrial enterprises in Mongolia, 91 in Bulgaria, 90 in Romania, but only 18 in Czechoslovakia and 16 in the G.D.R.

Although in theory co-operation in this form may cover any branch, at present it is to be found mainly in the power and extractive industry sectors where there is a high coefficient of capital and constructional work normally extends over a long period. Since Comecon as a whole runs a deficit in resources of power and raw materials, it is in the interest of the bloc to co-operate in large-scale projects designed to increase these resources.

Outside the U.S.S.R., Romania is the only country to produce oil and gas in abundance.[17] Bulgaria is rich in iron-ore but lacks coke, Poland has coal, but few ferrous and non-ferrous metals. That is why many projects have either been completed or are in the process of completion for the joint exploitation of natural resources. Without listing again vast operations such as the oil pipe-line Friendship or the unification of the electric power network, a few specific enterprises of this type are worth mentioning:

Poland and Czechoslovakia together built a power station at Nowy Dwor (Poland), with Czech machines and boilers, and heavy infrastructure provided by Poland. Czechoslovakia participated with Poland in developing the port of Szczecin and obtained certain concessionary rights in the port area. In the construction of an infrastructure for exploiting copper reserves in the region of Glogow-Lublin in Poland, Czechoslovakia provided credit which was repayable at 2% per annum in the form of copper-ore. After repayment, Czechoslovakia will continue to buy copper from Poland on the basis of a commercial agreement.

The G.D.R. and Poland are co-operating in the production of Polish brown coal. The G.D.R., Czechoslovakia and Romania co-operated in building in Romania (Braila) a combine producing cellulose from the reeds of the Danube. Poland supplied technical expertise for transporting the raw material and developing port installations. The G.D.R. equipped the factories. Czechoslovakia studied the use of by-products for obtaining sodium salts and supplied the driving machinery. Costs will be reimbursed in cellulose.

In 1959 Romania and Hungary completed the pipe-line carrying gas from Transylvania to Hungary (365 km and 200 million cubic metres per annum). Czechoslovakia supplied the U.S.S.R. with credit in the form of equipment for exploiting iron-ore and non-ferrous metal deposits. Since 1966 the credit has been repayable in ore. In 1966 she concluded an agreement with the U.S.S.R. to co-operate in developing the Soviet oil industry, receiving oil deliveries in return. By a further agreement in September 1968 Czechoslovakia will supply the U.S.S.R. with equipment for building a gas pipe-line on Soviet territory, in return for gas deliveries.

In 1963-5 the six socialist countries of Europe helped the U.S.S.R. to develop phosphorite reserves at Kingissepp in Estonia. Further important projects of the same type are planned for the decade 1970-80. Among these are the construction at Oust'Ilim in Siberia of a cellulose combine supplying 500,000 tons of cellulose a year, and an iron and steel complex with an annual capacity of 10-12 million tons of steel in the Koursk region. The second of these projects is linked to the building of mills producing sectional steels and sheet metal in the other European socialist countries.

These are some of the most conspicuous examples. In most cases participation means long-term credit (in equipment, technical assistance), repayable in quantities of the article jointly produced; deliveries continue after repayment on the basis of a normal commercial agreement. The enterprise constructed belongs to the country on whose territory it has been established (in the case of the Hungaro-Romanian gas pipe-line, the sections are the property of the country they are crossing).

The national character of socialist property is the main obstacle to the creation by socialist countries of mixed firms involving joint capital and management. At present there are relatively few mixed companies (Haldex, Intransmach, Agromach). The legislation of some socialist countries on foreign investment (Romania 1971, Hungary 1972) applies much more to joint ventures with capitalist participants than to collaboration within Comecon. Section 8 of the 1971 Programme forsees the establishment of joint enterprises with their own capital and recommends the creation of international management organisations, of which Interatominstrument (1972) is the first example. This does not exclude traditional forms of co-operation.

THE SUPPLY OF CREDIT

This form of co-operation may be linked to the preceding one, where credit is used for a joint investment project. More often it is linked to foreign trade, credit being extended to a state to allow it to buy goods from the lending country, repayment taking the form of commodity deliveries from the borrowing country. In exceptional cases co-operation takes the form of a loan in convertible exchange, which the borrower uses for purchases from capitalist countries. The U.S.S.R. sometimes practices this form of credit when it wishes to obtain certain goods on the world market without actually appearing on it.

Short-term credit was well-developed between member countries before the creation of the International Bank for Economic Co-operation. At present most intra-Comecon credit is medium- and long-term (less and more than five years respectively). The annual interest rate is usually 2%.

The absence of multilateralism characterises credit just as much as other forms of co-operation between Comecon countries. There is no joint credit policy. In this respect relations are normally bilateral, and more rarely trilateral. The biggest lender is the U.S.S.R. who extended more than 10 milliard roubles in credit to her partners between 1959 and 1968. The International Bank for Economic Co-operation does not engage in long-term credit, although it is legally empowered to do so.

In these conditions there is no common investment policy. Even when a venture is financed by several countries (e.g. the construction of the phosphorite combine at Kingissepp in the U.S.S.R.), capital is lent on an individual and not a collective basis. That is why the Thirteenth Session of the Council in April 1969 decided to create an Investment Bank of socialist countries. It was founded in 1970 and began operations in January 1971. In the first two years of its operation, the bank financed twenty-six projects, representing a total credit of 280 million roubles. 113 million of these were in convertible exchange (to pay for the purchase of equipment from capitalist countries). More than half the credit went to engineering, notably to modernise the Tatra car factories in Czechoslovakia and the Hungarian firm Ikarus, which supplies the whole of Comecon with buses. Most of these are medium-term operations (five to ten years). Countries to whom credit is extended must commit themselves to giving priority to the mobilisation of those domestic resources necessary for fulfilling the project. Credit is extended to the most efficient undertakings, preference being given to growth sectors and ventures interesting the whole or the majority of Comecon members.

An ancillary function of the bank will be to act as an instrument of multilateral aid to developing countries. A special fund will be set up for this purpose on 1 January 1974. Borrowers may be national banks, public or co-operative organisations, or private firms in the Third World.

SCIENTIFIC AND TECHNICAL CO-OPERATION

To go by the figures, mutual assistance in scientific and technical matters is highly developed. Between 1948 and 1968 the U.S.S.R. provided its partners with 75,000 files of documentation and received 22,000 in exchange. In the same period, the U.S.S.R. sent 23,000 specialists to other Comecon countries and received 44,000.

Agreements on scientific and technical co-operation have been drawn up between all the Comecon countries and the U.S.S.R., and also among the former. Co-operation is again mainly bilateral. Joint committees established as a result of these agreements meet twice a year alternately in the two capitals of the signatories and make recommendations to the states concerned.

Co-operation covers the following areas: communication of technical documents, plans and completed projects; loans of prototypes; the undertaking of surveys, tests and experiments; specialist missions to establish plans or explain the operation of exported equipment; co-operation between research institutes.

Certain countries specialise in particular branches of technical research: Czechoslovakia in the construction of machinery and in light industry, the G.D.R. in chemicals and mechanical engineering, Poland in metallurgy and power technology, Hungary in electro-technics, Romania in oil problems, and Bulgaria in the food industry.

The main obstacle to scientific co-operation has always been the contradiction between the elevated principles of socialist brotherhood and the down-to-earth realities of economic interest.

Up to the present time the exchange of documentation between Comecon countries has been effected without charge, without licences and without patents. This principle was established at the Second Session of Comecon held in Sofia in 1949 (the Sofia principle). At that time it was an effort on the part of the U.S.S.R. to help underdeveloped socialist countries in the process of industrialisation (60% of technical aid documents supplied by the U.S.S.R. went to the three least developed countries of Comecon: Bulgaria, Mongolia, Romania). The principle is now under fire since it tends to sterilise inventions, each country only passing on those from its third category. Suppose, for example, that country A sends an invention to country B free of charge; B manufactures a number of machines, thanks to this invention, and a proportion of them are eventually exported. A will lose on three counts: it obtains no part of the additional profit made by B from using the new machine; it loses in B a potential customer; it has to compete with B on the international market —all this without any compensation. It is obvious that if the invention is likely to be profitable, A will keep it, even if it cannot exploit its use with its own resources.

Numerous proposals have therefore been made that the Sofia principle should be scrapped and patents sold between socialist countries, either at world prices or at socialist prices within the bloc.

In 1968 some countries began to sign bilateral agreements on the sale of licences (U.S.S.R., G.D.R., Hungary). The 1971 Programme legalises this practice, stating that scientific and technical documents and information will be exchanged freely or for a financial consideration. In fact the granting of licences free of charge is implicitly reserved for technical assistance from developed Comecon countries to the less industrialised, since the latter will continue to receive inventions already amortised free of charge.

There are similar problems in the co-ordination of research. The only example of integrated research in Comecon is the joint Institute for Nuclear Research. In this case integration has been made easier by the almost exclusive position of the U.S.S.R. In principle co-ordination involves other areas as well, relevant plans having been made for 1966-70. But here again the co-ordination of work and the communication of results is usually on a bilateral basis. Collective financing and the concentration of researchers from different countries in international institutes is rare.

The 1971 Programme suggests improvements in the direction of greater co-operation: the creation of co-ordinating centres, of *ad hoc* research terms in specific areas and of international institutes of pure or applied research. Academic research will doubtless lend itself more easily to joint studies than development research, where member countries are more concerned about preserving their independence or technical advance.

In every field co-ordination between Comecon countries still appears to be very limited. On very rare occasions there are examples of joint policies. Institutions are never supra-national and expressions of support for the international control of production are mere pious wishes. The specialised institutions of Comecon themselves have no power. Intermetal, for example, set up in 1964, is in no way comparable to the steel branch of the E.C.S.C. It is mainly a centre for research and information in the iron and steel industry. Unless the structure and practice of Comecon are radically changed, it will be impossible to bring about socialist integration, if we understand by that a fusion of national economies with common planning and control.

The Integration of Socialist Economies

Until recently the concept of integration was applied exclusively to international relations in the capitalist world. A few weeks after the adoption by the Sixteenth Session of Comecon in June 1962 of the basic principles of the international socialist division of labour, Pravda published a document called 'Theses on imperialist integration in Western Europe' (26 August 1962). The aim was clearly to pinpoint the difference between on the one hand the new type of international relations of the socialist countries, based on the co-ordination of long-term plans without international planning being superimposed on domestic planning, and on the other the tendency towards supranationality in the community orientation of E.E.C. economic policy.

However a few weeks later in September 1962 Krushchev proposed a reinforcement of the powers of Comecon. These had already been increased in June 1962 when the Executive Committee replaced the former conference of representatives of Comecon countries. It is true that no direct reference was made to the ideas of supranationality and integration. But they were implicit. In 1963 the Romanian Communist Party fiercely opposed any authoritarian organisation of specialisation within Comecon which would keep the less developed countries (Bulgaria and Romania) in the position of permanent suppliers of agricultural products. Several times since 1964 the Romanian Communist Party has displayed its hostility to an integrated bloc of eight, a hostility which has shown itself in several ways. Faced in 1963 with the Soviet Union's refusal to participate in financing the construction of a large iron and steel complex at Galati, Romania turned to the West to obtain the equipment which the U.S.S.R. had refused to sell. The Soviet Union maintained that it would be irrational to establish in Romania a powerful metallurgical industry when other countries were better placed to specialise in this field and to cover the needs of others in steel. It is equally significant that Romania, an exporter of oil products, did not take part in building the pipe-line Friendship, which passes quite close to its borders.

The very idea of integration therefore began to arouse opposition even before the concept had been scientifically analysed. It seems that the expression was first used in an article by the Polish economist Z. Kamecki.[18] He distinguishes four basic types of integration: the economic integration of socialist countries, the integration of developed capitalist countries, the integration of developing non-socialist countries and the integration of a group of economically underdeveloped countries with an economically developed country. Later the expression was taken up in journals in other socialist countries, especially in the G.D.R. and Hungary.[19] But it was not until December 1968 that it appeared in a Soviet journal. The journal *Economic Questions* then published an article by G. Sorokin, director of the institute of the world socialist system in the U.S.S.R. Academy of Sciences, on 'The problems of the economic integration of socialist countries'. In January 1969 the Polish economic society organised a conference on the same subject in Warsaw.

How can socialist integration be defined? There are two counter-opposed concepts: market integration and production integration.

In the first case it would be a question of transforming Comecon into a real common market of the socialist countries. There is already considerable interpenetration of the socialist economies, since more than 60% of the total volume of their foreign trade is between themselves, but the free circulation of goods between countries is limited by the mechanism of national planning, and the international movement of labour and capital is almost non-existent. That is why the advocates of market integration insist on the creation of a common market, by means of more flexible national procedures where foreign trade is concerned, the development of direct agreements between economic units in different countries and the abolition of institutional obstacles to the flow of labour between states. Real multilateral trade would develop later, and would be channelled in particular directions by economic means. According to R. Nyers, secretary of the Central Committee of the Hungarian Socialist Workers' Party, writing in the Party daily *Népszabadsag* at the beginning of 1969: 'Our Party is in favour of creating a developed Comecon monetary system and a flexible prices system for foreign trade.'

Market integration is difficult. The integration of economic activity as a whole is even more problematical. As the Soviet economist G. Sorokin has pointed out, it effectively means mutual economic assimilation: 'In the course of building socialism and communism, in the process of concentrating production, of strengthening the international division of labour and extending economic ties between socialist countries, it becomes increasingly necessary to collaborate in developing the national economies, to introduce gradually a single structure for the world socialist economy, to interlock and weld together the various national economies.'[20] It is from such a system that an integrated socialist economy will emerge. Integration would be the final stage in plan co-ordination. Co-ordination is based on the principle of complete individual national sovereignty in domestic planning; integration implies limited sovereignty. But limited in what way? There is nowhere any reference to an eventual reform of the organs of Comecon. Perhaps repeated use of the word integration should be understood as a warning or a threat. This is how the Romanians at least seem to have taken it. In the knowledge that they have every guarantee under existing institutions, their opposition to any hint of limited sovereignty is complete.

The drafting of the Comecon Programme between April 1969 and July 1971 was characterised by these discussions on the direction that integration should take. The result has been a flexible document of both principle and action covering every form of co-operation. During the fifteen or twenty years after its adoption, co-operation will be strengthened and integration developed: by bilateral or multilateral agreements; by treaties between states and contracts between enterprises; and by short-, medium- or long-term operations. No supra-national organisation has been set up. Economic integration will not take in domestic planning, finance and management (section 1). The Programme reaffirms the principle of national sovereignty by reinforcing the terms of the Charter. It is realistic: integration will be a long process; it will be successful if it is in the interests of the states involved and gives a prior guarantee of their individual development; it will be the result of a series of measures, from mutual consultation on questions of economic policy to joint enterprises, and it will involve economic and technical co-operation and the development of trade. The efficacy of these measures will depend on their not being imposed on member countries.

Chapter 8

1. **Economic Relations between Comecon Countries and Developed Countries**
2. **Relations with Developing Countries**

RELATIONS BETWEEN SOCIALIST STATES AND THE OUTSIDE WORLD

In the previous chapter we looked at relations between member countries of Comecon. These relationships are dominant but not exclusive. Trade with the non-socialist world has increased enormously, especially since 1960.

Before analysing the main characteristics of these economic relations with the outside world, it is worth looking at an often neglected and little known area of international relations: exchanges between Comecon members and other socialist countries. These relations are heterogeneous and depend mainly on political factors. In the first place socialist countries outside Comecon differ from each other a great deal in their relations with their partners. Yugoslavia has grown closer to Comecon, especially since 1964 when she became an associate member. In 1961-3 25% of her total trade was with the socialist bloc. By 1964 this proportion had risen to 30%. Since then it has been stable at that level. Trade between Cuba and Comecon countries grew progressively from 1963, ending with the entry of Cuba into Comecon in 1972. Two-thirds of Cuba's foreign trade from 1966 was with Comecon, and 52% of this with the U.S.S.R. The socialist countries are the main outlet for Cuban sugar, following special agreements concluded in 1964-5 and renewed in 1972-3. The terms of these agreements guarantee Cuba a selling price which is well above the world price. 80% of Vietnam's trade is also with socialist countries which provide in this form and others the military and economic aid required by a period of war and reconstruction. Korea, which had no trading connections with non-socialist countries in 1955, has since regularly increased its trade with them (especially with Japan), but this does not represent more than 20% of its total trade. The nature and general structure of its relations with Comecon countries are very similar to those of Mongolia, a member of Comecon, with its partners.

The ideological conflict between the U.S.S.R. and the People's Republic of China since 1960 has been the main political factor determining the development of economic relations within the socialist world. In 1959 75% of China's foreign trade was with socialist countries, 50% of this with the U.S.S.R. In 1967 trade with socialist countries hardly exceeded 20% of the total. This withdrawal by China explains the sharp fall in the growth rates of the volume of foreign trade between socialist countries taken as a whole. The annual rate was 15% between 1951 and 1955, 14% between 1956 and 1960, and 6.9% between 1961 and 1965. This political factor is nevertheless not the only one in explaining the slower rate of growth of trade. During the last period exchanges within Comecon also tended to slacken off (average annual growth rates: 13% in 1951-5, 11% in 1956-60, 6% in 1961-6). This decline was linked to the fall in general economic growth in these countries and with the institutional obstacles to effective multilateral trade.

Political tensions within the socialist world have combined with the economic difficulties of Comecon to open up socialist markets to the outside world on an increasing scale. It was in 1953-5 that socialist markets were most inwardly orientated. At that time more than 80% of their total foreign trade was with each other. In 1966 this proportion had fallen to 63%, its lowest level since 1948. Since then it has been stable at around 65% to 70% (with the exception of China, Yugoslavia and Romania where 50% of trade is with non-socialist countries). It is striking that since 1961 the socialist countries' trade with capitalist countries has been evolving much more rapidly than their mutual trade: 9.6% per annum between 1960 and 1965, 11.4% between 1966 and 1970, as against 7.1% and 8.5% respectively for mutual trade.

The development of the trade of Comecon member countries as such tends to confirm these structural trends (*cf.* table 8.1).

1. ECONOMIC RELATIONS BETWEEN COMECON COUNTRIES AND DEVELOPED COUNTRIES

Foreign trade between member countries of Comecon and developed capitalist countries is growing at a rapid rate. For the period 1956-71 the average annual rate of growth of this trade was more than 11%. The level of trade is low however, making up from 2% to 3% of world exports and imports. This is the result of two opposite tendencies. On the one hand both socialist and capitalist countries, with a few exceptions, would like to develop mutual trade. On the other hand political, institutional and economic obstacles limit this growth. The interpenetration of these two tendencies will be looked at first

TABLE 8.1[1]

DEVELOPMENT OF THE STRUCTURE OF TRADE OF COMECON COUNTRIES

A=socialist bloc

B=developed capitalist countries

C=developing countries

Bulgaria

as a %

Exports				1960	1971
total	...	...	...	100	100
to A	...	...	...	84	79
B	...	...	...	13	14
C	...	...	...	3	7

Imports			1960	1971
total	...	...	100	100
from A	...	...	84	77.5
B	...	...	14	17
C	...	...	2	5.5

in millions of levs

Exports				1960	1971
total	...	...	...	669	2526
to A	...	...	...	562	2005
B	...	...	...	84	350
C	...	...	...	23	171

Imports			1960	1971
total	...	...	740	2432
from A	...	...	621	1885
B	...	...	102	408
C	...	...	17	139

Hungary

as a %

Exports				1960	1971
total	...	...	...	100	100
to A	...	...	...	71	69
B	...	...	...		25
(B/C)	...	...	...	29	
C	...	...	...		6

Imports			1960	1971
total	...	...	100	100
from A	...	...	70	66
B	...	...		29·5
(B/C)	...	...	30	
C	...	...		4·5

in millions of forints

Exports			1960	1971
total	...	...	10260	29479
to A	...	...	7319	20475
B/C	...	...	2941	1719

Imports			1960	1971
total	...	...	11455	34884
from A	...	...	8069	23423
B	...	...		9957
B/C	...	...	3386	
C	...	...		1504

Poland

as a %

Exports			1950	1960	1971
total	...	...	100	100	100
to A	...	...	62	62	63
B	...	...	35	30	30
C	...	...	3	8	7

Imports			1950	1960	1971
total	...	...	100	100	100
from A	...	...	61	63	67
B	...	...	36	30	27.5
C	...	...	3	7	5.5

in millions of zlotys

Exports			1950	1960	1971
total	...	...	2357	5302	15489
to A	...	...	1443	3321	9770
B	...	...	834	1568	4622
C	...	...	80	413	1097

Imports			1950	1960	1971
total	...	...	2673	5980	16151
from A	...	...	1633	3798	10883
B	...	...	995	1740	4407
C	...	...	85	442	861

G.D.R.

as a %

Exports			1950	1960	1971
total	...	...	100	100	100
to A	...	...	71	76	75
B ⎱	...	...		20	21
⎰	...	...	29		
C ⎰	...	...		4	4

in millions of marks

Exports			1950	1960	1971
total	...	...	1705	9200	21320
to A	...	...	1163	6262	15890
B ⎱	...	...		1859	4495
⎰	...	...	542		
C ⎰	...	...		379	935

Imports			1950	1960	1971
total	...	...	100	100	100
from A		...	76	75	69
B ⎱		...		21	27
⎰		...	24		
C ⎰		...		4	4

Imports			1950	1960	1971
total		...	1973	9113	20830
from A		...	1497	6736	14322
B ⎱		...		1994	5729
⎰		...	476		
C ⎰		...		383	779

Romania

as a %

Exports				1960	1971
total	...	...	...	100	100
to A	...	...	...	72	57
B	...	...	...	22	34
C	...	...	...	6	9

in millions of leu

Exports				1960	1971
total	...	...	...	4302	12606
to A	...	...	...	3139	7170
B	...	...	...	922	4302
C	...	...	...	241	1134

Imports				1960	1971
total	...	...	...	100	100
from A	...	...	...	72	54
B	...	...	...	25	39
C	...	...	...	3	7

Imports				1960	1971
total	...	...	...	3887	12616
from A	...	...	...	2842	6814
B	...	...	...	919	4956
C	...	...	...	126	846

Czechoslovakia

as a %

Exports				1960	1971
total	...	...	...	100	100
to A	...	...	...	72	70
B	...	...	...	17	20
C	...	...	...	11	10

in millions of crowns

Exports				1960	1971
total	...	...	...	13892	30095
to A	...	...	...	10041	21131
B	...	...	...	2316	6115
C	...	...	...	1535	2849

Imports				1960	1971
total	...	...	...	100	100
from A	...	...	...	71	70
B	...	...	...	19	24.5
C	...	...	...	10	5.5

Imports				1960	1971
total	...	...	...	13072	28870
from A	...	...	...	9316	20092
B	...	...	...	2477	7167
C	...	...	...	1279	1611

U.S.S.R.

as a %

Exports			1950	1960	1971
total	...	...	100	100	100
to A	...	...	83	76	65
B	...	...	15	18	20
C	...	...	2	6	15

in millions of roubles

Exports			1950	1960	1971
total	...	...	1615	5007	12425
to A	...	...	1350	3790	8116
B	...	...	236	913	2484
C	...	...	29	304	1825

Imports			1950	1960	1971
total	...	...	100	100	100
from A		...	78	71	66
B		...	15.5	20	23
C		...	6.5	9	11

Imports			1950	1960	1971
total	...	...	1310	5066	11231
from A		...	1023	3581	7359
B		...	204	1004	2601
C		...	83	481	1271

from the point of view of East-West trade as a whole, and then from that of specific relations between particular states.

The General Problems of East-West Trade

'Commercial problems between countries with different economic and social systems', to borrow a United Nations' phrase, can be classified under three heads: political, institutional and economic.

POLITICAL PROBLEMS

The fundamental principles which are generally recognised in East and West as lying at the basis of international economic relations are strikingly similar.

The principle of peaceful coexistence is for socialist states a fundamental principle governing international society. In the field of economic relations it assumes the 'development of economic and cultural co-operation on the basis of complete equality and mutual advantage' (C.P.S.U. text, December 1961). The United Nations Charter, in the aims of the organisation as defined in its first article, includes the aim of achieving international co-operation through solving international economic problems.

Economic competition between different social systems must respect peaceful coexistence and the freedom of commercial exchange: 'The Soviet Union and the other socialist countries reject policies of discrimination based on closed economic groupings. They uphold the most-favoured-nation principle, which has long shown itself to be the universal and generally accepted principle of international trade.'[2] The most-favoured-nation principle was incorporated into G.A.T.T. in 1947. The Agreement extends and completes it with the principle of non-discrimination and the prohibition of quantitative restrictions on exports and imports.

But this identity of views is to be found only at the level of general principles. Western countries have not applied the most-favoured-nation clause to their trade with socialist countries, which they have circumscribed with numerous restrictions. The socialist countries do not accept the legality of certain departures from the basic rules of international commerce contained in article 24 of the Agreement, in connection with regional integration, customs unions and free-trade areas.

Discrimination against Socialist Countries

That Western countries have not extended the principles of G.A.T.T. to socialist states is not because the Agreement was limited to relations between market economies. Originally most of the signatories to the Agreement were advanced capitalist countries. But articles 3 and 17 of the Agreement contain rules which can be applied to commerce with countries having a State monopoly of foreign trade. As an original member of G.A.T.T., Czechoslovakia has granted tariff concessions on 600 items and extended the most-favoured-nation clause to the other signatories who (with the exception of the United States) have responded in like fashion. Subsequently, in 1959, Poland and Yugoslavia[3] entered into relations with G.A.T.T. Yugoslavia became a provisional member in November 1962. After abolishing the State monopoly of foreign trade and loosening restrictions on imports and exports, she was able to become a full member in 1966. Poland joined G.A.T.T. in 1967 and Romania in 1971, with corresponding rights and obligations.[4]

There is therefore no obstacle of principle or organisation to the application of uniform rules for international East-West trade, analogous to those governing relations between market economies. However this trade still suffers from the discrimination and control introduced during the Cold War period (1948-52) under the instigation of the United States, and still formally in force in spite of the fact that numerous European states try either to limit or to avoid them.

Most important among the discriminatory measures introduced during the Cold War is the strategic embargo on exports. European countries have rarely applied discriminatory tariffs, and have formally extended most-favoured-nation treatment to socialist countries. This has had little practical effect however, since quota restrictions limit imports from these countries. Since 1951 only the United States has refused to make tariff concessions to communist regimes, with the exception of Yugoslavia after 1952 and Poland after 1956. Quotas, widely used in the beginning, are less systematically applied except by the United States and except for certain products, such as oil.

At the same time the embargo policy continues to block any real normalisation of East-West trade. Since 1947-8 the United States has placed a unilateral embargo on the export (and re-export) of strategic goods to communist countries. On the initiative of the U.S.A. a co-ordinating committee was set up in Paris in 1949 (Cocom), comprising the United States, West European countries in Nato and Japan. Its function was to draw up a list of products which members of the committee undertook not to export to communist countries directly or indirectly. The United States and her allies have always placed a different interpretation on the meaning of the embargo. For the United States the aim was to institute an economic blockade, so as to prevent the development of the socialist countries by depriving them of basic products or necessary equipment. For her partners the blockade had strictly military objectives. Initially the first approach was dominant: in 1952 the maximum Cocom list covered 50% of commodities in international trade. The list gradually shortened to the point where today it contains only military goods and supplies. The European countries have more or less abandoned the embargo, which they never really believed in (history shows that far from weakening the country under attack, economic blockade usually contributes in the long term to strengthening its productive potential by forcing it to become self-sufficient). The United States on the other hand continues to apply it, not only on the basis of the Cocom list but also in accordance with domestic legislation, particularly the 1949 Export Control Act. This act, revised in 1962, obliges the President of the United States to prohibit exports to communist countries if they tend 'to strengthen the military or economic potential' of a particular state.

Nowadays these arrangements tend rather to hinder Western countries in their trade with the East. When the Italian firm Fiat negotiated with the Soviet Ministry of Foreign Trade the construction of a car factory in the U.S.S.R. (August 1966), it first had to gain the approval of the American government, since some of the machinery necessary for equipping the factory had to be bought by Fiat from American firms (or their European subsidiaries) or else manufactured under American licence. The report delivered to the House of Representatives of the United States Congress, justifying the President's favourable response to the transaction, contains some interesting arguments: the machines in question are highly specialised, very costly and can only be used in car production; these machines will tend to involve the Soviet Union even more in the production of a highly popular consumer good whose manufacture absorbs considerable resources; direct Soviet expenditure on the expansion of car production should perhaps be considered as the beginning of a government policy allocating more resources to the consumer sector. In other words in this particular case the indirect export of American equipment to the U.S.S.R. is justified because it cannot strengthen Soviet military capacity and because it will on the contrary cause the U.S.S.R. to invest in the production of a consumer good and bring about a proportionate reduction in military expenditure.[5]

The Attitude of Socialist Countries to Regional Integration

The socialist countries are opposed in principle to all closed economic groupings and especially to the E.E.C. This opposition is based both on political considerations and on the belief that integration must reduce the volume of international trade and slow down its liberalisation. It might well be asked whether the U.S.S.R. and her Comecon partners do not constitute a closed group, but the socialist countries' reply to this is that the Council for Mutual Economic Assistance, unlike the E.E.C., has no common external tariff and no discriminatory protectionist policies comparable to the common agricultural policy of the E.E.C.

Can it be said that since 1957 East-West trade, and particularly inter-European commerce, has been checked by the creation of the Common Market? Statistics show that the opposite is the case. The period 1957-67 coincides with a very rapid expansion of trade between Comecon members and the countries of Western Europe (*cf.* statistics published in the U.N. documents quoted in the bibliography). At present it is not so much the rules of the Common Market which limit this trade as particular quantitative restrictions deriving from bilateralism between states. Just as there is no common Western policy on the part of Comecon, there is no common Eastern policy by the E.E.C., although in December 1969 the Six decided to strengthen the co-ordination of their activity relating to the socialist countries. These officially ignore the Community and approach each member country individually. For their part the European states attempt to derive maximum advantage from their negotiations with their contracting partners in the socialist bloc. In spite of certain declarations made by political personalities in the socialist countries, particularly in 1972, recognising the reality of the Common Market (e.g. Brejnev at the fourteenth Congress of Soviet trade unions), there is nothing in the present development of Comecon or its 1971 Programme intimating a future common policy *vis-à-vis* the Common Market. On the other hand from 1 January 1973 E.E.C. countries will have collectively to negotiate and conclude commercial agreements with socialist states. Present agreements will remain valid until the expiry of their term which for most of them is December 1974.

One example is particularly significant: the credit granted by European countries to socialist countries to allow them to pay for imports. In recent years the U.S.S.R. has been the chief beneficiary. In 1962 the Six decided informally not to grant anything more than five-year credits to socialist countries. The first infraction of this arrangement was made by France who sold entire factories to the U.S.S.R. in 1965 with a seven-year credit. The following year Italy agreed on a repayment period of eight and a half years for the cost of the factory built by Fiat in Togliattigrad. The repayment period was not to begin until 1971, when the first part of the project would be operational. The agreement between Germany and the Soviet Union in November 1969 on the delivery to the U.S.S.R. of large-diameter tubes for gas pipe-lines was accompanied by credit at 6% per annum, repayable within ten years from the date of delivery of the first section (end of 1972). Germany thus fell in line with the conditions granted by Great Britain at the end of 1968 when contracting to sell an ironworks. Britain of course was not bound by the unofficial agreement between the Six. Finally in March 1970 France granted even more favourable conditions to the U.S.S.R. in the form of credits of from seven to eight and a half years' duration. Moreover these were not for a single project but for two-thirds of the sales of French equipment specified in the five-year commercial agreement between France and the Soviet Union for 1970-4.

This type of one-upmanship shows quite clearly that the cohesion of the closed economic group of the Six *vis-à-vis* Comecon is not proof against individual commercial interest. According to an agreement of 1951 relations between West and East Germany come within the sphere of domestic trade and are not subject to the rules of international commerce. In 1967 the German Federal Republic decided on a programme to encourage these transactions. The result was to increase inter-German exchanges by 14% in 1968 in relation to the previous year, and by 16% in 1969. This privileged position might cause difficulties for Western Germany in her relations with Common Market partners. The conclusion of a basic treaty between the two Germanies in December 1972 makes no change in this arrangement, the main beneficiary being the G.D.R., since she can market her agricultural produce free of duty and other payments at West German prices, fixed by the E.E.C. above world prices.

INSTITUTIONAL PROBLEMS

The argument most frequently advanced by capitalist states when they refuse to extend all the advantages of the most-favoured-nation clause to socialist countries or when they refuse to lift quantitative restrictions on trade with them, concerns the institutional framework of socialist foreign trade.

It will be remembered that it has two main features: a State monopoly of foreign trade; the planning of foreign trade as a sub-division of the domestic macro-economic plan.

In countries outside the U.S.S.R., there has been a considerable relaxation of the State monopoly of foreign trade following the recent economic reforms, since socialist enterprises now have direct access to foreign markets. However, the right to intervene on these markets has been granted in each country only to a limited number of designated firms, and these are not entirely free in their negotiations, since they must take account of the foreign trade plan. Under these circumstances the most-favoured-nation clause does not have the same sense as in relations between market economies, where it allows foreign producers to compete amongst themselves as well as with the domestic products of the country to which they wish to sell. Even when socialist enterprises export individually to a capitalist market they have State backing. That is why they have often been accused of dumping. The accusation has been made in particular against Czechoslovakia in her relations with members of G.A.T.T., but has been proved in only a few isolated cases. But are things really so different in the West? When Fiat negotiated with the Soviet Union for the construction of a factory with a full-production capacity of 600,000 cars a year, are we really meant to assume that the Italian government took no interest in the transaction?

TABLE 8.2[6]

THE POSITION OF COMECON COUNTRIES IN THE WORLD IN 1967

(surface area, population, industrial production, foreign trade; world total=100)

	Surface area	Population	Industrial production	Volume of foreign trade
Developing countries	50.7	47.0	7.0	18.4
Advanced capitalist countries ...	23.4	18.4	55.0	69.0
Socialist countries (total)	25.9	34.6	38.0	12.6
Comecon	18.5	10.0	31.0	10.2

As we saw in the previous chapter it is the planning of foreign trade rather than the State monopoly which puts a brake on its expansion, even between socialist states. It is for this reason that the total volume of the foreign trade of member countries occupies such a minor place in world foreign trade: 10.2% in 1967, while supplying 31% of world gross industrial production (*cf.* table 8.2). Moreover this proportion shows a tendency to decline, falling below 10% at the beginning of the present decade, whereas Comecon's share in world industrial production is increasing constantly (estimated at 33% in 1972). Socialist countries rely as little as possible on foreign trade, even between themselves, to cover those needs revealed at the planning stage which cannot be satisfied from domestic production. They export just enough to cover imports. Within the framework of Comecon the tendency of each country towards autarky is counterbalanced by policies of plan co-ordination, co-operation and specialisation, policies which are proving very difficult to implement. Attempts are being made to replace bilateral exchanges with multilateral procedures in the field of payments and concerted action. These counterweights are absent in relations between Comecon countries and the West. Socialist countries only sell to industrialised capitalist countries because they need to buy, and try to achieve equilibrium in their balance of payments with each of their partners. The planned priority given to imports and the necessity of covering them by an equal total of exports explains the paradoxical behaviour of socialist countries describe by the American economist Franklyn Holzman[7] when referring to Soviet reactions during the Great Depression. From 1929 to 1932 the Soviet Union expanded its export of corn to the West in spite of the dizzy fall in prices (1932 prices being less than 40% of the 1929 level). This was because the Soviet Union found it essential to finance in this way her purchase of machinery, the price of which had fallen relatively less. Otherwise the first five-year plan would not have been fulfilled.

In the case of East-West trade Say's formula is applicable: products exchange against products. With a view to eliminating this barter mentality and stimulating trade, it is sometimes suggested in the West that in the absence of the real convertibility of socialist currencies an intra-European clearing system should be established. Such a system would have no effect as long as socialist foreign trade remains subordinated to the needs of the domestic plan. As Holzman has correctly pointed out in another study, the inconvertibility of socialist currencies is not merely monetary. It is above all real: purchases by foreign countries are limited because commodity flows are mainly planned and because it is difficult to buy goods not specifically earmarked for export.[8] Even if Western enterprises could acquire roubles or any other socialist currency they could not compete for the purchase of goods with national enterprises on the domestic socialist market. It is also because foreign trade is planned in kind that the difference between domestic and international prices can be maintained in the long term without jeopardising the internal equilibrium of the socialist countries.

This price gap explains the lack of drive of socialist enterprises on foreign markets. It has similar effects to the difference between wholesale prices at production level and retail prices on the domestic market. As was seen earlier these two price categories are determined separately and by different methods. Wholesale price variations have no effect on retail prices, and *vice-versa*. When the retail price rises, for example, the producer does not respond by increasing supply. Since the wholesale price usually remains unchanged, he has no incentive to do so. Similarly, in the field of international trade, world export or import price variations have no influence on the profitability of enterprises working for export or with imported products; they cannot bring about an increase or decrease in the supply of exported products or in the demand for imported goods.

A word of caution: at present only in the case of the Soviet Union is there a complete divorce between internal and external prices. In the other socialist countries economic reform has attempted to gear firms to increasing exports or restricting imports as a function of variations in world prices. This has meant supplementing the quantitative planning of foreign trade indicators with value indicators (at world prices), and instituting various formulae for interesting firms in foreign exchange revenue (or, in the case of imports, in economising on expenditure). However these procedures are very difficult to implement. They imply the conversion into foreign currency of magnitudes expressed in national currency, in a situation where the official exchange rates of socialist countries are highly arbitrary. Conversion coefficients are therefore necessary in almost every individual case, for both exports and imports and for the various monetary areas.

Even assuming greater flexibility by socialist countries in the planning of their foreign trade, there would not necessarily be an automatic expansion of East-West trade. The present economic structure of this trade does not favour further development.

ECONOMIC PROBLEMS

As can be seen from table 8.3, the exports of the socialist countries of Comecon to the West are composed essentially of raw materials and mineral fuels (35% to 40% of their sales to Western countries) together with food products (now stable at around 15% to 20% after a slight decline in recent years). On the other hand they export relatively few capital goods (less than 10% of sales to the West). The product composition of their trade with capitalist states is therefore typical of that of developing countries.

Such a situation can only bring long-term stagnation to trade between capitalist and socialist countries. Countries of the Eastern bloc, preoccupied above all with avoiding trade deficits with their capitalist partners, will have to increase sales to the West. Since they can hardly increase the proportion of their raw material and food product exports, it is vital for them to be able to

TABLE 8.3[9]

COMPOSITION OF THE FOREIGN TRADE OF COMECON MEMBERS
WITH DEVELOPED MARKET ECONOMIES IN 1970

	Exports of members of Comecon	Imports of members of Comecon
Raw materials and mineral fuels ...	36%	10%
Food products	17%	11%
Chemical products	5%	12%
Machinery, transport equipment ...	8%	34%
Other manufactured goods	25%	32%
Other	9%	1%

sell more manufactured and more capital goods on Western markets. This will require a considerable effort on their part to improve the quality of their products and to adapt production to the needs of eventual buyers. Some socialist economists have suggested greater international co-operation between enterprises, so little developed before 1968-70. Industrial co-operation would make it possible for socialist enterprises linked to capitalist firms to benefit from those production and marketing techniques which they lack.[10] But in the present state of East-West relations there are a large number of political and institutional obstacles standing in the way of further progress along this road.

According to the United Nations' Economic Commission for Europe, there were nearly 400 agreements on co-operation at the beginning of the 1970s between socialist and capitalist enterprises. However it is difficult to arrive at a precise figure, since it will depend on an agreed definition of what constitutes industrial co-operation. If we include everything going beyond a purely commercial transaction (sale or purchase of goods and services for money), agreements on industrial co-operation may assume various forms: the sale of whole factories, with deferred payment and the staggered delivery of equipment, supplemented by technical assistance and the transfer of know-how (e.g. the Fiat-U.S.S.R. agreement of 1966); the creation of mixed companies with shared capital; sub-contracting; joint ventures; manufacturing to order. Such intermediate forms as these are widely used in the socialist countries of Central Europe. An example of working to order is the manufacture of special types of rolled steels by the Galati iron and steel combine in Romania for the German firm Gütehoffnungshütte, in return for deliveries of iron and steel equipment and technical information. An example of sub-contracting is the assembly in Poland of Grundig tape-recorders, with some parts delivered by the German firm and others produced in Poland. A quantity of completed tape-recorders corresponding to the value of the parts supplied to Poland are returned to Grundig; the rest are marketed by Poland within Comecon. Participation is the form taken in the management of the hotels built by Intercontinental Hotels in Budapest and Bucharest; the property belongs to

Hungary and Romania, but part of the profit goes to the American firm as a function of the rate of hotel occupation by Western tourists. The mixed enterprise with shared capital is still the exception. Only in Romania (since 1971), Hungary (1972) and Yugoslavia is there legislation authorising foreign investment in national enterprises. Legislation in the other countries only permits joint enterprises outside national boundaries. Such firms have usually been established for marketing socialist products in Western countries.

These arrangements can be grouped into two categories. The first of these, which covers most of the contracts entered into by the U.S.S.R. with Western countries, involves on the one hand a socialist country with natural resources at her disposal and requiring the equipment and technology to develop them, and on the other a capitalist country requiring raw or semi-processed materials (especially fuel: oil and natural gas). The agreement consists of the delivery of equipment over a period of years for payment in kind. Examples of this type are the West German-U.S.S.R. tubes for gas contracts, or the contract between the American company Occidental Petroleum and the U.S.S.R. signed in April 1973. This contract is the most important case of East-West co-operation to date and comprises the delivery of factories in return for chemical products. The second group covers manufacturing concerns where the Western partner sees the chance of extending his market in the socialist world through sub-contracting tied to marketing agreements. At the same time he profits from a cheaper and more stable labour force than in the West. The socialist partner finds his advantage in mastering capitalist techniques in a product whose domestic supply is still inadequate (machinery and especially industrial consumer goods).

It appears to be a game which everybody wins. The capitalist countries widen their markets or consolidate their sources of supply. The socialist countries obtain the goods and techniques they need without loss of foreign currency. On the other hand the socialist countries do constitute a potential competitive threat to their capitalist partners on their own markets. While industrial co-operation makes it possible to economise on foreign currency, it does bring with it a degree of dependence on the advanced capitalist nations. Consequently, with the development of socialist integration, Comecon countries may in the future prefer to have recourse to collective loans on the Western money market (perhaps through the Investment Bank) rather than link themselves to capitalist firms for specific operations.

Trade between the U.S.S.R. and Industrialised Countries

The development of commercial relations between the Soviet Union and industrialised capitalist states illustrates the general trend of East-West trade.

The value of Soviet foreign trade rose from 2.9 milliard roubles in 1950 to 26 milliard in 1972. Since 1954 the share of non-socialist countries has been increasing constantly. In 1953 it was 17%, in 1972 35.5% (22.6% with industrialised countries). However Soviet trade as a proportion of world foreign trade is both low and constant: 4% between 1960 and 1972. In the same period the Soviet contribution to world industrial production rose from 19% to 20%.

The low level of Soviet foreign trade with industrialised countries (less than 1% of the volume of world foreign trade) is explained by the general factors limiting East-West trade. A further reason is the relative independence of the Soviet economy from foreign trade (the ratio of imports to national income being 3.5% in 1968).

From the point of view of the geographical structure of this trade, the most important partners of the Soviet Union among industrial countries in 1972 were, in order of importance: the German Federal Republic, Japan, Finland, Great Britain, France, the United States, Italy, Canada, Holland, Sweden, Belgium, Austria. The important position of Canada and the United States is due to the heavy purchases of wheat by the U.S.S.R. in 1972. Most of these countries have long-term commercial agreements with the Soviet Union. Great Britain has had trading relations with the U.S.S.R. longer than any other country. A provisional commercial agreement was signed in 1934. The Soviet Union has always been an important source of timber for England, and the two countries established a joint stock company with mixed capital well before the War. This was the Russian Wood Agency, comprising English brokers and representatives of the Soviet department responsible for timber exports. The British balance of trade with the Soviet Union has shown a substantial deficit for some years. Soviet trade with Japan was only resumed in 1957 and there was considerable expansion over the next ten years. The volume of trade multiplied fourteen times between 1958 and 1968, and apart from the usual commercial relations the two countries have developed various forms of economic co-operation, such as the development of Siberia and the ports on the Soviet eastern coast.[11] Finland was for a long time the privileged commercial partner of the U.S.S.R. for reasons of geographical proximity and political preference. But she lost her first place among capitalist countries in 1968. Soviet-Italian trade received a considerable boost from 1966 with the conclusion of the Fiat contract, followed by similar agreements in electronics (Olivetti), chemicals (Montedison), and Italy's commitment to buy large quantities of Soviet oil and gas. Commercial relations with the German Federal Republic have often been compromised for political reasons. In March 1963 for example Federal Germany suspended her deliveries of large-diameter tubes for oil pipe-lines to the U.S.S.R on account of the strategic embargo. In 1962 this item represented 22% of Soviet purchases. Six years later, in November 1969, the firms Thyssen and Mannesmann agreed to supply the Soviet Union with 1.2 million tons of large-diameter tubes for gas pipe-lines, coupled with a ten-year credit repayable from 1973 in the form of deliveries of natural gas to Germany (via a gas pipe-line to Bavaria passing through Czechoslovakia and Austria). A second contract of similar importance was signed with Mannesmann in July 1972. Brejnev's visit to Bonn the following year resulted in May 1973 in a general agreement on economic, industrial and technical co-operation which was in effect an extension of the 1972 commercial agreement.

The fact that France lies fifth among the industrial nations in the volume of trade done with the Soviet Union is not a true reflection of her importance on the Soviet market. France remains the second most important supplier of the Soviet Union in Western Europe, after being for several years the only great industrial power to run a surplus with the U.S.S.R. on its balance of trade. Franco-Soviet relations since 1966 have been developing in a very favourable political climate. It was in that year that an important agreement on scientific, technical and economic co-operation was signed. Various organs have been set up to implement the agreement.[12] The most important of these is a standing committee composed of French and Soviet representatives, whose function is to examine at least twice a year the practical problems arising from the commercial, economic and technico-scientific co-operation between the two countries. Commercial exchanges as such are effected on the basis of a long-term commercial agreement. The first of these was signed on 30 October 1964 and was renewed on 29 May 1969 for the period 1970–4. The main difficulty arises from the French balance of trade surplus with the U.S.S.R. The Soviet Union is only too ready to increase its purchases from France—provided it can cover them from sales. The expansion of these sales is limited by the capacity of the French market to absorb them (especially for finished products; France would be more willing to increase her imports of raw materials, oil and gas). A further obstacle is the lack of information in the hands of the French importers. The setting up in 1968 of a Franco-Soviet chamber of commerce to implement the 1966 agreement was an essential element in attempts to improve the information service.

But since 1971 trade has grown most of all with the United States. From 161 million roubles in 1970, trade grew to 184 million in 1971 and to 538 million in 1972. The turning-point came in May 1972 when the 'Fundamental principles of relations between the U.S.S.R. and the United States' were adopted on the occasion of President Nixon's visit to Moscow. In October 1972 the two countries signed an agreement regulating differences over war-time lease-lend, a commercial agreement for three years, and an agreement on methods of financing trade in which Exim Bank was authorised by the President of the United States to grant export credits to the U.S.S.R. In the meantime, during the summer, the U.S.S.R. had made large purchases of wheat. The spectacular and exceptional nature of these agreements should not be allowed to obscure the long-term improvement in commercial relations between the two countries. At the end of 1972 the Chase Manhattan Bank opened a branch in Moscow. The contract of April 1973 with Occidental Petroleum was preceded and followed by more modest though still significant agreements, from a contract for the sale of Pepsi-Cola in return for vodka to

Soviet purchases of equipment for the giant Kama lorry plant.

The product composition of Soviet trade presents the same general characteristics as that of the foreign trade of Comecon members as a whole. There is however an even higher proportion on the export side of raw materials and mineral fuels,[13] posing the same problems even more pointedly.

TABLE 8.4[14]

COMPOSITION OF SOVIET FOREIGN TRADE WITH EUROPEAN MARKET–ECONOMY COUNTRIES IN 1966

	Soviet Exports	Soviet Imports
Raw materials and mineral fuels:	81.3%	13.9%
Food products:	8.7%	10.3%
Machinery, transport equipment:	5.5%	44.0%
Chemical products:	2.0%	12.2%
Other manufactured goods:	0.9%	17.4%
Other:	1.6%	2.2%

Even a summary presentation of the different aspects of Soviet/capitalist trade should indicate some of the new elements in it, especially the development of the sale and purchase of licences which has been particularly active since 1965. But statistics on these transactions have not been published.

There is a similar lack of reliable data on the way in which the U.S.S.R. achieves equilibrium in its balance of payments, that is to say on its gold and capital movements. We know that the U.S.S.R. sells gold [15] of which it is an important producer to pay for its trade deficits, particularly through its banks abroad, the Moscow Narodny Bank in London (and its Bayreuth branch) and secondarily the Commercial Bank for Northern Europe in Paris.

2.   RELATIONS BETWEEN SOCIALIST AND DEVELOPING COUNTRIES

Relations between the socialist countries of Comecon and the non-socialist developing countries clearly have a political backcloth, just as do relations between developing countries and industrialised capitalist nations. The Third World is the stake in the competition between capitalism and socialism. To persuade the states of the Third World to follow the socialist road after freeing themselves from colonialism, it is not enough to demonstrate by example the advantages of the socialist economic system. It is also necessary to develop relations with them which are economically desirable from their point of view and which are politically free of all suspicion of colonialism or imperialism.

The ideology behind these relations has been defined in many documents emanating from the socialist countries collectively—which of course have had no past colonial connections with the Third World. An example is the following extract from the Declaration of the Conference of Representatives of Communist and Workers' Parties in 1960:

> The socialist countries are the sincere and faithful friends of peoples struggling for their independence or already liberated from the yoke of imperialist oppression. Rejecting in principle all forms of intervention in the internal affairs of young national states, they consider it their international duty to assist these countries in the struggle to consolidate their national independence. They help and support these countries as much as possible in their development, in the creation of a national industry, in the strengthening and expansion of their national economy, in the formation of skilled personnel, and co-operate with them in the struggle for world peace against imperialist aggression.[16]

This programme has been confirmed and its economic implications developed in the collective or individual contribution of representatives of socialist states at various international gatherings, especially at the sessions of the United Nations conference on trade and development at Geneva in 1964, New Delhi in 1968 and Santiago in 1972.

It is interesting to compare the socialist definition of support for developing countries with a quasi-official résumé of the objectives of United States' aid contained in a sub-committee report of Congress.[17] It states that since the end of World War II United States' aid has aimed at restoring economic stability in key countries; supplying arms and economic aid to halt the growth of communism, rebuilding the armed forces of allies threatened by communist aggression, encouraging technical co-operation and promoting economic development and humanitarian feelings.

Leaving aside the political denunciation of imperialist and communist aggression contained in the two texts, as well as the eulogies on socialist pacifism and Western humanitarianism, there remain significant differences in the aid programmes. In the socialist declaration it is the principle of national independence and non-intervention in internal affairs which is given priority. On the basis of this principle the socialist countries will not grant aid in the form of free gifts (with a few exceptions), since this type of assistance is usually linked to political or economic interference in the internal life of developing countries. On the other hand this is implicit in the American programme which is openly conceived as a riposte to communist infiltration, implying that aid will in the last analysis be proportionate to the political stand of the beneficiaries *vis-à-vis* communist regimes. Secondly, socialist countries favour the creation of national industry in the countries of the Third World. This of course is the strategy of industrial growth originally applied by the U.S.S.R.

to itself, and extended to the European socialist countries after World War II. The general philosophy of socialist aid might be summed up in the dictum, 'Help yourself and the communist world will help you.' Hence the insistence on the need for these countries to ensure *their* development, to strengthen *their* economy, to form *their* labour-force. The type of economic and technical co-operation ultimately decided on will reflect this concept. The American document confines itself to recommending the encouragement of economic development, without making any reference to specific efforts on the part of the beneficiaries. The final reference to humanitarian considerations implies that the Third World can be nothing more than the repository of Western good works.

The principles governing socialist foreign aid imply three consequences:
The relations between socialist and developing countries bring together partners with equal rights, an equality best reflected in the essentially commercial nature of the relationship;
The aid brought through an expansion of commercial relations will be completed by other forms of technical and economic co-operation, which will require some effort on the part of the beneficiaries towards making a positive contribution to their own development;
In the countries receiving socialist aid the objectives will be those economic sectors likely to promote economic growth, primarily the industrial sector.

Aid Through Trade

The expansion of commercial relations between socialist and developing countries really got under way round about 1955. From the time of the Russian Revolution the young Soviet state attempted to establish commercial links with several neighbouring states: with Afghanistan just after its independence (1919), then with Iran, Turkey and Mongolia (1921), and with China in 1924. There were also links with some Latin American states, particularly Argentina. But until the end of World War II the U.S.S.R. was the only socialist state. After the war the future countries of the socialist bloc had first of all to solve their own chronic problems before thinking of enlarging their international commitments. In addition, until the mid-1950s their relations with countries of the Third World were paralysed by the fact that most of these were still either colonial or mandated territories whose trade was channelled through the metropolitan countries or through foreign companies. Table 8.5 describes the development of trade between socialist and Third World countries between 1955 and 1966. During this period the average annual rate of growth of world foreign trade was 5.9%; that of trade between advanced capitalist states 9%; between the latter and developing countries 4.8%; between developing countries 2.8%; between socialist countries 8.4%; and between the latter and developing countries 12.6%.

TABLE 8.5[18]

THE DEVELOPMENT OF FOREIGN TRADE BETWEEN SOCIALIST AND DEVELOPING COUNTRIES (1955=100)

Countries	1956	1957	1958	1959	1960	1961	1962	1963	1964	1965	1966
All socialist countries	130	141	174	180	177	197	238	252	289	337	362
Comecon countries	127	154	176	178	190	228	277	284	308	364	391
U.S.S.R.	161	230	270	272	258	340	466	462	471	574	616

However trade between socialist countries and the Third World is a negligible proportion of the world total. It is likewise a low proportion of their own trade (12.5% of total socialist trade in 1966; 7.1% of that of developing countries of which 6.8% was represented by exports and 7.8% by imports). How can it be said that this trade is of any real help to the partners of the socialist camp? Trading advantages for the Third World derive from two causes: the structure of mutual trade and the system within which it operates.

THE STRUCTURE OF TRADE

This structure is especially favourable to developing countries: the socialist countries purchase their traditional exports (primary and agricultural products which Third World countries find increasingly difficult to sell on the right terms on saturated capitalist markets); the socialist countries sell machinery and capital goods needed by the Third World for industrialisation. Very often the credit arrangements linked to the commercial agreements provide for the loans accompanying these sales to be repaid either in traditional commodities or else in the products of the new industry of the Third World countries.

The U.S.S.R. for example sells complete factories, equipment and machinery (37% of her sales to the Third World in 1960, 50% in 1965–6), as well as other goods with a productive use (oil, metals). From them she buys traditional products: cotton (Afghanistan, U.A.R., Iran), wool (Turkey), rubber (Malaysia), jute (Pakistan), sisal, coffee (Brazil), tea (India, Ceylon), rice (Burmah), cocoa, etc. At the same time she is increasing her imports of craft products, cloth and manufactured goods. Such products however, form a modest proportion of Soviet purchases. An example is the commercial agreement with India for 1966–70, whereby the U.S.S.R. will be supplied with products from the electro-technical industry and engineering products.

This structure is likely to persist for the next decade. Can the socialist countries be accused of helping to maintain the developing countries in their position as suppliers of basic products of essentially agricultural origin, encouraging them in monoculture and arresting the diversification of their economies?

The socialist countries argue that initially it is not at all in the interest of developing countries to abandon the existing trade structure, and that on the contrary they must specialise in agriculture for export, by strengthening their monoculture sector if need be. Cuba for example returned to an economy based on sugar-cane production, when it had for a long time sought maximum economic diversification after the socialist revolution. Only under these conditions can a surplus be created for importing capital goods.

The usual objection to this reasoning is that such a policy puts the Third World at an ever greater disadvantage on account of the fall in the prices of primary products for export in relation to industrial import prices. Between 1952 and 1962, for example, whereas these countries raised the volume of their exports by 32%, the value of their sales rose by 8%.[19] That there has been a deterioration is clear. However it is far less important in relations between developing and socialist countries, since the former benefit from guaranteed stable markets and prices (in the form of long-term agreements). The problem of prices will be looked at again in relation to the forms of trade now in operation. As for the outlets offered by socialist countries, their share in Third World exports was 6.5% in 1965. This included 10.7% of their sales of agricultural produce and 11.9% of their sales of raw materials. Between 1960 and 1965 the socialist countries took 36% of the increase in the export of primary products by the Third World. Their reasons for continuing to do so are neither philanthropic nor mainly political. In the first place the socialist countries have not yet reached a standard of living where the market is saturated with tropical products – coffee, cocoa, tea, sugar, bananas. The planned rise in living standards over the next decade implies, among other things, a growing supply of these products for popular consumption. There will therefore be an increase in imports from tropical countries. In the second place the chemical industries of the U.S.S.R. and her Comecon partners have not yet reached their full potential. They do not produce great quantities of synthetic materials to compete with primary products (plastics, artificial fibres, etc.).

The socialist countries are particularly interested in obtaining supplies of oil and natural gas from the Third World. In the socialist bloc only the U.S.S.R. and Romania are important producers of these commodities. Until now the U.S.S.R. has covered almost all the needs of Comecon members in oil. Soon however she will no longer be able to do so. This is because domestic demand is growing as a result of the changing structure of her fuel consumption. In 1965 oil and gas covered 51% of domestic fuel consumption, 60% in 1970. There is a similar rise in demand by the other Comecon countries. Even Romania, long self-sufficient in oil, became a net importer in 1968. The programme of co-operation drawn up between certain countries of the Third World and the U.S.S.R. is directly geared to the more intensive exploitation of oil and gas fields. In the U.A.R. and Syria for example Soviet geologists contribute to the prospecting for oil reserves. In Algeria in 1964 the U.S.S.R.

organised and equipped an oil and gas institute and a technical school for training the personnel necessary to the oil industry. In India and Pakistan the U.S.S.R. is taking part in the search for new fields and the setting up of an oil industry, which would at least make these countries largely self-sufficient and independent of foreign supplies. In 1969 she began to take an interest in the working of Iraqi fields appropriated from the Iraq Petroleum Company. As far as gas is concerned, an important field was brought into service in Afghanistan in 1968. Half the production will be exported to the U.S.S.R. via a gas pipe-line crossing the Soviet republics of Central Asia. In the same year an agreement was concluded with Iran involving Soviet co-operation in the construction of a trans-Iranian gas pipe-line, Soviet equipment to be paid for in gas deliveries. The Soviet Union has even taken an interest in Latin American reserves. At the beginning of 1970 Soviet-Bolivian talks laid the foundations for deliveries to Eastern Europe of Bolivian oil, non-exportable to the United States since the nationalisation in 1969 of American oil companies in Bolivia.

Obviously the Third World can count for a long time to come on regular outlets in socialist countries for their traditional products.[20] In the longer term the structure of trade will change, as the countries of the Third World industrialise and modernise by their own efforts and with socialist help. It will be based on an international division of labour to which the introduction of elements of planning in these states will contribute. In other words the establishment of a public sector (not necessarily socialist) as a basis for State regulation of the economy will tend to facilitate an extension of foreign trade between socialist and developing countries. It represents a political and institutional back-cloth which should not be overlooked.

An example of the perspectives opened up by such collaboration is provided by the German-Egyptian agreements of 1965. The G.D.R. supplied the U.A.R. with technical assistance and equipment for building a cotton-spinning mill which is now the fourth largest in Egypt. A large part of its production is exported to the G.D.R. Later similar agreements were signed for equipping several other textile mills (combed wool, cotton). They imply long-term commercial commitments on both sides. But their main originality lies in a reorientation of production both in the country giving and in the country receiving the aid. The G.D.R. will in effect reduce her own production of natural textiles and concentrate more on the manufacture of artificial and synthetic fibres. She envisages an extension of this operation by contributing to the development in the U.A.R. of the first transformation stages of a petro-chemical industry. This is to the advantage of the G.D.R. since she will no longer import from the U.A.R. crude oil for her petro-chemical industry, but by-products for further transformation.

This co-operation, which will gradually spread to the whole of Comecon-Third World relations, will mainly take the form of credits granted by the socialist country to the beneficiary for extending the sector whose products it wishes to import. The developing country obtains aid which increases its potential for accumulation (in money and kind); the sector which has been stimulated is certainly orientated towards exports, but satisfies domestic demand as well; the long-term credit agreement guarantees markets and foreign exchange; the specific form of the credit maintains the independence of the two partners. Credit is therefore now one of the principal means of organising foreign trade between Comecon and the Third World.

THE FRAMEWORK OF COMMERCIAL RELATIONS

Exchange is carried out on the basis of long-term bilateral inter-state agreements (three to five years) which are renewable. Usually the two partners grant favoured-nation treatment to each other. The U.S.S.R. has gone even further. Applying the principle which she supported at the first United Nations' conference on trade and development at Geneva in 1964, according to which the developed nations should not only extend to Third World countries the treatment they reserve for each other but should give them additional advantages, the Soviet Union unilaterally abolished all import duties on products coming from the Third World on 1 January 1965.[21]

The commercial agreements concerning the nomenclature and quality of commodities to be exchanged impose binding obligations on both parties, further protocol modifying or completing the lists at a later date. Detailed and precise planning of these exchanges is necessary from the point of view of the socialist side, since the foreign trade plan is a sub-division of the domestic macro-economic plan. The same is true for the other country if it is committed to planning its economy, even on a limited scale.

The agreements stipulate stable prices. This is a guarantee for Third World countries against price fluctuation in primary products, which usually operates to their detriment.[22]

In principle the exchange must be in equilibrium. Where this is not the case, the agreements provide for payment of the balance either in national currency or in convertible exchange such as the American dollar or the pound sterling. Payment in convertible currencies is less favourable to the debtor country, usually the one from the Third World. This is not only because it reduces its foreign exchange reserves, but also because the burden of repayment can become very heavy if there is depreciation of the national currency. Consequently the agreements often stipulate that the agreed rate of exchange will be the official rate prevailing on the date of the agreement (the U.S.S.R. has agreements of this type with fifteen developing countries).

Short-term payment credits may be made to cover a temporary imbalance between the imports and exports of one party. The disadvantage of this procedure is that bilateral exchange, combined with the obligation on the debtor country to pay the balance at an early date, may limit the expansion of trade since the debtor will be tempted to reduce his indebtedness by restricting imports. That is why the socialist countries are resorting increasingly to long-term commercial credit linked to the delivery of equipment and repayable in commodities (traditional products or industrial goods manufactured with the help of the equipment supplied). However bilateralism is still the rule. Trade between Comecon and Third World countries would certainly expand much more if it could be organised on a multilateral basis.

All the same, present trading conditions are more favourable to developing countries than those between them and their capitalist partners. They sometimes lead to concessions by the capitalist countries. The Indo-Soviet agreement of 1960, for example, on the delivery of Soviet oil, led the other suppliers of oil to India to lower their prices.

Official forecasts of trade between the socialist and Third World countries are optimistic: in 1980 it is expected that the total value of this trade will be between 15 and 20 milliard dollars, 10 milliard of which will be composed of Soviet–Third World trade.

Socialist aid is thus mainly of a commercial type. However it is supplemented by other forms of co-operation.

Economic and Technical Co-operation

The socialist countries do not have recourse to certain forms of aid which are peculiar to the capitalist system: gifts or foreign investment. Gifts are only made in exceptional cases: in times of natural catastrophe or war (medical and food supplies to Vietnam for example). This attitude is justified in several ways: gifts are humiliating for the beneficiary and do him a disservice in that they are not calculated to involve him in a positive effort of his own; for developed countries gifts are often a means of getting rid of embarrassing surpluses which are non-existent in the socialist world; finally, gifts justify interference in the internal affairs of the beneficiaries, from which socialist countries bar themselves in principle.

Investment in the national enterprises of developing countries by capitalist states prejudices the independence of these countries. Such investment is usually private and cannot therefore by definition be applied by socialist states. Since 1970–1 however there has been some development of the mixed company between socialist enterprises and firms of the Third World. But these have been established mainly in the area of distribution and research, rather than for co-production as such.

The socialist states employ two forms of aid: credits for economic co-operation and technical assistance.

The first of these must not be confused with short-term and long-term commercial credits linked to commercial and payment agreements. They are mainly credits in kind: the borrowing country obtains credit to the value of the goods and services which it is to pay for (deliveries of equipment or complete industrial plant). The credit is therefore an important growth factor in so far as it tends to substitute the primitive accumulation which the country would otherwise be forced to initiate to promote development. It makes it possible to save time and to avoid that restriction of consumption inherent in the early stages of industrialisation.

Generally speaking the credits bear interest at 2.5% and are repayable in eight to twelve years. The repayment period begins from the time when all deliveries of equipment are complete or from the time when plant begins operating, in the case of the supply of complete factories. By way of comparison, it is interesting to note that the credits of the Export-Import Bank of the United States are granted for seven to eight years and bear interest at 5% to 5½% per annum. They are repayable in dollars, whereas most of the credit granted by the socialist countries is repayable in the form of commodity deliveries.

Between 1956 and 1967 the socialist countries granted more than 6 milliard roubles in credit, 4 milliard of which came from the U.S.S.R. In 1967 the latter had credit agreements with thirty-five developing countries. The main beneficiaries were India and the U.A.R., followed by Indonesia, Afghanistan and Algeria.

The loans are not linked to economic or military conditions. Their use is not subject to control. Nor do socialist countries share in the capital or profit of enterprises built with the help of the equipment supplied on credit.

Like commercial credit, credit for economic co-operation is advanced on the basis of inter-state bilateral agreements. The socialist countries take little part in international bodies for multilateral aid[23] which are the framework for aid supplied by capitalist states (through the intermediary of the United Nations, etc.). Nor is there any multilateral aid organisation within the socialist camp. It is undoubtedly one of the weaknesses of Comecon that it has not achieved greater co-ordination in this field and that co-operation between member countries is in this respect so little developed.

The further development of this form of aid is inhibited by the bilateral nature of the credit and by the fact that the beneficiaries are not always in a position to use it. In fact, and this is what distinguishes credit from a gift pure and simple, the borrowing country must make a minimal contribution to the operation financed by the credit so as to be able to reimburse it later. However many countries are in no position to do this. One explanation is the lack of trained technical personnel. Hence the importance of socialist technical aid.

This aid is in the first instance directed at infrastructure projects undertaken in developing countries with socialist credit and supplies. When these countries do not have the necessary work-force, teams of specialists are sent to co-operate with local labour as instructors and technical advisers (in prospecting natural resources or setting up equipment and plant). Personnel trained on the spot by the Soviet Union alone in the period 1955–65 has been estimated at 150,000.

Technical aid also covers the training of Third World personnel in establishments of higher and technical education in socialist countries. In 1966 for example the G.D.R. took 2,300 students from the Third World. In the same year the U.S.S.R. took 11,000, a large number of whom went to the Patrice Lumumba University in Moscow which specialises in this type of education.

Economic co-operation, technical assistance and the training of skilled personnel give a specific style to socialist aid: the beneficiaries must take an active part and free themselves from the gift mentality. Wherever possible national bodies assume responsibility for projects undertaken with socialist collaboration. In the U.A.R., for example, there is a body for implementing the five-year plan and one for the building of the Aswan dam; in Syria there is a council for economic development. The objectives of socialist aid are well defined: to restore the economies of the Third World through industrialisation based on an important public sector.

The Objectives of Socialist Aid

Socialist aid, in its commercial form or through economic and technical co-operation, claims to be disinterested. And it achieves this in so far as the advantages it affords (guaranteed markets, stable prices, favourable terms of credit, etc.) are not related to political or military conditions and do not involve control of the economy of the beneficiary. However it does have precise aims which explain its particular points of impact.

The geographical distribution of these countries is significant in itself. Can one detect a connection between the political orientation of countries receiving aid and the support they are given? Such a connection is far from clear. It is certainly true that each time a country of the Third World states its intention of following the road to socialism, the aid previously coming from the socialist camp is increased – if only to compensate for the fall in Western aid. Examples are the increasing support given to Algeria, Tanzania and the Sudan. Sudden reversals of policy in the opposite direction have a symmetrical effect: the substantial Soviet aid to Indonesia fell off following the *coup d'état* of September 1965 which was accompanied by violent anti-communist repression. Some countries however receive an equivalent amount of aid from both sides. India, for example, is the most important recipient of both American and Soviet aid. Between 1954 and 1965, she received more than one-seventh of total United States' aid granted to developing countries and a little less than one-fifth of the Soviet total.[24] The distribution by country of commercial relations and of co-operation between the Third World and members of Comecon is mainly a result of historico-geographical factors: the existence of previous traditional links (between the U.S.S.R. and Afghanistan or India, between Czechoslovakia and South-East Asia, between Bulgaria and the Near East, between Germany and Egypt); geographical proximity explains the predominance of Asia in trade and co-operation (from 40% to 60% according to the country), and the relative insignificance of Latin America (between 8% and 20%; although the European socialist countries have been trying to penetrate further into the American continent since 1960). Overall the U.A.R. and India have benefited most from socialist aid. The accumulated total of each of these two countries up to 1966 was more than 1 milliard roubles in credit, or one-third of the total coming from all socialist countries.

The objectives of socialist aid come through much more clearly in an examination of the economic sectors involved. The aim is to create a rational economic structure in the developing countries, a complex of enterprises and branches capable of forming the basis of heavy industry. This orientation corresponds to Soviet growth strategy, and contributes to the creation or strengthening of the public sector in Third World countries, since nationalisation policies tend to affect the infrastructure first (exploitation of natural resources, basic industries).

Table 8.6 illustrates this orientation, showing the distribution at the end of 1967 of the 2,500 projects completed or under construction in Third World countries by the socialist states as a whole (for the period 1955-67).

TABLE 8.6[25]

NUMBER OF PROJECTS COMPLETED OR UNDER CONSTRUCTION IN DEVELOPING COUNTRIES WITH THE HELP OF SOCIALIST STATES
(Situation at the end of 1967)

Iron and steel and non-ferrous metals	45
Power and coal	584
Engineering and metal processing	132
Chemical industry, oil, petro-chemicals	136
Iight and food industries	508
Building materials	112
Transport and communications	209
Geology	50
Agriculture	147
Teaching establishments and centres for professional and technical education	110
Other cultural and social establishments	223
Other	148
	2,404

It should perhaps be added that socialist aid, based on long-term commitments and usually expressed in kind (commercial agreements for the delivery of equipment, agreements on co-operation in industrial projects), is often more easily incorporated than Western aid into the planning, however rudimentary, of those Third World countries which have recourse to it.

Of the economic branches receiving socialist aid, first place is held by those which played a dominant rôle in Soviet growth: power, metals, mechanical engineering.

The power sector absorbs considerable credits for co-operation: for the participation of socialist countries in the prospecting of natural resources (oil and gas) and the building of thermal or hydro-electric power stations. Achievements in this last field have been spectacular, owing to the other effects of building a hydro-electric power station apart from the supply of power: irrigation, improved waterways, etc. The most well-known example is the Aswan dam project in Egypt. Building began in 1960 with Soviet aid, and the first section was finished in 1964. In the metal industry, the U.S.S.R. has set up some very large complexes. The first was the Bhilai combine in India for which credits were forthcoming in 1955 when the Soviet Union first began to channel aid to the Third World. The first stage began production in 1960 and had an annual capacity of 1 million tons, equal to the entire steel production of the country in 1947. An even bigger iron and steel works was constructed at Bokaro. This had an annual capacity of 4 million tons, so that the U.S.S.R. can be considered the founder of the Indian metal industry. She also contributed to creating or expanding this sector in Ceylon, the U.A.R., Algeria and Iran. Engineering offers more possibilities for joint co-operation between members of Comecon, and it is in this branch that one finds the greatest number of multi-lateral operations. For example the G.D.R., Romania, Czechoslovakia and the U.S.S.R. all participated in building the Khelouan industrial complex in the U.A.R. which includes an iron and steel works, a carbo-chemical factory and several heavy engineering plants. This project is significant for another reason. It constitutes an integrated programme of industrialisation, the engineering factories absorbing the output of the iron and steel complex.

In agriculture, socialist support has two aims: to contribute to the modernisation of this sector so as to raise agricultural exports (through the supply of machinery and fertilisers, the construction of irrigation networks, land improvement, etc.); to advise and help underdeveloped countries in diversifying their agriculture so as to make them self-sufficient in food production. Technical co-operation is very wide here. Experts usually accompany the materials delivered, not only to give instruction in the use of machinery, but also to suggest modifications in traditional methods of farming and structural transformations which will facilitate more rapid expansion: agrarian reform, the introduction of rudimentary forms of co-operation and collectivisation.

In the transport sector the socialist countries have mainly co-operated in the establishment of infrastructures: railways, roads, bridges, port installations, aerodromes. The main beneficiaries have been Iraq, Afghanistan and the U.A.R. Of the Comecon countries Hungary is the most important supplier of lorries and buses; the G.D.R. and Poland deliver ships.

Socialist co-operation thus aims at a radical transformation of the economies of underdeveloped countries. It might be asked whether this emphasis on industrialisation is particularly useful in countries where agriculture still accounts for 50% to 80% of national income and employs from 70% to 90%

of the work-force. If the industrial sector develops in isolation, apart from agriculture and without raising its productivity, the countries concerned will not profit in the long term from the aid which is supplied. From the socialist point of view it is here that the underdeveloped countries must make their own choice: the example of the socialist states, especially of the less-developed among them (hence the essentially political significance of Bulgarian aid for example), must show them that to get out of the rut they must develop the will to bring about a political and social transformation. The first step in this direction is the abolition of private property in the means of production on a scale large enough to make planning possible.

Apart from a few general indications no attempt has been made here to give figures for the total value of socialist aid. The figures have little meaning. It is certainly possible to estimate the volume of the foreign trade of socialist with developing countries. Value comparisons with exchanges between industrialised countries and the Third World are misleading because trade with the socialist bloc is mainly in the form of balanced exchanges in kind and on terms which are qualitatively advantageous. As for aid in the form of credits and gifts, estimates are even more hazardous. The same difficulties crop up: the problem of converting quantitative data into values; the evaluation of the qualitative advantages of this credit, such as low interest rates, long repayment periods and the ease of payment by debtor countries in local currency or commodities. There is a further unknown factor: the proportion of credits actually drawn on in relation to those advanced. Socialist country sources for the period 1955-66 show a total credit of 6 milliard roubles. 4 milliard of this came from the Soviet Union, 600 million from Czechoslovakia, and 400 from Poland. Western estimates evaluate aid from socialist countries since 1960 at about 5% of total international aid. Socialist writers reject this figure which they maintain is the result of a quantitative and qualitative under-estimate of socialist aid and an over-estimate of aid from the West.

CONCLUSION

Socialist ownership, or collective ownership by the whole people, of the basic means of production is the criterion defining the socialist economic systems. That was the point of departure of this book. Does this criterion still apply? For the author the reply must be yes. The socialist economies of Europe can certainly not be reduced to a single model. Their institutions, structures, policies and economic mechanisms are similar but by no means identical. They may be sub-divided into groups with distinguishing common features, the component parts of which also have their own originality. But in all of them the private appropriation of the essential means of production has disappeared and has been replaced by various forms of social appropriation (differing from country to country and from sector to sector). On this basis it has been possible to extend the principle of planning to all spheres of economic life, using a specialised administrative apparatus and methods of indirect intervention in the process of production and distribution.

The abolition of private property in the means of production is a step which most developing countries have not taken. It is a step which will perhaps be taken by those considered in the socialist bloc to be on the road to socialism (Tanzania is a case in point, to take a relatively old example of socialist commitment). The previous chapter showed how the Third World is one area of peaceful competition between the capitalist and socialist systems. It is just possible to consider the underdeveloped economies as outside both systems, or rather as within the ambit of the one or the other according to their particular orientation at any given moment. The instability of their political regimes often gives this orientation a provisional and reversible character.

At this point two questions arise. In the first place, does such a choice have any meaning; in other words, is there a convergence of the systems, gradually bringing modern developed economies closer together to the point where they blend into one industrial society, the variants of which can only be distinguished by secondary characteristics? Secondly, is there an optimal economic regime?

The form of the second question will depend on the reply given to the first. If the convergence theories are accepted the question will be about the objectives and functioning of the economic system they imply. If these theories are rejected the question is which of the two existing systems can best guarantee both economic growth and the satisfaction of human needs.

Theories of Convergence

Broadly speaking it is possible to isolate two theories of convergence: the hybridisation or the synthesis of the systems. According to the first version capitalism borrows its planning techniques from socialism, while socialism completes authoritarian and centralised direction of economic life with the regulative mechanisms of the market. The result of this cross-breeding is a hybrid species, a mixed socio-economic system. In the second version the technical features of modern large-scale industry radically transform the economic organisation of both systems and lead to a new social synthesis, as different from present systems as plastic is from its constituent elements.

Jan Tinbergen is the most eminent representative of the first version and has written many studies of it.[1]

In his view there have been remarkable changes in both systems, and they are not confined to the penetration of market factors into socialism or of planning into capitalism:

Within capitalism:
1.   Extension of the public sector, covering key branches, power, transport, banking and sometimes iron and steel; nationalisation effected after the War by governments of the left was usually left intact subsequently, even by later conservative governments. It therefore amounts to an almost irreversible process;
2.   The growing importance of the budget in the national income (one-quarter to one-third) which gives the State considerable financial means of intervention;
3.   Limitations on perfect competition between firms, either for economic reasons (ever-rising fixed costs) or because of systematic anti-trust legislation;
4.   The use of planning techniques either by large firms (United States) or by governments (France, Great Britain, Holland, etc.);
5.   Wages and prices control through anti-inflation policies;
6.   Market stabilisation policies (especially in agriculture);
7.   Regional development policies within the national framework over-riding considerations of short-term profitability in an effort to raise standards in underdeveloped areas;
8.   Extension of free or semi-free services, particularly in the field of education and health.

Within socialism:
1.   Growing professionalisation of enterprise management, leading to the creation of a class of specialised managers;

Economic planning is a form of subjective activity by individuals, a form of 'economic behaviour'. But like all voluntary and conscious economic activity by individuals, it is directly conditioned by the economic and social relations of production and reflects them. Socialist planning is the economic function of the socialist State and must guarantee macro-economic equilibrium. The possibility and necessity for a balanced development of the economy lie in historically determined property relations: the relations of social ownership of the means of production.

An analysis of the nature of programming shows why it cannot lead to a rational development of the capitalist economy. Programming is the economic function of the bourgeois State and exists to ensure the smoothest possible functioning of the capitalist economy . . .

The high level of capitalist 'socialisation' of production, which is reflected in the development of the public sector, the concentration in the hands of the State of a significant part of the national income, and the increase in the proportion of State investment in total accumulation, creates certain possibilities for a balanced regulation of the economy. However, the particular features of the collective interest of the monopoly bourgeoisie mean that these elements of regulation must develop within the framework of large monopolies in the different branches and sectors of the capitalist economy. That is why, in spite of the appearance of certain regulative mechanisms, the economy cannot develop in a balanced way in its totality: due to the dominance of private capitalist ownership of the means of production, contradictory class interests, and the anarchic form of economic activity corresponding to them.[7]

On the other hand a planned socialist economy does not evolve towards capitalism merely by using profit as a stimulant of economic activity. As was seen in chapter 2, in most socialist countries the maximisation of enterprise profit is linked to plan fulfilment. Even where this relationship is not a close one (as in Hungary and Czechoslovakia, where the profit motive is relatively independent of the plan), price control, taxation and regulations governing the use of residual enterprise profit ensure that profit retains its function as an instrument of economic policy, a criterion of success and a means of encouraging efficient management. In a system of socialist ownership, profit cannot be appropriated by private holders of capital.

The recognition of a specific cost to capital, which as we have seen has had an effect on price formation, on the calculation of investment efficiency, on enterprise management (through the criterion of profitability calculated as the ratio of profit to productive assets) and on taxation (through the imposition of a charge on these assets), is often used to support convergence theories. However this recognition does not involve rejecting the labour theory of value, according to which labour is the sole source of value. Capital represents indirect accumulated labour which creates a product and a specific value. To impose a charge on enterprise capital, or to use efficiency norms for selecting investment variants, means that this indirect labour, which is an amalgam of scarce resources, must be used judiciously so that its combination with direct labour can be as productive as possible. It means nothing more than that. At the level of production relations, the opposition between capital and labour in the capitalist system reflects that of two antagonistic classes, separated by the appropriation by one of them of the means of production. In the socialist system the contradiction cannot exist. That is why the very word 'capital' in this context is a misnomer, even though it may be convenient. As Khavina puts it:

> Socialist relations of production, and especially the basic relation of production, social ownership of the means of production, exclude the possibility of transforming these means into capital. These relations determine the difference of principle existing between the assets of socialist society and capital. The specifically socialist character of the means of production, in the form of productive assets, derives from the fact that they are the property of the whole of society and that they are used in its interest. In other words, they have a directly social character. The appropriation and disposal of these assets is monopolised by society. This ensures the economic equality of all its members in relation to the ownership of these assets. Although the latter are commodities, the vast mass of them cannot be purchased out of private income, nor can they become private property. That is why it is impossible for them to be used by a class, a strata or group of men in their personal interest, with the aim of appropriating surplus labour and product.[8]

The usual reply to this is that the concept is outmoded. Marxist theoreticians are still under the illusion that economic power belongs to the capitalists, to the private owners of capital. In reality both capitalism and socialism have been overtaken by the technological revolution, which is gradually creating a new society, a new industrial state. This second version of convergence is defended most clearly by the American economist J. K. Galbraith.

It is Galbraith's contention that the capitalist class has lost its dominant position once and for all, that there has been a transfer of power within the large firm from owners to managers.[9] Real power is in the hands of the technostructure, those participating in group decisions. This power is based on the information possessed by each member of the group, information which is synthesised by the organisation structuring the group itself. At the same time the technostructure is the inevitable product of any modern industrial society and determines the convergence of the systems. In other words convergence begins with the modern scale of production, the vast mass of capital required, the advanced technology and consequently the complexity of the organisation itself. It implies control over prices and the maximum possible management of purchases effected at those prices. In this sense planning must replace the market.[10]

The two systems are already advancing towards this new society. In each of them enterprises are tending to become oligarchies in the hands of their own staff, escaping on the one hand from the owners of capital and on the other from State or Party authorities. The consumer is no more sovereign in a socialist than in a capitalist system. In the former demand is directly orientated; in the latter it is conditioned by diverse forms of advertising. Prices and wages are authoritatively fixed in the East, and stabilised or even partially controlled by the State in the West. Finally the State everywhere orientates and organises professional and intellectual training, tending to produce the same result by different means: supplying the economy with the skilled personnel it needs. The effect is the convergence in all essential respects of two industrial systems which are ostensibly different.[11]

Galbraith's thesis is not new. In sociological rather than economic terms, it had been expressed a few years previously by Raymond Aron in his *Eighteen Lectures on Industrial Society:* 'Obviously some of the essential features of the division of labour are almost wholly determined by the techniques of production and are found in a similar form in every type of industrial society'.[12] But Aron is not led by this to subscribe to theories of convergence, an 'optimistic hypothesis' in his estimation which is by no means proven and is in many respects improbable. Like Galbraith he observes that in the large modern firm real power is in the hands of the managerial group. But he adds that the effects of this power are very different according to the type of enterprise (and particularly according to the mode of ownership of the means of production, which for him, together with the mode of control, is an essential factor in the opposition of capitalism and socialism).[13]

> 'In all industrial societies certain people occupy positions in which they have power over their fellows or enjoy prestige in relation to other members of the community. The organiser of the means of production, the managers of big industrial firms in the U.S.S.R., the U.S.A., or France, have power over those who work in the undertaking. Whatever the country, these managers also have ways of influencing the state. But the relationship between the managers of the instruments of production and those who hold power in the state is not the same in the Soviet Union and in the U.S.A.'[14]

The theory of technological convergence confuses industrial structures and economic systems. Nobody contests the fact that structures are growing closer together. But to deduce from that the emergence of a new society, a synthesis of the systems, is to ignore all the political, social and legal dimensions of a concrete social structure. J. Le Bourva probably comes close to the truth in his clear formulation of the problem. For him contemporary capitalist and socialist societies have one feature in common; they are:

> industrial, that is to say removed from the natural environment, no longer absorbed in subsistence production, and possessing a significant mass of productive capital and accumulated knowledge, which prepare the way for more capital and more knowledge. They stand opposed in relation to the system of ownership of this capital and consequently in relation to the distribution of power and the whole economic organisation.[15]

Since this contradiction between property systems appears to them to be irreducible, Marxist theoreticians maintain that relations between the two systems must continue within the framework of peaceful co-existence. This will be accompanied by competition in the field of economic growth, which will end when socialism has replaced capitalism and abolished private property in the means of production; in other words, after a radical transformation, a revolution, which need not necessarily be violent.

The Best Economic System

Soviet Russia appeared as the first concrete example of the socialist economy at about the same time as neo-classical political economy was formulating the theory of welfare, outlining the conditions necessary for a collective economic optimum. Pigou's *Economics of Welfare* was published in 1920, a little more than ten years after Pareto's *Manual of Political Economy* (1906), where a social optimum was first defined as a development of the consumer equilibrium theory enunciated by Walras at the end of the previous century.

Pareto's theory is that the optimum is achieved when it is no longer possible through a shift in the existing position to improve the welfare of one individual without reducing that of at least another. As long as that is possible the distribution of the community's resources is not consonant with optimum conditions which are realised automatically in a system of free competition (the main condition being the equalisation of the marginal productivity of each factor of production at its price, which is given by definition for all those with commodities to exchange and who can only adjust to this price).

The question of the optimum in a socialist system was posed in 1920 by the Austrian economist Ludwig von Mises in an article entitled 'Economic Calculation in Socialism'.[16] Von Mises categorically denied the possibility under socialism of rational economic calculation in the sense of an optimal allocation of resources. He maintained that in the absence of a market in the means of production, linked to their private ownership, prices would necessarily be fixed arbitrarily and could not therefore act as a guide in the rational distribution of capital goods. The principal condition for achieving the optimum would not be fulfilled.

An important doctrinal controversy followed this article during the inter-war period.[17] Two interpretations could be put on Mises' article, opening up two possible ways of refuting it. According to the first interpretation, economic calculation is impracticable in a socialist system. According to the second, it is irremediably irrational. Criticism was directed at both these versions, but did not question the formulation of the optimum as such. For most of the opponents of the liberal doctrine the best economic system was the one achieving the optimum defined by the doctrine itself, which for them was not capitalism but socialism. It might have been better to have criticised this particular conception of what constitutes an optimum. Such criticism was to come much later.

According to the first argument, economic calculation is not practicable in a socialist economy. For it to be so those adjustments which occur spontaneously through the market mechanism would have to be replaced by equivalent adjustments effected by the planner. The planner would have to know the quantity of all existing means of production, all the factor combinations actually applied in every enterprise and all consumer preferences. Given a knowledge of all production and demand functions, one could in theory work out the equations corresponding to optimal resource allocation. This possibility seemed to be excluded at the time of the great controversy. It became possible through the invention of linear programming. The work of Kantorovitch and Novojilov posed mathematically the problem of the choice of optimal production methods and solved it through the application of linear programming. They showed that the optimal plan in a socialist system does fulfil the conditions of the Pareto optimum (notably the equalisation of the weighted marginal productivities of factors of production). They have been able to demonstrate that after fixing the optimal plan it is perfectly feasible to establish rational prices for capital goods, even in the absence of a market. Soviet mathematical economists have therefore implicitly answered the criticism that economic calculation under socialism is impracticable. But is their argument convincing? Professor J. Marczewski doubts it. In his view the planner never has sufficient information at his disposal. But this is really avoiding the issue: hypothetically, he could have such information at his disposal. A second and much more serious objection is that linear programming is a limited method because it assumes that the objective function and its constraints appear in the form of linear expressions, which makes it impossible to take into account such phenomena as diminishing returns, economies of scale and external economies and diseconomies.[18] However even if linear programming cannot take these factors into consideration, neither can the market mechanism as defined in the hypothesis of welfare theory.

According to the second and probably the truest interpretation of Mises' thesis, economic calculation is not so much impracticable as impossible in the socialist system, where private property in the means of production has been abolished. Most of his opponents have certainly understood it in this way. In this case it could be shown that:

1. A real market in capital goods can exist under socialism, that is to say direct exchange relations between enterprises, even in the absence of private ownership;
2. Under this system the central planning department plays the rôle of a market for these goods and therefore fills any actual vacuum;
3. Rational economic calculation is possible in a socialist economy, but this rationality is specific, qualitatively different from the rationality of a market economy; consequently the hypothesis of a real or simulated market in capital goods can be abandoned.

We shall examine the second of these three theses which is attributable to Oskar Lange. The first was elaborated by the British economist H. Dickinson. At the time (1933) it appeared far removed from the mechanisms of any concrete socialist economy, of which the U.S.S.R. was the sole representative. Today, as we have seen, it has a basis in reality, since the economic reforms of the last decade are tending everywhere to institute direct contractual relations between enterprises for the purchase and sale of capital goods (even in the U.S.S.R., where the process is still least developed). The third, that of the Marxian socialist Maurice Dobb, goes so far in its justification of socialist rationality that it even denies the necessity for economic calculation. At the time[19] Dobb's conception of planning was of a highly centralised system, based on *ex ante* adjustments made by the planner whose aim was to realise the quickest possible economic growth. In other words he based his argument on the organisation and aims of the Soviet system as it existed under the first five-year plans. It should be added that it was not his intention to define a socialist conception of the optimum as such. Nor was he concerned with the Pareto optimum. As for the objectives of the best regime, he confined himself to showing that planning does not separate the optimal allocation of resources from income distribution, whereas the latter plays no part in the Pareto optimum.

The reason for dwelling now on the theses of Oskar Lange[20] is because they remain the doctrinal basis of much later discussions in Poland[21] on the possibilities of combining plan and market under socialism. In Czechoslovakia these discussions were taken further when economic reform was being prepared under the influence of Ota Sik, in an attempt to work out a theoretical synthesis known as market socialism.

Oskar Lange's 1936 synthesis might be summarised as follows: in the socialist system, assuming a knowledge of the population's preference scales, total productive resources and technological possibilities in factor combination (assumed to be constant in the short period), the central planning department can solve all the problems of economic calculation in the absence of a real market in capital goods. And this would be possible in either of two institutional environments: freedom of choice in consumer goods and jobs; no freedom of choice. In the first hypothesis individual, consumer and workers' choices would be free. Consumer goods prices would be determined by supply and demand; incomes would take the form of payments made by the social organisation as a function of the quantity of labour supplied and of a social dividend fixed by the State. Demand would therefore be known. Supply also; enterprise directors would in effect act like capitalist entrepreneurs, choosing that factor combination which would equalise the marginal productivity of all factors, and expanding production to the point where marginal cost and marginal revenue are equal; the prices of factors of production (labour and capital) being fixed by the State. But what guarantee is there that these prices are rational? This is the essence of the thesis. The planning department first fixes prices arbitrarily. Enterprises freely determine production programmes on this basis. The department itself uses these prices to determine investment programmes. Initially there is no reason to assume that these prices will be correct. It will be observed at the end of the reference period that supply and demand are not in equilibrium for a whole series of goods: there will be either too many or too few goods produced. The department will then correct its initial calculations. Through trial and error equilibrium will gradually be achieved. In other words, the department will have replaced the market and will exercise its functions, with the same original information. What Lange calls the 'parametric function of prices', instead of being elicited from individual choices, will result from choices made and imposed by the authority. Lange's second hypothesis refers to complete planning, including consumption and the labour market. The demonstration is the same, except that the parametric price function is also imposed in the consumption sector.

It was the first version which inspired later theories of market socialism. The decentralised model outlined by Brus in the work referred to earlier, the 'model of a planned economy with market mechanism', comes very close to Lange's concept (with a few differences, especially the choice of investment allocation, which Brus unlike Lange sees as made not on the basis of a parametric interest rate, but directly).

Similarly Ota Sik's theory as presented in his *Plan and Market under Socialism*[22] is based on the necessary organic interaction between market and planning. The plan fixes the basic structure of production programmes, technological policies and large investment projects, orientates professional training, determines the global distribution of national income (between consumption and investment) and regulates the prices of basic goods and the general price level. Within this framework there exists production for the market, since production is undertaken by independent units, individually manufacturing specific goods for a consumer (or user) who is relatively unknown, and basing their activity on material gain. The market is necessary for the consumer (user) to be able to endorse the final utility of the goods produced by purchasing them freely, since according to Sik nobody has yet invented a better way of controlling production.

Integration of plan and market in this form does not mean a return to capitalism. On the contrary it reinforces the efficiency of socialism. This is demonstrated by Brus in the *postface* to his *General Problems of the Functioning of the Socialist Economy*, written after the beginning of economic reform in the European socialist countries. It was also one of the platforms in the action programme of the Czechoslovak Communist Party in April 1968, moribund after August of the same year.

This model has not been applied concretely in any socialist country, except perhaps Yugoslavia and in this case one must have many reservations. In some respects the Yugoslav system goes much further in its decentralisation than all the theoretical decentralised models (investment decisions, enterprise freedom to establish new units). In other ways it is more authoritarian, especially in the field of prices. In principle prices for most goods are not subject to control. In fact the authorities reserve the right to prevent price rises. The consequence is a rigid price structure which prevents prices from playing the essential rôle conferred on them in the theoretical models. Finally the models do not contain the institutional hypothesis at the basis of the Yugoslav system, i.e. self-management. This is certainly a deficiency of the models. Is economic democracy (in the form of self-management or something else) not a necessary constituent of the optimum regime?

Jan Tinbergen gives a different version of the optimum, resulting from his studies on convergence. He again takes his point of departure as the optimum conditions defined in welfare theory. He finds it necessary to modernise this theory, which is defective in both the capitalist and socialist context if the classical hypotheses relating to the motivation and results of the activity of economic agents and to market structures are ignored. On this last point the models of market socialism assume implicitly that the socialist market established by the plan in the interests of planning is a competitive market. In fact it is no more competitive than the existing capitalist market, where the dominant type of structure is not competition but oligopoly.

One of the great difficulties encountered by welfare theory is the phenomenon of external economies or diseconomies. Here we have a situation where enterprise activity, far from being a matter of indifference to other units as the theory requires, involves them in disadvantages which are not compensated for (e.g. environmental pollution by some firms) or in advantages which are not paid for (e.g. the benefits accruing to new enterprises from an existing infrastructure designed to serve the needs of firms already established). In all these cases the operation of the market does not lead to a collective optimum. In fact it can lead to the elimination of marginal firms which are apparently unprofitable but which from the point of view of the collective interest should continue to function. On the other hand it serves to justify the existence of enterprises involving the community in very heavy expense.

In practice in capitalist economies, the State is intervening more and more in such situations, by subsidising marginal activities which are socially useful and by requiring anti-social enterprises to compensate the community for the risks or nuisances they incur. It is obvious that in this area a socialist state is much better placed. It can give direct support to unprofitable but necessary activities (the so-called planned deficit enterprises, for example), and can integrate external effects directly into the planning process instead of having to correct them *a posteriori*.

According to Tinbergen, therefore, an institutional factor has to be reintroduced into any definition of the optimum, taking account of the functions of the State. It will then be a question of working out a system of institutions which will maximise individual or collective well-being, taking account of constraints, especially of laws circumscribing the production process and of the cost of the institutions themselves. The optimum would be 'a set of institutions, each of them characterised by their behaviour or directives for the use of the instruments of policy or action parameters at their disposal.'[23] In general, this institutional system would include an important public sector, covering in particular those branches with considerable external effects, and a private sector whose activities would be orientated by the State, mainly through fiscal measures. In all cases the State would retain extensive decision-making rights in the field of investment.

Advanced societies are today still divided politically and economically into two great systems. Each system has its variants, and rightly or wrongly their citizens usually show a marked preference for one or other system, in which they either live or would like to live. The countries of the Third World, in the absence of any alternative mode of development, will have to opt for the one or the other. Apart from the possibility of getting help from both sides at once, neutralism is not a positive solution.

If the question is put in simple terms—which is the best economic system, socialism or capitalism?—capitalism would appear to be the holder of the title and socialism the challenger. However, in comparing the efficiency of the two systems it is essential to take account not only of their present achievements but also of their potential and their aims. The objection will doubtless be made that such a comparison is meaningless, since capitalism really exists, whereas there are only 'economies which have accomplished a socialist revolution' and no socialist economies as such.[24] But for the present writer the criterion of socialism is the collective appropriation of the means of production, the historical and institutional forms of which were analysed earlier.

The possibility of socialism's very existence and its subsequent efficiency as a system have been questioned, especially from the point of view of resource allocation. But other factors need to be considered as well: growth objectives, income distribution, the satisfaction of needs.

As far as the first of these is concerned, it must again be said (*cf.* chapter 4) that the growth of production cannot be the ultimate aim of socialist society. It is the means to an end, the fullest possible satisfaction of the material and cultural needs of the people. Economic policy in socialist countries has sometimes appeared to overlook this fact, practising a systematic strategy of growth to the detriment of consumption. It was perhaps necessary at certain periods in their history. However once this end is recognised the planning system makes possible the subordination of investment policy to it. In this respect socialism has a big advantage.

Income distribution is a constant and basic preoccupation of any socialist economic policy, as was seen in chapter 5, and even in those economies where market forces are important is never left to the free play of those forces. It is clear that such a policy cannot abolish inequality between individuals and that it may create new forms of inequality typical of socialism. But these inequalities are less marked than in systems with a market economy. Above all they are not sustained by antagonism between social classes, between worker and capitalist. The economic base of this antagonism is eradicated through the collectivisation of the means of production.

At this point we must return to a fundamental aspect of Marxist doctrine: the labour theory of value. This theory is usually analysed in conjunction with the principles of price formation (*supra*). Contrary to what is suggested (wishful thinking?) in certain versions of convergence theory, the 'ideological dogma' of the labour theory of value has not been abandoned in socialist economic thought. The thesis that the exchange value of goods is created by the social labour time necessary for their production and that it must serve as a basis for price formation has been retained in its entirety. It is not in a negation of the law of value that theorists like Bettelheim see a change in socialist principles, but in the fact that the law of value is now seen to operate in the socialist system as well. Soviet doctrine long held to the thesis that the law of value no longer obtained under socialism, that it was valid only as an explanation of the economic mechanisms of capitalism.

If it is admitted that value is created by labour, what conclusions can be drawn for the distribution of the net additional product? Under capitalism the distribution of surplus value is determined by the power relationship existing between holders of capital and workers. No economic norm can explain this division (hence the Marxist analysis of exploitation). Under socialism there is again no law guiding the distribution of net income and determining the options open to planning authorities. The socialisation of the means of production excludes private profit. It obviously does not imply the integral collective distribution of the profit created in each unit of production between the workers who contributed to its production. We have seen that even in the Yugoslav system the principle of self-management in no way authorises workers to appropriate the whole of enterprise revenue. The planner will therefore have discretion to designate the share of net income for the satisfaction of collective investment and consumption needs (discretionary but not arbitrary decisions, since this choice may be made after democratic consultation with citizens). The residue can then be distributed within production units, in the form of either increased individual incomes (bonuses) or other uses freely decided on by the workers. This theoretical outline corresponds more or less to the practice of existing socialist economies. In the opinion of the present writer, it ensures a more equitable distribution of income than the capitalist system, whatever reservations one may have about the more or less free and democratic nature of the corresponding decisions.

But it is said that socialism excludes freedom or, more precisely, consumer sovereignty. If consumer sovereignty means that the consumption chosen individually by each subject determines supply and leads to an equilibrium price, then this principle does not exist in socialist society. The planner acts on demand through his retail price policy and imposes specific patterns of consumption through the planning of production itself. But is the consumer really sovereign in the capitalist system? The extent of his sovereignty depends on the size of his income, which brings us back to the problem of distribution. At the same time advertising and the conditioning of taste compromise the very existence of this sovereignty. But it will be objected that in a market economy the individual is at least free to choose the structure of his consumption within the limitations imposed by his income. This is equally true in the socialist system for those articles of consumption on offer, which become increasingly varied as the socialist economies achieve higher levels of development. The main difference between the two systems is that the sovereignty of the individual consumer (as distinct from his freedom of choice) is not and never will be a socialist objective: 'to each according to his needs', the guiding principle of the communist society which must one day succeed socialism, does not mean 'to each according to his desires'.

NOTES AND REFERENCES

Introduction

1   André Garrigou-Lagrange, René Passet, *Economie politique. Systèmes et structures. Politiques de développement,* second edition, Paris, Précis Dalloz, 1969, p. 293.
2   Henri Chambre, *L'Economie planifiée,* second edition, Paris, P.U.F., coll. 'Que sais-je?', no. 329, 1968, p. 5.
3   It is to be found in the titles of numerous journals: e.g. *L'U.R.S.S. et les Pays de l'Est, Revue des Revues,* published from 1960 to 1968 by the Strasbourg Centre for research on the U.S.S.R. and Eastern countries (Editions du C.N.R.S.); *L'Est,* an Italian journal published by the Milan Centre for studies and research on social and economic problems. It is often found too in the names of institutions doing research on the socialist countries: e.g. the University of Brussels' Centre for studies on Eastern countries; numerous British and American institutes dealing with 'Soviet and East European Studies'; institutes in Federal Germany 'für Osteuropakunde' or 'für Ostforschung'.
4   Paris, Editions Ouvrières, 1968.
4   New York, MacGraw Hill, 1964.
6   *Cf.* Jean Marczewski, 'Planification et socialisme: réponse à Henri Denis' in *Annuaire de l'U.R.S.S. 1967,* Paris, Editions due C.N.R.S., 1968, p. 224: 'The main characteristic of a socialist economy is that it is geared entirely to the maximum satisfaction of the people's needs.'
7   *Cf.* the collection *Collectivist Economic Planning,* edited by F. von Hayek, London, 1935, especially the study by Ludwig von Mises, 'Economic Calculation in the Socialist Commonwealth'.
8   Constitutional law of the Czechoslovak Federation (27 October 1968), article 4: the economy of the Czechoslovak socialist republic will be planned within the framework of a socialist market.
9   The expression is applied to the French nationalised sector in the Nora Report, together with the term 'administered economy' (*Rapport sur les entreprises publiques,* April 1967, Documentation française, 1968, pp. 24 and 26, Working group of the Inter-ministerial Committee on nationalised enterprises).
10 Gregory Grossman, *Economic Systems,* Englewood Cliffs, Prentice Hall, 1967, p. 15.
11 Gregory Grossman, 'Notes for a theory of the command economy', *Soviet Studies,* vol. XV, 1963, no. 2, p. 105.
12 Benjamin Ward, *The Socialist Economy, A Study of Organizational Alternatives,* New York, Random House, 1967, p. 102.

13 'La théorie du calcul économique rationnel et la décentralisation de la planification socialiste', *Cahiers du Centre d'Etudes socialistes,* 1968, nos. 82-7, p. 24.
14 Wlodzimierz Brus, *Problèmes généraux du fonctionnement de l'èconomie socialiste,* Paris, Maspero, 1968, pp. 18-19.
15 Gregory Grossman, *Economic Systems,* p. 16.
16 P. J. D. Wiles, *The Political Economy of Communism,* Oxford, Basil Blackwell, 1964, p. 3.

Chapter 1

1 Programme of the Russian Communist Party (Bolshevik) adopted by the Eighth Party Congress, 18-23 March 1919.
2 *Kulak* means fist in Russian and was an expression used before the Revolution to describe the speculator who bought and resold on the rural market; profiteer (his 'clenched fist' over his ill-gotten gains).
3 N.E.P. = *novaïa ekonomitcheskaïa politika.*
4 *Manual of Political Economy,* volume 2, *Socialism,* Moscow, 1963, p. 31.
5 The last craft co-operatives were nationalised in 1960.
6 E. Preobrajensky, *De la N.E.P. au socialisme,* translated by the Strasbourg Centre for research on the U.S.S.R. and Eastern Countries, Paris, Ed du C.N.R.S., 1966, p. 57.
7 Text of the Programme, 1919, pp. 523-4.
8 *artel:* this word has been subject to various etymological interpretations. For some scholars it derives from the old Russian *rotit'sja,* to swear, the *artel* being a community of people bound together by oath. Others maintain that it comes from the Tartar *ortalyk,* community. For others, it was borrowed from the Italian *artieri,* worker, craftsman. In pre-Revolutionary times it indicated any organisation (of craftsmen, traders or independent workers) whose members pooled their labour, shared the profits and had joint and several liability.
9 Source: *The building of the foundations of the socialist economy in the U.S.S.R. (1926–1932),* Moscow, 1960, *passim.* For July 1931 a collection of statistics published in 1936 gives a figure of 211,100 *kolkhozy (Agriculture in the U.S.S.R.,* Moscow, 1936, p. 191), the same as for July 1932.
10 Source: G. M. Sorokin, *The planning of the Soviet economy,* Moscow, 1961, p. 102.
11 Sources: *The collective experience of building the socialist economy,* Moscow, 1968, p. 99; N. V. Faddeev, *The Council for Mutual Economic Assistance,* Moscow, 1969, p. 227; *Vestnik Statistiki,* 1969, 6, p. 92 (for Poland); *Vestnik Statistiki,* 1965, 11, p. 90, and *The economic development of Yugoslavia,* Belgrade, Notebooks, 1968, p. 34 (for Yugoslavia).
12 Dusan Kokavec, 'Socialist ownership', in *Czechoslovak Civil Law,* Bratislava, 1969, p. 50.
13 V. V. Laptev, 'Les institutions juridiques du gouvernement de l'économie soviétique', in *Les Institutions juridiques du gouvernement de l'économie dans les pays occidentaux et socialistes,* Brussels, Presses Universitaires, 1968, p. 21.
14 The expression is M. Mouskhely's, in M. Mouskhely, Z. Jedryka, *Le Gouvernement de l'U.R.S.S.,* Paris, P.U.F., 1961, p. 79. This principle was first applied to Party organisation before being adopted as a general principle of administration.
15 This is the usual practice of American Sovietologists, administrative law in their country being of little help to them on this point. *Cf.* Benjamin Ward, *The Socialist Economy, A Study of Organizational Alternatives,* p. 7: 'An organization has become more decentralized, with respect to choice, if the range of alternatives open to subordinates has increased'; similarly, Gregory Grossman, *Economic Systems,* p. 21.
16 Georges Vedel, *Droit administratif,* Paris, P.U.F., p. 561.

17 Strictly speaking, decentralisation is incompatible with the socialist theory of the State, which is based on the principle of the indivisibility of power, whether it is exercised at the level of national parliamentary assemblies or local representative councils. Decentralisation is therefore impossible by definition. This indivisibility of power does not of course preclude a differentiation of function, which in practice often reinforces the executive body.

18 Georges Vedel, *Droit administratif*, p. 560.

19 The demonstration could be applied to any other country. The U.S.S.R. has been chosen on account of its longer experience in experimenting with different systems.

20 The regional principle, which is a purely technical distinction, should not be confused with political forms of organisation determined by the federal structure of some states: U.S.S.R., Yugoslavia, Czechoslovakia since 1968.

21 Commentaries on the economic aspects of Soviet federalism always underline the inequalities of size and population of the various republics. But very little is made of the peculiar position of the R.S.F.S.R.: the capital of Russia is Moscow, as is that of the U.S.S.R.; all the central administrative institutions of the republic are in Moscow, as they are for the federal state also. In these conditions one might well ask how the particular interests of the Russian republic are safeguarded. No study has been made of this subject.

22 In Yugoslavia there is no specialised economic administration. This is a consequence of the principle of self-management. Enterprises (and all working establishments generally) manage themselves. Their activities are simply controlled by the organs of the general administration at commune, republic or federal level. Among the five chambers of the Federal Assembly (the Yugoslav Parliament) there is an economic chamber, but its competence is purely legislative (the drafting and voting of plans and laws concerning economic life).

Chapter 2

1 Some typical business behaviour of Soviet enterprise directors, based on interviews with Soviet émigrés in Federal Germany, is described by the American economist J. Berliner in an article 'The Informal Organisation of the Soviet Firm' published in the *Quarterly Journal of Economics*, August 1952, pp. 342–65. This behaviour has also been criticised in the Soviet press.

2 Source: *The Economy of the U.S.S.R. in 1968, Statistical Year-book*, Moscow, 1969, p. 184; for 1969, *Ekonomitcheskaïa Gazeta*, 1970, no. 3, p. 7.

3 Source: Statements on the implementation of annual plans by the Central Board of Statistics.

4 *Cf. infra*, chapter 6 on incomes policy.

5 Source: *Annuaire de l'U.R.S.S. 1969*, Paris, Ed. du C.N.R.S., 1970, pp. 674–5; *The Economy of the U.S.S.R. in 1968*, Moscow, 1969, p. 772.

6 His most important work is *Forms of Economic Management in Enterprises*, Moscow, Nauka, 1968.

7 *Notes et Etudes documentaires*, La Documentation française, 3 January 1969, no. 3551.

8 Source: *Yugoslav Survey*, vol. IX, November 1968, no. 4, p. 31.

Chapter 3

1 Sources: *Vestnik Statistiki*, 1967, no. 7, pp. 87–95; L. Kalinin, 'The Auxiliary Private Holding Under Socialism', Voprosy Ekonomiki, 1968, no. 11, pp. 52–53; *The Economy of the U.S.S.R. 1922–72, Statistical Year-book*, 1972, p. 2375.

Chapter 4

1 *The Political Economy of Socialism,* Moscow, Progress Publishers, 1967.

2 Source: N. V. Faddeev, *The Council for Mutual Economic Assistance,* Moscow, 1969, p. 237; V. Simtchera, *The Economy of Comecon Countries in the New Quinquenniad, Vestnik Statistiki,* 1971, 12; for Yugoslavia, OECD data.
   Note: Data relating to national income are established in socialist countries in either constant or current prices. Constant prices are used for calculating growth indices. All the countries concerned have changed the base year several times. At present prices for 1959 are used in Hungary, 1960 in Yugoslavia, 1962 in Bulgaria, 1963 in the G.D.R., and 1965 in Poland, Czechoslovakia and the U.S.S.R. For long series, indices are based on the prices of different years, but according to a methodology which is not usually explained in the statistical collections of the various countries. Current prices are used for calculating the structure of the national income. This may lead to difficulties in comparing different years if price variations have not been homogeneous in the various elements comprising the national income.
   Tables 4.1, 4.2, 4.3, 4.14 are therefore based on constant price data; tables 4.10 and 4.18 on current prices.

3 A. Gerschenkron, *Economic Backwardness in Historical Perspective,* Cambridge, Harvard University Press, 1962.

4 *Cf.* Peter Wiles, *The Political Economy of Communism,* chapter 13.

5 This basic point in the Marxist theory of value will be treated more fully in chapter 6; namely, that surplus value, or net additional product, must be entirely imputed to labour.

6 From V. S. Nemtchinov, *Models and Economico-mathematical Methods,* Moscow, 1962, p. 192.

7 In Lenin's view the appearance of crises could be temporarily delayed since department I, in conditions of extensive growth, required for its development not only constant capital *c* but also additional variable capital *v* (though proportionately less). That meant the employment of more labour, and thereby the creation of new outlets in the form of an increased demand for consumer goods. Rosa Luxemburg, a sharp critic of Marx on this point (in *The Accumulation of Capital,* 1913), held that capitalism can find much more significant and enduring outlets in markets outside the capitalist system.

8 M. Usievitch, 'Lenin's doctrine on the two divisions of the social product and the experience of building socialism in the countries of Comecon', *Voprosy Ekonomiki,* 1969, 1, pp. 111–22.

9 *Cf.* Alexander Erlich, *The Soviet Industrialisation Debate, 1924–8,* Cambridge, Harvard University Press, 1960.

10 E. H. Carr, on the other hand, in *Socialism, Capitalism and Economic Growth,* Cambridge University Press, 1967 ('Some random reflections on Soviet Industrialisation', p. 279) maintains that a decisive factor in industrialisation was the fear of capitalist encirclement experienced by Soviet leaders after the breaking-off of diplomatic relations between the U.S.S.R. and Great Britain in May 1927.

11 Naum Jasny, *Soviet Industrialisation, 1928–1952,* Chicago, The University of Chicago Press, 1961, p. 75.

12 Especially J. Goldman and K. Kouba, *Economic Growth in Czechoslovakia,* Prague, 1967; O. Sik, 'Contribution to the analysis of our economic development' in *Politicka Ekonomie,* 1966, 1, pp. 1–30 and *La Vérité sur l'économie tchécoslovaque,* Paris, Fayard, 1969. *Cf.* also an official document, the Action Programme of the Czechoslovak Communist Party of 5 April 1968: 'The Thirteenth Congress has approved the conclusions which state that the rehabilitation of our economy and the transition to intensive economic development cannot be effected through traditional means or through partial improvements in the system of management and planning, but only through a fundamental reform of

the mechanism of the socialist economy . . . Certain features of economic development in the last two years, the better use of factors of production, the reduction in the share of material costs in the social product . . . fully confirm the correctness of the conclusions adopted by the Thirteenth Congress.'

13 See E. Zaleski, *Planification de la croissance et fluctuations économiques en U.R.S.S.*, Paris, Sedes, 1962.

14 The first criticisms of Soviet growth strategy were in fact made following the first 'recession' in 1954–6, notably by the Polish economist B. Minc at an international conference of economists from socialist countries in November 1957.

15 Sources: *Problems of economic development in European socialist countries*, Kiev, 1968, p. 81; E. S. Kudrova, *National Income Statistics of European Socialist Countries*, Moscow, 1969, p. 73; *The Socialist World in Figures and Facts*, collection of statistics for 1967 to 1971 (edited in Moscow on the basis of national statistics).

16 Especially with analyses such as those of E. Denison for the United States and industrialised capitalist countries (*cf.* E. Denison, assisted by J. P. Poullier, *Why Growth Rates Differ*, Washington, 1967).

17 Sources: *The Economy of the Socialist Countries in 1968, Statistical Year-book*, p. 240; *The National Economy of the U.S.S.R. in 1970*, Moscow 1971, p. 758; *Statistical Year-book of Comecon*, 1972, p. 5.

18 Source: L. S. Degtiar, *Labour Resources and their Utilisation in Comecon Countries*, Moscow, 1969, p. 20 (from official statistical publications for socialist countries and United Nations data for capitalist countries).

19 Sources: L. S. Degtiar, *op. cit.*, p. 22; for the U.S.S.R. (1959 census figures), collection *World Population*, Moscow, 1965, p. 121.

20 *Yugoslav Survey*, vol. IX, May 1968, no. 2, p. 155.

21 Sources: For socialist countries, R. A. Galetskaïa, *The Industrialisation and Economic Structures of Socialist Countries*, Moscow, 1968, pp. 40, 42, 44; for the U.S.S.R., the collection of statistics *Labour in the U.S.S.R.*, Moscow, 1968, pp. 20; *Statistical Year-book of Comecon, 1972*, Moscow 1972, pp. 400–3.

22 Source: E. S. Kudrova, *National Income Statistics of European Socialist Countries*, Moscow, 1969, p. 89.

23 S. Strumilin. 'Fifty years of social progress in the U.S.S.R.', *Voprosy Ekonomiki*, 1969, 11, p. 71. This proportion appears rather high, but it is worth noting that in Strumilin's method of calculation the whole of the increase in national income in the period 1917–67 (index 57.2 in 1967 against a base of 1 in 1917) is due to the contribution of labour. This contribution is due to an increase in employment on the one hand (index 2.5 in 1967) and to higher productivity on the other (index 22.8 in 1967, from 57.2/2.5). *Cf.* the results obtained by E. Denison (*Why Growth Rates Differ*, p. 299) who attributes 30% of the increase in United States national income for 1950–62 to the contribution of the labour factor, 45.4% of this figure being due to the qualitative effects of education.

24 Sources: L. S. Degtiar, *Labour Resources and their Utilisation in Comecon Countries*, p. 150; I. P. Oleïnik, *The World Socialist Economy*, p. 119; K. I. Mikulskij, *Problems of Efficiency in the Socialist Economy*, Moscow, 1972, p. 170.

25 *Cf.* the ratio of gross investment/national income for 1955–62 in some developed countries: 18.5% in the United States, 19.7% in France, 23.4% in Italy, 27.2% in West Germany, 16.9% in Great Britain, from O.E.C.D. data quoted by Denison and Poullier, *Why Growth Rates Differ*, p. 118. On account of the great difference in methods of calculation, any comparison with the rates of socialist countries can be of only indicative value.

26 The rate of investment (calculated in current prices) has oscillated from a minimum of 14.3% (1956) to a maximum of 33.4% (1966) in Bulgaria, from 4.2% (1956) to 27.5% (1964) in Hungary, from 9.6% (1950) to 20.6% (1966) in the G.D.R., from 19.7% (1956) to 26.6% (1966) in Poland, from 10.5% (1956) to 27.0% (1965) in Romania, from 9.1% (1965) to 24.9% (1953) in Czechoslovakia. From E. S. Kudrova, *National Income Statistics of European Socialist Countries*, Moscow, 1969, p. 131.

382   *The Socialist Economies of the Soviet Union and Europe*

27   Sources: I. P. Oleïnik,*The World Socialist Economy*, Moscow, 1969, p. 130; R.
       A. Galetskaïa, *The Industrialisation and Economic Structures of Socialist
       Countries*, Moscow, 1968, p. 75. *Statistical Year-book of Comecon*, 1971, pp. 48–9
28   Sources: R. A. Galetskaïa, *The Industrialisation and Economic Structures of
       Socialist Countries*, op. cit., p. 53; for the U.S.S.R., from *The Economy of the
       U.S.S.R. in 1967, Statistical Year-book*, pp. 618–9; *Statistical Year-book of
       Comecon*, 1971, p. 141.
29   Sources: R. A. Galetskaïa, *The Industrialisation and Economic Structures of
       Socialist Countries*, op. cit., p. 52; for the U.S.S.R., *The Economy of the
       U.S.S.R. in 1967, Statistical Year-book*, p. 615; *Statistical Year-book of Comecon*,
       1971, pp. 170–171.
30   Besides, the ratio Y/K is the ratio of a flow to a stock and cannot have the
       symmetrical value of the ratio Y/L, expressing labour productivity, which is the
       ratio of two flows. *Cf.* Lavigne, 'Coefficient de capital et politique de l'investisse-
       ment dans l'industrie soviétique', *Annuaire de l'U.R.S.S. 1967*, Paris, Ed. du
       C.N.R.S., 1968, pp. 267–306.
31   If Y/L=labour productivity, K/Y=capital coefficient and K/L=coefficient of
       capital intensity, $K/Y=K/L \times L/Y$. Even if K/L increases, K/Y will decrease
       if L/Y diminishes, that is to say if labour productivity rises in a higher proportion.
32   Source: A. I. Antchichkin, V. Jaremenko, *Rates and Proportions of Economic
       Development*, Moscow, 1967, p. 100.
33   A. Nove gives examples in his article 'Le modèle explosif', *Annuaire de l'U.R.S.S.
       1967*, pp. 741–8.
34   Since 1956–60 the legal working week has been 41 hours, but the average length
       has been less; 40.6 hours in 1967, as against 48 legal and 47.8 average hours in
       1956.
35   It will be recalled that in Soviet analyses the capital coefficient K/Y and the
       productivity of capital Y/K are taken to be the inverse of each other, which is
       methodologically incorrect.
36   Studied in detail in chapter 7.
37   Sources: I. P. Oleïnik, *The World Socialist Economy*, Moscow, 1969, p. 300;
       Ju. Beljaev, L. S. Semenova, *Socialist Integration and the World Economy*,
       Moscow, 1972, p. 96.
38   Sources: R. A. Galetskaïa, *The Industrialisation and Economic Structures of
       Socialist Countries*, p. ´50; for the U.S.S.R., calculated from *The Economy of the
       U.S.S.R. in 1968, Statistical Year-book*, pp. 522–3.
39   Sources: I. P. Oleïnik, *The World Socialist Economy*, p. 123; for Romania, pre-
       war figures, J. M. Montias, *Economic Development in Communist Romania*,
       Cambridge, M.I.T. Press, 1967, p. 3; figures for 1955 and 1965, *Annual Statistical
       Abstract of the Socialist Republic of Romania*, Bucharest, 1969, p. 49; for the
       U.S.S.R., *Labour in the U.S.S.R.*, Moscow, 1968, pp. 24 and 124; for 1970,
       Statistical Year-book of Comecon, 1972, pp. 400 to 403 (the Year-book includes
       building under industry.)
40   Sources: (A): I. P. Oleïnik, *The World Socialist Economy*, pp. 135, 150; V.
       Simtchera, *The Economy of Comecon Countries in the New Quinquenniad*, p. 34.
       (B): I. P. Oleïnik, op. cit., pp. 132, 148, 150; V. Simtchera, op. cit., p. 36.
41   Sources: I. P. Oleïnik, op. cit., p. 121; R. A. Galetskaïa, *The Industrialisation
       and Economic Structures of Socialist Countries*, p. 61; *Statistical Year-book of
       Comecon*, 1972, pp. 48–9.
42   Except for Yugoslavia, where this principle was abandoned in 1952 for greater
       concentration on the consumer goods industry.
43   Sources: A. Sokolov, V. Terekhov, *The Economy of the Countries of Comecon:
       Results and Prospects*, Voprosy Ekonomiki, 1971, 9, p. 79; I. P. Oleïnik, *The
       World Socialist Economy*, p. 125.
44   Sources: I. P. Oleïnik, op. cit., p. 126; *Statistical Year-book of Comecon*, 1972,
       pp. 65–6.
45   Although the Soviet five-year plan for 1971–5 anticipates a faster rate of growth
       in group B than in group A, the actual trend since 1972 has again been in favour

of group A (a growth of 6.8% as against 6% for B). Moreover the 1973 plan forsees an increase of 6.3% for A and 4.5% for B (official data of the Central Board of Statistics of the U.S.S.R.).

46 Source: I. P. Oleïnik, *The World Socialist Economy*, p. 128.
47 *Cf*. F. Sellier, 'Durée du travail et système économique,' *Annuaire de l'U.R.S.S., 1969*, Paris, Ed. du C.N.R.S., 1970.
48 Source: K. I. Mikulskij, *Problems of Efficiency in the Socialist Economy*, p. 69.
49 For the U.S.S.R., see H. Chambre, *L'Aménagement du territoire en U.R.S.S.*, Paris-La Haye, Mouton, 1959; for the European socialist countries, the special number of *Economies et Sociétés*, volume III, January 1969, no. 1, 'Economie régionale et pays socialistes'.
50 *Cf*. the chapter on 'Kazakhstan: Soviet Third World?' in H. Chambre, *Union Soviétique et Développement économique*, Paris, Aubier Montaigne, 1967, pp. 259–369.
51 B. Colanovic, *The Development of Under-developed Regions in Yugoslavia*, Belgrade, 1966, p. 8.
52 Source: E. Zaleski, 'Le budget et les finances soviétiques en 1963', *L'U.R.S.S., Droit, Economie, Sociologie, Politique, Culture*, volume II, Paris, Ed. du C.N.R.S., 1964, pp. 256 and 258.

Chapter 5

1 *Cf*. the very similar definition given by J. Bénard, 'La théorie du calcul économique rationnel et la décentralisation de la planification socialiste', *Cahiers du centre d'Etudes socialistes*, nos. 82–7, June–September 1968, p. 22.
2 The eighteen regions do not cover all Soviet territory; this division leaves out the Republic of Moldavia, for a reason which is not explained in Soviet texts.
3 Source: *The Planning of the Soviet Economy*, Moscow, 1964, pp. 376–7.
4 Source: *The Planning of the Soviet Economy*.
Note to table 5.2: The notion of national income used in the accounting systems of socialist countries is contained in the formula for gross social product (*cf*. chapter 4):

National Income$=P-C=V+M$ (new value added).

National income therefore includes primary incomes, divided into two categories:
incomes from labour (or necessary product),
net incomes created by productive activity (or additional product).
Incomes from labour comprise the wages of workers in the productive sector, the incomes in money and kind of *kolkhoz* workers coming from their activity on the collective, and finally the incomes of workers, employees and *kolkhoz* members derived from their individual agricultural plots.
Net incomes from productive activity are subdivided into two categories: incomes from socialist enterprises (profits from industrial concerns, from building, transport and distributive enterprises; net receipts of *kolkhozy*); net revenue of the State, or turnover tax. The real meaning of this last item can only be appreciated from an understanding of the economic nature of the turnover tax as conceived by socialist theorists: *cf*. chapter 6. It follows that in the accounting system of socialist countries the notion of net national product at factor cost is non-existent. This is of course in conformity with Marxist theory, which denies the existence of several factors of production, labour being the sole creator of value; in general national income corresponds to the concept of net national product at current prices.
The structure of prices therefore has a considerable effect on the magnitudes making up the national income, especially in its breakdown into accumulation and consumption funds. Since the first of these funds comprises mainly capital goods and since their prices do not usually contain turnover tax, the share of the accumulation fund is statistically deflated.
For the annual macro-economic plan the national income balance is always

established in current prices for that year; for the five-year plan it is established in constant prices, the base year being the one the plan is drafted in (meaning that no account is taken of possible price changes during the five-year period).

5   Source: V. S. Sobol, *Study of the Problems of the Economic Balance,* Moscow, 1960.

6   The researchers took their inspiration from Marx's formulations on reproduction and especially from Quesnay's *Tableau économique.* W. Leontief played a part in drafting the 1923–4 balance. He emigrated a short time afterwards, and is accused by Soviet writers of systematically and deliberately refusing to acknowledge what he owes to his Russian experience in the construction of his input-output tables.

7   Explanations of this in Soviet works are not clear. It is sometimes stated that reserves (expenditure on replacements) should be placed at the edge of the first quadrant.

8   This method is based on the input-output analysis developed by Leontief. However Soviet statisticians and mathematicians attribute their initial inspiration not to Leontief's method, but to the analyses made at the beginning of this century by a remarkably gifted Russian writer called Dmitriev. Taking Walras' equilibrium theory as his point of departure, he formulated mathematically the concept of total input (by an equation of the total quantities of labour entering directly or indirectly into the production of one unit of a given good). See V. K. Dmitriev, *Economic Essays, Outline of an Organic Synthesis of the Labour Theory of Value and the Theory of Marginal Utility.*
For the analogy with the Leontief method, see H. Krier and J. Le Bourva, *Economie politique,* volume 1, Paris, Armand Colin, coll. 'U', 1968, pp. 208–16.

9   This is the reason why the totals of line and column are not identical for the same branch.

10   *Cf.* P. Massé, *Le Choix des investissements,* Paris, 1964.

11   It seems that this first ever work on linear programming had the following origin: shortly before the war a Leningrad plywood factory, using machines of different productivity for treating various types of wood, consulted the Institute of mathematics and mechanics at the University of Leningrad in an effort to solve the problem of distributing the different categories of wood between the machines so as to maximise their total productivity. It was on that occasion that Kantorovitch, then researching at the Institute and twenty-five years old, is supposed to have invented linear programming. *Cf.* A. Zauberman, *Aspects of Planometrics,* London, Athlone Press, 1967.

12   One of these studies has been translated into French: 'Mesure des dépenses de production et de leurs résultats en économie socialiste', *Cahiers de l'I.S.E.A.,* série G, number 19, February 1964, pp. 43–292.

13   On the history of planning, see E. Zaleski, *Planification de la croissance et fluctuations économiques en U.R.S.S.,* volume 1, Paris, S.E.D.E.S., 1962; H. Chambre, *Union soviétique et développement économique,* Paris, Aubier-Montaigne, 1968; C. Bobrowski, *Formation du système soviétique de planification,* Paris, Mouton, 1956.

Chapter 6

1   See H. Denis, *Histoire de la pensée économique,* Paris, P.U.F., coll. 'Thémis'.

2   For a more complete exposition, see text number 6 in H. Denis, *La formation de la science économique* (textes et documents), Paris, P.U.F., coll. 'Thémis', 1967.

3   The facts of the situation are often misrepresented: it is frequently maintained that in the so-called Stalinist period price formation was based on the law of value and that contemporary economic theory in the U.S.S.R. is developing concepts contrary to the law of value. The opposite is in fact the case.

4   *Cf.* their works quoted in the previous chapter.

5   An example of this policy is the fixing of vodka prices. Its cost of production is very low, a few kopeks a bottle; it could be reduced even further, but for 'moral' reasons the State makes little attempt to modernise production units. Wholesale price is fixed so as to just cover costs. But retail price is established at a very high level so as to discourage consumption. Through turnover tax vodka is an important source of State revenue. However it appears that price-elasticity of demand is very low, since the consumption of vodka hardly falls at all after price rises, the last of which (January 1970) increased the price per bottle sold in restaurants from 3 to 6 roubles.

6   *Cf.* V. Djacenko, 'Les facteurs de la formation des prix et les bases de leur classification', *Cahiers du monde russe et soviétique,* 1965.

7   Cf. J. Marczewski, 'Le rôle des prix dans un système planifié', *Economie appliquée,* 1966; 'Planification et socialisme: réponse à H. Denis', *Annuaire de l'U.R.S.S. 1967,* Ed. du C.N.R.S., 1968.

8   Source: *Incomes in post-war Europe,* Geneva, United Nations Economic Commission on Europe, 1967, chapter 8, p. 29.

9   *Ibid.,* p. 33.

10   Source: E. Berkovic, 'Differentiation of Personal Incomes', *Yugoslav Survey,* vol. X, number 1, February 1969, pp. 85, 86, 87.

11   The continuance of wage differentials under socialism was underlined by Marx in the *Critique of the Gotha Programme* in 1875, where he criticised the German workers' party programme for advocating a levelling of incomes in socialist society.

12   *Essays on planning methodology,* Moscow, 1964.

13   Sources: *Labour and Wages in the U.S.S.R.,* Moscow, 1968, p. 288; L. A. Kostin: *The Raising of Labour Efficiency under new conditions of Management,* Moscow, 1971, p. 88; *The State Five-Year Plan for Soviet Economic Development 1971–1975,* Moscow, 1972, p. 59–61.

14   Source: *Study of the Economic Position of Europe in 1971,* Geneva, United Nations Economic Commission on Europe, 1972, p. 81.

15   Sources: I. P. Oleïnik, *The World Socialist Economy,* p. 136; N. Varzin, 'The increase in labour productivity in Comecon counties', *Voprosy Ekonomiki,* 1973, 1, p. 72.

16   Source: *Incomes in post-war Europe,* chapter 7, p. 26.

17   Monthly family allowances as a percentage of wages: in Czechoslovakia, for one child, 5% of minimum wage; for three children, 30% of the minimum wage, 9% of the average wage in the highest income brackets; in the G.D.R., for each of the first three children, 3% of the average monthly wage in the industry, 11% for the fourth child; in Hungary, where allowances are only paid from the second child, 16.5% of the average wage for two children, 28.1% for three children. *Cf.* L. S. Degtiar, *Labour resources and their utilisation in Comecon countries,* Moscow, 1969, pp. 34–36.

18   Cf. P. Coulbois, *Eléments pour une théorie de la politique des revenus,* Paris, Dalloz, 1968.

19   Referred to evocatively as "monobank" by G. Garvy in *Money, Banking and Credit in Eastern Europe,* New York, Federal Reserve Bank, 1966.

20   Excluding Yugoslavia, where the structure of the banking system tends to differ from the 'socialist model', *cf.* chap. 2.

21   Sources: Z. V. Atlas, *The socialist monetary system,* Moscow, Finansy, 1969, p. 343; *Ekonomitcheskaia Gazeta,* 1973, 14, p. 21.

22   For the U.S.S.R., see F. Holzman, 'Soviet Inflationary Pressures, 1928–1957: Causes and Cures', *Quarterly Journal of Economics,* no. 2, May 1960, pp. 167–188; for Poland, *cf.* J. Montias, 'Bank Lending and Fiscal Policy in Eastern Europe', in *Money and Plan, op. cit.,* pp. 38–56.

23   Sources: *Economy of the U.S.S.R. in 1968, statistical year-book,* p. 775; V. Garbuzov, 'The budget in the decisive year of the five-year plan', *Finansy S.S.S.R.,* 1973, 1, pp. 3–16.
NOTE: Tables 6.14 and 6.15 include a certain percentage of unspecified expenditure and receipts. In the case of expenditure this proportion never exceeds 5%,

but for receipts is considerable. These unspecified receipts cover a series of taxes and other sources (entertainment tax, timber tax, customs duties, various local taxes and rates, net receipts from public services, etc.).

24   Ja. Liberman, 'Economic reform and financial planning', *Planovoe Khozjajstvo*, 1968, 3, pp. 52–61; B. Rakitskij, 'The economic functions of the tax on resources', *Voprosy Ekonomiki*, 1966, 12, pp. 17–28.

Chapter 7

1   New general terms were adopted in 1968 and applied from 1 January 1969.
2   Source: V. P. Sergeev, *Problems of Economic Rapprochement Between Comecon Countries*, Moscow, 1969, p. 229.
3   Sources: *Commerce Extérieur* (French edition of the Soviet journal *Vnechniaia Torgovlja*) 1969, 8, p. 26; *Comecon Year-books* (1971 and 1972) pp. 341–2 and 324–5; *Statistisches Jahrbuch der DDR*, 1972, annexe, p. 24.
4   Source: *Comecon Year-book*, 1972, p. 326.
5   Sources: V. P. Sergeev, *Problems of Economic Rapprochement Between Comecon Countries*, p. 228; *Le Courrier des Pays de l'Est*, January 1973, number 159, p. 17; *The Foreign Trade of the U.S.S.R. in 1971, Statistical Year-book*, Moscow 1972, p. 16.
6   Source: *The Foreign Trade of the U.S.S.R. in 1971*, p. 16.
7   Source: *Le Courrier des Pays de l'Est*, 1973, 1, pp. 24–5.
8   Cf. F. L. Pryor, *The Communist Foreign Trade System*, London, Allen and Unwin, 1963; numerous articles by F. Holzman, including 'Soviet Foreign Trade Pricing and the Question of Discrimination', *Review of Economics and Statistics*, May 1962; 'More on Soviet Bloc Trade Discrimination', *Soviet Studies*, July 1965, pp. 44–65.
9   This applies only to prices in intra-Comecon trade. Trade between socialist countries and Yugoslavia is based on world prices effective on the date of the agreement; in trade with Cuba, average world prices during the year before the agreement, with the exception of sugar purchased by the U.S.S.R. at a price above world prices.
10   S. Ausch, F. Bartha, 'Theoretical Problems of CMEA Intertrade Prices', in *Socialist World Market Prices*, Leyden, Sijthoff, 1969, pp. 61–100.
11   P. Wiles, *Communist International Economics*, p. 247.
12   An important international conference on this theme was organised by Comecon in Budapest in April 1967.
13   The Polish proposal is as follows: the permanent creditor nation (over a period to be defined) would convert 10% of its surplus transferable roubles into gold; conversely, the permanent debtor nation would be obliged to pay 10% of its debt in gold or convertible currencies; this percentage would be raised gradually, the final objective being to reach 100% convertibility.
14   Cf. G. Caire's article, 'Les critères de choix du commerce extérieur au sein du Conseil d'entraide économique', *Annuaire de l'U.R.S.S. 1968*, Paris, Ed. du C.N.R.S., 1969, pp. 401–26.
15   For details of this calculation, see G. Caire, *op. cit.*, p. 413.
16   Source: I. P. Oleïnik, *The World Socialist Economy*, p. 168.
17   She was a net exporter until 1968; since then an importer.
18   'Concepts and types of integration', published in the journal *Ekonomista*, 1967, number 1.
19   G. Kohlmey, in the journal *Wirtschaftswissenschaft*, 1967, number 8, speaks of *Marktintegration*, integration of socialist markets; I. Vajda, in the Hungarian journal *Kozgazdasagi Szemle*, 1968, number 4, analyses market and production integration.
20   *The Planning of the Soviety Economy*, pp. 77–8.

Chapter 8

1 Sources: *The Economy of the Socialist Countries in 1968,* Moscow 1969, pp. 254–5; *Foreign Trade,* 1969, no. 7, p. 54; *World Socialism and the Developing Countries,* Moscow 1969, *passim; National Statistical Year-books for* 1971. The figures in value are based on current prices for the corresponding years.

2 'Theses on imperialist integration in Western Europe', semi-official document published in *Pravda* and *Izvestia* on 26 August 1962.

3 *Note:* In the foreign trade statistics published by the United Nations, Yugoslavia is not classified as a planned economy.

4 Hungary and Bulgaria will probably join G.A.T.T. between 1973 and 1975; negotiations have already begun.

5 'The Fiat-Soviet Auto Plant', *Committee on Banking and Currency, U.S. House of Representatives,* Washington D.C., U.S. Government Printing Office, 1967, pp. 40–1.

6 Sources: *The Economy of the U.S.S.R. in 1967, Statistical Year-book,* p. 136; I. P. Oleinik, *The World Socialist Economy,* p. 250.

7 In his article in *Economies et Sociétés,* volume II, number 2, February 1968, quoted in the bibliography.

8 F. Holzman, 'The Foreign Trade Behaviour of Centrally Planned Economies', p. 243.

9 Source: CNUCED, 'Commercial relations between countries with different social and economic systems', Doc. Ronéotés, TD/B/410, 23 August 1972.

10 *Cf.* I. Vajda, 'The Problems of East-West Trade', *Acta Oeconomica,* 1968, number 3, pp. 243–56.

11 *Cf.* Z. Jedryka, 'Soviet-Japanese relations since the Second World War', *Annuaire de l'U.R.S.S. 1969,* Paris, Ed. du C.N.R.S., 1970, pp. 575–96.

12 A general outline of these organs can be found in the *Revue de Droit contemporain,* 1967, 2, pp. 12–19.

13 Even ignoring fluctuations in production; for example, following the bad harvest of 1963 Soviet cereal imports, which had been negligible during the preceding years, reached 7% of purchases in 1964; they fell in 1965, rose in 1966 to 6%, and then fell to 1.8% in 1967 and to 1.2% in 1968. In 1972 these imports were again significant, estimated at about 20 million tons.

14 Source: *Economic Bulletin on Europe,* United Nations, 1968, volume 20, number 1, p. 34.

15 Semi-official sources estimated Soviet sales of gold in 1963 at 550 million dollars, or 40% of known world production in that year (excluding the Soviet Union). *Economic Bulletin on Europe,* volume 16, 1964, number 1, p. 66.

16 Documents of the conference of communist and workers' parties, Moscow, 1960, quoted in *World Socialism and the Developing Countries,* Moscow, 1969, p. 6.

17 United States Congress, Senate Committee on Economic Relations, Report of the *ad hoc* sub-committee on the aid programme, Eighty-fifth Congress, First Session, Washington, 1957, p. 4, quoted by L. Tansky, *U.S. and U.S.S.R. Aid to Developing Countries, A Comparative Study of India, Turkey and the U.A.R.,* New York, Praeger, 1967.

18 Source: *World Socialism and the Developing Countries,* Moscow, 1969, p. 9.

19 Quoted by M. Rudloff, *Economie Politique du Tiers Monde,* Paris, Ed. Cujas, 1968, p. 225.

20 Even without taking political intervention into account, when socialist states make large-scale purchases of products temporarily unmarketable elsewhere. At the end of 1968, for example, the U.S.S.R. agreed to buy 5 million hectolitres of Algerian wine in both 1969 and 1970, or somewhat less than one-half Algerian production. The aim was to compensate for the reduction in French wine purchases which had created problems for the Algerian economy since 1967.

21   Which has no real significance (except as a political gesture) in a system where commercial exchanges are planned in kind and domestic prices fixed with no relationship to foreign prices.

22   There are occasions when the exporting country may suffer from this arrangement. H. Chambre (*Union Soviétique et développement économique*, p. 394) points out that Burma in its rice sales to the U.S.S.R. was unable to profit from the increase in the price of rice on the world market, since the Soviet-Burmese agreement had been signed when prices were very low.

23   When they do so their aid retains its bilateral character, since their contribution to these organs takes the form of non-convertible national currencies, which the beneficiary can only use with the donor country.

24   *Cf.* L. Tansky, *U.S. and U.S.S.R. Aid to Developing Countries, A Comparative Study of India, Turkey, and the U.A.R.*, pp. 18–19.

25   Source: *World Socialism and the Developing Countries*, Moscow, 1969, p. 16.

Conclusion

1   *Cf.*, especially, 'Do Communist and Free Economies Show a Converging Pattern?', *Soviet Studies*, volume 12, 1961, number 4, pp. 333–41, reproduced in *Comparative Economic Systems, Models and Cases*, edited by M. Bornstein, Irwin, 1969, pp. 432–41; 'Some Suggestions on a Modern Theory of the Optimum Regime', in *Socialism, Capitalism and Economic Growth*, edited by C. H. Feinstein, pp. 125–32.

2   Tinbergen observes that the 'levelling' thesis was abandoned in Soviet Russia very soon after the Revolution. We have seen that the present trend is again towards a narrowing of the wages' spectrum.

3   J. Tinbergen, 'Do Communist and Free Economies show a Converging Pattern?', p. 438.

4   *Economic Systems*, p. 111.

5   P. Wiles, 'Convergence: Possibility and Probability', in *Planning and the Market in the U.S.S.R.*, edited by A. Balinsky, Rutgers University, 1967, pp. 89–118.

6   Jan. S. Prybya, 'The Convergence of Western and Communist Economic Systems: a Critical Estimate', in *Comparative Economic Systems, Models and Cases*, edited by M. Bornstein, Irwin, 1969, pp. 442–52.

7   *Critique of Bourgeois Views of the Laws of Socialist Economic Management*, Moscow, 1968, pp. 89–90.

8   *Ibid.*, pp. 173–4.

9   J. K. Galbraith, *The New Industrial State*, 1967, London, Hamilton.

10   *Ibid.*

11   *Ibid.*

12   Weidenfeld and Nicholson, 1967, p. 232.

13   *Ibid.*, p. 80.

14   *Ibid.*, p. 233.

15   H. Krier, J. Le Bourva, *Economie politique*, volume 1, Paris, Armand Colin, coll. 'U', 1968, p. 62.

16   Published later in the collection edited by F. A. von Hayek, *Collectivist Economic Planning*, London, 1935.

17   The present author has analysed this controversy in *Le Capital dans l'économie soviétique*, Paris, S.E.D.E.S., 1961, pp. 20–33.

18   J. Marczewski, 'Le rôle des prix dans un système planifié', in *Economie appliquée*, 1966, 1, pp. 117–46 and 1967, 3, pp. 319–45.

19   He was to modify his views partially later; see especially *Welfare Economics and the Economics of Socialism. Towards a Commonsense Critique*, Cambridge, The University Press, 1969.

20   See 'On the Economic Theory of Socialism', *Review of Economic Studies*, volume 4, October 1936, number 1, pp. 53–71.

21 See especially the work of W. Brus.
22 *Plan and Market under Socialism,* New York, I.A.S.P., Prague, Academia, 1967; also, 'Socialist Market Relations and Planning', in *Socialism, Capitalism and Economic Growth,* edited by C. H. Feinstein, pp. 133–57; 'On Problems of the Plan and the Market', *Czechoslovak Economic Papers,* volume 10, 1968, pp. 125–37. For a Czech appraisal of this question: L. Rychetnik, O. Kyn, 'Optimal Central Planning in "Competitive Solution",' *Czechoslovak Economic Papers,* volume 10, 1968, pp. 29–46; K. Kouba, 'The Plan and the Market in a Socialist Economy', *Czechoslovak Economic Papers,* volume 11, 1969, pp. 27–42.
23 'Some Suggestions on a Modern Theory of the Optimum Regime', in *Socialism, Capitalism and Economic Growth,* edited by C. H. Feinstein, p. 127.
24 This is the position of C. Bettelheim, for whom there are only social formations in a state of transition to socialism. *Cf.* his work *La Transition vers l'économie socialiste,* Paris, Maspero, 1970, and his studies on 'Calcul économique, catégories marchandes et formes de propriété', in *Problèmes de planification,* Centre d'étude de planification socialiste, numbers 11 and 12.

GENERAL BIBLIOGRAPHY

1. Journals and Periodicals

IN FRENCH

Annuaire de l'U.R.S.S., droit, économie, sociologie, politique, culture, published by Centre de recherches sur l'U.R.S.S. et les pays de l'Est aux Editions du C.N.R.S.

Bulletin, Centre d'étude des pays de l'Est (Institut de sociologie de l'Université libre de Bruxelles); after 1968 *Revue* of the Centre d'Etude des pays de l'Est and the Centre national pour l'Etude des Etats de l'Est.

Bulletin économique pour l'Europe and *Etude sur la situation économique de l'Europe,* Commission économique pour l'Europe des Nations Unies.

Cahiers de l'Institut de science économique appliquée (since 1967 *Economies et Sociétés*), série G 'économie planifiée (textes et analyses)'.

Cahiers du monde russe et soviétique, published by the Centre de Documentation sur l'U.R.S.S. et les pays slaves, Ecole pratique des hautes études de Paris.

Commerce et coopération, Chambre de commerce franco-soviétique.

Commerce extérieur, ministère du commerce extérieur de l'U.R.S.S.

Documentation française. Le Secrétariat général du gouvernement, Direction de la documentation, including:-

    Chroniques étrangères U.R.S.S.; Revue U.R.S.S.; Problèmes politiques et sociaux, série U.R.S.S.;

    Courrier des pays de l'Est;

    Europe centrale et orientale;

    L'Europe de l'Est en . . .;

    Articles et Documents;

    Notes et Etudes documentaires;

    Problèmes économiques.

L'Europe orientale.

Problèmes de planification, Centre d'Etudes de la planification socialiste de l'Ecole pratique des hautes études.

La *Revue canadienne d'études slaves,* Montréal (Loyola College).

La *Revue de l'Est,* C.N.R.S.

La *Revue roumaine des sciences sociales, série des sciences économiques,* edited by the Institut d'économie de l'Academie des sciences de Roumanie.

Sciences sociales, Académie des Sciences de l'U.R.S.S.

L'U.R.S.S. et les pays de l'Est, Revue des revues, Editions du C.N.R.S.

IN ENGLISH

Acta Oeconomica, Hungarian Academy of Sciences.
Czechoslovak Economic Papers, Czechoslovak Academy of Sciences.
Eastern European Economics; Problems of Economics, International Arts and Sciences Press.
Economics of Planning, Norwegian Institute on International Questions.
Joint Publications Research Service, Translations on Eastern Europe, series Economic and Industrial Affairs, edited by the National Technical Information Service, Springfield, Virginia.
Slavic Review, American Association for the Development of Slavonic Studies.
Soviet Studies, published in Glasgow under the direction of Alec Nove.
Yugoslav Survey, Yugoslav Government publication.

IN GERMAN

Osteuropa, Osteuropa Wirtschaft, German Federal Republic.
Wirtschaftswissenschaft, German Democratic Republic.

IN ITALIAN

Documentazione sui paesi dell'Est., Centro studi e ricerche su problemi economico-sociali, Milan.
L'Est.

2. Books

IN FRENCH

GENERAL:

Le Dossier Russie, Verviers, Marabout Université, 1966.
Dossier de l'Europe de l'Est, Verviers, Marabout Université, 1968.
FEJTO, FRANCOIS, *Histoire des démocraties populaires,* Paris, Le Seuil, vol. I, 1952, vol. II, 1969.
Le Grand Défi, Encyclopédie Comparée, U.S.A.–U.R.S.S., Marc Saporta et Georges Soria, two vols., Paris, Laffont, 1967–8.
NETTL, J. P., *Bilan de l'U.R.S.S., 1917–1967,* Paris, Le Seuil, 1967.
SORLIN, PIERRE, *La Société soviétique, 1917–1967,* second edition, Paris, Armand Colin, coll. 'U', série 'Histoire contemporaine', 1967.

ON THE SOCIALIST ECONOMIC SYSTEM:

BETTELHEIM, CHARLES, *Problèmes théoriques et pratiques de la planification,* Paris, F. Maspero, 1966.
CHAMBRE, HENRI, *Union soviétique et développement économique,* Paris, Aubier-Montaigne, 1967.
Economie politique du socialisme, Moscow, Editions du Progrès, 1967.
MARCZEWSKI, JAN, *Planification et croissance économique des démocraties populaires,* Paris, P.U.F., 1956.
MASNATA, A., *Le Système socialiste-soviétique,* Neuchâtel, La Baconnière, 1965.
NIKITINE, P., *Manuel d'économie politique,* Moscow, 1961.

IN ENGLISH

BERGSON, ABRAM, *The Economics of Soviet Planning,* New Haven, Yale University Press, 1964.

BERGSON, ABRAM, *Essays in Normative Economics,* Cambridge, Harvard University Press, 1966.

BERLINER, J., *Economy, Society and Welfare,* New York, Praeger, 1972.

DOBB, MAURICE, *Papers on Capitalism, Development and Planning,* London, Routledge and Kegan, 1967.

DOBB, MAURICE, *Welfare Economics and the Economics of Socialism,* Cambridge, Cambridge University Press, 1969.

GROSSMAN, GREGORY, *Economic Systems,* Englewood Cliffs, New Jersey, Prentice Hall, 1967.

JASNY, NAUM, *Essays on the Soviet Economy,* New York, Praeger, 1962.

NOVE, ALEC, *The Soviet Economy,* London, Allen and Unwin, 1968.

SHERMAN, HOWARD J., *The Soviet Economy,* Boston, Little, Brown and Company, 1969.

SHERMAN, HOWARD J., *Radical Political Economy. Capitalism and Socialism from a Marxist Humanist Perspective,* New York and London, Basic Books, 1972.

WARD, BENJAMIN, *The Socialist Economy: A Study of Organizational Alternatives,* New York, Random House, 1967.

WILCZYNSKI, J., *The Economics of Socialism,* second edition, London, Allen and Unwin, 1972.

WILES, P. J. D., *Communist International Economics,* Oxford, Blackwell, 1967.

WILES, P. J. D., *The Political Economy of Communism,* Oxford, Blackwell, 1964.

Capitalism, Market Socialism and Central Planning. Readings in Comparative Economic Systems, edited by W. A. Leeman, Boston, Houghton Mifflin, 1963.

Communist Economy under Change, Studies in the Theory and Practice of Markets and Competition in Russia, Poland and Yugoslavia, London, Andre Deutsch, 1963.

The Communist World, Marxist and non-Marxist Views, edited by Harry Shaffer, New York, Appleton-Century-Crofts, 1967.

Comparative Economic Systems, Models a 'd Cases, edited by M. Bornstein, Homewood, Irwin, 1965; second edition 1969.

Comparisons of Economic Systems. Theoretical and Methodological Approaches, edited by A. Eckstein, Berkeley, Los Angeles, University of California Press, 1971.

Essays in Socialism and Planning in Honor of Carl Landauer, edited by G. Grossman, Englewood Cliffs, Prentice Hall, 1970.

Industrialization in Two Systems: Essays in Honor of A. Gerschenkron, edited by H. Rosovsky, New York and London, John Wiley, 1966.

New Currents in Soviet-Type Economies: A Reader, edited by George R. Feiwel, Scranton, International Textbook Company, 1968.

On Political Economy and Econometrics, Essays in Honour of Oskar Lange, London, Pergamon Press, Warsaw, Polish Scientific Publishers, 1969.

Planning and the Market in the U.S.S.R.: the 1960s, edited by A. Balinsky, New Brunswick, Rutgers University Press, 1967.

Readings on the Soviet Economy, edited by F. D. Holzman, Chicago, Rand McNally, 1963.

Socialism, Capitalism and Economic Growth, Essays Presented to Maurice Dobb, edited by C. H. Feinstein, London, Cambridge University Press, 1967.

Socialist Economics, Selected Readings, edited by Alec Nove and D. M. Nuti, London, Penguin Books, 1972.

The Soviet Economy. A Collection of Western and Soviet Views, edited by Shaffer, New York, Appleton-Century-Crofts, 1963.

Soviet Planning: Essays Edited in Honour of Naum Jasny, by Jane Degras and Alec Nove, Oxford, Blackwell, 1964.

The Soviet System in Theory and Practice, Selected Western and Soviet Views, New York, Appleton-Century-Crofts, 1965.

The Soviet Union and Eastern Europe, A Handbook, edited by G. Schöpflin, London, Anthony Blond, 1970.

INDEX

394 *The Socialist Economies of the Soviet Union and Europe*

demand 90, 106, 235, 273; evaluation of demand 268–9.
democratic centralism 26–7.
demography 144–8.
depreciation 55, 201, 236, 282.
devaluation 98, 263–6.
development, developing countries 348–360; strategy of development 129–143.
distribution 99–109.

economic administration, principles xiii, 26–32; organs, U.S.S.R. 32–42, 51–2, 56, 58, 63, 101–3, 113–4, socialist countries 42–8, 122–3.
economic branches, administration by 32, 35–9, 43; in the national income 173–5; inter-branch balances 199–206; wage differentials by branch 243, 244–5, 246–7; branch planning 190.
economic calculation xii, 208–9, 368–72.
economic contracts 58, 66, 67, 71, 104, 106.
economic delinquency 41–2.
economic efficiency 208–20, 368–73.
economic fluctuations 140, 141, 142.
economic growth xiv, 127–83; extensive and intensive 134, 139, 142–3, 155–6; growth factors 143–70; growth models 165–70; planning of growth 188; rate of growth 127–8, 136, 141, 142; theory of reproduction 130–7.
economic history, U.S.S.R. 1–17, 32–5, 128–9, 137–8, 220–2; socialist countries 17–24, 128–9.
economic institutions, general 25–32; U.S.S.R. 1–17, 32, 42; socialist countries 17–24, 42–8.
economic law 25–6, 59, 65–7.
economic laws xiv; priority growth of capital goods xiv, 131–7, 174.
economic ministries 33–9, 42–3, 65–7.
economic policy x–xi; agricultural 110, 112; of growth 137–43; financial 85–6, 276–7; monetary 272–6; prices 225–42; incomes 249–53, 258.
economic power x–xi, 27–9, 129, 186.
economic reforms, of the economic administration, U.S.S.R. 35–9, socialist countries 42–8; in agriculture, U.S.S.R. 118–22, socialist countries 122–4; in trade 99–109; of the enterprise, U.S.S.R. 59–80, socialist countries 80–98.
economic systems ix–xvii, 341, 348–50, 361–75.
economic theory, of investment 209, 212–7; of reproduction 130–7; of

value 226–34, 368–9.
employment, policy 150–3, 176, 244, 251.

family allowances 147, 257.
finance 277–89.
financial autonomy 51–2.

G.D.R. x, xiv, xvi, 1, 18–23, 43–47, 80–90, 105, 122–4, 127–8, 137, 139–42, 144–53, 156, 157–8, 165, 170–6, 208, 240, 246, 248, 252, 254, 257, 265, 289, 293–331 (Comecon), 336, 340–1, 353, 357, 359.
goods, consumer, distribution of 105–9; prices of 235; capital goods, distribution of, 101–5, law of priority growth 131–7, 174, prices of 231, 235.
Gosbank 2, 11, 67, 261–3, 266–72, 274–5.
Gosplan 33, 34, 38, 101–2, 188, 234.
Gosstroj 36, 39.
gross social product, "balance" 193; growth 137; definition 130–1, 165.

Hungary x, xvi, 1, 18–20, 22, 23, 43, 45–7, 80–90, 105, 122–4, 127–8, 137, 140, 141, 142, 144–53, 156, 158, 160, 170–6, 239, 240, 246, 252–3, 254, 257, 265, 272, 275–6, 288–90, 293–331 (Comecon), 335, 344–5, 359.

incomes policy 242–60, 274.
industrial associations, U.S.S.R. 9–10, 37–8, 66–7, 77–8, 79–80, 105, 211; Hungary 45; G.D.R. 43–4, 105; Czechoslovakia 44, 105; Yugoslavia 92–3.
industrial enterprise, U.S.S.R. 51–80, socialist countries 80–98; history of 5–11, 19–21; and supplies 101–5; and investment 209–11, 217; and prices 229–30, 237; relations with the budget 285–8; and wages 247–8, 251; legal status of, U.S.S.R. 10, 59.
industrialisation (policy of) 137–43, 171, 357–60.
industry, forms of property in, U.S.S.R. 2–3, 5–11, socialist countries 19–21; heavy 138, 173–4; labour-force 148–52, 172; prices 236–8; production 64, 141, 142, 170–1, 180; wages 243–53.
inflation 263, 272–6.
integration of socialist countries 329–31, 339–40.
interest (rate of) 60, 216, 228–9, 274,

275.

international credit, between socialist countries 315, 327; from capitalist to socialist countries 340; from socialist countries to countries of the Third World 355–7.

international division of labour 302, 316–29.

international economic relations, between socialist states 293–331, between socialist states and the outside world 333–60.

international law of the socialist states 294, 302–3.

international payments between socialist countries 303, 313–4.

international planning 318–29.

international prices within Comecon 303, 311–3.

investment efficiency 208–17, 241; enterprise, U.S.S.R. 54, 59, 61, 75–6, 216–7, 275–6, 281, 282, socialist countries 85–6, 94–5; financing 85–6, 210–11, 275–6; level and rate of 140, 157–61, 164, 211–2; planning 191; investment theory 133–4; joint investment of Comecon countries 298–9, 325–6.

Korea x, xvi, 265, 293, 307, 333.

kolkhoz 14–17, 110–21, 255, 267, 268, 269.

kulaks 3, 16, 23, 111.

labour, balances 203–6; and economic growth 143–56, 162–5; labour market 247–8; and value 130, 226–7.

labour-force, agricultural 148–52, 172; industrial 148–52, 172; in the enterprise 53, 71–2, 149, 153–5, 247–8, 251.

leisure 175–6, 256.

livestock breeding 110, 120.

loans 273, 285.

localisation 178.

marginalism 217–8, 231–2, 368–9.

market, market economy xii, 364, 368–71; kolkhoz market 110, 113, 116, 268, 269; market socialism 8–11, 98, 372; socialist market 312, 330–1.

material and technical supplies, U.S.S.R. 39, 67, 71, 101–4; socialist countries 104–5; for agriculture 117, 123–4.

mathematics, and doctrine 217–8, 231–2, 241; and planning 208, 219.

money 223–89; monetary policy 260–76.

Mongolia x, xv, xvi, 265, 293, 297, 306, 307, 316, 318, 325, 333, 350.

national accounting 130, 136, 149, 158–9, 165, 179–83, 192–206, 250, 319.

national income, "balance" 193–4; growth 127, 137, 141, 142, 143–4, 155–6, 180; definition 165–6, 193; structure 171–3.

nationalisation xv–xvi, 2–4, 8–11, 17–21, 358, 360, 364–5.

needs xi–xii, 127, 243, 253–4, 259.

N.E.P. 4–17, 137–8, 224, 262.

ownership of the means of production, co-operative 7–8, 12–17, 21–4, 113–24; state ix, xiv–xvi, 5–11, 17–20, 113; social (Yugoslavia) 90–1; socialist xiv–xvi, 361, 373.

patents 328–9.

peasants 110–24.

pensions and retirement, in agriculture, U.S.S.R. 120, 255, 283, socialist countries 124; in industry 147–8, 255, 258, 283.

plan, drafting 186–92; implementation 220–2; five-year plans 78, 89, 138, 207, 221.

planned economic indices, in agriculture 113, 115, 117, 118, 123; in trade 101–3, 106–7, 109; in industry 52–3, 59, 64–7, 70, 189.

planned economy xii–xiii, 185–6, 362–3.

planning, agricultural, U.S.S.R. 115, 117, 118–9; socialist countries 123; of foreign trade 308–11, 341–3; of growth 165–70; of distribution 100–9; in the enterprise, U.S.S.R. 52–3, 57, 58, 59–60, 68, 70–2, socialist countries 82–4; financial 276–80; methods 185–220 (U.S.S.R.); monetary 266–76; of prices 234–42; regional 34–9, 103, 190–1; of wages 243–53.

Poland x, xvi, 1, 19–24, 43, 45–7, 80–90, 105, 122–4, 127–8, 137, 139, 140–2, 144–52, 156, 158, 160, 170–6, 240, 246, 247, 252, 254, 265, 289, 293–331 (Comecon), 335, 338, 344, 359, 360.

popular democracies ix, 1, 17–24.

population, active 147–53, 172; total 143, 144.

prices, agricultural 115–6, 117, 119, 123, 239; retail 71, 235, 272–3, 285; wholesale 234–9; planning 191, 206, 234–6; reforms, U.S.S.R. 58, 62, 64,